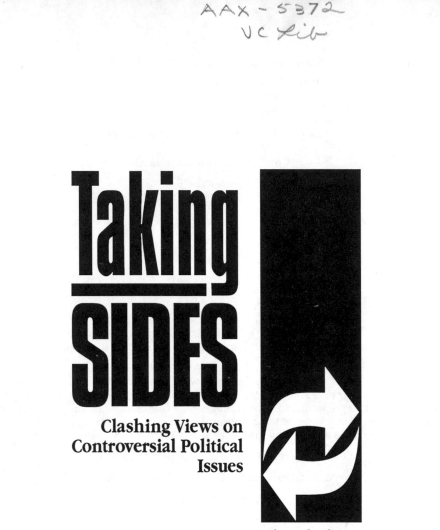

Taking SIDES

Clashing Views on Controversial Political Issues

Eleventh Edition

Edited, Selected, and with Introductions by

George McKenna
City College, City University of New York
and
Stanley Feingold
Westchester Community College

Dushkin/McGraw-Hill
A Division of The McGraw-Hill Companies

*In memory of Hillman M. Bishop and Samuel Hendel, masters of an
art often neglected by college teachers: teaching.*

Photo Acknowledgments

Cover image: © 1999 by PhotoDisc, Inc.

Cover Art Acknowledgment

Charles Vitelli

Manufactured in the United States of America

Eleventh Edition

10 9 8 7 6 5 4 3 2 1

Library of Congress Cataloging-in-Publication Data

Main entry under title:
    Taking sides: clashing views on controversial political issues/edited, selected, and with
    introductions by George McKenna and Stanley Feingold.—11th ed.
        Includes bibliographical references and index.
        1. United States—Politics and government—1945–. I. McKenna, George, *comp.* II. Fein-
    gold, Stanley, *comp.*

                                                                320'.973
        0-697-39146-9   ISSN: 1080-580X

 Printed on Recycled Paper

PREFACE

Dialogue means two people talking to the same issue. This is not as easy as it sounds. Play back the next debate between the talking heads you see on television. Listen to them try to persuade each other—actually, the TV audience—of the truth of their own views and of the irrationality of their opponents' views.

What is likely to happen? At the outset, they will probably fail to define the issue with enough clarity and objectivity to make it clear exactly what it is that they are disputing. As the philosopher Alasdair MacIntyre has put it, the most passionate pro and con arguments are often "incommensurable"—they sail past each other because the two sides are talking about different things. As arguments proceed, both sides tend to employ vague, emotion-laden terms without spelling out the uses to which the terms are put. When the heat is on, they may resort to shouting epithets at one another, and the hoped-for meeting of minds will give way to the scoring of political points and the reinforcement of existing prejudices. For example, when the discussion of affirmative action comes down to both sides accusing the other of "racism," or when the controversy over abortion degenerates into taunts and name-calling, then no one really listens and learns from the other side.

It is our conviction that people *can* learn from the other side, no matter how sharply opposed it is to their own cherished viewpoint. Sometimes, after listening to others, we change our view entirely. But in most cases, we either incorporate some elements of the opposing view—thus making our own richer—or else learn how to answer the objections to our viewpoint. Either way, we gain from the experience. For these reasons we believe that encouraging dialogue between opposed positions is the most certain way of enhancing public understanding.

The purpose of this 11th edition of *Taking Sides* is to continue to work toward the revival of political dialogue in America. As we have done in the past 10 editions, we examine leading issues in American politics from the perspective of sharply opposed points of view. We have tried to select authors who argue their points vigorously but in such a way as to enhance our understanding of the issue.

We hope that the reader who confronts lively and thoughtful statements on vital issues will be stimulated to ask some of the critical questions about American politics. What are the highest-priority issues with which government must deal today? What positions should be taken on these issues? What should be the attitude of Americans toward their government? Our

conviction is that a healthy, stable democracy requires a citizenry that considers these questions and participates, however indirectly, in answering them. The alternative is apathy, passivity, and, sooner or later, the rule of tyrants.

Plan of the book   Each issue has an issue *introduction,* which sets the stage for the debate as it is argued in the YES and NO selections. Each issue concludes with a *postscript* that makes some final observations and points the way to other questions related to the issue. In reading the issue and forming your own opinions you should not feel confined to adopt one or the other of the positions presented. There are positions in between the given views or totally outside them, and the *suggestions for further reading* that appear in each issue postscript should help you find resources to continue your study of the subject. We have also provided relevant Internet site addresses (URLs) on the *On the Internet* page that accompanies each part opener. At the back of the book is a listing of all the *contributors to this volume,* which will give you information on the political scientists and commentators whose views are debated here.

Changes to this edition   Over the past 20 years *Taking Sides* has undergone extensive changes and improvements, and we are particularly proud of this 11th edition. There are eight new issues in this volume: *Should Campaign Finance Be Reformed?* (Issue 3); *Investigating the President: Do We Need an Independent Counsel?* (Issue 6); *Should Judges Read Their Moral Views into the Constitution?* (Issue 7); *Is Welfare Reform Succeeding?* (Issue 13); *Is Socioeconomic Inequality Increasing in America?* (Issue 14); *Will America Dominate Tomorrow's Global Economy?* (Issue 17); *Does China Threaten Vital American Interests?* (Issue 18); and *Is Democracy Desirable for All Nations?* (Issue 20). In addition, for three other issues (political campaigns, the media, and abortion) we have replaced one of the selections to strengthen the argument. All told, there are 19 new selections—almost half the book is therefore new.

We worked hard on what we hope will be a truly memorable 11th edition, and we think you will like the result. Let us know what you think by writing to us care of Dushkin/McGraw-Hill, Sluice Dock, Guilford, CT 06437 or e-mailing us at GMcK1320@aol.com. Suggestions for further improvements are most welcome!

A word to the instructor   An *Instructor's Manual With Test Questions* (multiple-choice and essay) is available through the publisher. A general guidebook, called *Using Taking Sides in the Classroom,* which discusses methods and techniques for integrating the pro/con approach into any classroom setting, is also available. An online version of *Using Taking Sides in the Classroom* and a correspondence service for *Taking Sides* adopters can be found at www.cybsol.com/usingtakingsides/. For students, we offer a field guide to analyzing argumentative essays, *Analyzing Controversy: An Introduc-*

tory Guide, with exercises and techniques to help them to decipher genuine controversies.

Taking Sides: Clashing Views on Controversial Political Issues is only one title in the Taking Sides series. If you are interested in seeing the table of contents for any of the other titles, please visit the Taking Sides Web site at http://www.dushkin.com/takingsides/.

Acknowledgments   We received many helpful comments and suggestions from our friends and readers across the United States and Canada. Their suggestions have markedly enhanced the quality of this edition of *Taking Sides* and are reflected in the totally new issues and the updated selections.

Our thanks go to those who responded with suggestions for the 11th edition:

Michelle Bellini
University of Northern
   Colorado

Corlan Carlson
Whatcom Community
   College

Gary Donato
Three Rivers Community
   Technical College

Gerald Duff
Arizona State University

Lawrence Fleischer
City College, City University
   of New York

Peter Heller
Manhattan College

Willoughby Jarrell
Kennesaw State University

Steve Jenks
University of Central
   Oklahoma

Kenneth Kiser
Highland Community
   College

Patrice Mareschal
University of Oklahoma

Michelle Martin
Sierra College

Ted R. Mosch
University of Tennessee
   at Martin

Marion Moxley
El Camino College

David S. Myers
University of West Florida

Susan Rouder
City College of San Francisco

Harvey Strum
Sage Junior College of Albany

Paul Tesch
Spokane Community College

We also appreciate the spontaneous letters from instructors and students who wrote to us with comments and observations. We are grateful to David Dean, who served as list manager for the Taking Sides series for much of the period in which this edition was prepared, for his able editorial assistance;

to David Brackley, developmental editor; and to Rose Gleich, administrative assistant. Needless to say, the responsibility for any errors of fact or judgment rests with us.

George McKenna
City College, City University of New York

Stanley Feingold
Westchester Community College

CONTENTS IN BRIEF

CONTENTS

Writer Irving Kristol argues that America possesses a rich combination of ingredients that give it strength, resilience, and character. Freelance writer Daniel Lazare contends that America has become paralyzed in a constitutional straitjacket and that it needs radical reform.

Professor of political science Samuel L. Popkin argues that presidential election campaigns perform a unique and essential service in informing and unifying the American people. Political scientist Anthony King contends that American officeholders spend too much time and effort running for office, which detracts from their responsibility to provide good government.

Archibald Cox, a former special prosecutor and a law professor, argues that the increasing amount of money spent in elections corrupts government but that the public's faith in democratic self-government can be restored by

campaign finance reform. Bradley A. Smith, an associate professor at Capital University Law School, asserts that campaign contributions do not corrupt candidates, the biggest spenders do not always win, and the relatively modest amount that candidates spend is essential to educate voters and to increase their interest.

Journalist James Fallows contends that the information media put the profits of entertainment ahead of their responsibility to inform and educate the public. Media critic Jon Katz asserts that popular culture deals with social issues more effectively than traditional media do.

Columnist George F. Will argues that term limits will bring fresh perspectives into Congress and restore the spirit of citizen politics. Political consultant Victor Kamber contends that term limits for congressional members violate the spirit of democracy and will force Americans to accept inexperienced legislators.

Attorney General Janet Reno testifies that one part of the executive branch, the Department of Justice, should not be called upon to investigate another

and that Watergate and the Iran-Contra investigation demonstrated the value of an independent counsel. Supreme Court Justice Antonin Scalia holds that the independent counsel law violates the Constitution's absolute separation of powers and unconstitutionally restricts judicial control over subordinate officials within the executive branch.

Law professor Ronald Dworkin contends that judges must read the vaguer phrases of the Constitution with an eye toward what is best for the nation. Law professor Mary Ann Glendon warns of the perils of "romantic judging," which she argues usurps the role of legislatures and weakens the spirit of democracy.

James Wootton, president of Safe Streets Alliance in Washington, D.C., argues that mandatory sentencing sends a signal to would-be felons that they will pay heavily if they commit a crime. Judge Lois G. Forer contends that mandatory sentencing not only fails to deter crime, but it disrupts families, increases welfare costs, and hurts the poor and minorities.

Essayist Robert W. Lee argues that capital punishment is the only fair response to certain heinous crimes. Matthew L. Stephens, a prison chaplain, contends that the death penalty is motivated by revenge and is racist in its result.

Policy analyst Daniel Casse argues that the 1996 overhaul of welfare has encouraged long-term welfare clients to find meaningful jobs and to better their lives. Peter Edelman, a former adviser for the Clinton administration, maintains that the 1996 welfare overhaul will have a multitude of adverse consequences, including an increase in malnutrition, crime, drug and alcohol abuse, and family violence.

Economist Paul Krugman maintains that corporate greed, the decline of organized labor, and changes in production have contributed to a sharp increase in social and economic inequality in America. Christopher C. DeMuth, president of the American Enterprise Institute, asserts that Americans have achieved an impressive level of wealth and equality and that a changing economy ensures even more opportunities.

Legal scholar Robert H. Bork concludes that the semantics of "pro-choice" cannot hide the fact that aborting a fetus is killing an unborn child and that most abortions are performed for the woman's convenience. Writer Mary Gordon maintains that having an abortion is a moral choice that women are capable of making for themselves, that aborting a fetus is not killing a person, and that antiabortionists fail to understand female sexuality.

Essayist and editor Andrew Sullivan contends that legalizing gay marriage would be a profoundly humanizing step because such marriages, with their honesty, their flexibility, and their equality, could nourish the broader society as well. Social scientist James Q. Wilson asserts that to legalize homosexual

marriage would be to enter an untested area that could profoundly damage the already-fragile institutions of marriage and family.

Publisher Mortimer B. Zuckerman maintains that America's entrepreneurial genius will keep the nation economically dominant in the twenty-first century. Economist Paul Krugman asserts that American economic dominance in the world can easily be upset by even a mild national recession combined with moderate recovery in Europe and Asia.

Book critic Richard Bernstein and Ross H. Munro, director of the Asia program at the Foreign Policy Research Institute, argue that China, while disguising or minimizing its actual military expenditures, is rapidly modernizing its land, air, and naval forces and still pursues its aim of dominating East Asia. Professor of political science Robert S. Ross argues that China, with an obsolete air force, primitive missiles, and a miniscule navy with no aircraft carriers, has neither the means nor the will to challenge U.S. hegemony in the Pacific.

Daniel James, an adviser to Carrying Capacity Network in Washington, D.C., wants a moratorium on immigration, which, he claims, is causing Amer-

ica much social and economic harm. Economist Stephen Moore insists that immigrants have greatly enriched the American economy and culture.

Author and editor Robert Kagan argues that democracy has taken root in many nations that never had it before, in large measure due to American intervention, with desirable consequences for American security and prosperity. Foreign correspondent Robert D. Kaplan contends that recent experience demonstrates that not all nations have the conditions in which democracy can thrive, that some nations prosper without it, and that democracy may be less important in the future.

INTRODUCTION

Labels and Alignments in American Politics

George McKenna
Stanley Feingold

America's political vocabulary contains a rich variety of terms that have accumulated since the time of the country's founding in the eighteenth century —terms like *liberal, conservative, left wing, right wing, moderate, and extremist.* As we enter the twenty-first century, it is clear that the meanings of these terms have shifted over the past two and a half centuries. Some of the terms —*liberalism* is perhaps the best example—seem almost to have reversed their meaning. It is fair to ask whether these terms have any fixed, core meanings left in them. Are they now anything more than polemical weapons, useful for battering the enemy and rallying the faithful, or is there still something left in them? We believe that there is, but we caution that the terms must be used thoughtfully and with due regard for their origins and usage. Otherwise, the terms may end up obscuring or oversimplifying positions. Our purpose in this introduction is to explore the basic core meanings of these terms in order to make them useful to us as citizens.

LIBERALS VERSUS CONSERVATIVES: AN OVERVIEW

Let us examine, very briefly, the historical evolution of the terms *liberalism* and *conservatism.* By examining the roots of these terms, we can see how these philosophies have adapted themselves to changing times. In that way, we can avoid using the terms rigidly, without reference to the particular contexts in which liberalism and conservatism have operated over the past two centuries.

Classical Liberalism

The classical root of the term liberalism is the Latin word *libertas,* meaning "liberty" or "freedom." In the early nineteenth century, liberals dedicated themselves to freeing individuals from all unnecessary and oppressive obligations to authority—whether the authority came from the church or the state. They opposed the licensing and censorship of the press, the punishment of heresy, the establishment of religion, and any attempt to dictate orthodoxy in matters of opinion. In economics, liberals opposed state monopolies and other constraints upon competition between private businesses. At this point in its development, liberalism defined freedom primarily in terms of freedom *from.* It appropriated the French term *laissez-faire,* which literally

means "leave to be." Leave people alone! That was the spirit of liberalism in its early days. It wanted government to stay out of people's lives and to play a modest role in general. Thomas Jefferson summed up this concept when he said, "I am no friend of energetic government. It is always oppressive."

Despite their suspicion of government, classical liberals invested high hopes in the political process. By and large, they were great believers in democracy. They believed in widening suffrage to include every white male, and some of them were prepared to enfranchise women and blacks as well. Although liberals occasionally worried about "the tyranny of the majority," they were more prepared to trust the masses than to trust a permanent, entrenched elite. Liberal social policy was dedicated to fulfilling human potential and was based on the assumption that this often-hidden potential is enormous. Human beings, liberals argued, were basically good and reasonable. Evil and irrationality were believed to be caused by "outside" influences; they were the result of a bad social environment. A liberal commonwealth, therefore, was one that would remove the hindrances to the full flowering of the human personality.

The basic vision of liberalism has not changed since the nineteenth century. What has changed is the way it is applied to modern society. In that respect, liberalism has changed dramatically. Today, instead of regarding government with suspicion, liberals welcome government as an instrument to serve the people. The change in philosophy began in the latter years of the nineteenth century, when businesses—once small, independent operations—began to grow into giant structures that overwhelmed individuals and sometimes even overshadowed the state in power and wealth. At that time, liberals began reconsidering their commitment to the *laissez-faire* philosophy. If the state can be an oppressor, asked liberals, can't big business also oppress people? By then, many were convinced that commercial and industrial monopolies were crushing the souls and bodies of the working classes. The state, formerly the villain, now was viewed by liberals as a potential savior. The concept of freedom was transformed into something more than a negative freedom *from;* the term began to take on a positive meaning. It meant "realizing one's full potential." Toward this end, liberals believed, the state could prove to be a valuable instrument. It could educate children, protect the health and safety of workers, help people through hard times, promote a healthy economy, and—when necessary—force business to act more humanely and responsibly. Thus was born the movement that culminated in New Deal liberalism.

New Deal Liberalism

In the United States, the argument in favor of state intervention did not win an enduring majority constituency until after the Great Depression of the 1930s began to be felt deeply. The disastrous effects of a depression that left a quarter of the workforce unemployed opened the way to a new ad-

ministration—and a promise. "I pledge you, I pledge myself," Franklin D. Roosevelt said when accepting the Democratic nomination in 1932, "to a new deal for the American people." Roosevelt's New Deal was an attempt to effect relief and recovery from the Depression; it employed a variety of means, including welfare programs, public works, and business regulation —most of which involved government intervention in the economy. The New Deal liberalism relied on government to liberate people from poverty, oppression, and economic exploitation. At the same time, the New Dealers claimed to be as zealous as the classical liberals in defending political and civil liberties.

The common element in *laissez-faire* liberalism and welfare-state liberalism is their dedication to the goal of realizing the full potential of each individual. Some still questioned whether this is best done by minimizing state involvement or whether it sometimes requires an activist state. The New Dealers took the latter view, though they prided themselves on being pragmatic and experimental about their activism. During the heyday of the New Deal, a wide variety of programs were tried and—if found wanting—abandoned. All decent means should be tried, they believed, even if it meant dilution of ideological purity. The Roosevelt administration, for example, denounced bankers and businessmen in campaign rhetoric but worked very closely with them while trying to extricate the nation from the Depression. This set a pattern of pragmatism that New Dealers from Harry Truman to Lyndon Johnson emulated.

Progressive Liberalism

Progressive liberalism emerged in the late 1960s and early 1970s as a more militant and uncompromising movement than the New Deal had ever been. Its roots go back to the New Left student movement of the early 1960s. New Left students went to the South to participate in civil rights demonstrations, and many of them were bloodied in confrontations with southern police; by the mid-1960s they were confronting the authorities in the North over issues like poverty and the Vietnam War. By the end of the decade, the New Left had fragmented into a variety of factions and had lost much of its vitality, but a somewhat more respectable version of it appeared as the New Politics movement. Many New Politics crusaders were former New Leftists who had traded their jeans for coats and ties; they tried to work within the system instead of always confronting it. Even so, they retained some of the spirit of the New Left. The civil rights slogan "Freedom Now" expressed the mood of the New Politics. The young university graduates who filled its ranks had come from an environment where "nonnegotiable" demands were issued to college deans by leaders of sit-in protests. There was more than youthful arrogance in the New Politics movement, however; there was a pervasive belief that America had lost, had compromised away, much of its idealism. The New Politics liberals sought to recover some of that spirit by linking up with an older tradition of militant reform, which went back to the time of the Revolution. These new liberals saw themselves as the authentic heirs

of Thomas Paine and Henry David Thoreau, of the abolitionists, the radical populists, the suffragettes, and the great progressive reformers of the early twentieth century.

While New Deal liberals concentrated almost exclusively on bread-and-butter issues such as unemployment and poverty, the New Politics liberals introduced what came to be known as social issues into the political arena. These included: the repeal of laws against abortion, the liberalization of laws against homosexuality and pornography, the establishment of affirmative action programs to ensure increased hiring of minorities and women, and the passage of the Equal Rights Amendment. In foreign policy, too, New Politics liberals departed from the New Deal agenda. Because they had keener memories of the unpopular and (for them) unjustified war in Vietnam than of World War II, they became doves, in contrast to the general hawkishness of the New Dealers. They were skeptical of any claim that the United States must be the leader of the free world or, indeed, that it had any special mission in the world; some were convinced that America was already in decline and must learn to adjust accordingly. The real danger, they argued, came not from the Soviet Union but from the mad pace of our arms race with the Soviets, which, as they saw it, could bankrupt the country, starve our social programs, and culminate in a nuclear Armageddon.

New Politics liberals were heavily represented at the 1972 Democratic national convention, which nominated South Dakota senator George McGovern for president. By the 1980s the New Politics movement was no longer new, and many of its adherents preferred to be called progressives. By this time their critics had another name for them: radicals. The critics saw their positions as inimical to the interests of the United States, destructive of the family, and fundamentally at odds with the views of most Americans. The adversaries of the progressives were not only conservatives but many New Deal liberals, who openly scorned the McGovernites.

This split still exists within the Democratic party, though it is now more skillfully managed by party leaders. In 1988 the Democrats paired Michael Dukakis, whose Massachusetts supporters were generally on the progressive side of the party, with New Dealer Lloyd Bentsen as the presidential and vice-presidential candidates, respectively. In 1992 the Democrats won the presidency with Arkansas governor Bill Clinton, whose record as governor seemed to put him in the moderate-to-conservative camp, and Tennessee senator Albert Gore, whose position on environmental issues could probably be considered quite liberal but whose general image was middle-of-the-road. Both candidates had moved toward liberal positions on the issues of gay rights and abortion. By 1994 Clinton was perceived by many Americans as being "too liberal," which some speculate may have been a factor in the defeat of Democrats in the congressional elections that year. Since then, Clinton has gone to some lengths to shake off that perception, positioning himself as a "moderate" between extremes and casting the Republicans as an "extremist" party. (These two terms will be examined presently.)

Conservatism

Like liberalism, conservatism has undergone historical transformation in America. Just as early liberals (represented by Thomas Jefferson) espoused less government, early conservatives (whose earliest leaders were Alexander Hamilton and John Adams) urged government support of economic enterprise and government intervention on behalf of privileged groups. By the time of the New Deal, and in reaction to the growth of the welfare state since that time, conservatives had argued strongly that more government means more unjustified interference in citizens' lives, more bureaucratic regulation of private conduct, more inhibiting control of economic enterprise, more material advantage for the less energetic and less able at the expense of those who are prepared to work harder and better, and, of course, more taxes— taxes that will be taken from those who have earned money and given to those who have not.

Contemporary conservatives are not always opposed to state intervention. They may support larger military expenditures in order to protect society against foreign enemies. They may also allow for some intrusion into private life in order to protect society against internal subversion and would pursue criminal prosecution zealously in order to protect society against domestic violence. The fact is that few conservatives, and perhaps fewer liberals, are absolute with respect to their views about the power of the state. Both are quite prepared to use the state in order to further *their* purposes. It is true that activist presidents such as Franklin Roosevelt and John Kennedy were likely to be classified as liberals. However, Richard Nixon was also an activist, and, although he does not easily fit any classification, he was far closer to conservatism than to liberalism. It is too easy to identify liberalism with statism and conservatism with antistatism; it is important to remember that it was liberal Jefferson who counseled against "energetic government" and conservative Alexander Hamilton who designed bold powers for the new central government and wrote, "Energy in the executive is a leading character in the definition of good government."

Neoconservatism and the New Right

Two newer varieties of conservatism have arisen to challenge the dominant strain of conservatism that opposed the New Deal. Those who call themselves (or have finally allowed themselves to be called) neoconservatives are recent converts to conservatism. Many of them are former New Deal Democrats, and some like to argue that it is not they who have changed, it is the Democratic party, which has allowed itself to be taken over by advocates of progressive liberalism. They recognize, as did the New Dealers, the legitimacy of social reform, but now they warn against carrying it too far and creating an arrogant bureaucracy. They support equal opportunity, as they always did, but now they underscore the distinction between equal opportunity and equality of result, which they identify as the goal of affirmative action programs. Broadly speaking, neoconservatism shares with

the older variety of conservatism a high respect for tradition and a view of human nature that some would call pessimistic. During the cold war, neo-conservatives, like all conservatives, were also deeply concerned about the communist threat to America. They advise shoring up America's defenses and resisting any movement that would lead the nation toward unilateral disarmament.

A more recent and more politically active variant of conservatism is called the New Right. Despite the semantic resemblance between the New Right and neoconservatism, the two differ in important ways. Neoconservatives are usually lapsed liberals, while New Rightists tend to be dyed-in-the-wool conservatives—though ones who are determined to appeal to wider con-stituencies than did the "old" Right. Neoconservatives tend to be academics who appeal to other similar elites through books and articles in learned jour-nals. The New Right aims at reaching grassroots voters through a variety of forums, from church groups to direct-mail solicitation. Neoconservatives customarily talk about political-economic structures and global strategies; New Rightists emphasize the concerns of ordinary Americans, what they call family issues—moral concerns such as abortion, prayer in public schools, pornography, and what they consider to be a general climate of moral break-down in the nation. These family issues are very similar to the social issues introduced into the political arena by the advocates of progressive liberalism. This should not be surprising, since the rise of the New Right was a reaction to the previous success of the progressive movement in legitimizing its stands on social issues.

Spokesmen for progressive liberalism and the New Right stand as po-lar opposites: The former regard abortion as a woman's right; the latter see it as legalized murder. The former tend to regard homosexuality as a lifestyle that needs protection against discrimination; the latter are more likely to see it as a perversion. The former have made an issue of their support for the Equal Rights Amendment; the latter includes large num-bers of women who fought against the amendment because they believed it threatened their role identity. The list of issues could go on. The New Right and the progressive liberals are like positive and negative photographs of America's moral landscape. Sociologist James Davison Hunter uses the term *culture wars* to characterize the struggles between these contrary visions of America. For all the differences between progressive liberalism and the New Right, however, their styles are very similar. They are heavily laced with moralistic prose; they tend to equate compromise with selling out; and they claim to represent the best, most authentic traditions of Amer-ica. This is not to denigrate either movement, for the kinds of issues they address are indeed moral issues, which do not generally admit much com-promise. These issues cannot simply be finessed or ignored, despite the ef-forts of conventional politicians to do so. They must be aired and fought over, which is why we include some of them, such as abortion (Issue 15), in this volume.

RADICALS, REACTIONARIES, AND MODERATES

The label *reactionary* is almost an insult, and the label *radical* is worn with pride by only a few zealots on the banks of the political mainstream. A reactionary is not a conserver but a backward-mover, dedicated to turning the clock back to better times. Most people suspect that reactionaries would restore us to a time that never was, except in political myth. For many, the repeal of industrialism or universal education (or the entire twentieth century itself) is not a practical, let alone desirable, political program.

Radicalism (literally meaning "from the roots" or "going to the foundation") implies a fundamental reconstruction of the social order. Taken in that sense, it is possible to speak of right-wing radicalism as well as left-wing radicalism—radicalism that would restore or inaugurate a new hierarchical society as well as radicalism that calls for nothing less than an egalitarian society. The term is sometimes used in both of these senses, but most often the word *radicalism* is reserved to characterize more liberal change. While the liberal would effect change through conventional democratic processes, the radical is likely to be skeptical about the ability of the established machinery to bring about the needed change and might be prepared to sacrifice "a little" liberty to bring about a great deal more equality.

Moderate is a highly coveted label in America. Its meaning is not precise, but it carries the connotations of sensible, balanced, and practical. A moderate person is not without principles, but he or she does not allow principles to harden into dogma. The opposite of moderate is *extremist,* a label most American political leaders eschew. Yet there have been notable exceptions. When Arizona senator Barry Goldwater, a conservative Republican, was nominated for president in 1964, he declared, "Extremism in defense of liberty is no vice! ...Moderation in the pursuit of justice is no virtue!" This open embrace of extremism did not help his electoral chances; Goldwater was overwhelmingly defeated. At about the same time, however, another American political leader also embraced a kind of extremism, and with better results. In a famous letter written from a jail cell in Birmingham, Alabama, the Reverend Martin Luther King, Jr., replied to the charge that he was an extremist not by denying it but by distinguishing between different kinds of extremists. The question, he wrote, "is not whether we will be extremist but what kind of extremist will we be. Will we be extremists for hate, or will we be extremists for love?" King aligned himself with the love extremists, in which category he also placed Jesus, St. Paul, and Thomas Jefferson, among others. It was an adroit use of a label that is usually anathema in America.

PLURALISM

The principle of pluralism espouses diversity in a society containing many interest groups and in a government containing competing units of power. This implies the widest expression of competing ideas, and in this way, plu-

ralism is in sympathy with an important element of liberalism. However, as James Madison and Alexander Hamilton pointed out when they analyzed the sources of pluralism in their *Federalist* commentaries on the Constitution, this philosophy springs from a profoundly pessimistic view of human nature, and in this respect it more closely resembles conservatism. Madison, possibly the single most influential member of the convention that wrote the Constitution, hoped that in a large and varied nation, no single interest group could control the government. Even if there were a majority interest, it would be unlikely to capture all of the national agencies of government—the House of Representatives, the Senate, the presidency and the federal judiciary —each of which was chosen in a different way by a different constituency for a different term of office. Moreover, to make certain that no one branch exercised excessive power, each was equipped with "checks and balances" that enabled any agency of national government to curb the powers of the others. The clearest statement of Madison's, and the Constitution's, theory can be found in the 51st paper of the *Federalist:*

> It may be a reflection on human nature that such devices should be necessary to control the abuses of government. But what is government itself, but the greatest of all reflections on human nature? If men were angels, no government would be necessary.

This pluralist position may be analyzed from different perspectives. It is conservative insofar as it rejects simple majority rule; yet it is liberal insofar as it rejects rule by a single elite. It is conservative in its pessimistic appraisal of human nature; yet pluralism's pessimism is also a kind of egalitarianism, holding as it does that no one can be trusted with power and that majority interests no less than minority interests will use power for selfish ends. It is possible to suggest that in America pluralism represents an alternative to both liberalism and conservatism. Pluralism is antimajoritarian and antielitist and combines some elements of both.

SOME APPLICATIONS

Despite our effort to define the principal alignments in American politics, some policy decisions do not fit neatly into these categories. Readers will reach their own conclusions, but we may suggest some alignments to be found here in order to demonstrate the variety of viewpoints.

The conflicts between liberalism and conservatism are expressed in the opposing approaches of Lois Forer and James Wootton to the question of how to deal with crime (Issue 8). Wootton's defense of mandatory sentencing proceeds from the conservative premise that the best way to fight crime is to get criminals off of the streets and to show would-be criminals that punishment for crime will be swift and certain. Forer, who believes that most violent crime is impulsive, adopts the liberal view that society should aim to rehabilitate rather than simply punish criminals.

Robert Lee's defense of the death penalty (Issue 9) is a classic conservative argument. Like other conservatives, Lee is skeptical of the possibilities of human perfection, and he therefore regards retribution—giving a murderer what he or she "deserves" instead of attempting some sort of "rehabilitation" —as a legitimate goal of punishment. Another classic liberal/conservative split is on welfare. In 1996 Congress passed and President Clinton signed the Family Responsibility Act, which abolished Aid to Families with Dependent Children (AFDC), a New Deal–era welfare program that has been the target of conservatives for at least a quarter of a century. In Issue 13, Peter Edelman, a former Clinton official who resigned after Clinton signed the bill, calls the signing "the worst thing Clinton has done," while Daniel Casse contends that the new law has gotten people off welfare and into productive jobs. Issue 14, on whether or not the gap between the rich and the poor is increasing, points up another disagreement between liberals and conservatives. Most liberals would agree with Paul Krugman that socioeconomic inequality is increasing and that this undermines the basic tenets of American democracy. Christopher DeMuth, representing the conservative viewpoint, maintains that Americans are becoming more equal and that virtually all people benefit from increased prosperity because it takes place in a free market. Affirmative action (Issue 11) has become a litmus test of the newer brand of progressive liberalism. The progressives say that it is not enough for the laws of society to be color-blind or gender-blind; they must now reach out to remedy the ills caused by racism and sexism. New Deal liberals, along with conservatives and libertarians, generally oppose affirmative action, which they regard as racism in reverse.

Another progressive/New Deal split occurs between Mary Ann Glendon and Ronald Dworkin in Issue 7. Dworkin, who would not reject the *progressive* label, favors a kind of judicial activism based on judges' views of what outcome "does most credit to the nation." Glendon, echoing the concerns of New Deal liberals during the 1930s, fears that such activism upsurps the legislative function and enervates democracy.

Gay marriage (Issue 16) is also an issue that divides progressive liberals from conservatives. Andrew Sullivan defends gay marriage on the liberal grounds of equal treatment, while James Q. Wilson, whose views are more conservative, worries about what it might do to the institution of marriage. Another more or less predictable division between liberals and conservatives is on the issue of gun control (Issue 10). Liberals generally agree with Carl Bogus's view that stronger gun control laws than currently exist may reduce gun violence and at any rate are worth trying. Conservatives tend to agree with Daniel Polsby, who maintains that if gun control laws are tightened, criminals will be all the more tempted to use guns while committing crimes because they could then be reasonably sure that law-abiding citizens will not be carrying their own guns for self-defense.

This book contains a few arguments that are not easy to categorize. The issue on hate speech (Issue 12) is one. Liberals traditionally have opposed any

curbs on free speech, but Charles Lawrence, who would certainly not call himself a conservative, believes that curbs on speech that abuses minorities may be necessary. Opposing him is Jonathan Rauch, who takes the traditional liberal view that we must protect the speech even of those whose ideas we hate. Issue 20, on whether or not democracy is good for all countries, is also hard to classify. President Woodrow Wilson, a liberal, regarded World War I as a war to "make the world safe for democracy," but some latter-day liberals worry that exporting democracy to the ends of the earth is just as bad as pushing capitalism or other aspects of American life on other peoples. Robert Kaplan, who does not think democracy is the best form of government for all countries, is not necessarily a conservative, then, any more than Robert Kagan is a liberal for thinking that it is. Issue 15, on whether or not abortion should be restricted, also eludes easy classification. The pro-choice position, as argued by Mary Gordon, is not a traditional liberal position. Less than a generation ago legalized abortion was opposed by liberals such as Senator Edward Kennedy (D-Massachusetts) and the Reverend Jesse Jackson, and even today some liberals, such as former Pennsylvania governor Robert Casey and columnist Nat Hentoff, continue to oppose it. Nevertheless, most liberals now adopt some version of Gordon's pro-choice views. Opposing Gordon is former appeals court judge Robert Bork, who is clearly conservative, even if his argument here might be endorsed by liberals like Hentoff.

The arguments least likely to fit into a liberal-versus-conservative framework are the contrasting views of Attorney General Janet Reno and Supreme Court justice Antonin Scalia on the independent counsel law (Issue 6). Scalia, the conservative, opposes the law, as do many liberals today. But liberals were generally not opposed to the law in 1988, when Scalia wrote his opinion. Today, many conservatives who dislike President Clinton would agree with his attorney general's insistence on the need for an outside probe of possible wrongdoing in an administration—though few conservatives took that view in 1988, when Ronald Reagan was president.

Issues 17, 18, and 19 return us to the liberal/conservative arena of debate. In Issue 17, "Will America Dominate Tomorrow's Global Economy," Mortimer Zuckerman takes the conservative view that we are entering another "American century," while Paul Krugman warns (as liberals often do) of the dangers of patriotic "boasting." Issue 18 revisits the China debate, which periodically surfaces between liberals and conservatives. In 1972 President Nixon astounded friend and foe alike when he visited China and started melting the ice that had frozen the two countries into postures of confrontation. But Nixon was an exception among conservatives. Most have never stopped regarding "Red China" as a menace to the United States. This is the position taken by Richard Bernstein and Ross Munro, while Robert Ross takes a more liberal view in minimizing the danger posed by today's China. In Issue 19, "Should the United States Put More Restrictions on Immigration?" Daniel James worries about the effect of "newcomers" on the U.S. economy and culture, which is not a surprising view for someone who is deeply committed

to stability and continuity of culture, as conservatives are. Stephen Moore, in an argument that could have been made by liberals in the 1930s or the early 1900s, argues that America thrives on the energies brought to its shores by immigrants.

Obviously one's position on the issues in this book will be affected by circumstances. However, we would like to think that the essays in this book are durable enough to last through several seasons of events and controversies. We can be certain that the issues will survive. The search for coherence and consistency in the use of political labels underlines the options open to us and reveals their consequences. The result must be more mature judgments about what is best for America. That, of course, is the ultimate aim of public debate and decision making, and it transcends all labels and categories.

On the Internet . . .

The Federal Web Locator
Use this handy site as a launching pad for the Web sites of U.S. federal agencies, departments, and organizations. It is well organized and easy to use for informational and research purposes.
http://www.law.vill.edu/Fed-Agency/fedwebloc.html

The Library of Congress
Examine this Web site to learn about the extensive resource tools, library services/resources, exhibitions, and databases available through the Library of Congress in many different subfields of government studies.
http://www.loc.gov/

Scanned Originals of Early American Documents
Through this Emory University site you can view scanned originals of the Declaration of Independence, the Constitution, and the Bill of Rights. The transcribed texts are also available, as are the *Federalist Papers.*
http://www.law.emory.edu/FEDERAL/

Poynter Online
This research site of the Poynter Institute for Media Studies provides extensive links to information and resources about the media, including media ethics and reportage techniques. Many bibliographies and Web sites are included. *http://www.poynter.org/research/research.htm*

The Gallop Organization
Open this Gallup Organization page for links to an extensive archive of public opinion poll results and special reports on a huge variety of topics related to American society, politics, and government.
http://www.gallup.com/

U.S. Information Agency
This wide ranging page of the USIA provides definitions, related documentation, and a discussion of topics of concern to students of American government. It addresses today's hot topics as well as ongoing issues that form the foundation of the field. Many Web links are provided.
http://www.usia.gov/usis.html

PART 1

Democracy and the American Political Process

Democracy *is derived from two Greek words,* dēmos *and* kratia, *and means "people's rule." The issue today is whether or not the political realities of America conform to the ideal of people's rule. Are the people really running the country? Some contend that the democratic political system has failed. Is that a fair charge, or is it based on simplistic premises? Political campaigns have come under fire in recent years for failing to serve the best interests of American democracy. Is this true, or do campaigns effectively inform and unify the American public? Another issue generating controversy is the increasing amount of money being spent for political campaigns and the effect of this spending on the government. Does the current system of campaign finance need to be reviewed and reformed? Finally, in this section, we address the issue of the news media's role in the governmental process.*

■ Has the American Political System Succeeded?

■ Do Political Campaigns Promote Good Government?

■ Should Campaign Finance Be Reformed?

■ Are the Mass Media Degrading Political Discourse?

ISSUE 1

Has the American Political System Succeeded?

YES: Irving Kristol, from "On the Character of the American Political Order," in Robert L. Utley, Jr., ed., *The Promise of American Politics: Principles and Practice After Two Hundred Years* (University Press of America, 1989)

NO: Daniel Lazare, from *The Frozen Republic: How the Constitution Is Paralyzing Democracy* (Harcourt Brace, 1996)

ISSUE SUMMARY

YES: Writer Irving Kristol argues that America possesses a rich combination of ingredients that give it strength, resilience, and character.

NO: Freelance writer Daniel Lazare contends that America has become paralyzed in a constitutional straitjacket and that it needs radical reform.

"Some men," Thomas Jefferson wrote in 1816, "look at constitutions with sanctimonious reverence, and deem them like the ark of the Covenant, too sacred to be touched." Jefferson made it clear that he was no such person. In his view, "each generation is as independent as the one preceding, as that was of all which had gone before." Jefferson, therefore, put little stock in tradition or continuity, and even less in the Founding Fathers.

Ironically, Jefferson himself has become a sanctified figure, with his own marble memorial near the Capitol and countless tributes quoting his words as if they were scriptural. Indeed, in the popular mind Jefferson is often associated with the Constitution—a document that he played no role in drafting and about which he had some serious reservations.

American political folklore is full of these ironies. America's heroes and their ideas get yanked out of their historical settings and are thrown together into what appears to be a timeless realm of good feelings. Here are Jefferson and Lincoln sitting together, though the former kept slaves and the latter emancipated them. Over there Alexander Hamilton is talking to Teddy Roosevelt, whom the historical Hamilton probably would have regarded as a traitor to his class. Andrew Jackson seems to get along fine with Franklin Roosevelt, though the former hated centralized government and the latter expanded it further than anyone could have dreamed. It is the "Hall of the Presidents" in Disney World, except that the cordial, gesturing statues are not just presidents but also many others who have won their place in the

heavenly hall: Malcolm X and Martin Luther King, Jr., Abigail Adams and Eleanor Roosevelt, and Robert LaFollette and Robert Kennedy, for example.

Implicit—sometimes even explicit—in all this is the belief that America has a unique and coherent tradition, an "American way of life" that has carried the American people through a turbulent history and continues to guide them toward whatever lies ahead. It is a creed that celebrates "American exceptionalism," its special heritage; this belief does not rule out change, but it insists that changes are to be made by reaching back into the past and finding new wisdom there. Highest honors are usually reserved for the Founding Fathers, the men who set it going in the first place by their wise craftsmanship. Such talk would have embarrassed Jefferson, but it continues to touch deep chords whenever Americans gather to hear political speech.

The early years of the twentieth century marked a high point of national celebration; in 1909 the American writer Herbert Croly noted that "the faith of Americans in their own country is religious, if not in its intensity, at any rate in its almost absolute and universal authority." Yet a few years later, in 1913, historian Charles A. Beard published *An Economic Interpretation of the Constitution* (Free Press), which, far from portraying the founders as selfless, far-seeing patriots, depicted them as rather venal men bent upon protecting their own mercantile, investment, and manufacturing interests. For decades Beard's book was a favorite among debunkers of the Constitution and American exceptionalism. This current of dissent remained underground during much of the century, but in recent times, particularly since the Vietnam war, it has resurfaced. The last 30 years have seen numerous expressions of discontent with America and its heritage, from revisionist history to flag burning. In 1987 even a Supreme Court justice voiced some of these sentiments. Thurgood Marshall, the first African American to sit on the high court, suggested that the Framers of the Constitution drew up a document based upon "oudated notions of liberty, justice, and equality." In Marshall's view, the Constitution has been saved from obsolescence only by its amendments, particularly those that had been added since the Civil War. The founders themselves, he thought, deserve little credit for wisdom or foresight.

In the following selections, Irving Kristol upholds the "celebratory" view. America, he believes, possesses a rich mixture of ingredients that make it a successful polity, for which considerable credit should go to its founders. Opposing that view is Daniel Lazare, who suggests that the Constitution is no more suitable to present times than the horse-drawn vehicles that carried the Founding Fathers to Philadelphia in 1787.

YES

Irving Kristol

ON THE CHARACTER OF THE
AMERICAN POLITICAL ORDER

It is an interesting, if rather peculiar, fact about writings on the American political tradition that they are mainly what I would call Manichaean. Manichaeanism was a heresy of the early Christian centuries which held that the world was divided between a good god and a bad god and that the history of the world was the history of their conflict. It was a dualistic vision of reality and human history. Such a dualistic vision seems to be dominant in most interpretations of the American political tradition. Indeed, almost from the beginning, we have perceived the American tradition in terms of aristocrats versus republicans, the people versus the oligarchy, republicanism versus democracy, progressives versus the "special interests." From reading these dualistic interpretations of American history and American politics one would think our history has been particularly bloody, tumultuous, and ambiguous. That is not the case.

Our history has been, by most reasonable, let us say historical, standards not particularly tumultuous; and the American people seem never to have been torn by conflicting interpretations of the American political tradition, though scholars may be. Even our very bloody Civil War had surprisingly little effect on the course of American history. If one were to write an American history textbook with the chapter on the Civil War dropped out, to be replaced by a single sentence to the effect that slavery was abolished by constitutional amendment in 1865, very little in subsequent chapters, as now written, would need revision. The Civil War had even less effect on the American political tradition, since there never really was a distinctively Southern political tradition, nor did the war give rise to one. A textbook on American intellectual history could safely ignore the Civil War, were it not for the fact that one feels it to be almost sacrilegious that so much suffering should be so barren of consequence. The Civil War was and is a most memorable event—but not any kind of turning point in American history.

My thesis, in a nutshell, is that the American people have always understood the American political tradition in an instinctive way, whereas scholarly interpretations inevitably tend to emphasize one aspect of this tradition at

From Irving Kristol, "On the Character of the American Political Order," in Robert L. Utley, Jr., ed., *The Promise of American Politics: Principles and Practice After Two Hundred Years* (Tocqueville Forum, 1989). Copyright © 1989 by The University Press of America. Reprinted by permission.

the expense of all others. When I say that I think the American people have an instinctive understanding of the American political tradition, I mean that it is, as it were, "in their bones." I mean that almost literally. If we transported two or three thousand Americans to Mars to establish an American colony there and then left them alone, what would they do? They would do exactly what the original settlers of the West and the South did. They would behave like Americans. The first thing they would do is build a school. The second thing they would do is build a church. The third thing they would do is go out and make money. And the fourth thing they would do is have elections and form political parties —and fight like hell. They would just clone the American political process out there on Mars. In fact, if you look at the history of the settling of the West, you find a group of people—not all of them, by the way, native-born Americans, but it did not seem to matter—who all behaved in pretty much the same way, who established more or less identical villages which then became more or less identical cities.

So the question I wish to address is: what is the American political tradition as it is in practice, apart from all the theoretical arguments about it? Of course these arguments are very valuable. I really do not want to sound philistine; it is very important to study those arguments. But what I want to do is look at the American political tradition as it exists within American attitudes, within the American mind, within American habits of behavior, within, to put it in a cliché, "the American way of life." This is a cliché that has a lot of meaning, one which sums up all of the very different elements that go into making the American political tradition, as this tradition is apprehended by the American people. It is an extraordinarily mixed tradition. That is why it is possible for analysts to seize one aspect of it, for instance, the fact that it is capitalist, or that it is democratic, or that it is republican, and decide that is the basic aspect. Whereas the truth is that the American political tradition is simultaneously democratic, republican, capitalist, federal, and other things as well. It is, moreover, a political tradition whose roots are to be found in a Protestantized version of the Judeo-Christian tradition. I would like to take those elements of this mixture one by one, and see what they are.

"Democratic" is relatively simple. Ours is a political system and a political tradition that says that ultimately the will of the people will prevail. Ultimately, not instantly, because the will that is to prevail is presumed to incorporate the considered judgment of the people. Hence the separation of powers, the decentralization of authority, and the slow, cumbersome legislative process.

Moreover, because it is a democratic system, it is a system that prizes equality. But what does equality mean in the American political tradition? It means, to begin with, equality before the law. There is no question about that. It also means social equality; that is to say, a classless society, which we have. Many of us have studied sociology and have heard that we do not have a classless society. Sociology professors explain that we are really divided into four classes, seven classes, twenty-two classes, depending on what mode of analysis they use. But surely if we need a sociologist to tell us whether or not we live in a class society, then it is certain we do not live in a class society. People who live in class societies

know how many classes there are, and know exactly where they are within any particular class. There is no secret about it; it is the most obvious and important thing in anyone's life. The simple fact is that American society today is, in any reasonable sense of the term, a society of social equality. This does not mean economic equality. Social equality, not economic equality, is what our version of democracy is about.

Here, again, we can be misled by some learned men. My favorite learned misleader is Thorstein Veblen. He was an enormously gifted man who probably wrote more nonsense about America than any other gifted man in our history. Veblen's best known nonsense, about "conspicuous consumption," is studied soberly in sociology courses. By now the term has passed into the language. But if there is any fact that is obvious about the United States, it is how little conspicuous consumption there really is. I can prove this. Observe any stranger, and guess his income, or how wealthy his family is, or what his social class is. The fact is, you cannot. Almost all students are wearing blue jeans. You cannot tell what their incomes or backgrounds are. As for adults, go out to the parking lot. Can you really tell how much money a person has from his automobile? Professors drive foreign automobiles, businessmen drive American automobiles, and that's about all there is to say. If you see a Cadillac driving down the street, a car ninety feet long, can you tell what kind of person is driving it? Is it a doctor? Is it a pimp? It could be anybody. The truth is that in our kind of democracy there are no social classes by any reasonable definition of that term.

Ours, however, is not simply a democratic political tradition, it is also a re-publican political tradition. The late Martin Diamond wrote an excellent textbook called *The Democratic Republic.* It is one of the few textbooks I know which takes seriously both of those terms in relation to the American political tradition. What does the word "republic" mean when you say we are a democratic republic? It means that although we are democratic, we have no faith in democracy. Democracy, in the American political tradition, is not, or at least ought not to be, a matter of faith. There are lots of books written called something like "The Democratic Faith." That is the wrong phrase. There is no reason to have faith in democracy, which is simply one form of political government. Faith should be reserved for higher things than any political system. One should not have faith in *any* political system.

One cannot assume that where the will of the people is supreme, the people will do the right things. The republican aspect of our political tradition is the way in which we refine the will of the people through the principle of representation. For instance, it was always assumed, and even is assumed today, that our representatives, though common men, in a sense are also more than common men. Walter Bagehot said of Sir Robert Peel that he was not a common man but a common man could have been cut out of him. That is the way we feel, or should feel, about our representatives. They ought to represent us, be in tune with us, understand us. But they ought to be a little better than we are. They ought to be a little more elevated than we are—because then they elevate us.

We are republicans in that we have a Constitution which curbs the will of the people, forces the people to rethink, forces the people's representatives to de-

bate and consider, and forces the people to be reasonable. In other words, in a democratic republic the republican element is to be perceived when the people put constraints upon themselves because the people do not have any kind of democratic faith. People understand that they are capable of doing foolish things, and people therefore want institutional checks upon their own will, upon their own ultimate power.

Now to consider the federal element of the American political tradition. This is a very important element in the tradition, though often overlooked and, these days, underemphasized. The federal system is important because it institutionalizes the diffusion of power. I do not think anyone who has not experienced centralized power in other nations can understand how diffused power actually is in the United States. I well recall way back in 1970, during the Cambodian business, when some of my students at New York University announced to me that they were going down to Washington to seize power. I said, "How are you going to seize power?" They said, "We're going to take the Pentagon, that's what we're going to do." "Well, let's say the government leaves you the Pentagon," I said, "what are you going to do there?" "Well, we're going to give orders," they said. And I said, "Who's going to listen?"

It had not occurred to them that you cannot seize power in this country, you cannot even locate it. Perhaps in France it is possible to seize power by taking Paris. Suppose we had a revolution in New York City, and on the NBC nightly news broadcast from New York, the rebels proudly announced that a new regime had been established in City Hall. What would happen? The ratings would fall. People would say, "Oh, New York, you know what sort of things go on in New York," and it would not make the faintest bit of difference. It is very important, therefore, to preserve our federal system, so as to make unlikely any undue concentration and usurpation of power.

But there is a much more important aspect to the federal system, namely, the educational aspect. Local government and participation in local institutions is the way in which people learn the most important of all political truths, which is that the world is full of other people. It is a very sad political truth, a very disillusioning political truth. But people who do not understand it are engaged in a kind of utopian politics that is ultimately doomed. That the world is full of other people means that you may have a good idea, but it will often turn out that other people, somehow or other, for reasons which are inexplicable, do not see how good your idea is. It happens, not only does it happen, it is inevitable that it happens. Teaching us to live with other people is the function of the federal structure of our democracy. This kind of self-education can only occur through participation in local institutions, and it does not really matter how small they are. You really do not learn politics until you have the misfortune to be elected to your local school board. *Then* you understand what politics is about. In my own experience—I'm a New Yorker, we don't have local school boards, and if we did I couldn't get elected—I had the misfortune some years ago to be elected to the board of my cooperative apartment house. It was really very interesting to attend the annual meeting of this co-op. The residents were upper-income people, some very prominent socialists among them, some very prominent lawyers,

some very wealthy stock brokers. At the annual house meeting the board knew that for the first hour the tenants would get up and denounce the landlord. At the end of the hour it would occur to them that *they* were the landlord and then we would get down to business. It took them about three years before they stopped denouncing us, their elected and unpaid trustees, as the landlord. It was an educational process. Anyone who gets involved in local self-government discovers that the world is full of other people, that there is no point in being dogmatic about what you think is right, that you must come to terms with this world, a world which is what it is and is never going to differ radically from what it is.

One other major virtue of the federal system, which we are only now beginning to appreciate, is that it diffuses some absolutely insoluble problems, so that they fester on a local rather than on a national level. In this sense, I think the decision of the Supreme Court legalizing abortion was a political disaster, never mind the morality of it. It was a disaster because it made abortion a national issue. Until that time abortion had been a state issue and if the states wished, they could always devolve the responsibility for that issue upon local communities (as was and is done with an issue like prohibition). Now, abortion is not an issue you can compromise about. It is one of those issues that is ultimately divisive Therefore, you are better off diffusing the issue, making it a local issue, rather than importing it as a factor into national politics. As a result of the Supreme Court decision, we have imported a most divisive element into our national politics, one which cannot be compromised, and which we shall just have to live with.

It is deplorable that pornography also has now become nationalized as an issue, as a result of the courts' lack of wisdom. In my day, all the books that were banned in Boston were sold in New York. It was not such a bad system, people in both Boston and New York got what they really wanted and it didn't really matter all that much. Now the issue of pornography has become a matter of national significance, one on which national politicians are forced to make pronouncements, and this raises the question of national censorship. The best way to cope with the problems of pornography and censorship is to let local people solve it any way they want. Some will be permissive, some will not; some will have strict censorship, some will have lax censorship. That is all right. Indeed, that is just the way it is supposed to be. The whole point about federalism and decentralization is to see to it that such controversial issues do not distract national politics from its truly important concerns.

"Capitalist" is perhaps the most controversial of all the terms I have applied to our system. I do not see why it should be, since if anything is obvious, it is that we have been, certainly at least since the enactment of the Constitution, and in fact for many decades prior to that, a capitalist nation. A nation that believes that individual liberty is indissolubly linked to private property—that is what it means to be capitalist. We are a nation that believes that private property, and therefore a market economy (the two go together), are necessary, though not sufficient conditions for a political regime of liberty. Necessary but not sufficient. You can have private property and you can have a market economy in an authoritarian regime. Never in history, however, has there been what we would regard as

a free society, or a liberal society, or a regime of liberty that did not have private property and a largely market economy.

Capitalism is important not only because of the support it gives to liberty —it is *the* absolute precondition of liberty—but also because it promises and promotes economic growth. The ancient democracies of classical Greece were full of class strife; the *demos* versus the *aristoi*, the masses versus the oligarchy. If you do not have economic growth, all democracies fall into such class strife. It is economic growth that permits a democracy to avoid class struggles over the distribution of a pie of preestablished size. It does that by always creating a larger pie so that everyone benefits, however unequally, and you do not have to benefit at someone else's expense. You can acquire property without expropriating property. . . .

Our system is democratic, republican, federal, and capitalist. And it is also a system that has a religious basis. Let me explain what I mean. A democratic system where the will of the people rules supreme, and a capitalist system which regards the pursuit of self-interest in the marketplace as legitimate, needs religion to supply certain crucial, missing elements.

Traditional religion is to liberal democratic capitalism as the Old Testament is to the New. Let me explain this puzzling remark. There was a big fight within the Christian church during the first three centuries of its history as to whether or not the Old Testament should be included in Holy Scripture. There were some major movements (subsequently defined as heresies; the Marcionite heresy most notably) that said: "No, let's not bring the Old Testament into Holy Scripture. We have a New Testament, why do we need

the Old?" The church fathers, who were very wise men, said: "The New Testament, it's true, completes the Old; but there are things in the old which are not in the New, and which a church needs." The New Testament, after all, was not written with the establishment of the Christian church in mind—there is nothing about an established, authoritative Christian church in the New Testament. Therefore, the church fathers found they needed certain things in the Old Testament that are not in the New such as: the injunction to be fruitful and multiply, the pronouncement that God created the earth and saw it was good. In other words, the fathers needed certain theological premises to create an orthodoxy, to be able to tell its members that they can sanctify God in their daily lives, that they need not be hermits in the desert, they need not all become ascetic or aim at Christian perfection. These have all since been established as crucial affirmations of Christianity but, as it happens, are all to be found in the Old Testament, not in the New, since the people who wrote the New Testament took the Old Testament for granted.

It is not too much to say that the Judeo-Christian tradition, in its Protestantized form, is the Old Testament for liberal capitalism. It supplies things that liberal capitalism, liberal democratic capitalism, cannot itself supply; mainly what we call "values"—a moral code above all—and which the founders of capitalism simply took for granted. Precisely because a capitalist economy is one which does emphasize self-interest, it especially needs a very strong religious element in its culture in order to modify, complement and curb that self-interest.

Adam Smith wrote two books, *The Wealth of Nations* and a lesser known

book, *The Theory of Moral Sentiments.* *The Wealth of Nations* was about how people act in the marketplace. They act in the marketplace out of self-interest, and Adam Smith's great contribution was to show that these actions out of self-interest, nevertheless, in the longer term, served everyone's interest by promoting economic growth. In *The Theory of Moral Sentiments,* however, (a book which, incidentally, he never repudiated—he revised it after publishing *The Wealth of Nations,* but did not change it much) he said, "Fine, what happens when you have created wealth? What will wealthy people do?" He said that in the end, what wealthy people will do is try to earn the good opinion of their fellow citizens by acts of philanthropy, which is just what they are doing. Such acts of philanthropy, in this culture, come out of the Protestantized version of the Judeo-Christian moral tradition with which Adam Smith was familiar. . . .

I want to reassert that without this religious culture, the capitalist economic system becomes rather disgusting. Making money is fun; but, on the other hand, no one ever said it is an ennobling activity, no one ever said it is a heroic activity. It is, at best, a prosaic activity. In a society where most people are involved in commercial activities, you especially need a culture suffused with religious traditions that tell you what you are making money for, that tell you how to conduct yourself when you are making money, and that, above all, answer certain absolutely crucial and inevitable questions about the meaning of life and the meaning of death. It is this religious element that is the final and necessary constituent of the American political tradition.

. . . There is no point, in my view, in departing radically from that tradition —to socialism, for instance. The most important political fact of the twentieth century has been the death of socialism as an alternative model of society, as an alternative political tradition. There are still socialists to be found, but not in socialist countries. There are no socialists in Eastern Europe, no socialists in the Soviet Union, but there are socialists in American universities, French universities, German universities. The fact is, socialism as a serious political possibility is dead. There are about sixty official socialist countries in the world and not one of them is a place where you and I would want to live. Not one of them is a place where even their own people particularly want to live. They would all immigrate to the United States if given the opportunity. So the socialist ideal is dead. It lives as an academic idea, but as a reality it has been tried, and it does not work. It does not work because it is based upon a utopian vision of human nature, of what human beings are capable of. Because it is utopian it ends up trying to create utopia through coercion, since it cannot be created in any other way. But you cannot create utopia through coercion either; all you do is create a bureaucratic terrorist state.

So there is no alternative but to work within the American tradition. That is the test for the next generation —somehow to renew this tradition, perhaps revitalize it, perhaps amend it, perhaps revise it. But the tradition as I have described it—democratic, capitalist, federal, republican, religious—that is the tradition within which we shall have to work.

NO

Daniel Lazare

THE FROZEN REPUBLIC: HOW THE CONSTITUTION IS PARALYZING DEMOCRACY

America is a religious society caught up in a painful contradiction. On one hand, its politics rest on faith in the Founding Fathers—a group of planters, merchants, and political thinkers who gathered in a stuffy tavern in Philadelphia in 1787—and the document they produced during the course of that summer, the Constitution. These are the be-all and end-all of the American system, the alpha and the omega. On the other hand, the faith isn't working. Problems are mushrooming, conflicts are multiplying, and society seems increasingly out of control. As a result, Americans find themselves in the curious position of celebrating the Constitution and Founders, who comprise America's base, yet cursing the system of politics they gave birth to. The more the roof leaks and the beams sag, the more fervent the odes to the original architects and builders seem to grow.

This is curious but not unprecedented. In one form or another, Americans have been simultaneously praising the Constitution and cursing the government since virtually the moment George Washington took office. What is different, however, is the degree. Constitution worship has never been more fervent, while dissatisfaction with constitutional politics has never been greater. Yet rather than attempting to work through the contradiction—rather than wondering, for instance, whether the fact that the house is falling down doesn't reflect poorly on those who set it up—the general tendency over the last two decades or so has been to blame anyone and everyone except the Founders. If the original conception is pure and perfect—and it is an article of faith in America's civic religion that it is—then the fault must lie with the subsequent generations who allowed it to be trampled in the dust. We have betrayed the legacy by permitting politicians, the media, special interests, minorities, etc., to have their way. Therefore, our duty as loyal subjects of the Constitution is to pick it up, dust it off, and somehow restore it to its original purity.

This is the way religious societies think —when confronted with the problems of the modern world, their first instinct is to retreat to some long-lost Eden, where everything was good and clean and honest.... [I]t ain't necessarily so,... Eden was never what it was cracked up to be, and... the Founders were never as farseeing and all-wise as their followers allege. The problem with American politics... is not that they are the flawed expression of a perfect plan, but that they are the all too faithful expression of a flawed Constitution. Where the document devised in Philadelphia in 1787 neatly fit the needs of American society at the time, it proved woefully inadequate to the needs of American society in subsequent decades. In 1861, the constitutional system fairly disintegrated under the pressure of seventy years or so of pent-up change, unleashing one of the worst military conflicts of the entire nineteenth century. For approximately the next three-quarters of a century, it proved to be a political straitjacket, in which even the mildest social reform was prohibited on the grounds that it would interfere with the minority rights of bankers and industrialists; then, following a brief golden age after World War II, it has resulted in crippling gridlock and paralysis. The Constitution has performed this way not despite the Founders, but because of them. They created a system in which the three branches of government were suspended in almost perfect equipoise so that a move by one element in any one direction would be almost immediately offset by a countermove by one or both of the others in the opposite direction. The result was a counterdemocratic system dedicated to the virtues of staying put in the face of rising popular pressure. The more the system refused to budge,

the more the constitutional sages praised its essential immobility.

The problem with the Constitution lies not with any single clause or paragraph, but rather with the concepts of balance and immutability, indeed with the very idea of a holy, all-powerful Constitution. James Madison, who did more in Philadelphia than anyone else to shepherd the Constitution through to completion, saw the document as an anchor in a flyaway world. An anchor, however, is precisely what is holding American society back. There are times when society needs to fly away and leave the past behind—to cast off old assumptions, to adopt new theories, to forge new frameworks of politics and government. This is precisely what the Madisonian Constitution was designed to prevent and something it has succeeded all too well in doing. As a result, U.S. society is laboring under what is at best an eighteenth-century mode of government as it prepares to enter the twenty-first century.

America must cast off the constraints. At the same time, it has never seemed more unequal to the task. Society has never been more fragmented, politics have never been narrower or more shortsighted, while the extended constitutional priesthood—judges, eminent professors of constitutional law, op-ed columnists, and so forth—has never been more dogmatic. Even as they try to choke each other to death, liberals and conservatives have never been more united in their devotion to the secular religion that supposedly holds society together but is in fact tearing it apart. They are like Catholic and Protestant theologians of the sixteenth and seventeenth centuries, each one claiming to be more faithful to the Word than the other. The outlook

for reform seems grim as a consequence, which only makes it all the more *necessary*. What Americans need is less faith and more thought, less willingness to put their trust in a bygone political order and a greater realization that they, the living, are the only ones capable of maneuvering society through the storm. Instead of beginning with the Constitution as the essential building block, they should realize that there are no givens in this world and that all assumptions, beginning with the most basic, must constantly be examined and tested.

This must seem very strange to readers who have been trained from childhood to think of the Constitution as America's rock and foundation, without which it would disintegrate into an unthinking mob. Yet constitutional faith is a form of thoughtlessness, since it means relying on the thought of others rather than on one's own. The alternative is to emancipate oneself from the past, to wake up to the realization that two centuries of struggling and fighting have not been for naught and that we know a few things the Founders didn't as a consequence. Rather than continually deferring to their judgment, it means understanding that we are fully competent to make our way through the modern world on our own. This is not to say we should ignore Madison, Jefferson, et al., merely that there is no reason we should feel bound by their precepts.

... Government in America doesn't work because it's not supposed to work. In their infinite wisdom, the Founders created a deliberately unresponsive system in order to narrow the governmental options and force us to seek alternative routes. Politics were dangerous; therefore, politics had to be limited and constrained. But America cannot expect to survive much longer with a government that is inefficient and none too democratic by design. It is impossible to forge ahead in the late twentieth century using governmental machinery dating from the late eighteenth. Urban conditions can only worsen, race relations can only grow more poisonous, while the middle class can only grow more alienated and embittered. Politics will grow more irrational and self-defeating, while the price of the good life—that is, a nice home, good schools, a quiet street in a safe neighborhood—can only continue its upward climb beyond the reach of all but the most affluent. Rush Limbaugh, Howard Stern, and other demagogues of the airwaves will continue to make out like bandits, while the millions of people who listen to them will only grow angrier and more depressed. Eventually, every other society caught up in such a bind has snapped. Sooner or later, the United States will as well. The stays have already begun to fray....

If they are to emerge from their latest paralysis, Americans will have to resume the job they failed to finish in the 1860s. Rather than mindlessly cursing government and politicians, they will have to get to the bottom of the American predicament and figure out why politics in this country has grown so abysmal. Instead of rallying to this or that favorite son, they will have to figure out why even the best candidates wind up being defeated by the system they have vowed to change. Rather than relying on the Founding Fathers for answers, it means looking to themselves—to their own intelligence, their own analytical powers, their own creative abilities.

... [T]he underlying principle of checks and balances was much subtler than I had imagined. As every schoolchild knows,

the Founders had wanted a Constitution that would serve the people as "a safeguard against the tyranny of their own passions." As Supreme Court Justice Louis Brandeis put it in *Myers v. U.S.* (1926), "The doctrine of the separation of powers was adopted... not to promote efficiency but to preclude the exercise of arbitrary power"—which, put another way, meant that inefficiency was the price Americans had to pay for freedom and democracy. But there was a catch here. How was one to *evaluate* a system that was inefficient by design? What output criteria could one develop? If it was performing well, that is, efficiently, then it was performing in a way that was dangerous and threatening. If it was performing poorly, that is, *in*efficiently, then it was performing well. Bad was good and good was bad—a conundrum designed to stop even the most ardent reformer in his tracks.

Essentially, Madison and his colleagues in Philadelphia had created a puzzle palace in which logic was turned on its head. Or, rather, they had employed a different kind of logic, a pre-industrial version that would prove incomprehensible to citizens of the industrial era.... [N]ot only [is] the Constitution out of date but... by imposing an unchangeable political structure on a generation that has never had an opportunity to vote on the system as a whole, it amounts to a terrible dictatorship by the past over the present. Americans are prisoners, in effect, of one of the most subtle yet powerful systems of restraint in history, one in which it is possible to curse the president, hurl obscenities at Congress, and all but parade naked down Broadway, yet virtually impossible to alter the political structure in any fundamental way. They live in a system not only of limited government, but of limited democracy, which is why politics of late have become so suffocating and destructive. It is like a prison with no guards and no walls, yet from which no one ever escapes.

The answer is not less democracy—which is what term limits, a balanced-budget amendment, and other checks on legislative power represent—but more. Rather than checks and balances, the American people need to cast off constitutional restraints imposed more than two centuries ago and use their power *as a whole* to rebuild society as they see fit. This is not an invitation to lawlessness, but, quite the contrary, a call for the democratic majority to begin refashioning society along more rational and modern lines. Rather than less freedom, it is a plea for more, beginning with the freedom of the popular majority to modify its political circumstances in whatever way it sees fit. Rather than submitting to an immutable Constitution, Americans should cast off their chains and rethink their society from the ground up. They have nothing to lose —except one of the most unresponsive political systems this side of the former Soviet Union.

... Where the malapportioned U.S. Senate was a hot topic in the late nineteenth century, it has been all but forgotten by the late twentieth. Yet the disparities are worse than ever. Nine states account for more than half the total U.S. population, yet they account for less than twenty percent of the Senate vote. By the same token, a Senate majority can be gotten from twenty-six states representing less than one American in five. Twenty-one states, representing as little as one citizen in nine, are enough to filibuster any piece of legislation to death, while thirteen states, representing as little as 4.5 percent

of the population, are enough to stop a constitutional amendment in its tracks. This is a minority veto run amok. In other respects, the arrangement is deeply unfair as well. Because they are predominantly rural, the twenty-six smallest states have fewer blacks (in fact, about half the national average), fewer Asians, fewer gays, and, of course, fewer urban dwellers in general. Violations of one person–one vote have been barred at the state or municipal level ever since *Baker v. Carr* in 1962. Yet they are, for the moment, beyond challenge at the federal level.

Disparities like these are not just unfair—they are stupid and lazy. No comparable country puts up with anything like them, yet Americans seem oblivious. On the rare occasion when they do think about them, New Yorkers, Californians, et al. seem to just shrug. Commenting on how the Senate Republican minority had filibustered Clinton's economic-stimulus package in April 1993, the journalist Sidney Blumenthal observed matter-of-factly in the *New Yorker:*

> The Senate, of course, was designed to be unrepresentative; it incorporates the principle of the equality of states, not the equality of citizens. The forty-three Republicans do not represent forty-three percent of the people. Because they are clustered in the smaller states, the Senate Republicans represent less than a third of the population.

That little phrase "of course" sums up all that is fatalistic and unthinking in the American character, as presently constituted, that is. It represents uncritical obedience to the dictates of the Founders—to the notion that if the framers *wanted* the Senate to be unrepresentative, that's the way it shall be forevermore. A conscious decision, on the other hand, to abolish such disparities would mean the opposite. It would signal a determination to think through the problems of government ourselves, to take responsibility for where society is heading, and to put an end to drift and gridlock.

Needless to say, taking control of one's destiny can also be dangerous. Just as there is nothing to stop a young person who gets his own apartment and credit card from behaving irresponsibly, there is nothing to stop a nation either. By abolishing separation of powers and checks and balances, the House would liberate itself from judicial review. Even if the Bill of Rights were to remain in place, citizens would have no assurance that the House would abide by its provisions other than its own pledge to do so. Yet what the House promises one day, it can unpromise the next; it could thus abolish free speech and a free press at a stroke, with little more than a yelp of protest from the courts. The only thing that could stop them would be the people themselves, who would recognize that real majority rule is impossible outside of a framework of free and vigorous criticism and debate. The people would want to preserve democracy not for the sake of various beleaguered minorities, the justification presently cited by the ACLU, but for the sake of the majority, namely, its own. A demos that allowed democracy to be squashed would be a demos no longer, merely a collection of atomized prisoners of the status quo.

For a people who like their guarantees in writing, this may not sound like much. Yet the development of a modern, mass democratic consciousness, of a modern democratic *movement*, is the only assurance that democracy in the United States can even survive. Americans must

stop thinking of democracy as a legacy of the Founders and a gift of the gods, something that allows millions of voices to cry, "me! me! me!," while politicians and judges divide up the spoils according to some time-honored formula. Rather, they'll have to think of it as an intellectual framework that *they* create and continuously update, one that allows them to tackle the problems of the modern world not as individuals but as a society. If democracy is to survive, it must grow. And if it is to grow, it must detach itself from pre-democratic eighteenth-century norms and take its place in the modern world.

On the other hand, a young person who does not leave home will be stuck in a stage of attenuated adolescence forever. The same thing is true for Americans as a whole if they fail to emancipate themselves from dependence on a two-century-old legacy. "We're still Jefferson's children," Ronald Reagan once declared in a moment of ersatz piety. And as long as they continue to worship at the shrine of the Founders, Americans will remain in that childlike state indefinitely.

The alternative to taking responsibility and assuming risk is accepting the certainty of decline. There are any number of alternatives that one could imagine to the scenario of a democratic clean sweep sketched out above, none of them very pleasant. Rather than focusing their ire on the federal government, it's all too possible that Californians (not to mention Texans, New Yorkers, Pennsylvanians, etc.) might decide that it is more satisfying to fight among themselves along racial or geographic lines. The vast unfairness of the present arrangement in Washington might all too easily become lost in the mass of petty politics that is life in America, in which a scandal on the lo-

cal school board often looms larger than the scandalous inequality of the U.S. Senate. Fragmentation, after all, is what has allowed the system to survive the last two centuries, and it may be what allows it to limp along for two centuries more. Not unlike the British, Americans may opt for a variation on the theme of muddling through, in which the devil you know (complacency) is to be preferred over the one you don't (change). Small adjustments may be instituted to keep California from boiling over—a bit of military pork here, a federal boondoggle there, a tacit understanding that even if it is to have only two votes in the Senate, its wishes nonetheless will be accorded extra weight. Perhaps Congress will approve the division of the state into three parts so that residents will wind up electing six senators rather than the present two. It would not eliminate the disparities but would at least make them more tolerable. All the old problems would remain—gridlock, the absence of a coherent, systematic policy to deal with social problems, and so on—yet at least it would keep the ship of state from going to pieces when it is still miles from shore.

On the other hand, it would also mean continued long-term decline, and Americans do not seem to be the sort of people to put up with long-term decline. They are too volatile, too imbued with a sense of their own greatness, too angry with themselves and with each other. Checks and balances may persist in Washington, but, if so, political tension will undoubtedly rise to even more dangerous levels. For those who know their German history, there is already a whiff of Weimar in the air. Just as the prewar German constitution was pulled apart by unresolved tension between the executive and legislative branches, the American sys-

tem seems to be coming apart in a not-dissimilar way as well. True, the United States is not fragmented among a dozen or so political parties as Weimar was. Rather, thanks to the attenuated two-party system, it is fragmented among some 535 representatives and senators, each of whom recognizes no authority but his or her own. While Newt Gingrich has succeeded in imposing a remarkable degree of discipline on this motley crew, it is at the cost of increasing fragmentation below—between blacks and whites, the federal government and the states, the cities and suburbs, and so forth. H. Ross Perot's bizarre 1992 presidential bid is meanwhile an illustration of the authoritarian potential that has long been latent in the executive branch. "Presidential power is the power to persuade," political scientist Richard Neustadt once proclaimed. But what happens if H. Ross Perot transforms that power into the power to give orders and have Congress snap to attention?

The problem with the Constitution as it has developed over two centuries is that rather than engaging in a fundamental reordering, Americans have tried to democratize a predemocratic structure. As originally conceived, only one ruling institution—the House—was to be popularly elected and even then only by a fraction of what we now regard as the proper electorate (i.e., only, for the most part, by property-owning white males). The other ruling institutions—the Senate, the presidency, and the courts—were to be only indirectly chosen. But then Andrew Johnson helped democratize the presidency, the Seventeenth Amendment democratized the upper chamber to a degree by providing for the direct election of senators, and the furious confirmation battles over Robert Bork and Clarence Thomas have opened up the judiciary to an unprecedented level of popular pressure and inspection as well. The effect of separation of powers under such conditions has been to divide popular democracy against itself in such a way as to send the collective temperature shooting up to the boiling point. The electorate, as a consequence, is locked in a desperate internal struggle, which, as long as Madisonian checks and balances remain in effect, can never end. The results are tortuous, yet ultimately only two outcomes are possible. Either the body politic will keel over from exhaustion or it will explode.

POSTSCRIPT

Has the American Political System Succeeded?

On one point Kristol and Lazare seem to agree. "What Americans need," writes Lazare, "is less faith and more thought, less willingness to put their trust in a bygone political order and a greater realization that they, the living, are the only ones capable of maneuvering society through the storm." Kristol, too, disparages faith in politics: "Democracy, in the American political tradition, is not, or at least ought not to be, a matter of faith.... One should not have faith in *any* political system." Behind the apparent agreement of the two writers, however, there lies a deeper disagreement. For Lazare himself is not without faith; he shares Jefferson's faith in the ability of today's citizens to govern wisely without the restraints of the past. Of this faith Kristol is profoundly skeptical.

The tension between the two points of view in these arguments is that of continuity versus change. This has been a perennial theme in American thought. In the seventeenth century the Puritans who landed in New England saw themselves as carrying forward a reformation begun a century earlier on the European continent. Yet they also sensed that they were beginning something new. America was to be a brand new experiment, a "city upon a hill," as Puritan leader John Winthrop called it. Today, more than 350 years later, many Americans still regard it in that spirit.

Kristol's *Two Cheers for Capitalism* (Basic Books, 1978) spells out in greater detail some of the points he makes here, particularly that of the role of religion in counterbalancing capitalism. Michael Lind's *The Next American Nation* (Free Press, 1995) analyzes the development of American political thought from Jefferson's time to the present. Like Lazare, Lind believes in constant renewal, but he also stresses that renewal is bound to incorporate elements of the past. Richard Hofstadter's *The American Political Tradition and the Men Who Made It* (Vintage Books, 1989) was originally published in 1948, but it remains readable and provocative. Paul Johnson's massive *History of the American People* (HarperCollins, 1997) concludes that the American political system is constantly renewing itself, struggling valiantly with the ills that afflict it. "So the ship of state sails on," writes Johnson, "and mankind still continues to watch its progress, with wonder and amazement and sometimes apprehension, as it moves into the unknown waters of the 21st century and the third millenium."

ISSUE 2

Do Political Campaigns Promote Good Government?

YES: Samuel L. Popkin, from *The Reasoning Voter: Communication and Persuasion in Presidential Campaigns* (University of Chicago Press, 1991)

NO: Anthony King, from "Running Scared," *The Atlantic Monthly* (January 1997)

ISSUE SUMMARY

YES: Professor of political science Samuel L. Popkin argues that presidential election campaigns perform a unique and essential service in informing and unifying the American people.

NO: Political scientist Anthony King contends that American officeholders spend too much time and effort running for office, which detracts from their responsibility to provide good government.

Americans have the opportunity to vote more often to elect more officeholders than the citizens of any other democracy. Many elected officials serve two-year terms (members of the House of Representatives and many local and state officials), some serve four-year terms (the president, vice president, and other state and local officials), and only a few serve as long as six years (members of the Senate). In addition, voters may participate in primary elections to choose the candidates of the major parties for each of these offices. In the case of the presidential nominee, voters may select national convention delegates, whose election will determine who the party's nominee will be.

As a consequence, Americans are engaged in an almost ceaseless political campaign. No sooner is one congressional election over than another one begins. Given the long period required for organization and delegate-seeking prior to a presidential nomination, those who would be their party's nominee are off and running almost as soon as the last election has been decided.

Does this virtually nonstop campaigning serve the interests of American democracy? It surely makes for the most sustained appeal for public support by would-be candidates and those who finally win their party's support. During the height of the campaign season, lavish amounts of television time are bought for candidates' commercials, speeches, and sound bites on evening news broadcasts.

Voters who want to learn more about the candidates and their positions can expose themselves to more information than they can absorb in daily news-

papers, the news weeklies, talk radio, and C-SPAN. Less-interested adults cannot entirely escape political campaigns by switching their televisions to sitcoms and dramas, because they will be inundated with 30- and 60-second commercials for the candidates.

Yet despite this surfeit of information and advertisement, a smaller proportion of the eligible American electorate votes in presidential elections than did a century ago, and this proportion is smaller than those of other major democracies throughout the world. Just under 50 percent of the eligible electorate voted for president in 1996. An even smaller percentage votes in congressional, state, and local elections.

Declining voter turnout may derive in part from the reduced role of political parties, which once organized community rallies and door-to-door voter solicitation. In other democracies, party committees choose candidates; in the United States, candidates for national, state, and local office seek nomination by voters in primary elections. This diminishes the influence of parties and increases the amount and cost of campaigning.

In presidential campaigns, the national party convention used to be an exciting affair in which the delegates actually chose from among competing candidates. As a result of changes in the method of delegate selection, the winning nominee is now known long before the formal decision, and the convention has been reduced to a carefully scripted show without suspense or surprise. As a result, the television networks have cut back their coverage, and viewer interest has diminished.

Critics argue that television has not only supplanted traditional campaigning but has placed candidates in contrived settings and reduced issues to slogans. Furthermore, long campaigns become negative and candidates attempt to show their opponents in as bad a light as possible. Examples from recent campaigns abound, including mudslinging, character bashing, and the blatant misrepresentation of opponents' records.

Many supporters of the American electoral system believe that more campaigning is needed in order to educate potential voters and to inspire their participation. The campaign serves the invaluable function of illuminating the common interests of varied economic, social, ethnic, and racial groups in America's heterogeneous society. As for low voter turnout, some maintain that this represents satisfaction with the workings of American democracy. That is, if the two major parties do not represent diametrically opposed positions on the gravest issues, it is precisely because most Americans approve of moderate policies and few would be attracted to extreme views.

In the selections that follow, Samuel L. Popkin maintains that campaigns serve the purpose of bringing together a diverse population and that voters need to see more campaigning and fuller coverage, not less. Anthony King disagrees, asserting that the electoral system demonstrates an excess of democracy. To King, short terms, weak parties, open primaries, and expensive campaigns mean that officeholders spend more time and effort running for office than trying to provide good government.

YES
Samuel L. Popkin

THE REASONING VOTER

I believe that voter turnout has declined because campaign stimulation, from the media and from personal interaction, is also low and declining, and there is less interaction between the media and the grass-roots, person-to-person aspects of voter mobilization. The lack of campaign stimulation, I suggest, is also responsible for the large turnout gap in this country between educated and uneducated voters.

The social science research shows clear relations between the turnout and social stimulation. Married people of all ages vote more than people of the same age who live alone. And much of the increase in turnout seen over one's life cycle is due to increases in church attendance and community involvement. I believe that in this age of electronic communities, when more people are living alone and fewer people are involved in churches, PTA's, and other local groups, interpersonal social stimulation must be increased if turnout is to increase....

Political parties used to spend a large portion of their resources bringing people to rallies. By promoting the use of political ideas to bridge the gap between the individual "I" and the party "we," they encouraged people to believe that they were "links in the chain" and that the election outcome would depend on what people like themselves chose to do. Today, less money and fewer resources are available for rallies as a part of national campaigns. And parties cannot compensate for this loss with more door-to-door canvassing; in the neighborhoods where it would be safe to walk door-to-door, no one would be home.

Some of the social stimulation that campaigns used to provide in rallies and door-to-door canvassing can still be provided by extensive canvassing. This is still done in Iowa and New Hampshire. These are the first primary states, and candidates have the time and resources to do extensive personal campaigning, and to use campaign organizations to telephone people and discuss the campaigns. In research reported elsewhere, I have analyzed the effect of the social stimulation that occurs in these states. People contacted by one political candidate pay more attention to all the candidates and to the campaign events reported on television and in the papers. As they watch the

campaign they become more aware of differences between the candidates. And as they become more aware of the differences, they become more likely to vote.

This suggests a surprising conclusion: The best single way to compensate for the declining use of the party as a cue to voting, and for the declining social stimulation to vote at all, might be to increase our spending on campaign activities that stimulate voter involvement. There are daily complaints about the cost of American elections, and certainly the corrosive effects of corporate fund-raising cannot be denied; but it is not true that American elections are costly by comparison with those in other countries. Comparisons are difficult, especially since most countries have parliamentary systems, but it is worth noting that reelection campaigns to the Japanese Diet—the equivalent of the U.S. House of Representatives—cost over $1.5 million per seat. That would be equivalent to $3.5 million per congressional reelection campaign, instead of the current U.S. average of about $400,000 (given the fact that Japan has one-half the U.S. population and 512 legislators instead of 435). Although the differences in election systems and rules limit the value of such comparisons, it is food for thought that a country with a self-image so different from America's spends so much more on campaigning.

I believe that voters should be given more to "read" from campaigns and television, and that they need more interpersonal reinforcement of what they "read." Considering the good evidence that campaigns work, I believe that the main trouble lies not with American politicians but in the fact that American campaigns are not effective enough to overcome the increasing lack of social stimulation we find in a country of electronic as well as residential communities. This confronts us with some troubling questions. What kinds of electronic and/or social stimulation are possible today? To what extent can newspaper and television coverage provide the kinds of information citizens need to connect their own concerns with the basic party differences that campaigns try to make paramount? Is there a limit to what electronic and print stimulation can accomplish, so that parties must find a way to restore canvassing and rallies, or can electronic rallies suffice? Does watching a rally on television have the same effect as attending a rally? Could a return to bumper stickers and buttons, which have become far less prominent since campaigns began pouring their limited resources into the media, make a difference by reinforcing commitments and encouraging political discussions?

The problem may also be not simply a *lack* of social stimulation, but the growing *diversity* of social stimulation, and a resulting decline in reinforcement. In 1948, Columbia sociologists collected data about the social milieu of each voter and related the effects of the mass media on the voter to the political influences of family, friends, church, etc. They found that a voter's strength of conviction was related to the political homogeneity of the voter's associates. At that time, most voters belonged to politically homogeneous social groups; the social gulf between the parties was so wide that most voters had no close friends or associates voting differently from them. A decline in the political homogeneity of primary groups would lead to less social reinforcement; since the political cleavage patterns which exist today cut more across social groups,

voters are in less homogeneous family, church, and work settings and are getting less uniform reinforcement. Whether there is less overall social stimulation today, or whether there is simply less uniformity of social stimulation, the demands on campaigns to pull segments together and create coalitions are vastly greater today than in the past.

What Television Gives Us

Television is giving us less and less direct communication from our leaders and their political campaigns. Daniel Hallin, examining changes in network news coverage of presidents from 1968 to 1988, has found that the average length of the actual quote from a president on the news has gone from forty-five seconds in 1968 to nine seconds today. Instead of a short introduction from a reporter and a long look at the president, we are given a short introduction from the president and a long look at the reporter.

In the opinion of Peggy Noonan, one of the most distinguished speech-writers of recent years, who wrote many of President Reagan's and President Bush's best speeches, the change from long quotes to sound bites has taken much of the content out of campaigning: "It's a media problem. The young people who do speeches for major politicians, they've heard the whole buzz about sound bites. And now instead of writing ... a serious text with serious arguments, they just write sound bite after sound bite." With less serious argument in the news, there is less material for secondary elites and analysts to digest, and less need for candidates to think through their policies.

We also receive less background information about the campaign and less coverage of the day-to-day pageantry— the stump speeches, rallies, and crowds.

Moreover, as Paul Weaver has shown, the reporter's analysis concentrates on the horse-race aspect of the campaign and thus downplays the policy stakes involved. To a network reporter, "politics is essentially a game played by individual politicians for personal advancement ... the game takes place against a backdrop of governmental institutions, public problems, policy debates, and the like, but these are noteworthy only insofar as they affect, or are used by, players in pursuit of the game's rewards."

As a result of this supposedly critical stance, people are losing the kinds of signals they have always used to read politicians. We see fewer of the kinds of personalized political interactions, including the fun and the pageantry, that help people decide whose side they are on and that help potential leaders assemble coalitions for governing.

Gerald Ford went to a fiesta in San Antonio because he wanted Hispanic voters to see his willingness to visit them on their own ground, and to demonstrate that some of their leaders supported him. He also wanted to remind them of his willingness to deal respectfully with the sovereignty issues raised by the Panama Canal question. But when he bit into an unshucked tamale, these concerns were buried in an avalanche of trivial commentary. Reporters joked that the president was going after the "klutz" vote and talked about "Bozo the Clown." From that moment on, Ford was pictured in the media as laughably uncoordinated. Reporters brought up Lyndon Johnson's contemptuous jibe that Ford "was so dumb he couldn't walk and chew gum at the same time." Jokes circulated that he had played too much football without his helmet. For the rest of the campaign, his every slip was noted on the evening

news. Yet the news photos supposedly documenting the president's clumsiness reveal a man of remarkably good balance and body control, given the physical circumstances—not surprising for a man who had been an all-American football player in college and was still, in his sixties, an active downhill skier.

Similarly, during the 1980 campaign, Ronald Reagan visited Dallas and said, in response to a question, that there were "great flaws" in the theory of evolution and that it might be a good idea if the schools taught "creationism" as well. This statement was characterized in the media as the sort of verbal pratfall to be expected from Reagan, and much of the coverage related such gaffes *entirely* to questions about his intellectual capacity, not to the meaning of his appearance or the implications of the appearance for the coalition he was building.

What difference would it have made if press and television reporters had considered these actions by Ford and Reagan as clear and open avowals of sympathy for political causes dear to their hearts? What if Ford's political record on issues dear to Hispanics had been discussed, or if the guest list for the fiesta had been discussed to see which prominent Hispanics were, in fact, endorsing him? The nature of the gathering Reagan attended was noted at the time, but it was never referred to again. It was not until 1984 that Americans uninvolved in religious fundamentalism understood enough about what the Moral Majority stood for to read anything from a politician's embrace of Jerry Falwell, its president, or a religious roundtable such as the one Reagan attended in 1980. By 1988, as more people on the other side of the fundamentalism debates learned what the Moral Majority

stood for, the group was disbanded as a political liability.

Television, in other words, is not giving people enough to read about the substance of political coalition building because it ignores many important campaign signals. That rallies and other campaign events are "staged" does not diminish their importance and the legitimate information they can convey to voters. When Richard Nixon met Mao Tse Tung in 1972, the meeting was no less important because it was staged. And when Jesse Jackson praised Lloyd Bentsen by noting the speed with which he could go from biscuits to tacos to caviar, he was acknowledging another fact of great importance: in building coalitions, a candidate must consider the trade-off between offering symbols and making promises.

If politicians cannot show familiarity with people's concerns by properly husking tamales or eating knishes in the right place with the right people, they will have to promise them something. As Jackson noted, the tamales may be better than promises, because promises made to one segment of voters, or one issue public, will offend other groups and therefore tie the politician's hands in the future policy-making process.

Is it more meaningful when a governor of Georgia hangs a picture of Martin Luther King Jr., in the statehouse, or when a senator or congressman votes for a bill promising full employment? Is it better for a politician to eat a kosher hot dog or to promise never to compromise Israel's borders? When voters are deprived of one shortcut—obvious symbols, for example—obvious promises, for example —instead of turning to more subtle and complicated forms of information.

How good a substitute are electronic tamales for the real thing? Does watch-

ing a fiesta provide any of the stimulation to identification and turnout that attendance at a fiesta provides? How long does it take to bring us together, at least in recognizable coalitions? We need not have answers to these questions to see that they speak to the central issue of stimulating turnout and participation in elections in an age of electronic communities. The media *could* provide more of the kinds of information people use to assess candidates and parties. However, I do not know if electronic tamales provide the social stimulation of interacting with others, or the reinforcement of acting with others who agree, and I do not know how much more potent are ideas brought clearly to mind through using them with others. The demands placed on television are greater than the demands ever placed on radio or newspapers because the world is more diverse today and there are more segments which need to be reunited in campaigns.

OBJECTIONS AND ANSWERS

Two notable objections can be made to my suggestions for increasing campaigning and campaign spending. The first is the "spinmaster" objection: contemporary political campaigns are beyond redemption because campaign strategists have become so adept at manipulation that voters can no longer learn what the candidates really stand for or really intend to do. Significantly, this conclusion is supported by two opposing arguments about voter behavior. One objection is that voters are staying home because they have been turned off by fatuous claims and irrelevant advertising. A variant of this is that voters are being manipulated with great success by unscrupulous campaign advertising, so that their votes re-

flect more concern with Willie Horton* or school prayer or flag burning than with widespread poverty, the banking crisis, or global warming. The second objection is that popular concern with candidates and with government in general has been trivialized, so that candidates fiddle while America burns. In the various versions of this hypothesis, voter turnout is down because today's political contests are waged over small differences on trivial issues. While Eastern Europe plans a future of freedom under eloquent spokesmen like Vaclav Havel, and while Mikhail Gorbachev declares an end to the cold war, releases Eastern Europe from Soviet control, and tries to free his countrymen from the yoke of doctrinaire communism, in America Tweedledum and Tweedledee argue about who loves the flag more while Japan buys Rockefeller Center, banks collapse, and the deficit grows.

Both of these critiques of the contemporary system argue that campaigns themselves are trivial and irrelevant, that campaign advertising and even the candidates' speeches are nothing but self-serving puffery and distortion. This general argument has an aesthetic appeal, especially to better-educated voters and the power elite; campaign commercials remind no one of the Lincoln-Douglas debates, and today's bumper stickers and posters have none of the resonance of the Goddess of Democracy in Tiananmen Square. But elite aesthetics is not the test of this argument; the test is what voters learn from campaigns.

*[Willie Horton, a convicted murderer, escaped a prison furlough approved by then-governor of Massachusetts Michael Dukakis and committed a violent crime. George Bush exploited the incident in his campaign against Dukakis during the 1988 presidential race.—Eds.]

There is ample evidence that voters *do* learn from campaigns. Of course, each campaign tries hard to make its side look better and the other side worse. Despite that, voter perceptions about the candidates and their positions are more accurate. Furthermore, ... there is no evidence that people learn less from campaigns today than they did in past years. This is a finding to keep in mind at all times, for many of the criticisms of campaigns simplistically assume that because politicians and campaign strategists have manipulative intentions, campaigns necessarily mislead the voter. This assumption is not borne out by the evidence; voters know how to read the media and the politicians better than most media critics acknowledge.

... Voters remember past campaigns and presidents, and past failures of performance to match promises. They have a sense of who is with them and who is against them; they make judgments about unfavorable new editorials and advertisements from hostile sources, ignoring some of what is favorable to those they oppose and some of what is unfavorable to those they support. In managing their personal affairs and making decisions about their work, they collect information that they can use as a reality test for campaign claims and media stories. They notice the difference between behavior that has real consequences, on one hand, and mere talk, on the other.

... The ability of television news to manipulate voters has been vastly overstated, as one extended example will suggest. In television reporting—but not in the academic literature—it was always assumed before 1984 that winning debates and gaining votes are virtually one and the same. But on Sunday, October 7, 1984, in the first debate between Walter Mondale and Ronald Reagan, this assumption was shown to be flawed. Mondale, generally a dry speaker, was unexpectedly relaxed and articulate, and Reagan, known for his genial and relaxed style, was unexpectedly tense and hesitant. Mondale even threw Reagan off guard by using "There you go again," the jibe Reagan had made famous in his 1980 debate with Jimmy Carter. Immediately after the debate, the CBS News/*New York Times* pollsters phoned a sample of registered voters they had interviewed before the debate, to ask which candidate they were going to vote for and which they thought had done a better job in the debate. Mondale was considered to have "done the best job" by 42 percent to 36 percent, and had gained 3 points in the polls. As a result of similar polls in the next twenty-four hours by other networks and news organizations, the media's main story the rest of the week was of Mondale's upset victory over the president in the debate. Two days later, when another CBS News/*New York Times* poll asked voters about the debate and about their intended vote, Mondale was considered to have "done the best job" not by 42 percent to 36 percent margin of Sunday, but by 65 percent to 17 percent. Media reports, then, claimed that millions of voters had changed their minds about what they themselves had just seen days earlier. Yet in the three days during which millions changed their minds about who had won the debate, the same poll reported, few if any, changed their minds about how they would vote.

This example emphasizes just how complex the effects of television can be. Voters now have opinions about opinions. When asked who won the debate, they may say not what they think

personally, but what they have heard that the majority of Americans think. It is easier to change their opinions about what their neighbors think than to change their own opinions. And most important of all, it is clear that they understand the difference between a debater and a president, and that they don't easily change their political views about who they want to run the country simply on the basis of debating skills.

Critics of campaign spinmasters and of television in general are fond of noting that campaigners and politicians intend to manipulate and deceive, but they wrongly credit them with more success than they deserve. As Michael Schudson has noted, in the television age, whenever a president's popularity has been high, it has been attributed to unusual talents for using television to sell his image. He notes, for example, that in 1977 the television critic of the *New York Times* called President Carter "a master of controlled images," and that during the 1976 primaries David Halberstam wrote that Carter "more than any other candidate this year has sensed and adapted to modern communications and national mood.... Watching him again and again on television I was impressed by his sense of pacing, his sense of control, very low key, soft." A few years later this master of images still had the same soft, low-key voice, but now it was interpreted as indicating not quiet strength but weakness and indecision. Gerald Rafshoon, the media man for this "master of television," concluded after the 1980 campaign that all the television time bought for Carter wasn't as useful as three more helicopters (and a successful desert rescue) would have been.

As these examples suggest, media critics are generally guilty of using one of the laziest and easiest information shortcuts of all. Assuming that a popular politician is a good manipulator of the media or that a winner won because of his media style is not different from what voters do when they evaluate presidents by reasoning backward from known results. The media need reform, but so do the media critics. One cannot infer, without astonishing hubris, that the American people have been successfully deceived simply because a politician wanted them to believe his or her version of events. But the media critics who analyze political texts without any reference to the actual impact of the messages do just that.

Negativism and Triviality

Campaigns are often condemned as trivial—as sideshows in which voters amuse themselves by learning about irrelevant differences between candidates who fiddle over minor issues while the country stagnates and inner cities burn—and many assume that the negativism and pettiness of the attacks that candidates make on each other encourage an "a pox on all your houses" attitude. This suggests a plausible hypothesis, which can be given a clean test in a simple experiment. This experiment can be thought of as a "stop and think" experiment because it is a test of what happens if people stop and think about what they know of the candidates and issues in an election and tell someone what they know. First, take a random sample of people across the country and interview them. Ask the people selected what they consider to be the most important issues facing the country, and then ask them where the various candidates stand on these issues. Then ask them to state their likes and dislikes about the candidates' personal

qualities and issue stands, and about the state of the country. Second, after the election, find out whether these interviewees were more or less likely to vote than people who were not asked to talk about the campaign. If the people interviewed voted less often than people not interviewed, then there is clear support for the charge that triviality, negativism, and irrelevancy are turning off the American people and suppressing turnout.

In fact, the National Election Studies done by the University of Michigan's Survey Research Center, now the Center for Political Studies, are exactly such an experiment. In every election since 1952, people have been asked what they care about, what the candidates care about, and that they know about the campaign. After the election people have been reinterviewed and asked whether they voted; then the actual voting records have been checked to see whether the respondents did indeed vote.

The results convincingly demolish the triviality and negativism hypothesis. In every election, people who have been interviewed are more likely to vote than other Americans. Indeed, the reason the expensive and difficult procedure of verifying turnout against the voting records was begun in the first place was that the scholars were suspicious because the turnout reported by respondents was so much higher than either the actual turnout of all Americans or the turnout in surveys conducted after the election. So respondents in the national election studies, after seventy minutes of thinking about the candidates, the issues, and the campaign, were both more likely than other people to vote and more likely to try to hide the fact that they did not vote! Further, if people are reinterviewed in later elections, their turnout continues to

rise. Still further, while an interview cuts nonvoting in a presidential election by up to 20 percent, an interview in a local primary may cut nonvoting by as much as half.

The rise in no-shows on voting day and the rise of negative campaigning both follow from the rise of candidate-centered elections. When voters do not have information about future policies they extrapolate, or project, from the information they have. As campaigns become more centered on candidates, there is more projection, and hence more negative campaigning. Negative campaigning is designed to provide information that causes voters to stop projecting and to change their beliefs about a candidate's stand on the issues. "Willie Horton... was a legitimate issue because it speaks to styles and ways of governance. In that case Dukakis's."

As Noonan has also noted of the 1988 campaign, "There should have been more name-calling, mud slinging and fun. It should have been rock-'em-sock-'em the way great campaigns have been in the past. It was tedious." Campaigns cannot deal with anything substantive if they cannot get the electorate's attention and interest people in listening to their music. Campaigns need to make noise. The tradition of genteel populism in America, and the predictable use of sanitary metaphors to condemn politicians and their modes of communication, says more about the distaste of the people who use the sanitary metaphors for American society than it does about the failing politicians.

The challenge to the future of American campaigns, and hence to American democracy, is how to bring back the excitement and the music in an age of electronic campaigning. Today's campaigns

have more to do because an educated, media-centered society is a broadened and segmented electorate which is harder to rally, while today's campaigns have less money and troops with which to fight their battles.

* * *

When I first began to work in presidential campaigns I had very different ideas about how to change campaigns and their coverage than I have today. Coverage of rallies and fiestas, I used to think, belonged in the back of the paper along with stories about parties, celebrity fundraisers, and fad diets. Let the society editor cover banquets and rubber chickens, I thought; the reporters in Washington could analyze the speeches and discuss the policy implications of competing proposals.

I still wish that candidates' proposals and speeches were actually analyzed for their content and implications for our future. I still wish that television told us more about how elites evaluate presidential initiatives than what my neighbors said about them in the next day's polls. However, I now appreciate the intimate relationships between the rallies and governance which escaped me in the past. I now appreciate how hard it is to bring a country together, to gather all the many concerns and interests into a single coalition and hold it together in order to govern.

Campaigns are essential in any society, particularly in a society that is culturally, economically, and socially diverse. If voters look for information about candidates under streetlights, then that is where candidates must campaign, and the only way to improve elections is to add streetlights. Reforms can only make sense if they are consistent with the gut rationality of voters. Ask not for more sobriety and piety from citizens, for they are voters, not judges; offer them instead cues and signals which connect their world with the world of politics.

NO

Anthony King

RUNNING SCARED

To an extent that astonishes a foreigner, modern America is *about* the holding of elections. Americans do not merely have elections on the first Tuesday after the first Monday of November in every year divisible by four. They have elections on the first Tuesday after the first Monday of November in every year divisible by two. In addition, five states have elections in odd-numbered years. Indeed, there is no year in the United States—ever—when a major statewide election is not being held somewhere. To this catalogue of general elections has of course to be added an equally long catalogue of primary elections (for example, forty-three presidential primaries [in 1996]). Moreover, not only do elections occur very frequently in the United States but the number of jobs legally required to be filled by them is enormous—from the presidency of the United States to the post of local consumer advocate in New York. It has been estimated that no fewer than half a million elective offices are filled or waiting to be filled in the United States today.

Americans take the existence of their never-ending election campaign for granted. Some like it, some dislike it, and most are simply bored by it. But they are all conscious of it, in the same way that they are conscious of Mobil, McDonald's, *Larry King Live,* Oprah Winfrey, the Dallas Cowboys, the Ford Motor Company, and all the other symbols and institutions that make up the rich tapestry of American life.

To a visitor to America's shores, however, the never-ending campaign presents a largely unfamiliar spectacle. In other countries election campaigns have both beginnings and ends, and there are even periods, often prolonged periods, when no campaigns take place at all. Other features of American elections are also unfamiliar. In few countries do elections and campaigns cost as much as they do in the United States. In no other country is the role of organized political parties so limited.

America's permanent election campaign, together with other aspects of American electoral politics, has one crucial consequence, little noticed but vitally important for the functioning of American democracy. Quite simply, the American electoral system places politicians in a highly vulnerable position. Individually and collectively they are more vulnerable, more of the time,

From Anthony King, "Running Scared," *The Atlantic Monthly* (January 1997). Abridged and reprinted with permission of The Free Press, a division of Simon & Schuster, from *Running Scared: Why America's Politicians Campaign Too Much and Govern Too Little* by Anthony King (Martin Kessler Books, 1997). Copyright © 1997 by The Free Press.

to the vicissitudes of electoral politics than are the politicians of any other democratic country. Because they are more vulnerable, they devote more of their time to electioneering, and their conduct in office is more continuously governed by electoral considerations. I will argue that American politicians' constant and unremitting electoral preoccupations have deleterious consequences for the functioning of the American system. They consume time and scarce resources. Worse, they make it harder than it would otherwise be for the system as a whole to deal with some of America's most pressing problems. Americans often complain that their system is not sufficiently democratic. I will argue that, on the contrary, there is a sense in which the system is too democratic and ought to be made less so....

FEAR AND TREMBLING

Politics and government in the United States are marked by the fact that U.S. elected officials in many cases have very short terms of office *and* face the prospect of being defeated in primary elections *and* have to run for office more as individuals than as standard-bearers for their party *and* have continually to raise large sums of money in order to finance their own election campaigns. Some of these factors operate in other countries. There is no other country, however, in which all of them operate, and operate simultaneously. The cumulative consequences, as we shall see, are both pervasive and profound.

The U.S. Constitution sets out in one of its very first sentences that "the House of Representatives shall be composed of members chosen every second year by the people of the several states."

When the Founding Fathers decided on such a short term of office for House members, they were setting a precedent that has been followed by no other major democratic country. In Great Britain, France, Italy, and Canada the constitutional or legal maximum for the duration of the lower house of the national legislature is five years. In Germany and Japan the equivalent term is four years. Only in Australia and New Zealand, whose institutions are in some limited respects modeled on those of the United States, are the legal maximums as short as three years. In having two-year terms the United States stands alone.

Members of the Senate are, of course, in a quite different position. Their constitutionally prescribed term of office, six-years, is long by anyone's standards. But senators' six-year terms are not all they seem. In the first place, so pervasive is the electioneering atmosphere that even newly elected senators begin almost at once to lay plans for their re-election campaigns. Senator Daniel Patrick Moynihan, of New York, recalls that when he first came to the Senate, in 1977, his colleagues when they met over lunch or a drink usually talked about politics and policy. Now they talk about almost nothing but the latest opinion polls. In the second place, the fact that under the Constitution the terms of a third of the Senate end every two years means that even if individual senators do not feel themselves to be under continuing electoral pressure, the Senate as a whole does. Despite the Founders' intentions, the Senate's collective electoral sensibilities increasingly resemble those of the House.

Most Americans seem unaware of the fact, but the direct primary—a government-organized popular election to nominate candidates for public office—is, for

better or worse, an institution peculiar to the United States. Neither primary elections nor their functional equivalents exist anywhere else in the democratic world. It goes without saying that their effect is to add a further dimension of uncertainty and unpredictability to the world of American elective politicians.

In most other countries the individual holder of public office, so long as he or she is reasonably conscientious and does not gratuitously offend local or regional party opinion, has no real need to worry about renomination. To be sure, cases of parties refusing to renominate incumbent legislators are not unknown in countries such as France, Germany, and Canada, but they are relatively rare and tend to occur under unusual circumstances. The victims are for the most part old, idle, or alcoholic.

The contrast between the rest of the world and the United States could hardly be more striking. In 1979 no fewer than 104 of the 382 incumbent members of the House of Representatives who sought re-election faced primary opposition. In the following three elections the figures were ninety-three out of 398 (1980), ninety-eight out of 393 (1982), and 130 out of 409 (1984). More recently, in 1994, nearly a third of all House incumbents seeking re-election, 121 out of 386, had to face primary opposition, and in the Senate the proportion was even higher: eleven out of twenty-six. Even those incumbents who did not face opposition could seldom be certain in advance that they were not going to. The influence—and the possibility—of primaries is pervasive. As we shall see, the fact that incumbents usually win is neither here nor there.

To frequent elections and primary elections must be added another factor that contributes powerfully to increasing the electoral vulnerability of U.S. politicians: the relative lack of what we might call "party cover." In most democratic countries the fate of most politicians depends not primarily on their own endeavors but on the fate—locally, regionally, or nationally—of their party. If their party does well in an election, so do they. If not, not. The individual politician's interests and those of his party are bound together.

In contrast, America's elective politicians are on their own—not only in relation to politicians in most other countries but also in absolute terms. Party is still a factor in U.S. electoral politics, but it is less so than anywhere else in the democratic world. As a result, American legislators seeking re-election are forced to raise their own profiles, to make their own records, and to fight their own re-election campaigns.

If politicians are so vulnerable electorally, it may be protested, why aren't more of them defeated? In particular, why aren't more incumbent congressmen and senators defeated? The analysis here would seem to imply a very high rate of turnover in Congress, but in fact the rate—at least among incumbents seeking re-election—is notoriously low. How can this argument and the facts of congressional incumbents' electoral success be reconciled?

This objection has to be taken seriously, because the facts on which it is based are substantially correct. The number of incumbent congressmen and senators defeated in either primary or general elections *is* low. But to say that because incumbent members of Congress are seldom defeated, they are not really vulnerable electorally is to miss two crucial points. The first is that precisely because they are vulnerable, they go to prodigious lengths to protect themselves. Like work-

ers in nuclear-power stations, they take the most extreme safety precautions, and the fact that the precautions are almost entirely successful does not make them any less necessary.

Second, congressmen and senators go to inordinate lengths to secure re-election because, although they may objectively be safe (in the view of journalists and academic political scientists), they do not *know* they are safe—and even if they think they are, the price of being wrong is enormous. The probability that anything will go seriously wrong with a nuclear-power station may approach zero, but the stations tend nevertheless to be built away from the centers of large cities. A congressman or a senator may believe that he is reasonably safe, but if he wants to be re-elected, he would be a fool to act on that belief.

HOW THEY CAME TO BE VULNERABLE

American politicians run scared—and are right to do so. And they run more scared than the politicians of any other democratic country—again rightly. How did this come to be so?

The short answer is that the American people like it that way. They are, and have been for a very long time, the Western world's hyperdemocrats. They are keener on democracy than almost anyone else and are more determined that democratic norms and practices should pervade every aspect of national life. To explore the implications of this central fact about the United States, and to see how it came to be, we need to examine two different interpretations of the term "democracy." Both have been discussed from time to time by political philosophers, but they have never been codified and they certainly cannot be found written down in a constitution or any other formal statement of political principles. Nevertheless, one or the other underpins the political practice of every democratic country—even if, inevitably, the abstract conception and the day-to-day practice are never perfectly matched.

One of these interpretations might be labeled "division of labor." In this view, there are in any democracy two classes of people—the governors and the governed. The function of the governors is to take decisions on the basis of what they believe to be in the country's best interests and to act on those decisions. If public opinion broadly supports the decisions, that is a welcome bonus. If not, too bad. The views of the people at large are merely one datum among a large number of data that need to be considered. They are not accorded any special status. Politicians in countries that operate within this view can frequently be heard using phrases like "the need for strong leadership" and "the need to take tough decisions." They often take a certain pride in doing what they believe to be right even if the opinion of the majority is opposed to it.

The function of the governed in such a system, if it is a genuine democracy, is very important but strictly limited. It is not to determine public policy or to decide what is the right thing to do. Rather, it is to go to the polls from time to time to choose those who will determine public policy and decide what the right thing is: namely, the governors. The deciding of issues by the electorate is secondary to the election of the individuals who are to do the deciding. The analogy is with choosing a doctor. The patient certainly chooses which doctor to see but does not

normally decide (or even try to decide) on the detailed course of treatment. The division of labor is informal but clearly understood.

It is probably fair to say that most of the world's major democracies—Great Britain, France, Germany, Japan—operate on this basis. The voters go to the polls every few years, and in between times it is up to the government of the day to get on with governing. Electing a government and governing are two different businesses. Electioneering is, if anything, to be deplored if it gets in the way of governing.

This is a simplified picture, of course. Democratically elected politicians are ultimately dependent on the electorate, and if at the end of the day the electorate does not like what they are doing, they are dead. Nevertheless, the central point remains. The existing division of labor is broadly accepted.

The other interpretation of democracy, the one dominant in America, might be called the "agency" view, and it is wholly different. According to this view, those who govern a country should function as no more than the agents of the people. The job of the governors is not to act independently and to take whatever decisions they believe to be in the national interest but, rather, to reflect in all their actions the views of the majority of the people, whatever those views may be. Governors are not really governors at all; they are representatives, in the very narrow sense of being in office solely to represent the views of those who sent them there.

In the agency view, representative government of the kind common throughout the democratic world can only be second-best. The ideal system would be one in which there were no politicians or mid-dlemen of any kind and the people governed themselves directly; the political system would take the form of more or less continuous town meetings or referenda, perhaps conducted by means of interactive television. Most Americans, at bottom, would still like to see their country governed by a town meeting.

WHY THEIR VULNERABILITY MATTERS

In this political ethos, finding themselves inhabiting a turbulent and torrid electoral environment, most American elective officials respond as might be expected: in an almost Darwinian way. They adapt their behavior—their roll-call votes, their introduction of bills, their committee assignments, their phone calls, their direct-mail letters, their speeches, their press releases, their sound bites, whom they see, how they spend their time, their trips abroad, their trips back home, and frequently their private and families lives—to their environment: that is, to their primary and overriding need for electoral survival. The effects are felt not only in the lives of individual officeholders and their staffs but also in America's political institutions as a whole and the shape and content of U.S. public policy.

It all begins with officeholders' immediate physical environment: with bricks, mortar, leather, and wood paneling. The number of congressional buildings and the size of congressional staffs have ballooned in recent decades. At the start of the 1960s most members of the House of Representatives contented themselves with a small inner office and an outer office; senators' office suites were not significantly larger. Apart from the Capitol itself, Congress was reasonably comfortably housed in four buildings, known to

Washington taxi drivers as the Old and New House and Senate Office Buildings. The designations Old and New cannot be used any longer, however, because there are now so many even newer congressional buildings.

Congressional staffs have grown at roughly the same rate, the new buildings having been built mainly to house the staffs. In 1957 the total number of people employed by members of the House and Senate as personal staff was 3,556. By 1991 the figure had grown to 11,572—a more than threefold increase within the political lifetime of many long-serving members. [In 1996] the total number of people employed by Congress in all capacities, including committee staffs and the staffs of support agencies like the Congressional Research Service, was 32,820, making Congress by far the most heavily staffed legislative branch in the world.

Much of the growth of staff in recent decades has been in response to the growth of national government, to Congress's insistence on strengthening its policymaking role in the aftermath of Vietnam and Watergate, and to decentralization within Congress, which has led subcommittee chairmen and the subcommittees themselves to acquire their own staffs. But there is no doubt that the increase is also in response to congressional incumbents' ever-increasing electoral exposure. Congress itself has become an integral part of America's veritable "elections industry."

One useful measure of the changes that have taken place—and also an important consequence of the changes—is the increased proportion of staff and staff time devoted to constituent service. As recently as 1972 only 1,189 House employees—22.5 percent of House members'

personal staffs—were based in home-district offices. By 1992 the number had more than doubled, to 3,128, and the proportion had nearly doubled, to 42.1 percent. On the Senate side there were only 303 state-based staffers in 1972, making up 12.5 percent of senators' personal staffs, but the number had more than quadrupled by 1992 to 1,368, for fully 31.6 percent of the total. Since a significant proportion of the time of Washington-based congressional staffs is also devoted to constituent service, it is a fair guess that more than half of the time of all congressional staffs is now given over to nursing the district or state rather than to legislation and policymaking.

Much constituent service is undoubtedly altruistic, inspired by politicians' sense of duty (and constituents' understandable frustration with an unresponsive bureaucracy); but at the same time nobody doubts that a large proportion of it is aimed at securing re-election. The statistics on the outgoing mail of members of Congress and their use of the franking privilege point in that direction too. Congressional mailings grew enormously in volume from some 100 million pieces a year in the early 1960s to more than 900 million in 1984—nearly five pieces of congressional mail for every adult American. New restrictions on franking introduced in the 1990s have made substantial inroads into that figure, but not surprisingly the volume of mail emanating from both houses of Congress is still invariably higher in election years.

The monetary costs of these increases in voter-oriented congressional activities are high: in addition to being the most heavily staffed legislative branch in the world, Congress is also the most expensive. But there is another, nonmonetary cost: the staffs themselves be-

come one of the congressman's or senator's constituencies, requiring management, taking up time, and always being tempted to go into business for themselves. American scholars who have studied the burgeoning of congressional staffs express concern about their cumulative impact on Congress as a deliberative body in which face-to-face communication between members, and between members and their constituents, facilitates both mutual understanding and an understanding of the issues. Largely in response to the requirements of electioneering, more and more congressional business is conducted through dense networks of staffers.

One familiar effect of American politicians' vulnerability is the power it accords to lobbyists and special-interest groups, especially those that can muster large numbers of votes or have large amounts of money to spend on campaigns. Members of Congress walk the electoral world alone. They can be picked off one by one, they know it, and they adjust their behavior accordingly. The power of the American Association of Retired Persons, the National Rifle Association, the banking industry, and the various veterans' lobbies is well known. It derives partly from their routine contributions to campaign funds and the quality of their lobbying activities in Washington, but far more from the votes that the organizations may be able to deliver and from congressmen's and senators' calculations of how the positions they take in the present may affect their chances of re-election in the future—a future that rarely is distant. Might a future challenger be able to use that speech against me? Might I be targeted for defeat by one of the powerful lobbying groups?

A second effect is that American politicians are even more likely than those in other countries to engage in symbolic politics: to use words masquerading as deeds, to take actions that purport to be instrumental but are in fact purely rhetorical. A problem exists; the people demand that it be solved; the politicians cannot solve it and know so; they engage in an elaborate pretense of trying to solve it nevertheless, often at great expense to the taxpayers and almost invariably at a high cost in terms of both the truth and the politicians' own reputations for integrity and effectiveness. The politicians lie in most cases not because they are liars or approve of lying but because the potential electoral costs of not lying are too great.

At one extreme, symbolic politics consists of speechmaking and public position-taking in the absence of any real action or any intention of taking action; casting the right vote is more important than achieving the right outcome. At the other extreme, symbolic politics consists of whole government programs that are ostensibly designed to achieve one set of objectives but are actually designed to achieve other objectives (in some cases simply the re-election of the politicians who can claim credit for them).

Take as an example the crime bills passed by Congress in the 1980s and 1990s, with their mandatory-minimum sentences, their three-strikes-and-you're-out provisions, and their extension of the federal death penalty to fifty new crimes. The anti-drug and anti-crime legislation, by the testimony of judges and legal scholars, has been at best useless and at worst wholly pernicious in its effects, in that it has filled prison cells not with violent criminals but with drug users and low-level drug pushers. As for the death

penalty, a simple measure of its sheer irrelevance to the federal government's war on crime is easily provided. The last federal offender to be put to death, Victor H. Feguer, a convicted kidnapper, was hanged in March of 1963. By the end of 1995 no federal offender had been executed for more than thirty years, and hardly any offenders were awaiting execution on death row. The ferocious-seeming federal statutes were almost entirely for show.

The way in which the wars on drugs and crime were fought cannot be understood without taking into account the incessant pressure that elected officeholders felt they were under from the electorate. As one former congressman puts it, "Voters were afraid of criminals, and politicians were afraid of voters." This fear reached panic proportions in election years. Seven of the years from 1981 to 1994 were election years nationwide; seven were not. During those fourteen years Congress passed no fewer than seven major crime bills. Of those seven, six were passed in election years (usually late in the year). That is, there was only one election year in which a major crime bill was *not* passed, and only one non-election year in which a major crime bill *was* passed.

Another effect of the extreme vulnerability of American politicians is that it is even harder for them than for democratically elected politicians in other countries to take tough decisions: to court unpopularity, to ask for sacrifices, to impose losses, to fly in the face of conventional wisdom—in short, to act in what they believe to be their constituents' interest and the national interest rather than in their own interest. Timothy J. Penny, a Democrat who left the House of Representatives in 1994, put the point starkly, perhaps even too harshly, in *Common Cents* (1995).

> Voters routinely punish lawmakers who try to do unpopular things, who challenge them to face unpleasant truths about the budget, crime, Social Security, or tax policy. Similarly, voters reward politicians for giving them what they want—more spending for popular programs—even if it means wounding the nation in the long run by creating more debt....

WHAT, IF ANYTHING, MIGHT BE DONE?

Precisely because American politicians are so exposed electorally, they probably have to display—and do display—more political courage more often than the politicians of any other democratic country. The number of political saints and martyers in the United States is unusually large.

There is, however, no special virtue in a political system that requires large numbers of politicians to run the risk of martyrdom in order to ensure that tough decisions can be taken in a timely manner in the national interest. The number of such decisions that need to be taken is always likely to be large; human nature being what it is, the supply of would-be martyrs is always likely to be small. On balance it would seem better not to try to eliminate the electoral risks (it can never be done in a democracy) but to reduce somewhat their scale and intensity. There is no reason why the risks run by American politicians should be so much greater than the risks run by elective politicians in other democratic countries.

How, then, might the risks be reduced? What can be done? A number of reforms

to the existing system suggest themselves. It may be that none of them is politically feasible—Americans hold tight to the idea of agency democracy—but in principle there should be no bar to any of them. One of the simplest would also be the most radical: to lengthen the terms of members of the House of Representatives from two years to four. The proposal is by no means a new one: at least 123 resolutions bearing on the subject were introduced in Congress in the eighty years from 1885 to 1965, and President Lyndon B. Johnson advocated the change in his State of the Union address in January of 1966.

A congressman participating in a Brookings Institution round table held at about the time of Johnson's message supported the change, saying, "I think that the four years would help you to be a braver congressman, and I think what you need is bravery. I think you need courage." Another congressman on the same occasion cited the example of another bill that he believed had the support of a majority in the House. "That bill is not going to come up this year. You know why it is not coming up? . . . Because four hundred and thirty-five of us have to face election. . . . If we had a four-year term, I am as confident as I can be the bill would have come to the floor and passed."

A similar case could be made for extending the term of senators to eight years, with half the Senate retiring or running for re-election every four years. If the terms of members of both houses were thus extended and made to coincide, the effect in reducing America's never-ending election campaign would be dramatic.

There is much to be said, too, for all the reasons mentioned so far, for scaling down the number of primary elections. They absorb extravagant amounts of time, energy, and money; they serve little democratic purpose; few people bother to vote in them; and they place additional and unnecessary pressure on incumbent officeholders. Since the main disadvantage of primaries is the adverse effect they have on incumbents, any reforms probably ought to be concerned with protecting incumbents' interests.

At the moment, the primary laws make no distinction between situations in which a seat in the House or the Senate is already occupied and situations in which the incumbent is, for whatever reason, standing down. The current laws provide for a primary to be held in either case. An incumbent is therefore treated as though the seat in question were open and he or she were merely one of the candidates for it. A relatively simple reform would be to distinguish between the two situations. If a seat was open, primaries would be held in both parties, as now; but if the incumbent announced that he or she intended to run for re-election, then a primary in his or her party would be held only if large numbers of party supporters were determined to have one—that is, were determined that the incumbent should be ousted. The obvious way to ascertain whether such determination existed would be by means of a petition supervised by the relevant state government and requiring a considerable number of signatures. The possibility of a primary would thus be left open, but those who wanted one would have to show that they were both numerous and serious. A primary would not be held simply because an ambitious, possibly demented, possibility wealthy individual decided to throw his or her hat into the ring.

Any steps to strengthen the parties as institutions would be desirable on the same grounds. Lack of party cover in the United States means that elective officeholders find it hard to take tough decisions partly because they lack safety in numbers. They can seldom, if ever, say to an aggrieved constituent or a political-action committee out for revenge, "I had to vote that way because my party told me to," or even "I had to vote that way because we in my party all agreed that we would." Lack of party cohesion, together with American voters' disposition to vote for the individual rather than the party, means that congressmen and senators are always in danger of being picked off one by one.

BALLOT FATIGUE

What might be done to give both parties more backbone? Clearly, the parties would be strengthened—and elective officeholders would not need to raise so much money for their own campaigns —if each party organization became a major source of campaign funding. In the unlikely event (against the background of chronic budget deficits) that Congress ever gets around to authorizing the federal funding of congressional election campaigns, a strong case could be made for channeling as much of the money as possible through the parties, and setting aside some of it to cover their administrative and other ongoing costs.

The party organizations and the nexus between parties and their candidates would also be strengthened if it were made easier for ordinary citizens to give money to the parties and for the parties to give money to their candidates. Until 1986, when the program was abolished, tax credits were available for taxpayers who contributed small sums to the political parties. These credits could be restored. Larry J. Sabato, a political scientist at the University of Virginia, has similarly suggested that citizens entitled to a tax refund could be allowed to divert a small part of their refund to the party of their choice. Such measures would not, however, reduce candidates' dependence on donations from wealthy individuals and PACs [political action committees] unless they were accompanied by measures enabling the parties to contribute more generously to their candidates' campaigns. At the moment there are strict legal limits on the amount of money that national or state party organizations can contribute to the campaigns of individual candidates. The limits should be raised (and indexed to inflation). There is even a case for abolishing them altogether.

All that said, there is an even more straightforward way of reducing incumbents' dependence on campaign contributions. At present incumbents have to spend so much time raising funds because the campaigns themselves are so expensive. They could be made cheaper. This, of course, would be one of the effects of making U.S. elections less numerous and less frequent than they are now. Another way to lower the cost of elections would be to provide candidates and parties with free air time on television and radio.

POSTSCRIPT

Do Political Campaigns Promote Good Government?

The right of people to choose who governs them is the very essence of democracy. In that spirit Popkin argues that Americans need more democracy—that is, more participation by the people inspired by more campaigning and education of the public. King asserts that America has an excess of democracy and that the burden imposed by so many and so frequent elections is too great and leads to disillusion and more citizens not voting.

In order to stimulate greater voter participation, beginning in 1972 radical reforms were adopted to ensure that the presidential nominees of the two major parties would be those favored by the largest proportion of party members participating in the primaries and caucuses in which the national convention delegates were chosen. The local party organization plays a greatly reduced role because it no longer hand picks the delegates. The national convention plays a greatly reduced role because it no longer engages in any real deliberation regarding the choice of nominee. For better or worse, the electorate gets the presidential candidate endorsed by the largest number of delegates.

More directly, the people vote in primaries in order to designate candidates for all other elective offices. This means that voters are exposed to more and longer campaigns; they should therefore be motivated and informed both in the long primary campaign before the party choices are made and in the months leading up to the election before the officeholders are chosen.

A classic text that provides an overview of presidential campaigns is Nelson W. Polsby and Aaron Woldavsky, *Presidential Elections: Strategies and Structures of American Politics*, 9th ed. (Chatham House, 1995). Ever since Theodore White began his distinguished series of vivid accounts with *The Making of the President 1960* (Atheneum, 1961), each presidential election has produced a spate of books providing insightful analysis and insider revelations regarding the conduct of the campaign. One of the best is Richard Ben Cramer, *What It Takes: The Way to the White House* (Random House, 1992).

In the tradition of White's intimate journalism is Bob Woodward's account of the 1996 presidential campaigns of President Bill Clinton and Senator Bob Dole, *The Choice: How Clinton Won* (Simon & Schuster, 1997). More analytical and less anecdotal are the quadrennial volumes edited by Michael Nelson, *Election of 1996* (Congressional Quarterly Books, 1997), and Gerald M. Pomper, *The Election of 1996: Reports and Interpretations* (Chatham House, 1997). Stephen J. Wayne has updated his study of presidential campaigning in *The Road to the White House 1996: The Politics of Presidential Elections: Post-Election Edition* (St. Martin's Press, 1997).

ISSUE 3

Should Campaign Finance Be Reformed?

YES: Archibald Cox, from "Ethics, Campaign Finance, and Democracy," *Society* (March/April 1998)

NO: Bradley A. Smith, from "The Campaign-Finance Follies," *Commentary* (December 1997)

ISSUE SUMMARY

YES: Archibald Cox, a former special prosecutor and a law professor, argues that the increasing amount of money spent in elections corrupts government but that the public's faith in democratic self-government can be restored by campaign finance reform.

NO: Bradley A. Smith, an associate professor at Capital University Law School, asserts that campaign contributions do not corrupt candidates, the biggest spenders do not always win, and the relatively modest amount that candidates spend is essential to educate voters and to increase their interest.

The votes had hardly been counted in President Bill Clinton's successful bid for reelection in 1996 when charges of improper campaign financing began to swirl around the president. It was reported that large contributions could buy a night in the White House's Lincoln bedroom and that smaller contributions could buy coffee with the president in the Roosevelt Room. To many, this fund-raising seemed unseemly; sometimes it appeared sleazy, and when it concerned contributions from foreign nationals and corporations, it could have been illegal. Vice President Al Gore has been sharply criticized for soliciting contributions from the White House and raising money at a Buddhist temple luncheon. Predictably, when the Senate Committee on Governmental Affairs completed hearings early in 1998, the Republican majority castigated President Clinton, his aides, and the Democratic National Committee, while the Democratic minority charged that Republican leaders violated the laws.

Hundreds of millions of dollars are raised during each national campaign cycle, and the amount is increasing. By 1996 the average cost of winning a Senate seat was $4.5 million, while the average cost of winning a House seat was $660,000. In 1994, the most expensive congressional election ever, Senator Diane Feinstein (D-California) spent more than $14 million to turn back the challenge of Republican Michael Huffington, who spent $30 million. In her primary, Feinstein spent over $2 million to defeat her opponent, who spent $14,000. In his primary, Huffington spent nearly $6 million to defeat a rival, who spent $800,000.

What is wrong with candidates and parties' raising the large sums of money that are needed to present their messages in the form of television broadcasts and print advertisements? By the same token, what is wrong with voters' putting their money where their mouth is in politics? A great deal, say those who believe that the rampant spending on political campaigns discourages less-wealthy citizens from seeking office, diverts too much of a public officer's attention away from performing his or her duties to raising funds for the next campaign, and turns off voters who believe that money influences public policy more than their votes do. This last concern is exemplified by Roger Tamraz, an oil financier, who gained access to the White House through his $300,000 donation to the Democrats. Testifying before a congressional committee, he said that next time he would give $600,000, in the hope of having more influence.

After the 1996 election, major legislation to change the system of campaign finance was proposed by Senator John McCain (R-Arizona) and Senator Russell Feingold (D-Wisconsin). Perhaps the most prominent feature of the McCain-Feingold Bill was the effort to ban "soft money" contributions to political parties. Soft money is intended for party building and getting out the voters, but it is often closely tied in to particular candidates. Other reform proposals would give free television time to candidates who accept voluntary limits, lower the amounts that political action committees (PACs) can contribute to campaigns, and extend federal grants to candidates who limit their other campaign expenses.

Critics of these proposed reforms argue that campaign expenditures are really modest. Some suggest that much more should be spent in order to increase public awareness and turnout at the polls. One conservative strategy in opposing radical reforms was to urge a ban on contributions by trade unions without the prior approval of the union members. (A liberal retort was to oppose contributions by corporations without the prior approval of the stockholders.)

The most imposing objection to campaign finance reform is that it abridges the First Amendment's guarantee of freedom of political expression. In 1976 the U.S. Supreme Court considered a challenge to the campaign finance limitations of the Federal Election Campaign Act. In *Buckley v. Valeo* the Court concluded that spending limits violate the constitutional protection of free speech. The Court's reasoning was that to abridge political communication by restricting political expenditures "reduces the quantity of expression by restricting the number of issues discussed, the depth of their exploration, and the size of the audience reached."

In the following selections, Archibald Cox asserts that the present system of campaign finance creates improper political access and contributes to public cynicism regarding the democratic process. Bradley A. Smith maintains that both the cost and impact of campaign financing have been exaggerated and that proposed changes would abridge the people's First Amendment rights.

YES

Archibald Cox

ETHICS, CAMPAIGN FINANCE, AND DEMOCRACY

My subject is "Ethics, Campaign Finance, and Democracy." One need hardly argue to a thoughtful audience the general importance of high ethical standards in government. The dollars and cents costs of corruption are obvious. So is the unfairness to competitors. As the moral standards of a community affect the moral standards of political leaders, so do the moral standards of political leaders to an ever greater extent influence the moral standards of the community. But the prime goal is broader. At the beginning James Madison wrote in *The Federalist Papers:*

> The aim of every political constitution is, or ought to be to obtain for rulers men who possess the most wisdom to discern, and the most virtue to pursue, the common good of the society; and in the next place, to take the most effectual precautions for keeping them virtuous whilst they continue to hold their public trust.

How successful have we been in pursuing the second of Madison's aims over the past half century?

In the field normally suggested by the phrase "ethics in government" we seem to have made remarkable progress in writing laws and regulations well designed to set high ethical standards for members of Congress and officers and employees in the executive branch.

The progress began with Senator Douglas' work as chairman of a special subcommittee of the Senate Committee on Labor and Public Welfare. The subcommittee produced one of the first comprehensive reports—the first in the Senate—on the general field of ethical abuses in government. The Senator's Godkin Lectures, delivered at Harvard in 1952, became the classic treatment of the subject. In 1958 Congress enacted a very broad and loosely worded Code of Ethics for Government Service. Watergate gave new impetus to the movement. New Codes of Ethics were adopted by the Senate and House of Representatives in 1977, and a year later Congress enacted the Ethics in Government Act of 1978.

The Ethics in Government Act, as strengthened by amendments, supplies one of the foundation stones for assuring ethics in government: the individual detailed periodic financial reports required of the President and every officer in the executive branch and every employee compensated at or above the senior level, and also of Senators and Representatives in Congress and senior congressional staff. The publicity, like sunlight, both deters and corrects. In addition, the reports furnish a wealth of information for the press, reform groups and the public concerning practices tolerated by the current law and codes of ethics but damaging to the public good.

We have made good progress in stopping the flow of money from private interests with axes to grind directly into the personal bank accounts of senior government employees and elected and appointed officials. I refer to once widely accepted practices such as the large earnings for little work done outside one's government position, the honoraria paid in return for a short speech or perhaps simply attendance at a meeting of some trade association or other organization in the private sector. Gifts, transportation, travel expenses, a weekend or perhaps a week at a travel resort in return for a brief appearance at a convention fall in the same category. Senator Douglas explained the cost of such practices much more clearly than I can express it:

> Throughout this whole process, the official will claim—and may indeed believe—that there is no causal connection between the favors he has received and the decisions which he makes. He will assert that the favors were given and received on the basis of pure friendship unsullied by worldly considerations. He will claim that the decisions, on the other hand, will

have been made on the basis of the justice and equity of the particular case.

But—Senator Douglas emphasized:

> What happens is a gradual shifting of a man's loyalties from the community to those who have been doing him favors. His final decisions are, therefore, made in response to his private friendships and loyalties rather than to the public good.

Outside earnings have been sharply limited and the receipt of honoraria has been forbidden throughout the government. The Senate put the capstone on such legislation this summer by modifying its rules to forbid acceptance of travel expenses and of any but the most trifling entertainment. The House has not followed suit. On October 1, 1995 the House majority leader, Representative Armey, said that the Republican leadership would not bring a similar measure up for consideration that year. A week later, he reversed himself and said that a bill would be taken up in November. Any failure of the Republican leadership in the House to secure enactment of ethics reforms approved by every other part of the government could only be described as "shameful."

We have also made considerable progress in dealing with the evils of "the revolving door" through which officials, including members of Congress, regularly left government office only to walk back in to the Congress, or their former department or agency to use the friendships, influence and inside information acquired in government service as lobbyists for special interests. Senior personnel in the executive branch, for example, are now barred for one year from participating in any matter that was under their authority within a year prior to leaving the government. Former mem-

bers of Congress are barred from lobbying any present member of either House or any congressional staff for one year after leaving office. Similar but somewhat narrower limitations are laid upon other employees in both branches.

The measures are not a full remedy for the abuse of the "revolving door." There continues to be serious criticism of the practice of leaving Congress or high executive office and later becoming the lobbyist for a foreign government at any time. Much more important in my opinion, the one-year ban on lobbying is far too short either to eliminate the advantage of "inside information" or to ensure that the individual lobbied will not make his decisions "in response to his private friendships and loyalties [to his former colleagues turned lobbyist] rather than to the public good."

Taking all these reforms as a group, I think that we are thoroughly warranted in saying that, within the field conventionally denominated "ethics in government," we have made good progress in writing rules to keep our rulers virtuous in pursuit of the common good.

GROWING PUBLIC CYNICISM

Have we succeeded in Madison's aim to keep those chosen to govern virtuous in pursuit of the common good?

Surely, the answer is a resounding "No." Some will respond that the common good of which Madison, Jefferson and the Founding Fathers wrote was always an empty dream, meaningless in actuality, and that Congress has always been a place for striking a balance among the selfish interests of conflicting groups according to their political power. I grant you that pursuit of the common good was an ideal seldom wholly achieved and

often submerged in the battle of selfish interests. But I think that the ideal had its force, and that by any measure of achievement we have lost much ground in the past 20 years. Column after column, book after book, by such experienced observers as Elizabeth Drew, Al Hunt, William Greider and Kevin Phillips documents the proposition that "money-driven American politics stinks." A 1992 Gordon S. Black poll found that 75 percent of the registered likely voters agreed that "Congress is largely owned by special interest groups," while 85 percent agreed that "special interest money buys the loyalty of candidates." The 1994 elections resulted in a smashing defeat of the Democratic incumbents. The vote was a rejection of the performance of government and not just of the party in power. One therefore has to ask: What is to blame?

INFLUENCE OF LOBBYISTS

Surely the central cause of the current overwhelming public distrust of government, and of actual subordination of the common good to special interests, is the present system of campaign finance.

A few figures should be sufficient to recall the still swelling torrent of campaign money. In less than 20 years, spending in Senate races has increased more than five-fold. The average expenditure for a Senate winner was $610,026 in 1976 and $4.5 million in 1994, a seven-fold increase. In order to acquire $4.5 million for a campaign, a Senator must raise $14,423 a week each and every week of his six-year term. In 1976 the average spent by successful candidates for the House was $87,280. In 1994 it was $530,031—more than a six-fold increase. In 1994, 45 House

candidates spent more than $1 million apiece.

Special interest PAC [political action committee] contributions have become a dominant force in financing congressional campaigns, and consequently in congressional decision making. In 1994, 45 percent of the contributions of incumbent House candidates came from PACs. On the average, an incumbent Senate candidate raised $1.1 million from PACs in the 1994 election cycle. The 1994 elections brought many new members to both Senate and House, a switch to Republican control, and sweeping promises of reform; but the torrent of PAC money is still increasing. The 85 freshman members of the House raised just about $5 million in PAC contributions during the first six months of 1995, 25 percent higher than those of their predecessors in the corresponding first six months of 1993.

Nearly all PACs are affiliated with organizations that are concerned with government decisions and therefore maintain on-going lobbying. And while the law limits to $10,000 the amount any one PAC can contribute to any one member of Congress in a full election cycle, we must remember that large numbers of PACs will often be pressing the same issue. As former Senator Warren Rudman observed while in the House of Representatives:

> I call them wolf packs. Sure, the PACs can only give X amount of dollars, but you can take 10 PACs who are interested in defense or 10 PACs interested in energy or 10 PACs interested in agriculture or 10 PACs interested in trade issues and put them together and you have $100,000 between the primary and general election.

The medical industry PACs invested $45 million in campaign contributions in the decade 1983–1993; $18.6 million (44 percent) went to members of key committees who were still in office in 1993. Similarly, in the decade ending this spring communications industry PACs contributed in excess of $30 million, and communications interests and their executives added $8.6 million in "soft money" given to the Democratic and Republican national committees.

CAMPAIGN CONTRIBUTIONS AND POLITICAL ACCESS

The costs of this system of campaign finance are enormous.

First comes the substitution of money in place of ability to attract votes by character, program and record of public accomplishment as the driving force throughout our political system, ranging from elections to action and inaction by both Congress and the President.

Second, other experienced observers echo Senator Dale Bumpers' observation that "Every Senator knows I speak the truth when I say bill after bill has been defeated in this body because of campaign money."

Former Senator Packwood's diary provides examples. Similarly, outcomes are bound to have been affected by the tens of millions of dollars invested by the medical and communications interests while Congress was working on basic legislation affecting them.

Efforts to analyze the effect of special interest contributions upon key votes point to the same conclusion. Consider the dairy subsidy. Three huge dairy cooperatives had been showering political contributions upon members of Congress. Of those who had received

more than $30,000, all voted for the subsidy at the high level. Of those who received from $20,000 to $30,000, 97 percent chose the high level; from $10,000 to $20,000, 81 percent. On the other hand, of those Congressmen who received from $1 to $2,500, only 33 percent voted for the higher subsidy, along with 23 percent of those who received no dairy industry money. The higher subsidy carried the day at a cost of $1 billion to the taxpayers. The effect of the special interest money seems plain whether one infers that it bought votes in Congress or that it made the difference in congressional elections in an age when the key factor is usually the ability to outspend one's opponent in buying skilled campaign managers, pollsters, "packagers" and television spots.

The defenders of large campaign contributions often acknowledge that the contributions buy "access" to Senators and Representatives but deny that they buy votes. But buying and selling access itself changes the very basis of our political system. No one would tolerate a legal system in which the judge heard only the evidence and arguments of one side. Why should the Congress be different? The irresistible forces so well described by Senator Douglas in speaking of gifts and entertainment also come into play:

> What happens is a gradual shifting of man's loyalties from the community to those who have been doing him favors. His final decisions are, therefore, made in response to his private friendships and loyalties rather than to the public good.

The access and the loyalties engendered by large campaign contributions also win innumerable opportunities to advance the special interest in ways less apparent than key votes: the appointment

of A rather than B to the staff of a key committee, absence from a hearing, a slight verbal change in a complex 240 page bill, the insertion at midnight of an apparently small, technical exemption into a tax or appropriations bill thus securing some interest in the millions of dollars.

Hand in hand with the torrent of PAC money flowing to the newly elected Republican members of Congress, there has come closer and closer participation by lobbyists in the legislative process. The *Wall Street Journal* reports that while the House Science Committee was writing a regulatory overhaul bill earlier this year, the committee's general counsel was surrounded by lobbyists for businesses vitally interested in the legislation and that one night the majority staff turned its computer over to the business interests. The same account reports that during a House Resources subcommittee hearing on Bureau of Reclamation activities, the lobbyist for a private firm that oversees the Central Arizona project, former Arizona Congressman John Rhodes, actually sat on the dais with the chairman of the subcommittee.

Confronted by these and countless other examples, it is no wonder that a study done for the Kettering Foundation found that:

> People believe two forces have corrupted democracy. The first is that lobbyists have replaced representatives as the primary political actors. The other force seen as more pernicious is that campaign contributions seem to determine political outcomes more than voting.

The third cost of the present system of campaign finance is the shrinking and ultimate loss of faith in democratic self-government. When money and lobbyists are seen to govern, men and women

drop out of the political process; they take no interest and cease to vote. Only 55.2 percent of the eligible population voted in 1992, the year of the last presidential election; only 39 percent voted in 1994. Many of those who do vote learn less each year about the issues and candidates. The package gotten up by the professional advertiser, the thirty-second sound bite with its pretested slogans, and the attack message, all received by television, replace informed discussion. The cynicism that accompanies the feeling of powerlessness discourages active citizenship.

Fourth among the costs and first in importance, I would list the loss of faith in a common good of society—of which Madison wrote when he said that one aim of every political constitution should be to keep those elected virtuous in pursuit of the "common good." I return to the point a little later. For the moment it is enough to say that even if the skeptics are right in saying that in a self-governing democracy, elections and the halls of Congress are no more than the places where selfish groups strike an equilibrium of self-interests, still it is a disastrous step back to have money become the sole determinant of where the balance is struck.

REFORMING AMERICAN POLITICS

To restore confidence in representative government by turning our elected governors' focus away from special interests and back to the common good, we need first to reform the system of campaign finance. Solid reform would comprise five elements.

1. First, reform must provide viable candidates with substantial public campaign resources in return for their agreement to observe strict spending limits. I

couple the two because the U.S. Supreme Court has held that although Congress violates the First Amendment by setting a limit on what one may spend to get elected, Congress may offer public financing to those candidates who subscribe to spending limits, as indeed the present law provides in presidential general elections. There are various forms in which the public financing might be provided: direct grants, matching payments, publicly funded communications vouchers, and so forth. My personal preference is for direct grants large enough to run an effective campaign without becoming indebted to special donors, the kind of plan established in 1974 for presidential general elections.

2. The second essential of campaign finance reform is tighter restriction of PAC contributions. The PAC contributions, unlike many personal contributions, are plainly and simply financial investments made in the hope that they will yield earnings in favorable government decisions. The ceiling on individual PAC contributions to individual candidates should be reduced from the present $5,000 limit to $1,000. The total amount an individual candidate receives from all PACs should also be limited. The influence of the special interest lobbyists would be greatly weakened.

3. Limits upon PAC contributions will be effective only if the reform measure includes as a third component a prohibition against "bundling." Normally a PAC obtains individual contributions to the PAC and then makes PAC contributions to candidates. In the 1980s PACs began to have their contributors write checks to designated individual candidates instead of the PAC but to leave the checks with the PAC. The PAC then bundles together and delivers the checks to each candidate

whom it chooses to support. The PAC thus receives the credit and the gratitude from the candidate, and the access and influence that go with it. Nevertheless, today the PAC is held to have made no contribution, and it can thus circumvent even the present $5,000 statutory limit. Closing the bundling loophole is essential to any effective PAC limits.

4. Fourth, it is important to stop the flow of "soft money" from wealthy individuals, corporations, and labor unions into the coffers of the political parties which spend it for the benefit of presidential and congressional candidates outside the existing statutory limits. The present system of funding presidential campaigns worked well until the mid-1980s when the Federal Elections Commission sanctioned the practice whereby a wealthy donor gives unlimited monies to a national political party, normally Democratic or Republican, and the national party then channels those dollars to its state organizations, which spend them for the benefit of the presidential ticket in ways that can be labeled "party building." The whole process escapes federal law.

In the 1991–1992 election cycle George Bush and the Republican National Committee raised $49.6 million in this fashion. Each of 69 contributors gave $100,000 or more. Clinton and the Democratic National Committee raised $35.3 million from 72 contributors, with each giving $100,000 or more. The money was spent in excess of the public funds provided to them on condition that they receive no private contributions. You will have read of the public controversy aroused by President Clinton's offer of personal access to himself and to Vice President Gore and others in return for contributions of $100,000 to the Democratic National Committee. Obviously, no reform of campaign finance can be effective unless it closes this gaping loophole.

5. The last essential major element in any effective reform is reconstitution of the Federal Elections Commission. The present commission has done an admirable job in gathering and publishing information about the financing of election campaigns, but it has done little as an enforcement agency. The requirement that there be six members, three Republicans and three Democrats, means that all too often the commission is deadlocked along party lines. The present practice of appointing members closely linked to the political parties also means that the commission is at best slow to challenge ways of raising and spending ever larger funds in excess of the statutory limits. Consider the gaping loopholes left by the commission's rulings on bundling and "soft money."

RESTORING CONFIDENCE

To outline legislation reforming our present system of financing election campaigns is much easier than to persuade Congress to enact it. On the one hand, the vast majority of the people desires reform: 83 percent according to a *USA Today*/CNN poll. On the other hand, the Senators and Representatives who vote upon a reform bill, the president who must sign it, and the political parties to which they belong, are all beneficiaries of the present system and indebted to the special interests that supply such large proportions of their funds. Most of them cannot know how their personal positions and power and their party's fortunes would be affected by reform. This makes for resistance.

Yet there are also encouraging signs. In 1992 a sound measure was blocked only by a veto by President Bush. In 1993 the Senate and the House passed different measures but the differences were never ironed out in conference. In May 1995 the Senate rebuffed an effort by the Republican leadership to gut the existing system of public financing for presidential campaigns. A strong bipartisan bill sponsored by senators John McCain and Russell Feingold has been filed in the Senate. In July 1995 the Senate, over the strong resistance of the Republican leadership led by Senator Dole, voted its commitment to the consideration of campaign finance reform during the present Congress. The picture in the House was confused. Representatives Linda Smith, Chris Shays and Martin Meehan have introduced a strong bi-partisan bill similar to the McCain-Feingold bill in the Senate. In early October 1995 the Majority Leader said that reform would not be considered by the Congress. Later, he indicated that a reform measure would be brought forward in the spring of 1996. Speaker Gingrich proposed in November 1995 that a large commission be appointed to study not only campaign finance, but the status and future of political parties, the effect of media oligarchies, etc. The minority leader expressed approval. As Representative Linda Smith said, "The old boys and old establishment came together to stall for time."

Our ability to add to the voices and votes for reform and thus obtain reform depends upon exercising the privileges and accompanying duties of true representative government: informing not only ourselves but friends, neighbors, and others in the community, enlisting in or building civic associations for a grass roots movement to lobby for early reform, registering our wills with our chosen representatives and holding them accountable if they do not work for and then accomplish real reform.

Five or six decades ago when the philosopher Alfred North Whitehead was asked how he would explain the extraordinary achievements of the American people, he answered that no other people in the history of mankind had shown such innate qualities of toleration and cooperation. It was the spirit of toleration and cooperation that gave birth to the extraordinary number and variety of associations observed by de Tocqueville during his travels in America. The hardships of the wilderness taught our forebears that, essential though individual liberty might be, they were all fellow voyagers in the same boat; that no one could move very far towards individual goals unless the vessel moved; and that the vessel would not move if some voyagers pulled ahead, others backed water, others demanded a new boat, and more and more dropped out to go ashore. Toleration and cooperation flowed from belief in the value of common enterprise— belief in "the common good of society" of which James Madison wrote.

Today the prevailing style is often confrontational. The language is too often of demand and of "rights," not of cooperation and consensus. By the same token, the old voluntary civic associations are shriveling up: Boy Scouts and Red Cross volunteers, the labor unions, the Lions, the Elks, and even the PTA. Men and women drop out and factions too often seem to press their separate aims, not through general progress, but by taking from each other.

Earlier I counted the people's growing loss of confidence in the government as the most serious cost of the power

achieved by lobbyists for special interests under present methods of campaign finance. Confidence in the government is closely related to confidence in representative democracy and to its *sine qua non*, belief in a common good. The link is symbiotic. A marked decline of belief in the working of self-government weakens, and if the decline continues, could destroy, belief in a common good. Happily, the converse is also true. The effective working of government in ways that build confidence in the system, while by no means the only influence, will tend to revive the belief in a common good.

I am confident that our politics, our institutions of self-government, will be purged of the corrupting cancer of today's system of campaign finance. The American people have never resigned themselves to endless corruption. Corruption and reform go in cycles. The ethics measures which I tried briefly to describe were developed over the course of three decades, each in response to evidence of the abuse. The efforts of truly committed Senators and Representatives expressing the will of 83 percent of the people will surely prevail if enough of us care enough not to be deluded by pretenses of reform and to register our wills.

May we also look forward to revival of the belief in the "common good of society" of which Madison and other Founding Fathers so often wrote, and from which flowed the tolerance and cooperation and voluntary civic associations that were hallmarks of the American people? I find guidance in the words of my great teacher, Judge Learned Hand, speaking of the path of mankind from the dark swamp in which our remote ancestors blundered:

Day breaks forever, and above the eastern horizon the sun is now about to peep. Full light of day? No, perhaps not ever. But yet it grows lighter and the paths that were so blind will, if one watches sharply enough, become hourly plainer. We shall learn to walk straighter. Yes, it is always dawn.

NO

Bradley A. Smith

THE CAMPAIGN-FINANCE FOLLIES

In 1974, Congress passed amendments to the Federal Elections Campaign Act that, for the first time in our nation's history, seriously undertook to regulate political campaigns. Most states followed suit, and virtually overnight, politics became a heavily regulated industry.

Yet we now see, on videotape and in White House photos, shots of the President of the United States meeting with arms merchants and drug dealers; we learn of money being laundered through Buddhist nuns and Indonesian gardeners; we read that acquaintances of the President are fleeing the country, or threatening to assert Fifth Amendment privileges to avoid testifying before Congress. Regulation, we were told two decades ago, would free our elected officials from the clutches of money, but they now seem to devote more time than ever before to pursuing campaign cash. The 1974 reforms, we were promised, would open up political competition, yet the purely financial advantage enjoyed by incumbents in congressional races has increased almost threefold. Regulation was supposed to restore confidence in government, yet the percentage of Americans who trust their government to "do what is right most of the time" is half what it was before the 1974 act, and campaigns themselves seem nastier and less informative.

Well, say apologists for the law; if we have failed, it is only because our labors have just begun. If our goals seem farther away, we must redouble our efforts. We must ban political action committees (PAC's). We must prevent "bundling," a procedure whereby a group collects contributions from its members and delivers them all at once to a candidate's election committee. We must ban large contributions to political parties ("soft money"). We must, in the words of former Vice President Walter Mondale and former Senator Nancy Kassebaum, learn to distinguish between "campaign endorsements or attacks and [speech] that genuinely debates issues," and we must restrict the former while encouraging the latter. Senators John McCain (R.-Arizona) and Russell Feingold (D.-Wisconsin), the most prominent reformers in today's Washington, have proposed enacting all of these measures at once.

If existing regulation has failed so spectacularly, and existing laws are being broken seemingly at will, is more regulation the solution? Before we rush off

on another round, it may be worthwhile to examine the premises on which the impulse to regulate campaign finance is based. Each of them is severely flawed.

* * *

The first assumption underlying proposals for campaign-finance regulation is that too much money is being spent on political campaigning. The amounts are often described in near-apocalyptic terms. Candidates, we are informed, amass "huge war chests" from "fat cats" who "pour their millions" into campaigns and "stuff the pockets" of representatives in an "orgy" of contributions. Expenditures "skyrocket," leaving legislators "awash" in "obscene" amounts of cash.

Hyperbole aside, however, the amount spent each year on all political activity in the United States, from every ballot referendum to races for every office from dog catcher to President, is less than the amount spent on potato chips. Total spending of congressional races in 1995–96 was less than what is spent annually on Barbie dolls. Total PAC contributions in federal elections in 1995–96 were just about equal to the amount needed to produce the most recent *Batman* movie.

On a per-voter basis, our expenditures are equally low: less than $2.50 per eligible voter per year, or about the cost of a single video rental, for all congressional races, including all primaries. Looked at as a proportion of gross domestic product, total spending on all political activity in this country amounts to approximately five-hundredths-of-one-percent —less than is spent in nations as varied as Canada, Germany, and Venezuela.

Perhaps more relevant than any of these comparisons are the amounts spent on political campaigning versus other types of advertising. In 1996, the Home Depot corporation alone spent more on advertising than federal law allowed Bill Clinton, Bob Dole, and Ross Perot put together to spend on the general election. Although Michael Huffington was roundly criticized for "exorbitant" spending in his 1994 race for a Senate seat from California, it cost him less than what Sony International spent in the same year to promote a single compact disc by Michael Jackson. Unilever NV, a company most people have never heard of, devotes more money each year to advertising its wares than has ever been spent in any two-year election cycle by all candidates for the House and Senate.

The plain truth is that it costs money to communicate, and there is no reason to expect that political communication should come free. This is the crucial insight of the Supreme Court's 1976 decision in *Buckley* v. *Valeo*, a case issuing from a challenge to the 1974 Federal Elections Campaign Act by a broad coalition of groups ranging from the ACLU to the Conservative and Libertarian parties. There the Court struck down mandatory limits on campaign spending as well as limits on what a candidate could spend from his own personal funds. The Court did not say, as its critics have alleged, that money equals speech; rather, it recognized that limits on spending can restrict speech just as surely as can a direct prohibition. Imagine, for example, if newspapers were limited to $100,000 a year for publishing costs: most would go out of business, and those that remained would become very thin indeed. (This consideration has hardly stopped the *Washington Post*, the *New York Times*, and *USA Today* from ridiculing the *Buckley* decision.)

Spending on political advertisements is important to educate voters, increasing

their interest in elections and their knowledge of candidates and issues. Repetition plays an important part in this process: the electorate's hatred of 30-second campaign ads is surpassed only by its desire to get its political information by means of those same ads. And the ads cost money.

Although campaign-finance reformers often appeal to the public's unhappiness with negative ads, negativity has long been a feature of political campaigns, and money is not the source of it. (As long ago as 1796, the presidential candidate Thomas Jefferson was attacked as "an atheist, anarchist, demagogue, coward, mountebank, trickster, and Franco-maniac," and his followers as "cutthroats who walk in rags and sleep amidst filth and vermin.") In fact, if the goal is to have positive campaigns, even *more* money would be needed, for the simple reason that positive ads are less memorable than negative ones and hence need to be repeated more frequently. Besides, a limit on spending would mean that candidates would have to depend more on the media to get their message across, and the press is often more negative in its campaign coverage than the contestants themselves.

There is, finally, no objective criterion by which to measure whether "too much" is being spent on political campaigns. But as we have seen, spending in this country is not high. Considering the vital importance of an informed electorate to democratic government, it is hard to discern why it should be lower.

* * *

The hidden premise behind the idea that too much is being spent on campaigns is that money "buys" election results —a second assumption of reformers. It is true that the candidate who spends the most money wins most of the time. But the cause-and-effect relationship between spending and victory is nowhere near so straightforward as this might suggest.

For one thing, the formulation neglects the desire of donors to give to candidates likely to win. In other words, it may be the prospect of victory that attracts money, not the other way around. (What that money does and does not buy is treated below.) Or a candidate's fund-raising edge may simply reflect the relative status of his popularity, later to be confirmed or disconfirmed at the polls.

Even when the ability to raise and spend money actually succeeds in changing the outcome of a race, it is ballots, not dollars, that ultimately decide who wins, and ballots reflect the minds of voters. All that spending can do is attempt to change those minds. It would be a strange First Amendment that cut off protection for speech at the point where speech began to influence people's views, and it reflects a remarkable contempt for the electorate to suggest that it is incapable of weighing the arguments being tendered for its consideration.

Indeed, there is ample evidence that the electorate does so discriminate, and that higher spending in behalf of a losing argument will not necessarily translate into electoral triumph. In the Republican takeover of Congress in 1994, for example, the 34 victorious challengers spent, on average, just two-thirds of the amount spent by their Democratic opponents, who also enjoyed the inherent advantage of incumbency. By contrast, in the 1996 race for the Republican presidential nomination, Phil Gramm, who raised the most money, was the first to have to drop out. As Michael Malbin of

the Rockefeller Institute of Government has observed, "Having money means having the ability to be heard; it does not mean that voters will like what they hear."

The key variable in elections is not which candidate spends the most, but whether or not challengers are able to spend enough to overcome the advantage of incumbency and make their names and issues known to voters. Once they reach this threshold, races are up for grabs. For example, in the 1996 House races, 40 percent of challengers who spent over $600,000 won, as opposed to just 3 percent who spent less than $600,000. Once the threshold was crossed, it mattered little whether or not the challenger was outspent, or by how much. The problem, if it can be called that, is not that some candidates "buy" elections by spending too much, but that others spend too little to get their message to the voters.

* * *

Still another assumption of reformers is that, if we truly cared about self-government and participatory democracy, we would be better off if campaigns were funded by many small contributors rather than by fewer large ones.

In fact, the burden of financing political campaigns has *always* fallen to a small minority, both in the United States and in other democracies. Nearly eighteen million Americans now make contributions to a political party, candidate, or PAC during an election cycle. Although this figure is higher than at any other time in American history, and represents a broader base of voluntary public support than has been enjoyed by any other system of campaign funding anywhere, it still comes to less than 10 percent of the voting-age population.

Which sorts of candidates are typically able to raise large sums of money in small amounts, as the reformers prefer? In the years prior to federal funding of presidential campaigns, the two most successful in this respect were Barry Goldwater and George McGovern. The former raised $5.8 million from over 400,000 contributors in 1964, only to suffer a landslide defeat, while the latter, who raised almost $15 million from donors making average contributions of about $20, lost in an even bigger landslide eight years later. More recently, Oliver North raised approximately $20 million, almost all from small contributors, for his 1994 U.S. Senate race, outspent his rival by almost four to one, and still lost to a candidate plagued by personal scandal—primarily because the electorate, rightly or wrongly, viewed him as too "extreme."

What these examples suggest is that the ability to raise large sums in small contributions can be a sign less of broad public support, as reformers assert, than of fervent backing by an ideological minority. Other groups positioned to exert influence by this means tend to be those (like unions) in possession of an ongoing structure for mobilizing their constituents or those we usually call "special interests." It is the inchoate, grass-roots public that more often fails to make its interests known, and is therefore frequently reliant on individuals with large fortunes to finance movements that will represent it. Ross Perot forced the deficit to the forefront of attention in 1992, and Steve Forbes brought about a debate on the flat tax in 1996. Both were real issues, but each lacked an organized constituency, a problem Perot and Forbes were able to overcome only by means of their own substantial resources.

Ironically, the banning of large contributions, which means that no single gift is likely to make much difference in a political race, gives potential donors little incentive to become involved. A radical campaign can overcome this difficulty: its supporters tend to be motivated more by ideology than by rational calculations of a candidate's chances of winning. But this just further underscores the way in which banning large contributions can help render the political system more rather than less vulnerable to forces on the fringes of the mainstream—hardly, one presumes, the result the reformers have in mind.

A corollary fallacy entertained by reformers is that the financial resources placed at a candidate's disposal should ideally reflect his level of popular support. But this is to confuse the purpose of elections with the purpose of campaigns. The former do measure popular support. The latter, however, are about something else: persuading voters, and *improving* one's level of support. This, as we have seen, requires monetary expenditures, and it is a sign of health in a democracy when such expenditures are forthcoming.

When Steve Forbes declared his candidacy for the presidency in the fall of 1995, few Americans had heard of him or given much thought to the idea of a flat tax. Forbes's standing in the polls for the Republican nomination was in the vicinity of 2 percent. If his spending had been limited to his preexisting level of support, the flat-tax debate would probably not have occurred. Yet such debates are what campaigns ought to be about, and the more we regulate campaign money, the fewer of them there are likely to be.

* * *

Perhaps no belief is more deeply rooted in the psyche of reformers—and of the public at large—than that the money drawn into the system through political campaigns corrupts not only the campaigns themselves but, once a candidate is elected, the entire legislative process. Many officeholders have themselves complained about the influence of money in the legislature. But political scientists and economists who have studied this matter have consistently concluded otherwise. As John Lott and Stephen Bronars, the authors of one such study, conclude: "Our tests strongly reject the notion that campaign contributions buy politicians' votes.... Just like voters, contributors appear able to sort [out] politicians who intrinsically value the same things that they do."

The primary factors affecting a legislator's voting record are personal ideology, party affiliation, and constituent wishes —not contributions. Does anybody really think Phil Gramm would suddenly drop his opposition to gun control if the National Rifle Association (NRA) ceased contributing to his campaigns? Of course not: the NRA supports Gramm *because* he opposes gun control, and so, almost certainly, do many if not most of his Texas constituents.

This makes perfect sense. Individuals who enter politics usually do so because they have strong views on political issues; party support is almost always more important to election than any one contribution; and, to repeat, a legislator wins with votes, not dollars. For a politician to adopt an unpopular or unwise position that will cost him voter support in exchange for a $5,000 campaign contribution—the maximum

amount allowed under federal law—would be counterproductive, to say the least.

This is not to say that other factors never come into play. A legislator may be concerned about how his vote will be reported in the press, or whether an opponent can easily caricature him in a negative ad. Personal friendships may affect a voting decision, as may the advice of aides and staff, itself often influenced by ideology. Money is another such secondary factor, but it is only one, and not necessarily the political commodity of greatest value. Many of the most influential Washington lobbying groups, including the American Association of Retired Persons, the National Education Association, and the American Bar Association, do not make political contributions. The NRA does have a large PAC, but it also has nearly two million members who care intently about its issues. Although gun-control advocates complain that the NRA outspends them, the more important fact is that it also outvotes them.

Finally, most issues find well-financed lobbies on both sides. A seemingly dull proposal to introduce a one-dollar coin, for example, may line up metal companies, vending-machine manufacturers, and coin laundries on one side, paper and ink companies on the other. Similarly with higher-profile issues like tort reform, where well-financed insurance interests take one position and equally well-financed trial lawyers the other. At least one set of these contributors, and often both, will suffer enormous *losses* in the legislative process, a fact often ignored by reformers.

When push comes to shove, even the most ardent reformers are rarely able to point to a specific instance of corruption. Ask a reformer to name which of our 535 Congressmen and Senators are acting contrary to what they believe to be the public good, or to what their constituents desire, because of campaign contributions, and the answer every time is some variation of "It's the system that's corrupt." But if we cannot name individuals corrupted by the system, on what basis are we to conclude that corruption is a problem intrinsic to the "system"?

* * *

When it came time to fight the American Revolution, the founders of this nation did not go to the king seeking matching funds with which to finance their revolt. Instead, in the Declaration of Independence, they pledged their fortunes as well as their lives and sacred honor.

Today, in order to cure the alleged problem of fortunes in politics, reformers offer a variety of complex schemes aimed at *preventing* private citizens from demonstrating their commitment to democratic political change. Former Senator Bill Bradley and House Minority Leader Richard Gephardt claim that we need a constitutional amendment to overturn the *Buckley* decision. In Gephardt's sweeping formulation, there is a "direct conflict" between "freedom of speech and our desire for healthy campaigns in a healthy democracy," and "you can't have both." Their proposed amendment, if enacted, would grant a greater degree of protection to commercial speech, flag burning, and Internet porn than to the discussion of political candidates and issues.

Meanwhile, "moderate" reformers continue to push the McCain-Feingold bill, lately shorn of a ban on PAC's that even its sponsors admit was "probably" unconstitutional. Even so, this bill would

place vast new limits on the freedom of political discussion, ban most contributions to political parties to pay for voter registration, slate cards, rallies, and get-out-the-vote drives, and restrict speech in ways directly prohibited by standing Supreme Court decisions.

If it is not the case that too much money is spent on campaigns, or that money, rather than the character of a handful of elected officials, is the source of political corruption, or that large contributors buy elections or in some way frustrate "true democracy," why should we tolerate such gross infringements of traditional First Amendment freedoms? What would be accomplished by measures like those being proposed by the reformers that would not be better accomplished by minimal disclosure laws that simply require the reporting of all sources of financial support?

Of course, disclosure laws may also be broken, as they appear to have been in the 1996 campaign. Character matters, and the rule has yet to be invented that someone will not succeed in violating. But what all the reformers overlook, from the most extreme to the most moderate, is that we already have, in the First Amendment, a deeply considered response to the problems inherent in democratic elections—and one that is far superior to the supposedly enlightened system of regulation with which we are now saddled.

By assuring freedom of speech and the press, the First Amendment allows for exposure of government corruption and improper favors, whether these consist of White House meetings with drug dealers or huge tax breaks for tobacco companies. By keeping the government out of the electoral arena, it allows for robust criticism of government itself, and prevents incumbents from manipulating the election-law machinery in their own favor. It frees grass-roots activists and everyday speech alike from suffocating state regulation, thereby furthering the democratic aim of political discussion. And it allows candidates to control their own message rather than having to rely on the filters of the press or the vagaries of bureaucrats and judges called upon to decide which forms of speech are to be limited as "endorsements or attacks," and which allowed as "genuine debate."

In the vast muddle that has been made by our decades-old regulatory folly, the only real question concerns whose logic we will now follow: the logic of those who gave us our existing campaign-finance laws and who, despite a disastrous record, now want license to "reform" them still further, or the logic of the founders who gave us the First Amendment. For most Americans, I suspect, the choice would be an easy one.

POSTSCRIPT

Should Campaign Finance Be Reformed?

As is often the case when one examines a complex issue, there are several interrelated questions that must be answered in examining campaign finance: Do large contributors have an unfair influence on public policy? Is there a preferable method of raising money, such as through small contributions by less-affluent voters? The problem with this approach is the indifference of much of the electorate, reflected in the failure of the scheme by which voters can make a token contribution to political campaigns through their income tax returns.

Should incentives be created for people of more modest means to run for public office? Just as the U.S. Supreme Court has invalidated poll taxes (the payment of a state fee in order to vote), so too has it struck down high filing fees for primary candidates because "potential office seekers lacking both personal wealth and affluent backers are in every practical sense precluded from seeking the nomination of their chosen party." Beyond this, the U.S. Supreme Court in *Buckley v. Valeo* seemed to preclude any other action to make candidates more financially equal. Upholding limits on contributions, the Court rejected any limits on expenditures by more-affluent candidates.

Does existing campaign finance law give an unfair advantage to the candidate who outspends a rival? Consider that over 85 percent of winners in recent Senate and House elections outspent their rivals. This is partly due to the fact that in less competitive districts, contributors are more likely to give to the incumbent or probable winner. There are, however, conspicuous examples of candidates' winning despite their spending less.

Would free television time create a more level political field? What happens if a trade union, corporation, or other interest wishes to purchase television advertising to support a candidate or an issue? Could such independent expenditures be barred close to the election? What about candidate endorsements in publications or on billboards? Is public financing of congressional elections an alternative? Is there public support for such an expenditure? Would it rule out independent campaigning by individuals who are not formally affiliated with the campaign? When all the knotty political questions have been considered, there remains the constitutional question: Can campaign finance be limited without limiting political speech?

Liberals have found these questions particularly difficult. Numerous articles in *The American Prospect* have approached the issue of campaign reform from different perspectives. The coeditors of this liberal, bimonthly periodical take opposing positions on this question in the January/February 1998 issue: Robert Kuttner favors campaign finance reform in "Rescuing Democracy

from 'Speech,' " while Paul Starr argues against limiting campaign spending in "The Loophole We Can't Close." Similarly, *The Progressive*, another liberal publication, carried a debate on campaign finance in its December 1997 issue, featuring Bob Schiff, "The First Amendment Is Not a Stop Sign Against Reform," and Laura W. Murphy, "We Refuse to Sacrifice the First Amendment in a Desperate Attempt to Adopt Reform Legislation."

Herbert E. Alexander has written for many years on campaign finance, and his judicious treatment is available in *Reform and Reality: The Financing of State and Local Campaigns* (Twentieth Century Fund, 1991). Frank J. Sorauf, in *Inside Campaign Finance: Myths and Realities* (Yale University Press, 1994), provides an excellent introduction. Finally, Thomas Gais, in *Improper Influence: Campaign Finance Law, Political Interest Groups, and the Problem of Equality* (University of Michigan Press, 1996), offers a scholarly critique of the existing rules.

ISSUE 4

Are the Mass Media Degrading Political Discourse?

YES: James Fallows, from *Breaking the News: How the Media Undermine American Democracy* (Pantheon Books, 1996)

NO: Jon Katz, from "Rock, Rap and Movies Bring You the News," *Rolling Stone* (March 5, 1992)

ISSUE SUMMARY

YES: Journalist James Fallows contends that the information media put the profits of entertainment ahead of their responsibility to inform and educate the public.

NO: Media critic Jon Katz asserts that popular culture deals with social issues more effectively than traditional media do.

Just a few years ago it was unimaginable that the respectable information media would publish and broadcast sexual charges and rumors directed against a public official. Now newspapers, news weeklies, and television news and talk shows contain language that, until recently, would have been censored. Is public discourse degraded or appropriately informed by this change?

A broader cause of concern is the charge that the mass media are drowning as well as degrading political discourse in an endless flood of trivia and titillation. Magazine racks contain few periodicals with a single article that deals with genuine political issues, and the weekly papers at the supermarket checkout counter are as bizarre as they are prurient.

Worse, network television, which most people rely upon for political news, offers hours of soap operas, situation comedies, and game shows but schedules only a half-hour (approximately 24 minutes plus commercials) of national and world news without any real analysis or effort at understanding. Of course, there are the local news programs, whose major criterion is human interest (a child who has fallen in a well, domestic violence, the weather) and whose political coverage does not extend much beyond noting a politician's attendance at a local barbecue.

The impact of television is not entirely insignificant. Television gave sharp focus to the civil rights movement—its marches, speeches, and violence—in ways that the print media could not. It brought the fictional sitcom family of Bill Cosby into white homes and, in doing so, may have altered racial atti-

tudes. Television coverage played a major role in shaping American attitudes toward the war in Vietnam. And in presenting law professor Anita Hill's accusation of Supreme Court nominee Clarence Thomas as well as Thomas's refutation, television contributed to the beginning of an ongoing national debate on sexual harassment.

Several significant mass media changes have occurred in recent years. First, ownership of print and television media has become more concentrated. Currently, seven corporations own the 6 broadcast networks, 42 of the 50 cable channels that are most often subscribed to, and many of the leading motion picture studios, major publishers, and other important media.

Second, although fewer corporations control a larger proportion of information and entertainment media, there has also been a sharp increase in media sources. The public can choose from among a staggering number of cable TV and radio stations, more current magazines and recent books than any book store could possibly stock, and more new movies than there are theaters in which to show them. One consequence of this proliferation of media choices is that the three major television networks have shown a steady decline in the size of their audiences.

The newest and fastest-growing medium of information and entertainment is the Internet, as accessed through computers. The Internet offers seemingly limitless possibilities for expression, but no one knows what role it will play in our lives or the extent to which it may supersede other media in conveying information and thought. Some critics argue that despite, or perhaps because of, this ever-increasing choice among media, there is a decreasing likelihood that uncommitted adults will often if ever encounter serious political news and opinion.

Television has become the primary forum in which political issues are discussed, but instead of long speeches, the candidates speak in very short sound bites, brief, catchy statements designed to be broadcast on the evening news. Under the circumstances, no exploration of issues is possible. Even when interviewers ask hard questions, candidates often give prepared answers that are only tangentially related or that entirely evade the questions. Most speakers at the major party conventions in 1996 were limited to five minutes, but the large number of speeches meant that few would be broadcast or excerpted in television news summaries or newspaper accounts.

Is anybody listening? Network television sharply curtailed the time it devoted to covering the national party conventions in 1996, and a majority of the electorate did not tune in. It should not have come as a surprise, however, because between March 1995 and April 1996, the proportion of under-30 voters watching the network nightly news dropped from 36 to 22 percent.

In the following selections, James Fallows, a veteran correspondent and editor, asserts that the press prefers conflict over content and would rather entertain the public than engage it. On the contrary, *Rolling Stone* media critic Jon Katz argues, popular culture defines the real political issues far better than the media that he rejects as the "Old News."

YES

James Fallows

HOW THE MEDIA UNDERMINE AMERICAN DEMOCRACY

Americans have never been truly fond of their press. Through the last decade, however, their disdain for the media establishment has reached new levels. Americans believe that the news media have become too arrogant, cynical, scandal-minded, and destructive. Public hostility shows up in opinion polls, through comments on talk shows, in waning support for news organizations in their showdowns with government officials, and in many other ways. The most important sign of public unhappiness may be a quiet consumers' boycott of the press. Year by year, a smaller proportion of Americans goes to the trouble of reading newspapers or watching news broadcasts on TV. This is a loss not only for the media but also for the public as a whole. Ignoring the news leaves people with no way to prepare for trends they don't happen to observe themselves, no sense of what is happening in other countries or even other parts of their own town, no tools with which to make decisions about public leaders or policies. Evidently many people feel that these losses represent a smaller sacrifice than being exposed to what the news offers.

The big American institutions that have failed in the recent past often wasted years blaming others for their problems. The U.S. military was near collapse in the immediate aftermath of the Vietnam War. Many members of the military felt stabbed in the back and blamed their problems on weak political leaders and ungrateful fellow citizens. The Big Three automakers of Detroit, with their dinosaurlike vehicles, were unprepared in the 1970s for the sudden rise in world oil prices or for competition from Japan. They complained about the unfairness of oil producers in the Middle East, regulators in Washington, and car makers in Japan.

There was some truth in such complaints. But the larger truth is that these institutions reversed their decline only when they recognized and corrected defects in their own internal values. In the early 1970s, control of the auto companies had passed from "car men," who had been trained to design and build automobiles, to "money men," who knew all about quarterly profits and stock options but very little about making cars. In the face of Japanese competition, the Big Three floundered until they put "car men" back in charge. The

American military of the same era was damaged by an ethic of careerism directly at odds with its older tradition of service. Officers bucked for promotion by being yes-men to their superiors and helping get defense contracts approved. In the field in Vietnam, enlisted men often limited their goal to surviving their 365 days "in country" and officers tried mainly to get a combat-command ticket punched. Then, during the decade after Vietnam, the military examined its ethics more deeply and honestly than any other American institution, and it corrected much of what was wrong.

The media establishment is still in the denial stage. Many of today's journalists are all too aware of the pressures pushing their profession in a direction they don't want to go. But they have not been able to deal with outside complaints honestly enough to begin the process of reform. In response to suggestions that the press has failed to meet its public responsibilities, the first instinct of many journalists is to cry "First Amendment!," which is like the military's reflexive use of "national security" to rebut outside criticism of how it does its work.

Criticize reporters or editors for their negativity, and you will be told that they are merely reflecting the world as it is. Objecting to news coverage, they say, is merely "blaming the messenger"; the press claims no responsibility for the world that it displays. Accuse a publication of left-wing bias, and its editors will reply that they are often accused of being right-wing, too—or of being pro-black, or anti-black, or pro-business, or nuttily pro-environment, or of being biased in every other conceivable way. If people are complaining from all sides, the editors reason, it must mean that they've got the balance just about right. Say that coverage is shallow or sensationalistic, and reporters will reply that they are already serving up more extensive, thoughtful news analysis than a lazy public will bother to read. If they don't feature crime and gore on the local TV news or run celebrity profiles in the paper, they'll lose their audience to competitors that do. Complain that reporters are insulated and elitist, being more committed to the values of the powerful politicians they cover than to the interests of the audience they supposedly serve, and journalists will say that even if the charge was accurate it would be irrelevant. They are "insulated," they feel, only in the sense that research scientists are, devoting all their effort to understanding an exotic subject. They can better serve the public by getting a close-up view of power than by artificially keeping their sources at arm's length.

There is some truth in journalism's complaints and excuses. But the larger truth is that the most influential parts of the media have lost sight of or have been pushed away from their central values.... [T]he values of journalists have changed,... their current practices undermine the credibility of the press, and... they affect the future prospects of every American by distorting the processes by which we choose our leaders and resolve our public problems. Many journalists have noted the crisis in their profession, and a number of them have begun reform efforts....

Everyone knows that big-time journalists have become powerful and prominent. We see them shouting at presidents during White House press conferences. We hear them offering instant Thumbs Up/Thumbs Down verdicts a few seconds after a politician completes a speech.

We know that they swarm from one hot news event to the next—from a press conference by Gennifer Flowers, to a riot site in Los Angeles, to congressional hearings on a Supreme Court nominee, to the arraignment of Tonya Harding.

Yet from outside the business it may be hard to understand the mixture of financial, social, and professional incentives that have produced this self-aggrandizing behavior. Some of the changes have been underway for decades, and others have taken effect in the last three or four years. Together they have turned the internal values of elite journalism upside down.

Any organization works best when the behavior that helps an individual get ahead is also the behavior that benefits the organization as a whole. Any organization suffers when what is good for the individual is bad for the group. As journalism has become more star-oriented, individual journalists have gained the potential to command power, riches, and prestige that few of their predecessors could have hoped for. Yet this new personal success involves a terrible bargain. The more prominent today's star journalists become, the more they are forced to give up the essence of real journalism, which is the search for information of use to the public. The effects of this trade-off are greatest at the top of the occupational pyramid, which is why the consequences are so destructive. The best-known and best-paid people in journalism now set an example that erodes the quality of the news we receive and threatens journalism's claim on public respect.

The harm actually goes much further than that, to threaten the long-term health of our political system. Step by step, mainstream journalism has fallen into the habit of portraying public life in America as a race to the bottom, in which one group of conniving, insincere politicians ceaselessly tries to outmaneuver another. The great problem for American democracy in the 1990s is that people barely trust elected leaders or the entire legislative system to accomplish anything of value. The politicians seem untrustworthy while they're running, and they disappoint even their supporters soon after they take office. By the time they leave office they're making excuses for what they couldn't do.

Deep forces in America's political, social, and economic structures account for most of the frustration of today's politics, but the media's attitudes have played a surprisingly important and destructive role. Issues that affect the collective interests of Americans—crime, health care, education, economic growth—are presented mainly as arenas in which politicians can fight. The press is often referred to as the Fourth Branch of Government, which means that it should provide the information we need so as to make sense of public problems. But far from making it easier to cope with public challenges, the media often make it harder. By choosing to present public life as a contest among scheming political leaders, all of whom the public should view with suspicion, the news media helps bring about that very result.

While creating new obstacles for American politics, today's media outlets have also put themselves in an impossible position. They increasingly present public life mainly as a depressing spectacle, rather than as a vital activity in which citizens can and should be engaged. The implied message of this approach is that people will pay attention to public affairs only if politics can be made as interest-

ing as the other entertainment options available to them, from celebrity scandals to the human melodramas featured on daytime talk programs. In attempting to compete head-to-head with pure entertainment programs, the "serious" press locks itself into a competition it cannot win. Worse, it increases the chances of its own eventual extinction. In the long run, people will pay attention to journalism only if they think it tells them something they must know. The less that Americans care about public life, the less they will be interested in journalism of any form. . . .

* * *

The media branches by themselves could not entirely correct the sense of cynical mistrust that threatens American politics. This requires the efforts of politicians and of the public as well. Journalists could, however, recognize how much they are contributing to a mood of fatalistic disengagement. If they recognized that this mood was the fundamental challenge not just to a functioning democracy but to their own professional survival as well, many other decisions would fall into place. They would understand why they should take public complaints seriously. They would understand the importance of changing their habits soon. And they would have an idea of the kinds of changes they should make.

The changes would all be in the direction of making it easier for citizens to feel a connection to their society's public life. This would mean an improvement in politics. . . . It would also mean salvation for the press itself. The truth that today's media establishment has tried to avoid seeing is that it will *rise or fall with the political system.*

The ultimate reason people buy the *New York Times* rather than *People,* or watch *World News Tonight* rather than *Entertainment Tonight,* is a belief that it is worth paying attention to public affairs. If people thought there was no point even in hearing about public affairs—because the politicians were all crooks, because the outcome was always rigged, because ordinary people stood no chance, because everyone in power was looking out for himself— then newspapers and broadcast news operations might as well close up shop too, because there would be no market for what they were selling. If people have no interest in politics or public life, they have no reason to follow the news. It doesn't concern them. They might as well spend their time going shopping or watching baseball. They might as well confine their viewing to sitcoms and daytime talk shows, and their reading to computer magazines and diet books.

Mainstream journalism has made the mistake of trying to compete with the pure entertainment media—music, TV celebrities, movies—on their own terms. But this is a losing game. Between January and September of 1995, the network news programs devoted an astonishing amount of airtime to the O. J. Simpson trial. News about O. J. made up fully 15 percent of the *NBC Nightly News* during this period. (It was 13 percent for the *CBS Evening News,* and 9 percent of *ABC's World News Tonight.*) Yet no matter how much time the networks dedicate to the Simpson trial—or the Menendez brothers, or Tonya Harding, or whatever future scandal occupies our attention— they can never match *Hard Copy* or *Inside Edition.* They are locking themselves into a competition they are bound to lose. If the public is looking for pure celebrity or entertainment, it will go for the real thing.

If public life continues to lose its claim on America's attention, so—inevitably—will journalism. What will be left is more restrained versions of *Hard Copy*. . . .

* * *

Today's journalists can choose: Do they want merely to entertain the public or to engage it? If they want to entertain, they will keep doing what they have done for the last generation. Concentrating on conflict and spectacle, building up celebrities and tearing them down, presenting a crisis or issue with the volume turned all the way up, only to drop that issue and turn to the next emergency. They will make themselves the center of attention, as they exchange one-liners as if public life were a parlor game and make fun of the gaffes and imperfections of anyone in public life. They will view their berths as opportunities for personal aggrandizement and enrichment, trading on the power of their celebrity. And while they do these things, they will be constantly more hated and constantly less useful to the public whose attention they are trying to attract. In the long run, real celebrities—singers, quarterbacks, movie stars—will crowd them off the stage. Public life will become more sour and embittered, and American democracy will be even less successful in addressing the nation's economic, social, and moral concerns.

NO   Jon Katz

ROCK, RAP AND MOVIES
BRING YOU THE NEWS

It's a shame Oliver Stone wasn't running one of the networks when the Bush administration decided journalists couldn't cover the gulf war. Nobody denied that conspiracy. Stone would have surely gone berserk, storming past the blue cabanas, over the berms and into the desert with his own camera-armed legions to bring back riveting pictures and shocking notions, like war is hell.

It's a shame, too, that Sinéad O'Connor wasn't providing network commentary in place of one more former general touting new weapons. When she refused to have the national anthem played at her concerts, she went further out on a limb than any of the major news organizations did on behalf of their silenced correspondents.

Too bad, as well, that instead of one of those evening-news suits, Bruce Springsteen isn't reporting on the economy. Springsteen seemed to know years ago that the jobs weren't coming back. The networks are still waiting for confirmation from the White House.

Straight news—the Old News—is pooped, confused and broke. Each Nielsen survey, each circulation report, each quarterly statement, reveals the cultural Darwinism ravaging the news industry. The people watching and reading are aging and dying, and the young no longer take their place. Virtually no major city daily has gained in circulation in recent years (The *Washington Post* is one of the few exceptions). In the last decade, network news has lost nearly half its audience. Advertising revenues are drying up.

In place of the Old News, something dramatic is evolving, a new culture of information, a hybrid New News—dazzling, adolescent, irresponsible, fearless, frightening and powerful. The New News is a heady concoction, part Hollywood film and TV movies, part pop music and pop art, mixed with popular culture and celebrity magazines, tabloid telecasts, cable and home video.

Increasingly, the New News is seizing the functions of mainstream journalism, sparking conversations and setting the country's social and political agenda. It is revolutionizing the way information reaches people and moves

among them. It is changing the way Americans evaluate politicians and, shortly, elect them.

Think of Walter Cronkite or Ted Koppel if you want to get an image of the Old News. The voice is grave, resonant with the burden of transmitting serious matters—White House communications strategies, leaks from State Department sources, leading economic indicators. The stories are remote (from Yugoslavia, Nairobi, Beijing) or from institutions that feel as remote (Congress, Wall Street, the Supreme Court). The reporters of the Old News cluster there, talking to one another, mired in an agenda that seems increasingly obtuse and irrelevant.

In January 1992, the New News is absorbed with a different agenda: On the eve of Martin Luther King's birthday, Public Enemy focuses the country's attention on his broken dream through its furious new video, an imagined enactment of the killing of Arizona state-government officials. In New York City, inner-city parents are taking their children to see *Juice* to educate them about the consequences of street violence. *JFK*—assaulted for weeks by the Old News as reckless and irresponsible—has prompted the chairman of a congressional committee that investigated the assassination to ask for the release of all government documents on the slaying. The kids on *Beverly Hills, 90210*— "The only show on TV that portrays teen life as it really is," says the editorial director of *16* magazine—are struggling with divorce, sex and AIDS. . . .

* * *

Once, the borders were clear and inviolate: Newspapers, newscasts and newsmagazines covered serious events; pop culture entertained us. But in the past generation, the culture sparked by rock & roll, then fused with TV and mutated by Hollywood, ran riot over the traditional boundaries between straight journalism and entertainment.

Now the list of issues addressed by the New News—far from the front pages and evening newscasts—is growing steadily. We're exposed to gender conflict in *Thelma & Louise;* money blues, sexual conflicts and working-class stress on *Roseanne;* motherhood, corporate takeovers and journalistic ethics on *Murphy Brown.*

Bart Simpson's critique of society is more trenchant than that of most newspaper columnists. Movies like *Boyz n the Hood* and *Straight Out of Brooklyn* and rappers like Public Enemy and Ice Cube deal with race more squarely than *Nightline.* No wonder Chuck D calls rap the CNN of black America.

In the same way that middle-class blacks rarely appear in the traditional media, disaffected working-class whites don't seem to exist in the world Old News covers. Analysts looking for clues to David Duke's popularity would do better to listen to Guns n' Roses and Skid Row songs than to scan newscasts and newspapers for the source of white resentment.

The country's ascendant magazine is not a newsmagazine. *Entertainment Weekly* focuses on what editors used to call the back of the book—the arts and culture material once ghettoized behind the important stuff. But today, the back of the book is the book. In its January 17th cover story, "JFK: The Film and the Furor, What's Behind the Backlash," *EW* dramatically illustrated how popular culture and major stories have steadily converged on one another over the past three decades, redefining what news is and who gets to cover it.

It didn't happen overnight—more like thirty years. Bob Dylan's vision of rock & roll helped mainstream music move from entertainment to political expression, an Op-Ed page for millions of kids who would never have dreamed of reading— or agreeing with—a newspaper editorial. Following in the tradition of shows like *All in the Family,* TV producers and writers broke free of the censors and produced broadcasts like *Hill Street Blues, St. Elsewhere* and *L.A. Law,* presenting life more and more as viewers experienced it, not as the networks wanted it seen.

So did tabloid telecasts and made-for-TV movies, which dramatized, reenacted and reinterpreted issues like sexism, child abuse, alcoholism and homosexuality. Hollywood helped define Vietnam in *Apocalypse Now,* racial hatred in *Do the Right Thing,* the takeover culture in *Wall Street.* Emerging cable technology gave viewers and programmers vastly more choices, breaking open the New News. Pop culture—America's most remarkable invention since the car—spawned a new information culture.

* * *

The modern news media—the Old News —was formed in the years after World War II. Major newspapers and instantly powerful network-news divisions chose Washington and New York as their headquarters, and presidential politics, the economy and foreign affairs—the cold war, mostly—as their preeminent beats. In its heyday, the Old News showed us the murder of John Kennedy, took us to the moon, then helped drive a president from office and end a war.

Other stories—the sexual revolution, the role of race, dramatic changes in the relationship between people and their jobs, the evolution of pop culture, a rebirth of spiritualism—were covered sporadically and incompletely by the Old News. They often sprang up away from well-staffed bureaus in a handful of major cities, thus making them harder for Old News to cover. They were a sideline, never the main event.

But for the New News—and for much of America—they were *the* event. Women, blacks, Hispanics, gays and Asians had launched an ongoing political and cultural revolution against middle-class white males, who continue to dominate most institutions, including the news media. In some countries, revolutions are violent, blood affairs settled in the streets. In America, they were slugged out in music videos, movies and cable shows....

The Old News seems bewildered and paralyzed by the dazzling new technologies competing for its audience, clucking like a cross old lady chasing noisy kids away from her window. Editors and producers prefer "serious topics" to the New News culture. In the same way they once fussed over rock & roll, most newspapers and news shows were too busy attacking Nintendo addiction to notice that more than 50 million entertainment systems had taken up residence in American homes, literally redefining what a TV set was and what it did. In 1991, the Nintendo hot line got 2 million calls from players needing help in ascending yet another level of Tetris or Super Mario Bros. 3.

All the while, news organizations puzzled about why kids were leaving in droves. Interactive video-jukebox systems and sports channels, round-the-clock local-news channels, video shopping and scores of movie and entertainment channels helped to create a new video culture for the young, a profound

change in leisure time that the Old News kissed off as a teen fad.

Stung by the mounting evidence that Americans' passions and concerns increasingly lie elsewhere, Old News institutions do appear unnerved. They've launched promotional campaigns, experimented disdainfully with color, commissioned marketing studies. ("Perhaps we should start a kids' page?") But it's mostly fussing. Every time real change is broached ... the guardian crows of the old order shriek the innovators into submission.

The networks sneered as CNN haltingly began to construct the most efficient and responsive electronic news-video-gathering machine in history. The newspaper industry's most dramatic response to the New News—*USA Today* —was greeted by the business with the same enthusiasm with which the human body greets a foreign invader. It was dubbed McPaper and dismissed as insubstantial, shallow and, worst of all, TV-like.

Its owner, Gannett, which owns eighty-one newspapers and admits to being alarmed about newspapers' shrinking and aging circulation, recently published a handbook for its editors. It says with shocking bluntness that papers have failed to recognize "key topics that shape readers' lives" and are filled with "dull, formula-based writing" and that newsrooms are "isolationist, elitist and afraid of change."

* * *

All the facts add up to a story that, Gannett's urgings notwithstanding, journalism doesn't want to hear. The Old News has clung desperately to the view that New News culture, like pornography, is nothing but trash and will eventually just go away. Yet journalistically, the New

News is often superior to the old at spotting major stories and putting them into context....

There is ... almost no story Old News has struggled to come to grips with more dramatically and unsuccessfully than race. America seems continually stunned by episodic explosions of racial hatred—by the murder of Yusuf Hawkins in New York, the violent black-Hasidic confrontations in Brooklyn last summer [1991], the chord struck by David Duke.

Still overwhelmingly owned, staffed and run by whites, and white males in particular, the media are stymied and discomfitted by racial issues. After decades of ignoring brutal racism, they seem to have lurched from one extreme to the other. Now they're so desperate to avoid the appearance of racism that they seem frozen by the subject.

The members of the media are able to quote demagogues and activists, but they're unable to advance the country's understanding of ghetto fury, to portray and represent the view of the black middle class or to explore white anger and confusion. Few issues in American life generate so much mythology, yet the intrigues of the White House chief of staff are covered in far greater detail. Spike Lee is far ahead of his mainstream journalistic competitors on racial issues. So is Ice Cube: "They have the authority/To Kill a minority/F——ing with me cause I'm a teenager/With a little bit of gold and a pager."

Police advocates don't make many albums, but there's plenty of white backlash to racial tensions evident in white rock, as well as worry about bleak economic futures. Perhaps the leading white working-class New News columnists at the moment are the members of Guns n' Roses, whose "Right Next Door to Hell,"

from *Use Your Illusion I*, is a national anthem for working-class anger:

When your innocence dies
You'll find the blues
Seems all our heroes were born to lose
Just walkin' through time
You believe this heat
Another empty house another
    dead-end street

Skid Row sounds like John Chancellor in comparison. From the album and song *Slave to the Grind*: "You got me forced to crack my lids in two/I'm still stuck inside the rubber room/I gotta punch the clock that leads the blind/I'm just another gear in the assembly line." . . .

* * *

The most explosive assault the New News has made on the Old is Oliver Stone's *JFK*. Its release has sparked less a free-for-all discussion of a recent historical event than a modern-day heresy trial. Stone set out to upend conventional wisdom, centering his film on Jim Garrisons' largely discredited theories. It is unclear why so many Americans remain skeptical about the Warren Commission's findings—only nineteen percent believe in the lone-gunman theory, according to polls—yet clearly they do. Whatever the accuracy of his theory, Stone—whose *Platoon, Wall Street* and *Born on the Fourth of July* were dramatically journalistic in their efforts to reflect different cultures at crucial times—has tapped into this dark strain in American life.

The Old News condemns Stone as irresponsible because he is advancing disproved theories and crackpot speculation as truth. The Old News is crying foul, incensed that someone has crossed over into their turf.

Yet it is Stone's movie, not years of columnizing by the Old News, that is likely to force the release of Kennedy-assassination documents the government is keeping under wraps. The license Stone took—and the risk—in reinventing a seminal story in the country's history illustrates why the New News is gaining so dramatically on the old: It is willing to heed and explore the passionate and sometimes frightening undercurrents in American life. . . .

Mainstream journalism frequently checkmates itself. In worshipping balance over truth, objectivity over point of view, moderation over diversity and credibility over creativity, the Old News gives consumers a clear choice. Consumers can have a balanced discussion, with every side of an issue neutralizing the other, or they can turn to singers, producers and filmmakers offering colorful, distinctive, often flawed but frequently powerful visions of their truth. More and more, Americans are making it clear which they prefer.

Younger audiences raised on New News traditions of outspokenness and hyperbole appear to understand that Public Enemy and Oliver Stone are not always to be taken literally. These New News communicators speak to states of mind, to anger at real issues like poverty and hopelessness, to disenchantment with jingoistic institutions and to a common perception that mainstream news organizations don't tell the whole truth or at least don't much reflect their truth.

Stone's *JFK* will have to stand the ultimate capitalist media test, the same one every newspaper, TV station, magazine and Nintendo dealer faces: People will buy it, watch it, read it, believe it. Or not. At least Stone has made it clear where he stands.

POSTSCRIPT

Are the Mass Media Degrading Political Discourse?

The media are criticized for emphasizing the political contest while neglecting political content. Not only are political campaigns trivialized as very long horse races, but the media apply peculiar tests to judge victory. Responding to a newspaper attack upon his wife and himself during the 1972 Democratic primary in New Hampshire, Edmund Muskie wept, and the media said that he had lost, even though Muskie received 46 percent, while George McGovern was declared the winner with 37 percent. When a presumed primary favorite falls short of expectations, the media label him a loser; when a candidate exceeds expectations, he is declared a winner. In this way, the media influence public behavior in later primaries. This may be due to what Larry Sabato, in *Feeding Frenzy: How Attack Journalism Has Transformed American Politics* (Free Press, 1991), asserts is the media's preference for sensationalism to thoughtful analysis.

Perhaps it is simply the inevitable superficiality of the mass media. Talk radio and television are superficial in format and sensational in their pursuit of a larger audience. Howard Kurtz, in *Hot Air: All Talk, All the Time* (Times Books, 1996), critically examines the content and impact of talk shows, including those of Rush Limbaugh, Phil Donahue, Don Imus, Michael Kinsley (a former cohost of *Crossfire*), and the McLaughlin Group. Thomas E. Patterson, in *Out of Order: How the Decline of the Political Parties and the Growing Power of the News Media Undermine the American Way of Electing Presidents* (Random House, 1993), deplores news coverage that is given to empty phrases (e.g., "Read my lips: No new taxes!") and real or imagined personality traits. Jeff Greenfield's review in *The Washington Monthly* (January/February 1994) rejects Patterson's view that the press exercises much power over elections.

Fallows's criticism of the press aroused sharp opposition, as evidenced by Howard Raines, "The Fallows Fallacy," *The New York Times* (February 25, 1996) and David Remnick, "Scoop," *The New Yorker* (January 29, 1996). The impact of the increasing corporate concentration of media ownership is examined in Ben H. Bagdikian, *The Media Monopoly*, 5th ed. (Beacon Press, 1997).

In *The Roar of the Crowd: How Television and People Power Are Changing the World* (Times Books, 1993), Michael J. O'Neill, former editor of the *New York Daily News* and past president of the American Society of Newspaper Editors, concludes that American journalism deals better with controversy than with the forces of reform. However, the media can effect change. The impact of the new media upon a democratic society is the subject of *The Electronic Republic: Reshaping Democracy in the Information Age* by Lawrence Gossman (Viking,

1995). Gossman, a former network executive, is optimistic about the power of instant communications to remake the democratic process.

Studies of public attention to major news stories have shed light on what events the public follows. The most closely watched news story between 1986 and 1996 was the explosion of the space shuttle *Challenger*, which 80 percent of the American public followed closely. Two-thirds closely followed American involvement in the Gulf War against Iraq. By contrast, only 40 percent followed the 1996 presidential campaign at its height, and a much lower percentage of the population paid close attention earlier in the year. Only one in five Americans follows closely the early presidential primaries. Perhaps the fault for any decline in political discourse lies not in our media but in ourselves.

On the Internet . . .

http://www.dushkin.com

The Supreme Court/Legal Information Institute

Open this site for current and historical information about the Supreme Court. The LLI archive contains many opinions issued since May 1990 as well as a collection of nearly 600 of the most historical decisions of the Court.

http://supct.law.cornell.edu/supct/index.html

U.S. House of Representatives

This page of the U.S. House of Representatives will lead you to information about current and past House members and agendas, the legislative process, and so on. You can learn about events on the House floor as they happen.

http://www.house.gov/

U.S. Senate

This page of the U.S. Senate will lead you to information about current and past Senate members and agendas, legislative activities, committees, and so on.

http://www.senate.gov/

The White House

Visit the White House page for direct access to information about commonly requested federal services, the White House Briefing Room, and the presidents and vice presidents. The Virtual Library allows you to search White House documents, listen to speeches, and view photos.   *http://www.whitehouse.gov/WH/Welcome.html*

PART 2

The Institutions of Government

The Constitution provides for three governing bodies: the president, Congress, and the Supreme Court. Over the years, the American government has generated another organ with a life of its own: the bureaucracy. In this section, we examine issues that concern all the branches of government (executive, legislative, and judicial). Many of these debates are contemporary manifestations of issues that have been argued since the country was founded.

■ Should There Be Term Limits for Members of Congress?

■ Investigating the President: Do We Need an Independent Counsel?

■ Should Judges Read Their Moral Views into the Constitution?

ISSUE 5

Should There Be Term Limits for Members of Congress?

YES: George F. Will, from *Restoration: Congress, Term Limits and the Recovery of Deliberative Democracy* (Free Press, 1992)

NO: Victor Kamber, from *Giving Up on Democracy: Why Term Limits Are Bad for America* (Regnery, 1995)

ISSUE SUMMARY

YES: Columnist George F. Will argues that term limits will bring fresh perspectives into Congress and restore the spirit of citizen politics.

NO: Political consultant Victor Kamber contends that term limits for congressional members violate the spirit of democracy and will force Americans to accept inexperienced legislators.

In America's early years, members of Congress were only part-time legislators. Congress met for only a few months of the year, and the rest of the time its members worked back in their home states and districts as farmers, lawyers, businessmen, or in some other private pursuit. Congressional pay was low, and it was not anticipated that members would serve many years in Congress. The ideal, much touted in the eighteenth and early nineteenth centuries, was of citizen lawmakers serving their nation in Congress for a few years before returning to local affairs and private employment. The expectation was that there would be frequent rotation in office and that nobody would think of congressional service as a full-time career.

For more than a century, actual practice approximated this model. The turnover of congressional seats was high, averaging 40 to 50 percent in each election; typically, members of Congress served a few terms, then moved out of Washington. In this century, however, particularly since World War II, Washington has become a city of career politicians: bureaucrats, lobbyists, congressional staffers—and members of Congress. Except for a few brief recesses, Congress meets year-round, and members spend most of their lives in Washington. Turnover in Congress is now very low; even 10 percent is a rare event in any election year. To be sure, the 1994 congressional elections brought in a large crop of newcomers—almost all of them Republican— and by 1996 it was clear that some of them occupied precarious positions. Nevertheless, the turnover rate in Congress today does not even approach the rate that it was in the nineteenth century.

How do voters react to this state of affairs? Their attitude is unclear, even contradictory. On one hand, voters are responsible for the low turnover in Congress. They are the ones who keep reelecting their representatives, and voter loyalty is remarkable: even legislators caught up in scandals often survive electoral challenges by appealing to constituents' attachment to "their congressman." On the other hand, voters in several states have indicated in unmistakable terms their unhappiness with the status quo. In 1992, 14 states had ballot initiatives calling for mandated term limits (most of them specifying a maximum of 12 years) for U.S. senators and representatives. Not only did all of these initiatives pass, in 13 of the 14 states they passed by huge margins. (Florida's and Wyoming's, for example, passed by a margin of 77–23.) These initiatives were challenged in the courts, and in 1995 the Supreme Court ruled that they were unconstitutional. One item in the Republicans' "Contract With America"—their campaign document in the 1994 congressional elections—was the promise of a constitutional amendment setting term limits. Once installed in 1995, the new Republican Congress attempted to pass the amendment but failed to muster the necessary two-thirds majority in even one house. Regardless of their party, senior members of Congress are generally unenthusiastic about voting to end their careers.

Self-interest aside, however, are there valid reasons for members of Congress to oppose term limits? What right have the voters to limit the number of terms for which a person can run for office? Aren't those who demand term limits not only hurting their representatives but also hurting *themselves* by denying themselves, at some point, the freedom to reelect a worthy public servant? Supporters of term limits reply by pointing to the enormous resources available to congressional incumbents: name recognition, free mailings, rewards that can be reaped by doing favors for constituents, access to the media, and the ability to raise large sums of money from wealthy interests. Term limits, the argument goes, are the only way of countering these advantages and preventing the indefinite reelection of incumbents.

But what is wrong with reelecting incumbents? Proponents of term limits contend that Washington needs an infusion of fresh blood and a restoration of the old spirit of citizen politics; term limits, they believe, will help to realize these goals. Opponents of term limits insist that in today's world we need experienced men and women to represent us in Congress and that term limits will remove legislators just when they start to become most useful to their constituents. In general terms, these are the respective positions of George F. Will and Victor Kamber in the following selections.

YES

George F. Will

RESTORATION

A strong, and itself sufficient, reason for term limits is that they would re-store to the legislative branch the preeminence and luster that it rightly should have. There is a kind of scorched-earth, pillage-and-burn conservatism that is always at a rolling boil, and which boils down to a brute animus against gov-ernment. Those who subscribe to this vigorous but unsubtle faith have had jolly fun in the early 1990s as public esteem for government, and especially for Congress, has plummeted. However, that is not my kind of conservatism. I do not fathom how any American who loves the nation can relish the spectacle of the central institutions of American democracy being degraded and despised. Patriotism properly understood simply is not compatible with contempt for the institutions that put American democracy on display.

Congressional supremacy is a traditional tenet of American conservatism. It had better be, because it also is a basic constitutional fact. The Constitution begins with a brisk fifty-two-word preamble about why we, the people, are constituting ourselves. Then the Constitution buckles down to business, the first item of which—Article I—defines the composition, duties and powers of the legislative branch.

It is altogether appropriate that the home of this branch, the Capitol, is the noblest public building in daily use anywhere in the world. And it is fitting that this building sits at the conjunction of the four quadrants of the Federal City. That setting symbolizes the fact that Congress is and ought to be the epicenter of the political expression of the nation's collective life. But in modern America, and in the context of today's Leviathan-like federal govern-ment, Congress can be entrusted with that centrality only if it is reformed by term limits. This is so because only term limits can break the nexus between legislative careerists and the capacity of the modern state to be bent to the service of their careerism.

This nexus, degrading to Congress and demoralizing to the country, is one reason why government performs so poorly and is therefore so disdained. Contemporary evidence confirms what reason suggests: A permanent class of career legislators is inherently inimical to limited government—government that is discriminating in its ends and modest in its methods. Interest in term

From George F. Will, *Restoration: Congress, Term Limits and the Recovery of Deliberative Democracy* (Free Press, 1992). Copyright © 1992 by George F. Will. Reprinted by permission of The Free Press, a division of Simon & Schuster, Inc. Notes omitted.

limits has risen as government's record of practical achievements has become steadily less impressive.

Furthermore, any attempt to understand the waning of respect for government in general, and for the Congress in particular, should begin with this fact: As government has become more solicitous, it has not become more loved or respected. As government has become more determinedly ameliorative, it has fallen in the esteem of the public whose condition it toils to improve. There is a perverse correlation between the increasing role of compassion in the rhetoric of governance and the decreasing regard for government on the part of the compassionated public. And there is a causal relation between many of the government's failures and the motives, attitudes and actions of legislative careerists. So to begin the argument for term limits, let us turn to the behavior of Congress that has imparted such momentum to the term limits movement....

"LIKE A STRONG WIND"

... [H]ow probable is it that a Congress operating under term limits will do worse than the Congress that has collaborated with the production of $400 billion deficits, the savings and loan debacle, and many other policy wrecks, and has driven away in despair many of its best members?

Consider a baseball analogy. In 1988 the Baltimore Orioles (on whose board of directors I sit) were dreadful. They were somewhat like today's Congress— expensive and incompetent. They lost their first twenty-one games, a record, and went on to lose a total of 107. After the season the Orioles' management had a thought: Hey, we can lose 107 games with inexpensive rookies. The 1989 Orioles were major league baseball's youngest team and had the smallest payroll and came within a few October pitches in Toronto of winning the American League East.

Increasingly, the principal argument against term limits turns out to be a somewhat serpentine assertion. It is that limits would be both harmful and redundant —harmful because rotation depletes the reservoir of wisdom, and redundant because there already is a healthily high amount of rotation. Tom Foley, the [former] Speaker of the House of Representatives, arrived on Capitol Hill (actually arrived there for a second time; he had previously been an aide to Senator Henry Jackson) in 1965. He was part of the bumper crop of new congressmen produced by the anti-Goldwater tide. By 1992 Foley was fond—rather too fond— of noting that 93 percent of the members of the House had arrived since he did, that 81 percent had arrived since the thunderous post-Watergate election of 1974, and that 55 percent had come since Reagan rode into town in 1981. However, a more pertinent number is this: Of the 1,692 congressmen who have sat since 1955, when Democratic control of the House began, 35.7 percent of the members, or 604 congressmen, have served seven terms or more. Of the current members of the 102d Congress (1991–92), 37.5 percent are already in at least their seventh term. In the last four elections (1984–90) the turnover in the House due to death, retirement or—much the least important cause—defeat averaged about 10 percent per election.

Much of the turnover comes not from the defeat of incumbents in competitive elections but from the voluntary departure of members who despair of enjoy-

ing useful service in a Congress geared to the service of careerism. The leadership of Congress—the ruling class that runs the committees and subcommittees that are the primary instruments for self-promotion—has not been changed nearly as much as Foley's numbers lead people to believe. Systematic changing by term limits would make serious service possible more quickly than it now is. Hence term limits would make Congress more attractive to serious people. In 1991 the economists W. Robert Reed of the University of Oklahoma and D. Eric Schansberg of Indiana University at New Albany argued that term limitations, while eliminating the possibility of long careers, would increase access to leadership positions. Representatives would be eligible for leadership positions much sooner than at present. "Currently," they said, "it takes sixteen years to reach the 80th percentile of seniority." On the basis of certain assumptions about how many members serving under term limitations will choose to serve the maximum permissible number of terms, and how many will die or be defeated, Reed and Schansberg calculated that under a six-term limit the time required to reach the 80th percentile would be cut in half, to eight years.

Some opponents of term limits say that limits are a recipe for institutionalizing ignorance. They say that if all congressional careers are short, no one will have time to master the subtleties and mysteries of the government's vast and increasing penetration of society, a penetration carried out by subsidies, taxation and regulation. But that argument tends to turn around and bite its authors, as follows: If government now is so omnipresent (because it strives to be omniprovident) and so arcane that it makes a permanent legislative class indispensable, that is less an

argument in favor of such a class than it is an argument against that kind of government. It is an argument for pruning the government's claims to omnicompetence. It is an argument for curtailing government's intrusiveness at least enough so that the supervision of the government can be entrusted to the oversight of intelligent lay people. Or amateurs. Sometimes called citizens.

Critics of term limitation worry that compulsory rotation of offices will mean that a substantial number of representatives and senators will always be looking ahead to their next employment. This, say the critics, means, at best, that these legislators will be distracted from the public business, and it may mean that they will be corrupted by the temptation to use their last years in power to ingratiate themselves with potential employers. Both of these possibilities are, well, possible. But the critics must confront a question: Would such corruption be worse—morally more reprehensible, and more injurious to the public weal—than legislative careerism has proved to be? Careerism, after all, is the legislator's constant surrender—with an easy conscience—to the temptation to use every year in power to ingratiate himself with all the factions useful to his permanent incumbency.

Also, people who would come to Congress under term limits would be less susceptible than cynics think to the temptation to misuse their congressional service to court future employers. After all, people who will choose to spend a necessarily limited span of time in Congress are apt to come from serious careers and will want to return to them. Furthermore, the political incentive for private interests to hire politically influential people from the ranks of ex-

congressmen will be radically reduced by the term limits that will swell those ranks. Think about it. One reason ex-legislators are hired by private interests today is to take advantage of their relationships with ex-colleagues who remain in Congress. But term limits will guarantee that those relationships are short-lived. Those ex-colleagues will soon be ex-congressmen.

Would term limits deplete the pool of talent from which we draw presidents? History, which is all we have to go by, says otherwise. Presidents are rarely launched from long legislative careers. How many people have become president after serving twelve or more consecutive years in the House or the Senate? Just three, and two became president by accident. The three are James Polk, Lyndon Johnson and Gerald Ford.

Unquestionably term limits would substantially increase the number of competitive congressional races. It is highly probable that this would lead to increased rates of voting. People are apt to vote at the end of campaigns that they have been talking and arguing about. They are more apt to talk and argue about campaigns when the outcomes are in doubt. Every four years the presidency provides the electorate with an election to argue about. Congress could be a much more prolific producer of wholesome arguments. Every four years Congress offers voters 936 elections —two elections of the 435 members of the House and elections of two-thirds of the one hundred senators. Term limits, by reducing the number of incumbents running, would increase the number of competitive races and would thereby enliven the nation's civic conversation....

* * *

In the famous first paragraph of the first of the Federalist Papers, Alexander Hamilton said that Americans, "by their conduct and example," will decide whether government by "reflection and choice" shall supplant government by "accident and force." Since that was written the world has turned many times, and many democracies have been born. America's sense of uniqueness, and hence of mission, has been somewhat diminished by this multiplication of democracies.

It has been diminished, but not extinguished. Ours is the oldest democracy and remains much the most important. By virtue of our relative antiquity, our example carries special saliency. And because of the material power we possess, which we have from time to time been called upon to deploy in defense of democracy, we feel, and are, more implicated than any other nation in the world's political evolution. Therefore how we do at the day-to-day business of democracy matters. It matters mostly to us, but not only to us. The world is watching.

NO

Victor Kamber

GIVING UP ON DEMOCRACY: WHY TERM LIMITS ARE BAD FOR AMERICA

MANDATORY ROTATION: THE HISTORY OF A BAD IDEA

The people are the best judge who ought to represent them. To dictate and control them, to tell them whom they shall elect, is to abridge their natural rights.

—Robert Livingston

Like many other bad ideas, term limits has been around a long time. In fact, we've already had term limits, and they didn't work.

After winning independence from England and before crafting the Constitution, Americans established a government under the Articles of Confederation. Because the former British subjects were suspicious of centralized power, they instituted a weak central government, with most of the power residing in the states. The only federal governmental body created by the Articles was the Continental Congress, but it could do nothing without the approval of at least nine of the thirteen states. The Continental Congress could not tax or regulate commerce, and although it could "requisition" money, it had no power to collect it. Another restraint on the body's power, which ultimately proved crippling, was term limits.

The result of term limits was a system of independent states under a dangerously weak central government. The economic and political crises resulting from this lack of central power threatened the stability, even the viability, of the new republic. Armed insurrections, including Shays's Rebellion, during which starving veterans of the Revolutionary Army marched on Boston, led the nation's leaders to reconsider such a loosely organized confederation of states....

The Constitutional Debate Over Term Limits

Despite the difficulties caused by term limits in the Articles, the first draft of the Constitution presented at the opening of the Constitutional Convention did have a provision for them. The "Virginia Plan" would have barred mem-

bers of the House of Representatives from office for an unspecified number of years after their terms expired. But that provision was quickly, and *unanimously*, deleted....

The Framers of the Constitution wanted experienced legislators who would use their wisdom and expertise to provide leadership for the fledgling country. They had no objections to politicians being repeatedly returned to office, as long as they performed honestly and effectively and maintained their voters' support. In *The Federalist* No. 53, Madison explained the convention's rationale:

> A few of the members [of Congress]... will possess superior talents; will by frequent reelections, become members of long standing; will be thoroughly masters of the public business, and perhaps not unwilling to avail themselves of those advantages.

The convention's reasoning for excluding limits is as powerful and relevant today as it was two hundred years ago. Despite their attempts to link term limits to the original intent of the Framers of the Constitution, the term limiters cannot dress up history enough to alter the basic facts.

The Case Against Term Limits

Why did the Framers of the Constitution reject term limits? Because they believed that frequent elections were a form of natural term limits: they required legislators to go repeatedly before the voters to earn their support. Frequent elections were the best way to prevent abuse of power by Congress. James Madison called regular elections "the cornerstone of liberty," and argued in *The Federalist Papers* that effective legislators should be returned to office frequently. He believed that experience was necessary for a legislator to perform in the people's best interests:

> No man can be a competent legislator who does not add to an upright intention and a sound judgment a certain degree of knowledge of the subjects on which he is to legislate. A part of this knowledge may be acquired by means of information which lies within the compass of men in private as well as public stations. Another part can only be attained, or at least thoroughly attained, by actual experience in the station which requires the use of it.

While the proponents of term limits sneer at "professional politicians," the Framers of our Constitution thought that experienced and capable legislators were the best guarantors of freedom. And they were wary of inexperienced legislators. "The greater the proportion of new members, and the less the information of the bulk of the members, the more apt will they be to fall into the snares that may be laid for them," argued the writers of *The Federalist*.

Term limits are specifically addressed in *The Federalist* No. 72, written by Alexander Hamilton, whose understanding of what motivated politicians was so uncanny that one might speculate such wisdom came from self-reflection as well as observation. He felt that one ill effect of term limits would be "a diminution of the inducements to good behavior. There are few men who would not feel much less zeal in the discharge of a duty, when they were conscious that the advantages of the station with which it was connected must be relinquished at a determinate period."

Hamilton was no Pollyanna; he knew that "the desire for reward is one of the strongest incentives of human conduct... the best security for the fidelity of mankind is to make their

interest coincide with their duty." Term limits would reduce the rewards for public service, since leaders would not be able to see their policies through and, therefore, would either find their agendas unfulfilled or would get no credit for them if they were ultimately enacted.

Imagine if you were given a job and told that you will be taken off the job at a certain point in time, no matter how well you do it. What will be your incentive to work hard? In the same way, if legislators are allotted only a certain number of terms and are not able to see many of their goals achieved, they will have little incentive to do more than keep their seats warm and show up for roll call votes. Or worse, they can wreak havoc, since they won't be around to suffer the consequences.

Open elections have the positive incentives that Hamilton mentions, giving legislators the opportunity to pursue their ambitions. And they also create negative incentives—if a politician does not perform or violates the public trust, the people can throw him or her out of office.

Madison correctly saw the reelection process as a means of popular discipline, accountability, and control of elected officials. "[Officeholders] will be compelled to anticipate the moment when their power is to cease, when their exercise of it is to be reviewed, and when they must descend to the level from which they are raised; there forever to remain *unless* a faithful discharge of their trust have established their title to a *renewal* of it."

Hamilton also saw the temptations that would result from a mandatory limit on officeholding. Even a venal or ambitious legislator who is facing a reelection would not take as much advantage of the office as he would if he knew he were leaving, never to return. As Hamilton put it, "His avarice might be a guard against his avarice."

Experience was also crucial to Hamilton. "That experience is the parent of wisdom, is an adage the truth of which is recognized by the wisest as well as the simplest of mankind. What more desirable or more essential than this quality in the governors of nations?"

During the debate for ratification in his home state of New York, Hamilton repeatedly made the following points:

1. The people have the right to judge whom they will and will not elect to public office.
2. Rotation reduces the incentives for political accountability.
3. Rotation deprives the polity of experienced public servants.

These arguments were powerful enough in their time to convince the delegates to reject term limits. Their strength has not diminished in the two centuries since they were composed. . . .

Coming to a Legislature Near You

Now all of a sudden the issue of term limits has returned, more radical and more popular than ever. Why is that?

People are frustrated with the political system. There are many problems that seem insoluble, and Congress at times does not appear willing to address them effectively. Drugs, crime, the economy, health care, the looming crises in Social Security and Medicare, the federal deficit, the breakdown of our schools and other public institutions—all these are serious and dramatic problems, and the American people are justly worried about them.

But term limits aren't going to make things any better. They're only going to

make these problems even more difficult to address politically. With a Congress hampered by term limits and filled with rookie legislators still learning the ropes and short-term "veterans" angling for jobs when their terms run out, it will be next to impossible to get meaningful and effective legislation out of Congress.

Despite the historical record, term limits are being sold as a quick and painless cure to everything that ails our body politic. The people behind term limits are promising one easy solution to a variety of complex problems. The Framers knew that there are no quick fixes, and they found out the hard way that term limits do not deliver as promised. That's why they refused to put term limits in the Constitution, and that's why we should honor their wisdom and foresight by keeping elections open to everyone, even experienced politicians.

POPULISM OR ELITISM?

We already have term limits. They're called elections.

Every two years you can vote to end the term of your representative. Every six years you can vote to kick your senator out of office. No one is forcing you to vote for incumbents, but legally imposed term limits will deprive you of the right to vote for them if you want to.

What if you went to a car dealer and were told that you can buy any car that you want, as long as it isn't the same one that you had before, even if it had served you well?

What if you went into the hardware store and the salesperson said that you can get any color house paint, as long as it doesn't match the color of your house?

What if you went to the video store and the clerk told you that you can't rent "Casablanca" because you've already seen it before?

That's exactly what term limits advocates are telling you. They don't want you to make your own choices, because they assume you can't be trusted with your own vote.

Power Over People

Arguments for term limits are often filled with pseudopopulist rhetoric. "The strength of our society has never been experts dictating to the people from Washington, but rather, our greatness has always been due to the common sense and the common decency of the American people. Trust the people." So says Paul Jacob, the head of U.S. Term Limits.

But behind the rhetoric is the reality: Term limits are profoundly elitist. We have already seen how a few rich and powerful people were able to convince Oklahomans to vote against their best interests and impose term limits on their state legislators. That's happened in every state where term limits have passed —a few people with their own ideological and personal motivations (joined in some cases by well-meaning but ill-informed citizens) have sold everyone else a phony bill of goods. But the elitism of term limits is about more than just money and power. It's about someone telling you how to vote.

Right now you can vote for any candidate you choose. But under term limits your right to vote for the candidate of your choice will be severely compromised. You won't be able to vote for your own representatives simply because they proved themselves popular and effective by winning previous elections.

While the supporters of term limits run the ideological gamut from the far Right (where most of them are) to the activist Left, they share one thing in common: They don't believe that you can be trusted with your vote. If they succeed in selling term limits to the rest of the country, there's no telling where it will end. Free and democratic elections are the only guarantee of liberty. Once they are compromised, our other rights are threatened.

POSTSCRIPT

Should There Be Term Limits for Members of Congress?

Will contends that "a permanent class of career legislators is inherently inimical to limited government." But Kamber, who also believes in limited government, writes that "free and democratic elections are the only guarantee of liberty," and he indicates that term limits undermine such elections. Both authors share the same goals but differ on which means are best for achieving those goals.

In addition to Will's book, James K. Coyne and John H. Fund's *Cleaning House: America's Campaign for Term Limits* (Regnery Gateway, 1992) also makes a conservative case for term limits; the authors argue that such limits would result in the downsizing of government. Political scientist Nelson W. Polsby, in an article entitled "Congress-Bashing for Beginners," *The Public Interest* (Summer 1990), argues that term limits would "limit the effectiveness of the one set of actors most accessible to the people." Paul S. Herrnson's *Congressional Elections* (Congressional Quarterly Press, 1995) is an account of the campaign process that, among other things, indicates how difficult it is for newcomers to defeat incumbents.

Would term limits be more beneficial to Democrats than to Republicans? To liberals more than to conservatives? On one hand, term limits would end the careers of many long-term members, and most incumbents are Democrats. On the other hand, it would make it more possible for newcomers to enter Congress, and many of these newcomers are likely to be African Americans, Latinos, and other minorities, who in turn are likely to be Democrats. Yet shorter terms would mean less time for members of Congress to create new social programs, which would probably make conservatives happy. But the promise of fresh blood and new thinking—one of the chief selling points of term limits—seems more in keeping with the liberal ethos.

ISSUE 6

Investigating the President: Do We Need an Independent Counsel?

YES: Janet Reno, from Hearing Before the Committee on Governmental Affairs, U.S. Senate (May 14, 1993)

NO: Antonin Scalia, from Dissenting Opinion, *Morrison, Independent Counsel v. Olson et al.,* U.S. Supreme Court (1988)

ISSUE SUMMARY

YES: Attorney General Janet Reno testifies that one part of the executive branch, the Department of Justice, should not be called upon to investigate another and that Watergate and the Iran-Contra investigation demonstrated the value of an independent counsel.

NO: Supreme Court justice Antonin Scalia holds that the independent counsel law violates the Constitution's absolute separation of powers and unconstitutionally restricts judicial control over subordinate officials within the executive branch.

No one could have suspected that when burglars were caught breaking into the Democratic Party's campaign headquarters in 1972, this would lead to a president's resignation in disgrace and the enactment of a law establishing a special prosecutor (later called an independent counsel) to investigate wrongdoing by the president and other members of the executive branch of the national government. The scandal that was gradually uncovered came to be known as Watergate, named after the the apartment and hotel complex in which the initial break-in occurred.

When the Watergate investigations began to implicate officials close to him, President Richard Nixon appointed a special prosecutor, Archibald Cox, who vigorously pursued his investigation. When Nixon sought to have Cox removed, the attorney general and deputy attorney general resigned because they refused to fire the special prosecutor. It was left to the Department of Justice's third-in-command, Solicitor General Robert Bork, to dismiss Cox.

Cox's successor, Leon Jaworski, was no less determined than his predecessor to uncover the truth, and this ultimately led him to demand that the president turn over the newly discovered, secretly recorded tapes from the Oval Office of the White House. When Nixon refused, the Supreme Court (in *U.S. v. Nixon* in 1974), with no dissent, agreed with the special prosecutor. The tapes clearly implicated the president in participating in the cover-up of

the Watergate burglary, and their revelation prompted the first resignation by a president in American history.

In order to regularize the procedure for investigation of the executive branch, Congress adopted the Ethics in Government Act in 1978, which provides that the attorney general should, upon due cause, request the appointment of a special counsel by a three-judge panel of the District of Columbia Court of Appeals. In the first 20 years of the law, 18 investigations were begun and only 3 resulted in indictments.

The largest number of independent counsel investigations, including several involving members of the cabinet, has been initiated during the Clinton presidency. The most far-reaching, known as Whitewater, began with allegations regarding a failed land investment in Arkansas by then-governor Bill Clinton, Mrs. Clinton, and their associates in this venture. Several of their associates were indicted and convicted of various crimes, but no charges were made against the president or Mrs. Clinton prior to the expiration of the Little Rock, Arkansas grand jury. Much of the focus of the probe switched to Washington as it expanded into an inquiry into the suicide of a presidential counsel and allegations of Clinton's extramarital sexual behavior before and during his presidency. The legal issues have been obscured by partisan reactions to what some characterize as the stonewalling of a president who would not be candid and what others characterize as the improper, overzealous, and perhaps illegal conduct of independent counsel Kenneth Starr.

Clinton argued that the independent counsel law violates the separation of powers. Presidents have invoked the claim of executive privilege on the ground that conversations with their aides must be confidential or else they risk losing the candid expression of judgment that is essential to decision making. For the most part, the courts have honored that claim, but from Watergate to Whitewater, independent counsels have argued that there are investigations that require an abridgment of executive privilege.

In 1988 the Supreme Court upheld the right of a special counsel appointed under the Ethics in Government Act to compel testimony regarding the conduct of officers of the executive branch. *Morrison v. Olson* concerned a special counsel's investigation of whether or not former Justice Department official Theodore B. Olson had misled Congress in a dispute over alleged political manipulation of the toxic waste cleanup program. Justice Antonin Scalia's outspoken dissent—from which the second of the following selections has been taken—has become the leading position of those who believe that the law violates the separation of powers and runs the risk of prosecutorial abuse.

A few months after Clinton took office in 1993, Attorney General Janet Reno vigorously supported reauthorizing the independent counsel law for another five years. At the same time, she opposed its extension to members of Congress as a violation of the separation of powers. Attorney General Reno's remarks in the following selection include her responses to questions and observations by members of the Senate Committee on Governmental Affairs, before which Reno was testifying.

YES

Janet Reno

TESTIMONY OF JANET RENO

ATTORNEY GENERAL RENO: Thank you very much, Mr. Chairman. Mr. Chairman and members of the Committee, I appreciate the invitation to be here to present the views of the Department of Justice and the administration on the enactment of the new Independent Counsel Act. After consideration of the issues and options available to us, I am pleased to announce that the Department and the administration fully support reenactment of the Act, and we will work closely with this Committee and Congress to pass this every important piece of legislation.

I am well aware of the depth of the controversy that has surrounded this Act since its inception. While there are legitimate concerns about the costs and burdens associated with the Act, I have concluded that these are far, far outweighed by the need for the Act and the public confidence it fosters.

As you have pointed out, the Independent Counsel Act was originally adopted in 1978 after Congress first passed the Special Prosecutor Act that changed the terminology and now uses the phrase "Independent Counsels," in the belief that the title better reflects the balanced, impartial role of the office. The Act has twice been reauthorized. The constitutionality of the statutory scheme has been upheld by the Supreme Court. Last year, the legislation was permitted to lapse. It is proper that this Committee is now moving to fill that void.

It is my firm conviction that the law has been a good one, helping to restore public confidence in our system's ability to investigate wrongdoing by high-level Executive Branch officials. In 1975, after his firing triggered the Constitutional crisis that led to the first version of this Act, Watergate special prosecutor Archibald Cox testified that an independent counsel was needed in certain limited cases and he said, "The pressure, the divided loyalty, are too much for any man, and as honorable and conscientious as any individual might be, the public could never feel entirely easy about the vigor and thoroughness with which the investigation was pursued. Some outside person is absolutely essential." Now, nearly two decades later, I could not state it any better.

From U.S. Senate. Committee on Governmental Affairs. *Independent Counsels*. Hearing, May 14, 1993. Washington, DC: Government Printing Office, 1993.

It is neither fair nor valid to criticize the Act for what politics has wrought, nor to expect the Act to solve all our crises. The Iran-Contra investigation, far from providing support for doing away with the Act, proves its necessity. I believe that this investigation could not have been conducted under the supervision of the Attorney General and concluded with any public confidence in its thoroughness or impartiality.

The reason that I support the concept of an independent counsel with statutory independence is that there is an inherent conflict whenever senior Executive Branch officials are to be investigated by the Department and its appointed head, the Attorney General. The Attorney General serves at the pleasure of the President. Recognition of this conflict does not belittle or demean the impressive professionalism of the Department's career prosecutors, and permit me to say again I have been so impressed with the lawyers in the Department of Justice at every level. They are non-political, they are splendid lawyers, and they have enjoyed the opportunity to work with your staff on this legislation.

I appreciate what Senator Cohen, and I don't think I have been here long enough for you to confirm your judgment, but even if I were here for a long time and you decided that you were absolutely right, I still think that there will be a need for it based on my experience for 15 years in Dade County.

It is absolutely essential for the public to have confidence in the system and you cannot do that when there is conflict or an appearance of conflict in the person who is, in effect, the chief prosecutor. There is an inherent conflict here, and I think that that is why this Act is so important.

It is worth noting that only a few matters that have been investigated by independent counsels over the last decade resulted in convictions. Far more covered individuals accused of wrongdoing have been cleared at the close of an independent counsel's investigation. This role of declining to prosecute a Government official is, I suggest, as important a part as any process in the prosecution. The credibility and public confidence engendered by the fact that an independent and impartial outsider has examined the evidence and concluded that prosecution is not warranted serves to clear a public official's name in a way that no Justice Department investigation ever could.

It is telling that on occasion covered individuals, including former Attorney General Edwin Meese, have called for an appointment of an independent counsel to investigate the allegations against them. I doubt the public would have accepted with confidence the decision not to prosecute had each of those individuals been cleared not by an impartial outside prosecutor but by the Attorney General and his Justice Department.

The Independent Counsel Act was designed to avoid even the appearance of impropriety in the consideration of allegations of misconduct by high-level Executive Branch officials and to prevent, as I have said, the actual or perceived conflicts of interest. The Act thus served as a vehicle to further the public's perception of fairness and thoroughness in such matters, and to avert even the most subtle influences that may appear in an investigation of highly-placed Executive officials.

Three months ago, the Senate Judiciary Committee undertook an extensive study of everything I had done for the

last 15 years, and the fact that governors of Florida, independent of me, could appoint special prosecutors when anybody said boo about me was oftentimes, I think, what gave credibility to the process of those 15 years.

It is a measured, appropriate response to a limited but serious problem, and the administration therefore supports the Independent Counsel Act's reenactment. My conclusion upon review [of] the history and operation of the Independent Counsel Act is that the statute has served the country well. This does not mean, however, that the statute functions without flaws or without imposing real costs and burdens. Based on the recommendations of those career prosecutors who work with the Act on a daily basis, and after the Department's 15 years of experience with the Act, I am prepared to suggest a number of changes that I believe will significantly improve the Act. I will discuss these proposals in general terms today and we at the Department stand ready to work together with your staffs in every way possible throughout this process.

Senate bill 24 proposes to expand the Attorney General's discretion to utilize the Act with respect to any investigation of a Member of Congress. I do not believe this change is necessary, as the Attorney General has that power right now under 591(c) of the Act. This section provides that investigations of non-covered persons may be handled under the provisions of the Act in cases in which there may be a personal, financial or political conflict of interest.

You have asked me to discuss why I oppose a mandatory extension of the Act to the members of Congress. Consistent with the doctrine of separation of powers, Congress is separate from the

Executive Branch and there is no inherent conflict between the Executive Branch and Congress. They are two independent branches of Government and if we were to suggest a conflict, I would start worrying about whether we had separation of powers. I feel very strongly, particularly after the experience of the last 3 months, that we do.

The Act was designed to address conflicts of interest which exist when the Executive Branch attempts to investigate itself. The Act does provide a procedural mechanism, as I have pointed out, for removing criminal investigations from a forum wherein there might be a real or institutional conflict of interest to an independent forum.

In 1982, Congress gave the Attorney General the power to invoke the provisions of the Act on a discretionary basis, should she or he conclude that a conflict of interest exists. Since that time, the Attorney General has never found it necessary or appropriate to invoke the discretionary provision with respect to a Member of Congress, and throughout this period, during both Democratic and Republican administrations, the Department has successfully investigated and, where need be, prosecuted numerous members of Congress. Therefore, mandatory coverage certainly is unwarranted.

Senate bill 24 proposes also that independent counsels be periodically reappointed by the Special Division of the court based on the court's assessment of the status of the investigation. We believe that this procedure would be too great an intrusion by the court into the investigation of the independent counsel. While the current limited role of the court in appointing the independent counsel is appropriate, any continuing oversight of the progress or scope of the investigation

would be constitutionally suspect and unwise as a matter of policy, and I recommend against that provision.

I want to emphasize my commitment to a productive and efficient working relationship between the Justice Department and the independent counsels. The need for an independent, unbiased decisionmaker is no reason for hostility between the Department and the independent counsel. We must not work at cross-purposes. Independent counsels are Federal prosecutors whose mission is the same as mine, to determine whether Federal crimes have been committed and, if so, to prosecute the perpetrators.

The Department has much to offer any independent counsel, ranging from resources to prosecutorial experience to institutional memory. It is inefficient and ultimately harmful to the interests of justice for any independent counsel to be left to reinvent the wheel on a difficult legal or policy issue. Therefore, I would suggest that the Committee consider whether the statute should require that the independent counsel consult on issues of law and Department policy and practices with the appropriate components of the Department, unless the independent counsel concludes that the unique needs of the particular stage of the investigation mandate not only independence but secrecy from his or her fellow prosecutors in the Department of Justice. I believe that regular and frequent contact by independent counsels with the prosecutors in the Department will foster productive working relationships and serve to help avoid many of the problems that have occurred in the past.

I also want to emphasize efficiency and effectiveness in the process. For example, the 15-day period for initial inquiries has proven too short, I am told, to resolve the complex issues raised and to cover the inevitably long distance between my prosecutors' word processors and my desk. I think this period should be changed to 30 days, with an option to extend the inquiry for an additional 30 days on notice to the Special Division.

The Act historically covered all allegations of both felonies and most misdemeanors. I believe that this coverage could be narrowed to felonies and those few misdemeanors that are routinely prosecuted by the Department, particularly if I have broad discretion to utilize the Act in other appropriate cases.

In addition, the ambiguity of the provision concerning campaign officials continues to cause difficulties in interpretation and application, sometimes requiring a full-scale investigation simply to determine whether an individual who served on the campaign, "exercised authority at the National level."

In conclusion, I want to confirm my full support for the reauthorization of the Independent Counsel Act. Public support for our Government is predicated on the belief that the Government is fair and just. The Independent Counsel Act is a crucial element of ensuring public confidence. I believe that in the spirit of cooperation, we will pass this important legislation and I look forward to working with you and would be happy to answer any questions.

SENATOR LEVIN: Thank you, Ms. Reno. First, a question about prosecutorial experience has been raised by some who suggest that perhaps we should write into the law a requirement that independent counsels have prosecutorial experience. In fact, all, independent counsels, I think, except one have *had* that prosecutorial experience, but it is not

a requirement of the law. What is your reaction to that suggestion?

ATTORNEY GENERAL RENO: Senator, I basically think that that should be left to the Special Division. You have splendid, wonderful lawyers who may not have had tremendous prosecution experience, but have a reputation for fairness, objectivity and excellence as lawyers, and I think they can fulfill that role.

SENATOR LEVIN: Another criticism has been the length of the investigations. Some of them have taken a long time, some of them have not. Complex Federal criminal cases often take years to investigate. . . .

Are you aware of any evidence that any of the 13 independent counsels who have been appointed over the last 14 years have engaged in foot-dragging for any improper purpose?

ATTORNEY GENERAL RENO: I have heard no evidence to that effect, Senator. I certainly have not investigated each one carefully to answer that question in an informed manner, but I have heard no evidence to that effect. And I will tell you again, based on my 15 years, I have sometimes been accused by others of foot-dragging and all it was was an attempt to answer every question, to make sure that innocent people weren't charged, and sometimes delay is in the interest of justice if it is to do that and if you do it with all deliberate speed.

SENATOR LEVIN: Now, there has been a suggestion that the tenure of independent counsels be limited by statute to a specific time period, such as 2 years, and if they don't file an indictment within 2 years, then that is it. One of the concerns we have about that proposal is that it would create an undue incentive for defense attorneys to engage in dilatory tactics in order to outlast the deadline, so we do not have a statute of limitations in this bill.

But what we do is require that the Special Court review the work, not renew the mandate, but just simply review the work of the independent counsel every 3 years to see if the work is done and as to whether or not the independent counsel should be terminated by the Special Court. So we don't have a renewal requirement, but simply a 3-year review to see if there is a basis for terminating the independent counsel by the court. What is your reaction to that 3-year review we have in the bill?

ATTORNEY GENERAL RENO: As I stated in my statement, I am concerned about courts interfering with investigations, but I think the court probably would have inherent Constitutional power if there was an abuse of due process.

SENATOR LEVIN: Even without that explicit authority, they could do that in any event?

ATTORNEY GENERAL RENO: As I indicated in my opening remarks, I think the latter might be the better way to go because if judges were constantly telling prosecutors, stop investigating this, I don't think you are going anywhere, that could have some real Constitutional implications. . . .

SENATOR COHEN: . . . Ms. Reno, you are, I think, the first Attorney General to ever appear before Congress to endorse the Independent Counsel Act. That marks a real change in past policy, and that is true under Democratic administrations and Republican administrations. Is this your view or does that reflect those directly subordinate to you within the Justice Department itself?

ATTORNEY GENERAL RENO: Well, I haven't asked those directly subordinate. I thought you were going to ask me the same question others have been asking me. Is it the fellow down the street?

SENATOR COHEN: You mean at 1600 Pennsylvania Avenue?

ATTORNEY GENERAL RENO: This is very emphatically my view based on my 15 years' experience. You and I at the confirmation hearing addressed this issue and I was working through it, but you will recall my very express statement to you at the time that it is based on my knowledge as a prosecutor. I have tried to use it very, very sparingly, but as I mentioned to you at the time, under Florida's structure, the governor could appoint another State attorney, not a special prosecutor, so it was an independent State attorney, to handle a matter when either he or the State attorney found they should be recused.

It did so much to do exactly what you all are trying to do by this Act, which is to give the public confidence, and sometimes I would [do] it and then at the end somebody would say, but so-and-so did this and they were related to the person that was doing the investigation, and I would say, fine, have somebody else look at it. I just think again, in the line of trying to be accountable and trying to be as open as possible and saying we don't have anything to hide, it does a great deal toward giving the public confidence in the system....

SENATOR COCHRAN: ... While I haven't finally made a decision about the bill introduced by the Chairman and Senator Cohen, I was very much impressed with the arguments made by former Attorney General Katzenbach, who I know is testifying later at this hearing, to the effect that we should not renew this in-dependent counsel law; that the Attorney General is a person of integrity. When the President selects the Attorney General, he ordinarily—and we can expect him to and he should under his responsibility as the Chief Executive of the country, seek out someone who is a person of unquestioned integrity and nominate them for this office. Then the Senate has the power and the responsibility to review the qualifications, the background, to ensure that the person is someone who can be trusted to carry out the duties of this office. That is a very thorough review of qualifications, of a person's integrity, background and experience, and fitness for the office.

I dare say the independent prosecutor or special counsel or independent counsel undergoes no such rigorous review of his or her qualifications in the process of selection by the court here in the District of Columbia, or if the Attorney General participates in that. I don't know that there is any participation as a practical matter. But in the past when Attorney Generals would select a special prosecutor under the powers of the office, I doubt if the investigation of a special prosecutor ever rose to the level of the investigation of the Attorney General himself or herself.

So without going into all the details of the article and the expected testimony of General Katzenbach, I want to ask you what makes the independent counsel so sacrosanct as a trustworthy individual. Under normal circumstances, why can't the Attorney General be expected to conduct an investigation, bring an indictment or present facts for an indictment, and carry a prosecution and still maintain the confidence in the process?

ATTORNEY GENERAL RENO: I don't know that anything is sacrosanct, and I don't know that there is any perfect

answer. I can answer based on my 15 years' experience where the people of Dade County elected me 5 times, and I was reported to be, from what I understand and what people talk about around here, an honest prosecutor who was accountable to the people.

But I was also a prosecutor who was not afraid to have other people look me over, and the people of Florida only had the opportunity to do that every 4 years and cases arose during that period of time where there might be questions. I would analogize it, what if my 5 chief assistants whom I appointed were the subject of an investigation. What if Mr. Katzenbach's assistant attorneys general had been the subject of an investigation? I don't think he ever envisioned that that would happen, and I certainly never envisioned that any 1 of my 5 chief assistants would be the subject of an investigation.

But if they were and if I conducted that investigation and cleared them, the people of Dade County would say, Janet just whitewashed it. If I prosecuted them, some would say—some critics would say, Janet didn't prosecute them vigorously enough; she just filed misdemeanors against them.

SENATOR COCHRAN: I understand that. What procedure did you use in Florida in such situations?

ATTORNEY GENERAL RENO: Well, I never had that situation, but wherever I felt that there was a legitimate conflict or an appearance of conflict—and I used the process less than most other State attorneys. Under our law, you could recuse yourself and ask the governor to, by executive assignment, appoint one of the 19 other State attorneys elected in the 19 other circuits to Dade County.

Wherever anybody implied that it was a political situation, I always asked the governor to appoint a Republican. I asked the Republican governor to appoint a Republican so that there would be no question that politics was not a part of it.

It is not sacrosanct, senator, but if there is one reason that the Judiciary Committee could look at what I had done and not come up with anything that would cause them to vote against me, I think it was because we tried to use that wisely over that period of time to avoid appearances and to let people look at what we had done. I can think of two or three instances where we worked with the Senate Judiciary Committee staff and said, here is the special prosecutor's report, here is what they found, this is what was done; it is all here, you can look us over.

SENATOR COCHRAN: Right, and the point is that that system works very well in Florida, does it not?

ATTORNEY GENERAL RENO: It worked well for me. I can't speak to the other State attorneys.

SENATOR COCHRAN: Well, I think you make the point for me. You do not have an independent counsel law in the State of Florida. You do not have the same kind of law you are coming here today asking us to reauthorize. In my judgment, we have some very serious problems with the current state of affairs. If an independent counsel staffs up, he necessarily has a large staff if it is a big prosecution. Look at the Walsh prosecution, for example. I don't know how many lawyers were hired, but a lot of people talked about the fact that it was a huge staff.

How is this person who is the independent counsel going to monitor, supervise, direct the work of that entire staff of prosecutors to ensure that they bring to the task the same level of independence and integrity and competence that the independent counsel personally has? There is no way in the world to do that.

There were a lot of suspicions, and I don't know whether there is any truth to the suspicions or not, that many of the staff of this recent independent counsel were out to leak information to the press, to embarrass the Bush administration during the campaign for reelection, to try to ensure that indictments were brought as quickly as they could be, supported by facts, for political purposes. These were suspicions. I don't know whether there is any truth to those suspicions or not, but they were very serious. If they were true, those were very serious charges.

How would you go about keeping that kind of thing from happening if you were an independent counsel?

ATTORNEY GENERAL RENO: Well, Senator, I have to disagree with you because you are concerned about an independent counsel supervising his staff. The people that investigated me were independent State attorneys who were not beholden to me in any way, whom I did not appoint, who oftentimes were of the other political party who could have embarrassed me until the cows came home, and who not only had to supervise the staff that they designated to come to Dade County to investigate whatever the issue was in our office—on only one or two occasions was it some allegation against me—they not only [had] to do that, they had to supervise their office back home and they were capable of doing that.

NO

Antonin Scalia

DISSENTING OPINION OF ANTONIN SCALIA

MORRISON v. OLSON ET AL.

It is the proud boast of our democracy that we have "a government of laws and not of men." Many Americans are familiar with that phrase; not many know its derivation. It comes from Part the First, Article XXX, of the Massachusetts Constitution of 1780, which reads in full as follows:

> "In the government of this Commonwealth, the legislative department shall never exercise the executive and judicial powers, or either of them: The executive shall never exercise the legislative and judicial powers, or either of them: The judicial shall never exercise the legislative and executive powers, or either of them: to the end it may be a government of laws and not of men."

The Framers of the Federal Constitution similarly viewed the principle of separation of powers as the absolutely central guarantee of a just Government. In No. 47 of The Federalist, Madison wrote that "[n]o political truth is certainly of greater intrinsic value, or is stamped with the authority of more enlightened patrons of liberty." Without a secure structure of separated powers, our Bill of Rights would be worthless, as are the bills of rights of many nations of the world that have adopted, or even improved upon, the mere words of ours.

The principle of separation of powers is expressed in our Constitution in the first section of each of the first three Articles. Article I, § 1, provides that "[a]ll legislative Powers herein granted shall be vested in a Congress of the United

From *Morrison, Independent Counsel v. Olson et al.*, 108 S. Ct. 2597 (1988). Case citations omitted.

States, which shall consist of a Senate and House of Representatives." Article III, § 1, provides that "[t]he judicial Power of the United States, shall be vested in one supreme Court, and in such inferior Courts as the Congress may from time to time ordain and establish." And the provision at issue here, Art. II, § 1, cl. 1, provides that "[t]he executive Power shall be vested in a President of the United States of America."

...[T]he Founders conspicuously and very consciously declined to sap the Executive's strength in the same way they had weakened the Legislature: by dividing the executive power. Proposals to have multiple executives, or a council of advisers with separate authority were rejected. Thus, while "[a]ll legislative Powers herein granted shall be vested in a Congress of the United States, which shall consist of a Senate *and* House of Representatives," U.S. Const., Art. 1, § 1 (emphasis added), "[t]he executive Power shall be vested in *a President of the United States*," Art. II, § 1, cl. 1 (emphasis added).

That is what this suit is about. Power. The allocation of power among Congress, the President, and the courts in such fashion as to preserve the equilibrium the Constitution sought to establish— so that "a gradual concentration of the several powers in the same department," Federalist No. 51, can effectively be resisted. Frequently an issue of this sort will come before the Court clad, so to speak, in sheep's clothing: the potential of the asserted principle to effect important change in the equilibrium of power is not immediately evident, and must be discerned by a careful and perceptive analysis. But this wolf comes as a wolf.

...[I]t is ultimately irrelevant *how much* the statute reduces Presidential control.

The case is over when the Court acknowledges, as it must, that "[i]t is undeniable that the Act reduces the amount of control or supervision that the Attorney General and, through him, the President exercises over the investigation and prosecution of a certain class of alleged criminal activity." It effects a revolution in our constitutional jurisprudence for the Court, once it has determined that (1) purely executive functions are at issue here, and (2) those functions have been given to a person whose actions are not fully within the supervision and control of the President, nonetheless to proceed further to sit in judgment of whether "the President's need to control the exercise of [the independent counsel's] discretion is *so central* to the functioning of the Executive Branch" as to require complete control (emphasis added), whether the conferral of his powers upon someone else "*sufficiently* deprives the President of control over the independent counsel to interfere impermissibly with [his] constitutional obligation to ensure the faithful execution of the laws" (emphasis added), and whether "the Act give[s] the Executive Branch *sufficient* control over the independent counsel to ensure that the President is able to perform his constitutionally assigned duties" (emphasis added). It is not for us to determine, and we have never presumed to determine, how much of the purely executive powers of government must be within the full control of the President. The Constitution prescribes that they *all* are. . . .

Is it unthinkable that the President should have such exclusive power, even when alleged crimes by him or his close associates are at issue? No more so than that Congress should have the exclusive power of legislation, even when what is at issue is its own exemption from the

burdens of certain laws. No more so than that this Court should have the exclusive power to pronounce the final decision on justiciable cases and controversies, even those pertaining to the constitutionality of a statute reducing the salaries of the Justices. A system of separate and co-ordinate powers necessarily involves an acceptance of exclusive power that can theoretically be abused. As we reiterate this very day, "[i]t is a truism that constitutional protections have costs." While the separation of powers may prevent us from righting every wrong, it does so in order to ensure that we do not lose liberty. The checks against any branch's abuse of its exclusive powers are twofold: First, retaliation by one of the other branch's use of *its* exclusive powers: Congress, for example, can impeach the executive who willfully fails to enforce the laws; the executive can decline to prosecute under unconstitutional statutes; and the courts can dismiss malicious prosecutions. Second, and ultimately, there is the political check that the people will replace those in the political branches ... who are guilty of abuse. Political pressures produced special prosecutors—for Teapot Dome and for Watergate, for example—long before this statute created the independent counsel.

The Court has, nonetheless, replaced the clear constitutional prescription that the executive power belongs to the President with a "balancing test." What are the standards to determine how the balance is to be struck, that is, how much removal of Presidential power is too much? Many countries of the world get along with an executive that is much weaker than ours—in fact, entirely dependent upon the continued support of the legislature. Once we depart from the text of the Constitution, just where short of that do we stop? The most amazing feature of the Court's opinion is that it does not even purport to give an answer. It simply *announces*, with no analysis, that the ability to control the decision whether to investigate and prosecute the President's closest advisers, and indeed the President himself, is not "so central to the functioning of the Executive Branch" as to be constitutionally required to be within the President's control. Apparently that is so because we say it is so. Having abandoned as the basis for our decision-making the text of Article II that "the executive Power" must be vested in the President, the Court does not even attempt to craft a *substitute* criterion—a "justiciable standard," however remote from the Constitution—that today governs, and in the future will govern, the decision of such questions. Evidently, the governing standard is to be what might be called the unfettered wisdom of a majority of this Court, revealed to an obedient people on a case-by-case basis. This is not only not the government of laws that the Constitution established; it is not a government of laws at all.

In my view, moreover, even as an ad hoc, standardless judgment the Court's conclusion must be wrong. Before this statute was passed, the President, in taking action disagreeable to the Congress, or an executive officer giving advice to the President or testifying before Congress concerning one of those many matters on which the two branches are from time to time at odds, could be assured that his acts and motives would be adjudged—insofar as the decision whether to conduct a criminal investigation and to prosecute is concerned—in the Executive Branch, that is, in a forum attuned to the interests and the policies of the Presidency. That was one of the

natural advantages the Constitution gave to the Presidency, just as it gave Members of Congress (and their staffs) the advantage of not being prosecutable for anything said or done in their legislative capacities. It is the very object of this legislation to eliminate that assurance of a sympathetic forum. Unless it can honestly be said that there are "no reasonable grounds to believe" that further investigation is warranted, further investigation must ensue; and the conduct of the investigation, and determination of whether to prosecute, will be given to a person neither selected by nor subject to the control of the President—who will in turn assemble a staff by finding out, presumably, who is willing to put aside whatever else they are doing, for an indeterminate period of time, in order to investigate and prosecute the President or a particular named individual in his administration. The prospect is frightening (as I will discuss at some greater length at the conclusion of this opinion) even outside the context of a bitter, interbranch political dispute. Perhaps the boldness of the President himself will not be affected—though I am not even sure of that. (How much easier it is for Congress, instead of accepting the political damage attendant to the commencement of impeachment proceedings against the President on trivial grounds—or, for that matter, how easy it is for one of the President's political foes outside of Congress—simply to trigger a debilitating criminal investigation of the Chief Executive under this law.) But as for the President's high-level assistants, who typically have no political base of support, it is as utterly unrealistic to think that they will not be intimidated by this prospect, and that their advice to him and their advocacy of his interests before a hostile Congress will not be affected, as

it would be to think that the Members of Congress and their staffs would be unaffected by replacing the Speech or Debate Clause with a similar provision. It deeply wounds the President by substantially reducing the President's ability to protect himself and his staff. That is the whole object of the law, of course, and I cannot imagine why the Court believes it does not succeed.

Besides weakening the Presidency by reducing the zeal of his staff, it must also be obvious that the institution of the independent counsel enfeebles him more directly in his constant confrontations with Congress, by eroding his public support. Nothing is so politically effective as the ability to charge that one's opponent and his associates are not merely wrongheaded, naive, ineffective, but, in all probability, "crooks." And nothing so effectively gives an appearance of validity to such charges as a Justice Department investigation and, even better, prosecution....

* * *

The purpose of the separation and equilibration of powers in general, and of the unitary Executive in particular, was not merely to assure effective government but to preserve individual freedom. These who hold or have held offices covered by the Ethics in Government Act are entitled to that protection as much as the rest of us, and I conclude my discussion by considering the effect of the Act upon the fairness of the process they receive.

Only someone who has worked in the field of law enforcement can fully appreciate the vast power and the immense discretion that are placed in the hands of a prosecutor with respect to the objects of his investigation. Justice Robert Jackson, when he was Attorney General under

President Franklin Roosevelt, described it in a memorable speech to United States Attorneys, as follows:

> "There is a most important reason why the prosecutor should have, as nearly as possible, a detached and impartial view of all groups in his community. Law enforcement is not automatic. It isn't blind. One of the greatest difficulties of the position of prosecutor is that he must pick his cases, because no prosecutor can even investigate all of the cases in which he receives complaints. If the Department of Justice were to make even a pretense of reaching every probable violation of federal law, ten times its present staff will be inadequate. We know that no local police force can strictly enforce the traffic laws, or it would arrest half the driving population on any given morning. What every prosecutor is practically required to do is to select the cases for prosecution and to select those in which the offense is the most flagrant, the public harm the greatest, and the proof the most certain.
>
> "If the prosecutor is obliged to choose his case, it follows that he can choose his defendants. Therein is the most dangerous power of the prosecutor: that he will pick people that he thinks he should get, rather than cases that need to be prosecuted. With the law books filled with a great assortment of crimes, a prosecutor stands a fair chance of finding at least a technical violation of some act on the part of almost anyone. In such a case, it is not a question of discovering the commission of a crime and then looking for the man who has committed it, it is a question of picking the man and then searching the law books, or putting investigators to work, to pin some offense on him. It is in this realm—in which the prosecutor picks some person whom he dislikes or desires to embarrass, or selects some group of unpopular persons and then looks for an offense, that the greatest danger of abuse of prosecuting power lies. It is here that law enforcement becomes personal, and the real crime becomes that of being unpopular with the predominant or governing group, being attached to the wrong political views, or being personally obnoxious to or in the way of the prosecutor himself."

Under our system of government, the primary check against prosecutorial abuse is a political one. The prosecutors who exercise this awesome discretion are selected and can be removed by a President, whom the people have trusted enough to elect. Moreover, when crimes are not investigated and prosecuted fairly, nonselectively, with a reasonable sense of proportion, the President pays the cost in political damage to his administration. If federal prosecutors "pick people that [they] thin[k] [they] should get, rather than cases that need to be prosecuted," if they amass many more resources against a particular prominent individual, or against a particular class of political protesters, or against members of a particular political party, then the gravity of the alleged offenses or the record of successful prosecutions seems to warrant, the unfairness will come home to roost in the Oval Office. I leave it to the reader to recall the examples of this in recent years. That result, of course, was precisely what the Founders had in mind when they provided that all executive powers would be exercised by a *single* Chief Executive. As Hamilton put it, "[t]he ingredients which constitute safety in the republican sense are a due dependence on the people, and a due responsibility." The President is directly dependent on the people, and since there is only *one* President, *he* is responsible. The people know whom to blame,

whereas "one of the weightiest objections to a plurality in the executive ... is that it tends to conceal faults and destroy responsibility."

That is the system of justice the rest of us are entitled to, but what of that select class consisting of present or former high-level Executive Branch officials? If an allegation is made against them of any violation of any federal criminal law (except Class B or C misdemeanors or infractions) the Attorney General must give it his attention. That in itself is not objectionable. But if, after a 90-day investigation without the benefit of normal investigatory tools, the Attorney General is unable to say that there are "no reasonable grounds to believe" that further investigation is warranted, a process is set in motion that is *not* in the full control of persons "dependent on the people," and whose flaws cannot be blamed on the President. An independent counsel is selected, and the scope of his or her authority prescribed, by a panel of judges. What if they are politically partisan, as judges have been known to be, and select a prosecutor antagonistic to the administration, or even to the particular individual who has been selected for this special treatment? There is no remedy for that, not even a political one. Judges, after all, have life tenure, and appointing a surefire enthusiastic prosecutor could hardly be considered an impeachable offense. So if there is anything wrong with the selection, there is effectively no one to blame. The independent counsel thus selected proceeds to assemble a staff. As I observed earlier, in the nature of things this has to be done by finding lawyers who are willing to lay aside their current careers for an indeterminate amount of time, to take on a job that has no prospect of permanence and little prospect for promotion. One thing is certain, however: it involves investigating and perhaps prosecuting a particular individual. Can one imagine a less equitable manner of fulfilling the executive responsibility to investigate and prosecute? What would be the reaction if, in an area not covered by this statute, the Justice Department posted a public notice inviting applicants to assist in an investigation and possible prosecution of a certain prominent person? Does this not invite what Justice Jackson described as "picking the man and then searching the law books, or putting investigators to work, to pin some offense on him"? To be sure, the investigation must relate to the area of criminal offense specified by the life-tenured judges. But that has often been (and nothing prevents it from being) very broad—and should the independent counsel or his or her staff come up with something beyond that scope, nothing prevents him or her from asking the judges to expand his or her authority or, if that does not work, referring it to the Attorney General, whereupon the whole process would recommence and, if there was "reasonable basis to believe" that further investigation was warranted, that new offense would be referred to the Special Division, which would in all likelihood assign it to the same independent counsel. It seems to me not conducive to fairness. But even if it were entirely evident that unfairness was in fact the result—the judges hostile to the administration, the independent counsel an old foe of the President, the staff refugees from the recently defeated administration—*there would be no one accountable to the public to whom the blame could be assigned.*

I do not mean to suggest that anything of this sort (other than the inevitable self-selection of the prosecutory staff)

occurred in the present case. I know and have the highest regard for the judges on the Special Division, and the independent counsel herself is a woman of accomplishment, impartiality, and integrity. But the fairness of a process must be adjudged on the basis of what it permits to happen, not what it produced in a particular case. It is true, of course, that a similar list of horribles could be attributed to an ordinary Justice Department prosecution —a vindictive prosecutor, an antagonistic staff, etc. But the difference is the difference that the Founders envisioned when they established a single Chief Executive accountable to the people: the blame can be assigned to someone who can be punished.

The above described possibilities of irresponsible conduct must, as I say, be considered in judging the constitutional acceptability of this process. But they will rarely occur, and in the average case the threat to fairness is quite different. As described in the brief filed on behalf of three ex-Attorneys General from each of the last three administrations:

> "The problem is less spectacular but much more worrisome. It is that the institutional environment of the Independent Counsel—specifically, her isolation from the Executive Branch and the internal checks and balances it supplies— is designed to heighten, not to check, all of the occupational hazards of the dedicated prosecutor; the danger of too narrow a focus, of the loss of perspective, of preoccupation with the pursuit of one alleged suspect to the exclusion of other interests."

It is, in other words, an additional advantage of the unitary Executive that it can achieve a more uniform application of the law. Perhaps that is not always

achieved, but the mechanism to achieve it is there. The mini-Executive that is the independent counsel, however, operating in an area where so little is law and so much is discretion, is intentionally cut off from the unifying influence of the Justice Department, and from the perspective that multiple responsibilities provide. What would normally be regarded as a technical violation (there are no rules defining such things), may in his or her small world assume the proportions of an indictable offense. What would normally be regarded as an investigation that has reached the level of pursuing such picayune matters that it should be concluded, may to him or her be an investigation that ought to go on for another year. How frightening it must be to have your own independent counsel and staff appointed, with nothing else to do but to investigate you until investigation is no longer worthwhile—with whether it is worthwhile not depending upon what such judgments usually hinge on, competing responsibilities. And to have that counsel and staff decide, with no basis for comparison, whether what you have done is bad enough, willful enough, and provable enough, to warrant an indictment. How admirable the constitutional system that provides the means to avoid such a distortion. And how unfortunate the judicial decision that has permitted it.

* * *

The notion that every violation of law should be prosecuted, including —indeed, *especially*—every violation by those in high places, is an attractive one, and it would be risky to argue in an election campaign that that is not an absolutely overriding value. *Fiat justitia, ruat caelum.* Let justice be done, though the heavens may fall. The reality is, how-

ever, that it is not an absolutely overriding value, and it was with the hope that we would be able to acknowledge and apply such realities that the Constitution spared us, by life tenure, the necessity of election campaigns. I cannot imagine that there are not many thoughtful men and women in Congress who realize that the benefits of this legislation are far outweighed by its harmful effect upon our system of government, and even upon the nature of justice received by those men and women who agree to serve in the Executive Branch. But it is difficult to vote not to enact, and even more difficult to vote to repeal, a statute called, appropriately enough, the Ethics in Government Act. If Congress is controlled by the party other than the one to which the President belongs, it has little incentive to repeal it; if it is controlled by the same party, it dare not. By its shortsighted action today, I fear the Court has permanently encumbered the Republic with an institution that will do it great harm.

Worse than what it has done, however, is the manner in which it has done it. A government of laws means a government of rules. Today's decision on the basic issue of fragmentation of executive power is ungoverned by rule, and hence ungoverned by law. It extends into the very heart of our most significant constitutional function the "totality of the circumstances" mode of analysis that this Court has in recent years become fond of. Taking all things into account, we conclude that the power taken away from the President here is not really *too* much. The next time executive power is assigned to someone other than the President we may conclude, taking all things into account, that it *is* too much. That opinion, like this one, will not be confined by any rule. We will describe, as we have today (though I hope more accurately) the effects of the provision in question, and will authoritatively announce: "The President's need to control the exercise of the [subject officer's] discretion *is* so central to the functioning of the Executive Branch as to require complete control." This is not analysis; it is ad hoc judgment. And it fails to explain why it is not true that—as the text of the Constitution seems to require, as the Founders seemed to expect, and as our past cases have uniformly assumed—all purely executive power must be under the control of the President.

POSTSCRIPT

Investigating the President: Do We Need an Independent Counsel?

If not an independent counsel, then who? Can any administration be trusted to conduct a vigorous and impartial inquiry into its own conduct, one that might result in political embarrassment or the uncovering of criminal acts? If there had been no special prosecutor, would the Watergate scandal have been uncovered? These are questions that critics must confront.

Given the broad subpoena power with which an independent counsel must be vested, how can overzealous inquiries that recklessly impugn or destroy the reputations of innocent individuals or pry into private lives be curbed? How can the confidentiality that the president and his aides must have be guaranteed? Can some constraints be placed on the length and cost of an investigation? These are questions that supporters of an independent counsel must consider.

Media coverage of Whitewater and other allegations against President Clinton has been so extensive that an interested reader will have to select carefully. Perhaps the most objective accounts can be found in the frequent news articles in the *Congressional Quarterly Weekly Report,* particularly its November 15, 1997, analysis of the way in which the appointment of a special counsel is triggered, the investigations that have been conducted, and proposals for reform or repeal. An excellent brief summary of the operation of the Ethics in Government Act can be found in Linda Greenhouse, "Ethics in Government: The Price of Good Intentions," *The New York Times* (February 1, 1998).

Katy J. Harriger, in *Independent Justice: The Federal Special Prosecutor in American Politics* (University Press of Kansas, 1992), examines political practices and constitutional issues from the antecedents of the independent counsel (in the investigation of the Teapot Dome scandal of the Harding administration) to Watergate. Historical background for the limits on presidential power within the American separation of powers can be found in Charles O. Jones, *The Presidency in a Separated System* (Brookings Institution, 1994). Who investigates the independent counsel when charges are made against his conduct? That question is raised by Jane Mayer, in "How Independent Is the Counsel?" *The New Yorker* (April 12, 1996).

The Watergate scandal has been the subject of many books and several motion pictures (most famously, *All The President's Men,* based on the journalistic coup by Bob Woodward and Carl Bernstein). There is much reflective material in Ken Gormley, *Archibald Cox: Conscience of a Nation* (Addison-Wesley, 1997). Approving of the independent counsel, Watergate prosecutor Cox believes that the law should set a higher standard than "reasonable grounds" to

warrant further investigation and that alleged wrongdoing prior to running for or occupying the presidency should be left to ordinary investigation.

As the final arbiters of the meaning of the Constitution, the Supreme Court can curb the power of the president. President Harry S. Truman's wartime seizure of steel mills in order to prevent a curtailment of necessary military supplies was struck down by the Supreme Court. This great conflict between the executive and judicial powers is recounted in Alan F. Westin, *The Anatomy of a Constitutional Law Case: Youngstown Sheet and Tube Company v. Sawyer: The Steel Seizure Decision* (Columbia University Press, 1990).

ISSUE 7

Should Judges Read Their Moral Views into the Constitution?

YES: Ronald Dworkin, from "The Moral Reading of the Constitution," *New York Review of Books* (March 21, 1996)

NO: Mary Ann Glendon, from "Partial Justice," *Commentary* (August 1994)

ISSUE SUMMARY

YES: Law professor Ronald Dworkin contends that judges must read the vaguer phrases of the Constitution with an eye toward what is best for the nation.

NO: Law professor Mary Ann Glendon warns of the perils of "romantic judging," which she argues usurps the role of legislatures and weakens the spirit of democracy.

"It is emphatically, the province and duty of the judicial department, to say what the law is." This assertion lay at the heart of Chief Justice John Marshall's opinion for the U.S. Supreme Court in the landmark case *Marbury v. Madison* (1803). Marshall was building a case for judicial review—the authority of federal courts to strike down congressional laws or presidential rulings that, in their view, violate the Constitution. Most lawmakers at that time accepted the supremacy of the Constitution, but, many asked, why should courts have the last say in interpreting the Constitution?

The answer, said Marshall, is that judges have no choice: they *cannot* blind their eyes to the Constitution when somebody before the court is accused of a federal crime. Suppose someone is condemned to death for treason on the basis of an unconstitutional statute, such as a law that said that the testimony of one witness is enough for conviction (the Constitution says that there must be two). Now suppose he appeals to the courts. Should the courts ignore his appeal and let him be hanged for violating an unconstitutional statute?

Marshall's argument for judicial review would be unanswerable if every case of unconstitutionality were as clear-cut as the one just mentioned. Where Marshall's argument becomes problematic is in cases where the language of the Constitution is not clear-cut but fuzzy. For example, what is an "establishment of religion," which is prohibited by the First Amendment? Does it mean an established church, such as they have in England, or is it broad enough to include nondenominational prayers in public schools? And what of the Fourteenth Amendment's guarantee of "equal protection of the laws"?

How broad should that protection be? Does it encompass not only blacks but women, homosexuals, disabled people, and unborn children? The Constitution itself does not say. Why, then, should a court's interpretation be preferred over the interpretation of Congress or the president?

Chief Justice Marshall implied that there are objective legal principles for interpreting the Constitution in such disputed cases, though he never spelled them out. Down through the years, other jurists and commentators have tried to devise guiding principles. Appeals court judge Learned Hand (1872–1961) thought that the Supreme Court should assume final authority to interpret the Constitution only when it was absolutely necessary to resolve competing claims of the other two branches of the federal government. In a somewhat similar mode, Justice Felix Frankfurter (1882–1965), who served on the Supreme Court from 1939 to 1962, preached a doctrine that he called "judicial self-restraint." Only if a federal law is clearly unconstitutional, Frankfurther believed, should it be struck down; in doubtful cases the Court should defer to the elected branches of government and presume that the law is constitutional.

During the Reagan administration in the 1980s, former appeals court judge Robert H. Bork became embroiled in controversy because of his doctrine of "original intent." Bork believes that the most objective way of interpreting some of the vaguer and fuzzier clauses in the Constitution is to go back and examine the intent of those who originally wrote those clauses. Bork's views offended many feminists and civil rights activists, and when President Ronald Reagan nominated him to the Supreme Court in 1987, they feared that he would roll back abortion rights and affirmative action. His nomination was therefore defeated in the Senate.

In the following selections, philosopher Ronald Dworkin rejects Bork's "originalism" as well as the "self-restraint" approach of Hand and Frankfurter. Dworkin's view is that judges, in interpreting some of the vaguer phrases in the Constitution, must ultimately decide "which conception does most credit to the nation." This broadly moralistic approach to constitutional interpretation worries Mary Ann Glendon, who occupies the Learned Hand professorship at Harvard Law School. Characterizing it as "romantic judging," she argues that it usurps the function of legislatures and weakens the spirit of democracy.

YES

Ronald Dworkin

THE MORAL READING OF
THE CONSTITUTION

It is patent that judges' own views about political morality influence their constitutional decisions, and though they might easily explain that influence by insisting that the Constitution demands a moral reading, they never do. Instead, against all evidence, they deny the influence and try to explain their decisions in other—embarrassingly unsatisfactory—ways. They say they are just giving effect to obscure historical "intentions," for example, or just expressing an overall but unexplained constitutional "structure" that is supposedly explicable in nonmoral terms.

This mismatch between role and reputation is easily explained. The moral reading is so thoroughly embedded in constitutional practice and is so much more attractive, on both legal and political grounds, than the only coherent alternatives, that it cannot readily be abandoned, particularly when important constitutional issues are in play. But the moral reading nevertheless seems intellectually and politically discreditable. It seems to erode the crucial distinction between law and morality by making law only a matter of which moral principles happen to appeal to the judges of a particular era. It seems grotesquely to constrict the moral sovereignty of the people themselves—to take out of their hands, and remit to a professional elite, exactly the great and defining issues of political morality that the people have the right and the responsibility to decide for themselves.

That is the source of the paradoxical contrast between mainstream constitutional practice in the United States, which relies heavily on the moral reading of the Constitution, and mainstream constitutional theory, which wholly rejects that reading. The confusion has had serious political costs. Conservative politicians try to convince the public that the great constitutional cases turn not on deep issues of political principle, which they do, but on the simpler question of whether judges should change the Constitution by fiat or leave it alone. For a time this view of the constitutional argument was apparently accepted even by some liberals. They called the Constitution a "living" document and said that it must be "brought up to date" to match new circumstances and sensibilities. They said they took an "active" approach to the

From Ronald Dworkin, "The Moral Reading of the Constitution," *New York Review of Books* (March 21, 1996). Copyright © 1996 by NYREV, Inc. Notes omitted.

Constitution, which seemed to suggest reform, and they accepted John Ely's characterization of their position as a "noninterpretive" one, which seemed to suggest inventing a new document rather than interpreting the old one. In fact, this account of the argument was never accurate. The theoretical debate was never about whether judges should interpret the Constitution or change it—almost no one really thought the latter—rather it was about how it should be interpreted. But conservative politicians exploited the simpler description, and they were not effectively answered.

The confusion engulfs the politicians as well. They promise to appoint and confirm judges who will respect the proper limits of their authority and leave the Constitution alone, but since this misrepresents the choices judges actually face, the politicians are often disappointed. When Dwight Eisenhower, who denounced what he called judicial activism, retired from office in 1961, he told a reporter that he had made only two big mistakes as President—and that they were both on the Supreme Court. He meant Chief Justice Earl Warren, who had been a Republican politician when Eisenhower appointed him to head the Supreme Court, but who then presided over one of the most "activist" periods in the Court's history, and Justice William Brennan, another politician who had been a state court judge when Eisenhower appointed him, and who became one of the most liberal and explicit practitioners of the moral reading of the Constitution in modern times.

*　*　*

Presidents Ronald Reagan and George Bush were both intense in their outrage at the Supreme Court's "usurpation" of the people's privileges. They said they were determined to appoint judges who would respect rather than defy the people's will. In particular, they (and the platform on which they ran for the presidency) denounced the Court's 1973 *Roe* v. *Wade* decision protecting abortion rights, and promised that their appointees would reverse it. But when the opportunity to do so came, three of the justices Reagan and Bush had appointed between them voted, surprisingly, not only to retain that decision in force, but to provide a legal basis for it that much more explicitly adopted and relied on a moral reading of the Constitution. The expectations of politicians who appoint judges are often defeated in that way, because the politicians fail to appreciate how thoroughly the moral reading, which they say they deplore, is actually embedded in constitutional practice. Its role remains hidden when a judge's own convictions support the legislation whose constitutionality is in doubt—when a justice thinks it morally permissible for the majority to criminalize abortion, for example. But the ubiquity of the moral reading becomes evident when some judge's convictions of principle—identified, tested, and perhaps altered by experience and argument—bend in an opposite direction, because then enforcing the Constitution must mean, for that judge, telling the majority that it cannot have what it wants....

THE MORAL READING

The clauses of the American Constitution that protect individuals and minorities from government are found mainly in the so-called Bill of Rights—the first ten amendments to the document—and the

further amendments added after the Civil War. (I shall sometimes use the phrase "Bill of Rights," inaccurately, to refer to all the provisions of the Constitution that establish individual rights, including the Fourteenth Amendment's protection of citizens' privileges and immunities and its guarantee of due process and equal protection of the laws.) Many of these clauses are drafted in exceedingly abstract moral language. The First Amendment refers to the "right" of free speech, for example, the Fifth Amendment to the process that is "due" to citizens, and the Fourteenth to protection that is "equal." According to the moral reading, these clauses must be understood in the way their language most naturally suggests: they refer to abstract moral principles and incorporate these by reference, as limits on government's power.

There is of course room for disagreement about the right way to restate these abstract moral principles, so as to make their force clearer to us, and to help us to apply them to more concrete political controversies. I favor a particular way of stating the constitutional principles at the most general possible level. I believe that the principles set out in the Bill of Rights, taken together, commit the United States to the following political and legal ideas: government must treat all those subject to its dominion as having equal moral and political status; it must attempt, in good faith, to treat them all with concern; and it must respect whatever individual freedoms are indispensable to those ends, including but not limited to the freedoms more specifically designated in the document, such as the freedoms of speech and religion. Other lawyers and scholars who also endorse the moral reading might well formulate the constitutional principles, even at a very general level,

differently and less expansively than I just have however, and though here I want to explain and defend the moral reading, not my own interpretations under it, I should say something about how the choice among competing formulations should be made.

Of course the moral reading is not appropriate to everything a constitution contains. The American Constitution includes a great many clauses that are neither particularly abstract nor drafted in the language of moral principle. Article II specifies, for example, that the President must be at least thirty-five years old, and the Third Amendment insists that government may not quarter soldiers in citizens' houses in peacetime. The latter may have been inspired by a moral principle: those who wrote and enacted it might have been anxious to give effect to some principle protecting citizens' rights to privacy, for example. But the Third Amendment is not itself a moral principle: its *content* is not a general principle of privacy. So the first challenge to my own interpretation of the abstract clauses might be put this way. What argument or evidence do I have that the equal protection clause of the Fourteenth Amendment (for example), which declares that no state may deny any person equal protection of the laws, has a moral principle as *its* content though the Third Amendment does not?

This is a question of interpretation or, if you prefer, translation. We must try to find language of our own that best captures, in terms we find clear, the content of what the "framers" intended it to say. (Constitutional scholars use the word "framers" to describe, somewhat ambiguously, the various people who drafted and enacted a constitutional provision.) History is crucial to that

project, because we must know something about the circumstances in which
a person spoke to have any good idea
of what he meant to say in speaking
as he did. We find nothing in history,
however, to cause us any doubt about
what the framers of the Third Amendment meant to say. Given the words they
used, we cannot sensibly interpret them
as laying down any moral principle at all,
even if we believe they were inspired by
one. They said what the words they used
would normally be used to say: not that
privacy must be protected, but that soldiers must not be quartered in houses in
peacetime.

* * *

The same process of reasoning—about
what the framers presumably intended
to say when they used the words they
did—yields an opposite conclusion about
the framers of the equal protection clause,
however. Most of them no doubt had
fairly clear expectations about what legal consequences the Fourteenth Amendment would have. They expected it to end
certain of the most egregious Jim Crow
practices of the Reconstruction period.
They plainly did not expect it to outlaw official racial segregation in school
—on the contrary, the Congress that
adopted the equal protection clause itself maintained segregation in the District
of Columbia school system. But they did
not *say* anything about Jim Crow laws
or school segregation or homosexuality
or gender equality, one way or the other.
They said that "equal protection of the
laws" is required, which plainly describes
a very general principle, not any concrete
application of it.

The framers meant, then, to enact
a general principle. But which general
principle? That further question must be

answered by constructing different elab-
orations of the phrase "equal protection
of the laws," each of which we can recognize as a principle of political morality
that might have won their respect, and
then by asking which of these it makes
most sense to attribute to them, given
everything else we know. The qualification that each of these possibilities must
be recognizable as a political *principle* is
absolutely crucial. We cannot capture a
statesman's efforts to lay down a general
constitutional principle by attributing to
him something neither he nor we could
recognize as a candidate for that role.
But the qualification will typically leave
many possibilities open. It was once debated, for example, whether the framers
intended to stipulate, in the equal protection clause, only the relatively weak
political principle that laws must be enforced in accordance with their terms, so
that legal benefits conferred on everyone,
including blacks, must not be denied, in
practice, to anyone.

History seems decisive that the framers
of the Fourteenth Amendment did not
mean to lay down only so weak a
principle as that one, however, which
would have left states free to discriminate
against blacks in any way they wished so
long as they did so openly. Congressmen
of the victorious nation, trying to capture
the achievements and lessons of a terrible war, would be very unlikely to settle
for anything so limited and insipid, and
we should not take them to have done
so unless the language leaves no other
interpretation plausible. In any case, constitutional interpretation must take into
account past legal and political practice
as well as what the framers themselves
intended to say, and it has now been settled by unchallengeable precedent that
the political principle incorporated in the

Fourteenth Amendment is not that very weak one, but something more robust. Once that is conceded, however, then the principle must be something *much* more robust, because the only alternative, as a translation of what the framers actually *said* in the equal protection clause, is that they declared a principle of quite breathtaking scope and power: the principle that government must treat everyone as of equal status and with equal concern.

* * *

Two important restraints sharply limit the latitude the moral reading gives to individual judges. First, under that reading constitutional interpretation must begin in what the framers said, and, just as our judgment about what friends and strangers say relies on specific information about them and the context in which they speak, so does our understanding of what the framers said. History is therefore plainly relevant. But only in a particular way. We turn to history to answer the question of what they intended to *say*, not the different question of what *other* intentions they had. We have no need to decide what they expected to happen, or hoped would happen, in consequence of their having said what they did, for example; their purpose, in that sense, is not part of our study. That is a crucial distinction. We are governed by what our lawmakers said—by the principles they laid down—not by any information we might have about how they themselves would have interpreted those principles or applied them in concrete cases.

Second, and equally important, constitutional interpretation is disciplined, under the moral reading, by the requirement of constitutional *integrity*. Judges may not read their own convictions into the Constitution. They may not read the abstract moral clauses as expressing any particular moral judgment, no matter how much that judgment appeals to them, unless they find it consistent in principle with the structural design of the Constitution as a whole, and also with the dominant lines of past constitutional interpretation by other judges. They must regard themselves as partners with other officials, past and future, who together elaborate a coherent constitutional morality, and they must take care to see that what they contribute fits with the rest. (I have elsewhere said that judges are like authors jointly creating a chain novel in which each writes a chapter that makes sense as part of the story as a whole.) Even a judge who believes that abstract justice requires economic equality cannot interpret the equal protection clause as making equality of wealth, or collective ownership of productive resources, a constitutional requirement, because that interpretation simply does not fit American history or practice, or the rest of the Constitution.

Nor could he plausibly think that the constitutional structure commits any other than basic, structural political rights to his care. He might think that a society truly committed to equal concern would award people with handicaps special resources, or would secure convenient access to recreational parks for everyone, or would provide heroic and experimental medical treatment, no matter how expensive or speculative, for anyone whose life might possibly be saved. But it would violate constitutional integrity for him to treat these mandates as part of constitutional law. Judges must defer to general, settled understandings about the character of the power the Constitution assigns them. The moral reading asks them to find the best conception of constitutional moral principles—the best understand-

ing of what equal moral status for men and women really requires, for example —that fits the broad story of America's historical record. It does not ask them to follow the whisperings of their own consciences or the traditions of their own class or sect if these cannot be seen as embedded in that record. Of course judges can abuse their power—they can pretend to observe the important restraint of integrity while really ignoring it. But generals and presidents and priests can abuse their powers, too. The moral reading is a strategy for lawyers and judges acting in good faith, which is all any interpretive strategy can be.

I emphasize these constraints of history and integrity, because they show how exaggerated is the common complaint that the moral reading gives judges absolute power to impose their own moral convictions on the rest of us. [English historian Thomas Babington] Macaulay was wrong when he said that the American Constitution is all sail and no anchor, and so are the other critics who say that the moral reading turns judges into philosopher-kings. Our constitution is law, and like all law it is anchored in history, practice, and integrity. Still, we must not exaggerate the drag of that anchor. Very different, even contrary, conceptions of a constitutional principle —of what treating men and women as equals really means, for example— will often fit language, precedent, and practice well enough to pass these tests, and thoughtful judges must then decide on their own which conception does most credit to the nation. So though the familiar complaint that the moral reading gives judges unlimited power is hyperbolic, it contains enough truth to alarm those who believe that such judicial power is inconsistent with a republican

form of government. The constitutional sail is a broad one, and many people do fear that it is too big for a democratic boat.

WHAT IS THE ALTERNATIVE?

Constitutional lawyers and scholars have therefore been anxious to find other strategies for constitutional interpretation, strategies that give judges less power. They have explored two different possibilities. The first, and most forthright, concedes that the moral reading is right—that the Bill of Rights can only be understood as a set of moral principles. But it denies that judges should have the final authority themselves to conduct the moral reading—that they should have the last word about, for example, whether women have a constitutional right to choose abortion or whether affirmative action treats all races with equal concern. It reserves that interpretive authority to the people. That is by no means a contradictory combination of views. The moral reading, as I said, is a theory about what the Constitution means, not a theory about whose view of what it means must be accepted by the rest of us.

This first alternative offers a way of understanding the arguments of a great American judge, Learned Hand. Hand thought that the courts should take final authority to interpret the Constitution only when this is absolutely necessary to the survival of government—only when the courts must be referees between the other departments of government because the alternative would be a chaos of competing claims to jurisdiction. No such necessity compels courts to test legislative acts against the Constitution's moral principles, and Hand therefore thought it wrong for judges to claim

that authority. Though his view was once an open possibility, history has long excluded it; practice has now settled that courts do have a responsibility to declare and act on their best understanding of what the Constitution forbids. If Hand's view had been accepted, the Supreme Court could not have decided, as it did in its famous *Brown* decision in 1954, that the equal protection clause outlaws racial segregation in public schools. In 1958 Hand said, with evident regret, that he had to regard the *Brown* decision as wrong, and he would have had to take the same view about later Supreme Court decisions that expanded racial equality, religious independence, and personal freedoms such as the freedom to buy and use contraceptives. These decisions are now almost universally thought not only sound but shining examples of our constitutional structure working at its best.

The first alternative strategy, as I said, accepts the moral reading. The second alternative, which is called the "originalist" or "original intention" strategy, does not. The moral reading insists that the Constitution means what the framers intended to say. Originalism insists that it means what they expected their language to *do*, which as I said is a very different matter. (Though some originalists, including one of the most conservative justices now on the Supreme Court, Antonin Scalia, are unclear about the distinction.) According to originalism, the great clauses of the Bill of Rights should be interpreted not as laying down the abstract moral principles they actually describe, but instead as referring, in a kind of code or disguise, to the framers' own assumptions and expectations about the correct application of those principles. So the equal protection clause is to be understood as com-

manding not equal status but what the framers themselves thought was equal status, in spite of the fact that, as I said, the framers clearly meant to lay down the former standard not the latter one.

The *Brown* decision I just mentioned crisply illustrates the distinction. The Court's decision was plainly required by the moral reading, because it is obvious now that official school segregation is not consistent with equal status and equal concern for all races. The originalist strategy, consistently applied, would have demanded the opposite conclusion, because, as I said, the authors of the equal protection clause did not believe that school segregation, which they practiced themselves, was a denial of equal status, and did not expect that it would one day be deemed to be so. The moral reading insists that they misunderstood the moral principle that they themselves enacted into law. The originalist strategy would translate that mistake into enduring constitutional law.

That strategy, like the first alternative, would condemn not only the *Brown* decision but many other Supreme Court decisions that are now widely regarded as paradigms of good constitutional interpretation. For that reason, almost no one now embraces the originalist strategy in anything like a pure form. Even Robert Bork, who remains one of its strongest defenders, qualified his support in the Senate hearings following his nomination to the Supreme Court—he conceded that the *Brown* decision was right, and said that even the Court's 1965 decision guaranteeing a right to use contraceptives, which we have no reason to think the authors of any pertinent constitutional clause either expected or would have approved, was right in its result. The originalist strategy is as indefensible in prin-

ciple as it is unpalatable in result, more-over. It is as illegitimate to substitute a concrete, detailed provision for the abstract language of the equal protection clause as it would be to substitute some abstract principle of privacy for the concrete terms of the Third Amendment, or to treat the clause imposing a minimum age for a President as enacting some general principle of disability for persons under that age.

* * *

So though many conservative politicians and judges have endorsed originalism, and some, like Hand, have been tempted to reconsider whether judges should have the last word about what the Constitution requires, there is in fact very little practical support for either of these strategies. Yet the moral reading is almost never explicitly endorsed, and is often explicitly condemned. If neither of the two alternatives I described is actually embraced by those who disparage the moral reading, what interpretive strategy do they have in mind? The surprising answer is: none. Constitutional scholars often say that we must avoid the mistakes of both the moral reading, which gives too much power to judges, and of originalism, which makes the contemporary Constitution too much the dead hand of the past. The right method, they say, is something in between which strikes the right balance between protecting essential individual rights and deferring to popular will. But they do not indicate what the right balance is, or even what kind of scale we should use to find it. They say that constitutional interpretation must take both history and the general structure of the Constitution into account as well as moral or political philosophy. But they do not say why history or structure, both of which, as I said, figure in the moral reading, should figure in some further or different way, or what that different way is, or what general goal or standard of constitutional interpretation should guide us in seeking a different interpretive strategy.

So though the call for an intermediate constitutional strategy is often heard, it has not been answered, except in unhelpful metaphors about balance and structure. That is extraordinary, particularly given the enormous and growing literature in American constitutional theory. If it is so hard to produce an alternative to the moral reading, why struggle to do so? One distinguished constitutional lawyer who insists that there must be an interpretive strategy somewhere between originalism and the moral reading recently announced, at a conference, that although he had not discovered it, he would spend the rest of his life looking. Why?

I have already answered the question. Lawyers assume that the disabilities that a constitution imposes on majoritarian political processes are antidemocratic, at least if these disabilities are enforced by judges, and the moral reading seems to exacerbate the insult. If there is no genuine alternative to the moral reading in practice, however, and if efforts to find even a theoretical statement of an acceptable alternative have failed, we would do well to look again at that assumption.

NO

Mary Ann Glendon

PARTIAL JUSTICE

As late as the early 1960's, Justice William O. Douglas was widely regarded as a disgrace to the bench even by many lawyers who shared his social and economic views. Douglas's contempt for legal craftsmanship was seen as sloppiness; his visionary opinions were taken as evidence that he was angling for the presidency; and his solicitude for those he considered underdogs was perceived as favoritism.

By the end of the 1960's, however, a new and very romantic ideal of judging had begun to take shape. In eulogies, tributes, law-review articles, and legal journalism, judges began to be praised for qualities that would once have been considered problematic: compassion rather than impartiality, boldness rather than restraint, creativity rather than craftsmanship, and specific results regardless of the effect on the legal order as a whole. In the 1990's, Douglas would surely have basked in the "Greenhouse Effect"—a term (named after the *New York Times*'s Linda Greenhouse) for the warm reciprocity between activist journalists and judges who meet their approval.

This great change was set into motion by the appointment of Earl Warren as Chief Justice in 1953. President Eisenhower's choice of Warren was an unusual move, for the new Chief Justice had spent almost all his professional life in electoral politics. After serving as California's attorney general, he became a power in the state Republican party and then a popular governor. He was Thomas E. Dewey's running mate in 1948, and a serious contender for the Republican presidential nomination himself in 1952.

Nothing in Warren's background had prepared him for the fine-gauge work of opinion writing. He was impatient with the need to ground a desired outcome in constitutional text or tradition. As described by an admirer, Warren was a man who brushed off legal and historical impediments to the results he felt were right; he was not a "look-it-up-in-the-library" type.

What he was, above all, was a statesman, and although scholars may argue about its foundations in constitutional text and tradition, the Warren Court's decision in *Brown* v. *Board of Education* was indeed a great act of statesmanship. Those academics who downplay the importance of *Brown* in the struggle for racial justice have underrated its effects on attitudes about race relations—

effects that in turn helped to bring about important political changes like the Civil Rights Act of 1964 and voting-rights legislation. The Warren Court laid its prestige on the line in a bid not only to dismantle official segregation, but to delegitimate racially discriminatory attitudes. That wager was successful. Though racial prejudice has not been eradicated, it has no respectability at all in contemporary American society.

The effects of *Brown* on the legal profession and on the legal order as a whole were another matter. And here it was not Warren but William Brennan, appointed to the Supreme Court by Eisenhower in 1956, who came to incarnate those less salutary effects most fully.

* * *

Brennan was of humble origins. The son of Irish immigrants, he made his way to Harvard Law School—encouraged by his trade-unionist father who told him that a lawyer could do a lot for working people. Brennan did go into labor law, but enlisted on the other side of the cause that had meant so much to his father. After some years as a successful corporate practitioner in New Jersey, he became a trial judge and rose in time to the New Jersey Supreme Court. On the U.S. Supreme Court, he became a towering hero to those who shared his view that the Court had not only the power but the duty to promote social and political change.

Described by his biographer, Kim Eisler, as neither the most brilliant nor the best writer on the Court, Brennan during his long tenure may nevertheless have had the most influence on the general direction of its decisions. Few lawyers would disagree with the *New Yorker's*

evaluation, on Brennan's retirement in 1990, that he had come "to personify the expansion of the role of the judiciary in American life."

Even toward the end of his career, as the composition and mood of the Court changed, Brennan was often able to beat the odds and further his vision. As portrayed by Bob Woodward and Scott Armstrong in *The Brethren,* Brennan "cajoled in conference, walked the halls constantly and worked the phones, polling and plotting strategy with his allies." In later years, when his colleagues declined to follow him on such excursions as judicially banning capital punishment or abolishing the custom of prayer at the opening of legislative sessions, Brennan went out on the hustings, calling on state courts to take up the cudgels.

In speeches and writings, Brennan encouraged state judges to exercise their powers of constitutional review in new and creative ways. State courts, he pointed out, could interpret their own constitutions so as to provide even more rights than are afforded under the federal Constitution. Like the fox in Aesop's fable, the wily Brennan cajoled whole flocks of jurists into dropping their reserve. "State courts cannot rest," he wrote, "when they have afforded their citizens the full protections of the federal Constitution. State constitutions, too, are a font of individual liberties, their protections often extending beyond those afforded by the Supreme Court's interpretation of federal law."

Unlike many adventurous judges, Brennan had well-developed views of judging and did not mind discussing them. Here he is in a 1988 essay:

> The Constitution is fundamentally a public text—the monumental charter of

a government and a people—and a Justice of the Supreme Court must apply it to resolve public controversies. For, from our beginnings, a most important consequence of the constitutionally created separation of powers has been the American habit, extraordinary to other democracies, of casting social, economic, philosophical, and political questions in the form of lawsuits, in an attempt to secure ultimate resolution by the Supreme Court.... Not infrequently, these are the issues on which contemporary society is most deeply divided. They arouse our deepest emotions. The main burden of my 29 years on the Supreme Court has thus been to wrestle with the Constitution in this heightened public context, to draw meaning from the text in order to resolve public controversies.

* * *

That passage can instructively be compared with views often expressed in the past by Justices Oliver Wendell Holmes and Louis D. Brandeis. Holmes insisted that legislatures, no less than courts, were the ultimate guardians of the liberties and welfare of the people. "About 75 years ago," he said as a very old man, "I learned that I was not God. And so, when the people want to do something I can't find anything in the Constitution expressly forbidding them to do, I say, whether I like it or not, 'Goddammit, let 'em do it.'"

Brandeis for his part emphasized that, where vexing social problems were concerned, it would often be more advantageous to leave state and local governments free to experiment than to impose uniform and untested federal mandates upon the entire country. The states, he said, were like "laboratories" where innovative approaches to novel problems could be tested and refined or rejected.

Although one of the opinions of which Brennan was proudest was on legislative reapportionment, he maintained an uncharacteristic silence on the role of the elected branches in resolving the issues on which "society is most deeply divided." The reason must be that the way he saw his own life's work, as indicated in the above passage, put him in direct competition with the popular branches. Quoting Justice Robert Jackson, he made no bones about his position that, right or wrong, the Court was to have the last word: "The Justices are certainly aware that we are not final because we are infallible; we know that we are infallible because we are final."

Brennan's approach to judging could not be more remote in spirit from Holmes's structural restraint. Nor did Brennan have much use for the prudent avoidance of the appearance of judicial imperialism that was characteristic of the first great shaper of the Court, John Marshall. Brennan did not hesitate to claim, regarding the Court's powers: "The course of vital social, economic, and political currents may be directed."

Energized and prodded to no small degree by Brennan, majorities on the Warren and Burger Courts actively pursued a high-minded vision of empowering those individuals and groups they perceived as disadvantaged. When deference to the elected branches served those ends, as in many affirmative-action cases, Brennan deferred as humbly as any classical judge. When the decisions of councils or legislatures got in his way, he invoked expansive interpretations of constitutional language to brush them aside.

While Brennan was not one to let text or tradition stand in the way of a desired result, he knew how to turn his

corners squarely. But he did not share the devotion to judicial craftsmanship that characterized the work of colleagues like John Marshall Harlan or Byron White. Nor did he show much concern about the probable side-effects of a desired result in a particular case on the separation of powers, federal-state relations, or the long-term health of political processes and institutions. With respect to such matters, he was impatient with what he considered to be abstractions and technicalities.

When it came to compassion, Brennan had plenty for those he made (or wished to make) winners, but he showed little sensitivity toward those he ruled against. His heart went out to Native Americans when a Court majority permitted the federal government to build a road through sacred Indian places on public land. But in striking down a longstanding and successful New York City program providing remedial math and reading teachers to poor, special-needs children in religious schools, Brennan was pitiless. It took a dissent by Justice Sandra Day O'Connor to point out that the majority ruling, written by Brennan, had sacrificed the needs and prospects of 20,000 children from the poorest families in New York, and thousands more disadvantaged children across the country, for the sake of a maximalist version of the principle of separation of church and state.

* * *

The new model of bold, assertive judging has also had its exemplars in the lower courts. One federal appellate judge famed for his crusading decisions was the late J. Skelley Wright. Looking back on his role in expanding landlords' liability for the condition of leased premises, he wrote in 1982:

I didn't like what I saw, and I did what I could to ameliorate, if not eliminate, the injustice involved in the way many of the poor were required to live in the nation's capital. I offer no apology for not following more closely the legal precedents which had cooperated in creating the conditions that I found unjust.

The romantic ideal also fired the imaginations of judges in the capillaries of the legal system, the sites of the everyday administration of justice described in *The Federalist* as "the great cement of society." A longtime District of Columbia Superior Court judge, Sylvia Bacon, told the American Society for Public Administration that "There is a sense among judges that there are wrongs to be righted and that it is their responsibility to do it." As for the role of the Constitution and the law in guiding the judge's sense of right and wrong, Judge Bacon brusquely remarked: "Legal reasons are often just a cover for a ruling in equity (basic fairness)."

By "fairness," Judge Bacon apparently did not mean anything so prosaic as keeping an open mind to the arguments, and applying the relevant law without regard to the identity of the litigants and without regard to a particular outcome. Her notion was more visceral: "Plain and simple sense of outrage by the judge." Such views were no impediment to Judge Bacon's election to a seat on the American Bar Association's board of governors in the 1980's.

Yet they would have been anathema to the Founders, for whom impartiality was the *sine qua non* of judicial justice. Massachusetts, adopting John Adams's

words, built the concept into its Bill of Rights:

> It is essential to the preservation of the rights of every individual, his life, liberty, property, and character, that there be an impartial interpretation of the laws, and administration of justice. It is the right of every citizen to be tried by judges as free, impartial, and independent as the lot of humanity will admit.

From the early years of the Republic to the present day, every American judge has taken a vow to carry out his duties without fear or favor:

> I do solemnly swear that I will administer justice without respect to persons, do equal right to the poor and to the rich, and that I will impartially discharge and perform all the duties incumbent upon me, according to the best of my abilities and understanding agreeably to the Constitution and laws of the United States, so help me God.

Some critics of the world view implicit in this oath say that judging "without respect to persons" can lead to inhumane results by ignoring important differences —between men and women, rich and poor, black and white, strong and weak. If the critics had their way, the oath would be revised to read something like this:

> I affirm that I will administer justice with careful attention to the individual characteristics of the parties, that I will show compassion to those I deem disadvantaged, and that I will discharge my duties according to my personal understanding of the Constitution, the laws of the United States, and such higher laws as may be revealed to me.

Besides, the critics observe, impartiality is often just a mask covering various sorts of bias. They point to historical research that has found more than a little clay on the feet of classical idols. It may well have been Holmes's obnoxious eugenic views, for example, rather than his vaunted restraint, that prompted him to uphold a state statute providing for the forced sterilization of mental patients— with the cruel comment that "three generations of imbeciles are enough."

But are judicial compassion and responsiveness viable substitutes for the elusive ideal of impartiality? Few would dispute that judges should be able to empathize with the people who come before them. But in the early years of this century, adventurous judges were extremely tender-hearted toward big business, while showing little compassion for women and children working long hours in factories.

* * *

Let us acknowledge that until someone figures out how to make judges from other than human material, neither classical nor romantic feet will be a pretty sight. The real question, then, is which judicial attributes, systematically cultivated, offer the most protection against arbitrariness and bias.

Whatever one may conclude about the right mix of qualities for the special circumstances of the Supreme Court, it is hard to imagine that the routine administration of justice can benefit from an increase of compassion at the expense of impartiality. A close-knit, relatively homogeneous community can perhaps get along with a system where village elders reach decisions on the basis of their personal sense of fairness and their informed concern for the parties and the community. But that pastoral model cannot serve for an ethnically and ideologically diverse nation where litigants are strangers to the judge

and often to each other. Under such conditions, the liberties and fortunes of citizens cannot be left to the mercy of each judge's personal sense of what procedures are fair, what outcome is just, who needs protection, and who deserves compassion.

In constitutional cases, romantic judging also exacts a toll on the democratic elements in our form of government. When Warren and Burger Court majorities converted the Constitution's safety valves (the Bill of Rights, due process, equal protection) into engines with judges at the controls, they wreaked havoc with grass-roots politics. The dismal failures of many local authorities in dealing with racial issues became pretexts for depriving citizens everywhere of the power to experiment with new approaches to a wide range of problems that often take different forms in different parts of the country. Constitutional provisions designed to protect individuals and minorities against majoritarian excesses were increasingly used to block the normal processes through which citizens build coalitions, develop consensus, hammer out compromises, try out new ideas, learn from mistakes, and try again.

Elected officials have offered little resistance to judicial inroads on their powers. On hot issues, they often are only too happy to be taken off the hook by the courts. But each time a court sets aside an action of the political branches through free-wheeling interpretation, self-government suffers a setback. Political skills atrophy. People cease to take citizenship seriously. Citizens with diverse points of view lose the habit of cooperating to set conditions under which all can flourish. Adversarial legalism supplants the sober legalistic spirit that, in the 19th century, Alexis de Tocqueville

admired in the American people. For, as Abraham Lincoln warned,

> if the policy of the government, upon vital questions, affecting the whole people, is to be irrevocably fixed by decisions of the Supreme Court, ... the people will have ceased to be their own rulers, having, to that extent, practically resigned their government into the hands of that eminent tribunal.

* * *

In retrospect, one can see that the rise of bold judging proceeded for the most part with good intentions. Earlier in the century, state-court judges often had to take the initiative to keep judge-made law abreast of social and economic changes. In the wake of the New Deal, federal judges had to improvise techniques for dealing with regulatory law. Then in *Brown*—and also in the one-man, one-vote cases—the Supreme Court had to exercise statesmanship in addressing legal aspects of the country's most pressing social problems.

The achievements of gifted judges in meeting those challenges made it difficult for some of them—as well as for their less capable colleagues—to resist the impulse to keep on doing justice by their own lights. That those lights were not always powered by authoritative sources was easy to disguise, even from themselves. It was a case of successes leading to temptations, of a good thing taken to extremes.

In finding our way back from these extremes, the beginning of wisdom is to recognize that, whatever the pros and cons of adventurous judging by the Supreme Court on momentous occasions, romantic ideals are a poor guide to how judges throughout the system should comport themselves as a general matter.

The unique political role of the nation's highest court may require its members at times to show the sorts of excellence that are traditionally associated with executives or legislators—energy, leadership, boldness. But, day in and day out, those qualities are no substitute for the ordinary heroism of sticking to one's last, of demonstrating impartiality, interpretive skill, and responsibility toward authoritative sources in the regular administration of justice.

As things now stand in the topsy-turvy world of legal journalism, however, a judge will win no plaudits for such heroism, and may even earn contempt for not being interesting enough. When Byron White stepped down from the Supreme Court in 1993, the *New Republic*'s cover story called him "a perfect cipher." Admitting that White was "a first-rate legal technician," a writer for that magazine sneered at him for being "uninterested in articulating a constitutional vision." To this writer, it was evidence of White's "mediocrity" that he was hard to classify as a liberal or a conservative.

What made White hard to classify, of course, were the very qualities that made him an able and conscientious judge— his independence and his faithfulness to a modest conception of the judicial role. His "vision," implicit in nearly every one of his opinions, was not that difficult to discern. As summed up by a former clerk, it was one

> in which the democratic process predominates over the judicial; [and] the role of the Court or any individual Justice is not to promote particular ideologies, but to decide cases in a pragmatic

way that permits the political branches to shoulder primary responsibility for governing our society.... The purpose of an opinion ... is quite simply to decide the case in an intellectually and analytically sound manner.

Though White's competence, independence, and integrity did not make for lively copy, he was a model of modern neoclassical judging. As for the future, it is heartening that White's replacement, Ruth Bader Ginsburg, took the occasion of a speech shortly after her appointment to embrace the model of the "good judge" as represented by Learned Hand. Quoting Hand's biographer, Justice Ginsburg said:

> The good judge is "open-minded and detached ... heedful of limitations stemming from the judge's own competence and, above all, from the presuppositions of our constitutional scheme; [the good] judge ... recognizes that a felt need to act only interstitially does not mean relegation of judges to a trivial or mechanical role, but rather affords the most responsible room for creative, important judicial contributions."

As Justice Ginsburg's former colleague Robert Bork has observed, the key check on judicial authoritarianism will always be the judge's own understanding of the scope and limits of judicial power— and the insistence of a vigilant citizenry on having judges who will resist the temptation to remake the constitutional design for government and who will wholeheartedly comply with the judicial oath's promise to do equal justice without respect to persons.

POSTSCRIPT

Should Judges Read Their Moral Views into the Constitution?

At some point, every critic of the moralistic judicial activism advocated by Dworkin must take a stand on the case *Brown v. Board of Education* (1954), which struck down state-imposed racial discrimination. The *Brown* Court did so by taking an extremely broad interpretation of the Fourteenth Amendment's "equal protection" clause, an interpretation that (as Dworkin concedes) far exceeded the apparent intentions of the Framers. Yet who today would say that the *Brown* decision was wrong? Glendon herself admits that it greatly advanced the cause of racial justice. Her concern is that it may have tempted jurists to go even further, continually stretching the Constitution to make it fit their own moral views.

Glendon argues some of her points at greater length in *A Nation Under Lawyers: How the Crisis in the Legal Profession Is Transforming American Society* (Farrar, Straus, & Giroux, 1994), as does Dworkin in *Freedom's Law: The Moral Reading of the American Constitution* (Harvard University Press, 1996). Three recent books provide accounts of factional and personal fights inside the Supreme Court: Phillip J. Cooper's *Battles on the Bench: Conflict Inside the Supreme Court* (University of Kansas Press, 1995) illuminates battles behind the scenes in the Court since John Marshall's time; James F. Simon's *The Center Holds: The Power Struggle Inside the Rehnquist Court* (Simon & Schuster, 1995) celebrates the defeat of "conservatives" on the Rehnquist Court; and Bernard Schwartz, in *Decision: How the Supreme Court Decides Cases* (Oxford University Press, 1996), relies on cases and anecdotes to reveal what goes on behind the scenes when the Supreme Court justices deliberate.

Glendon quotes with approval this famous quip of Justice Oliver Wendell Holmes: "About 75 years ago I learned that I was not God." Yet, for better or worse, Supreme Court justices have to act as if they *were* mortal gods. They have come to be designated the final interpreters of the Constitution's meaning. Even if the Court decides to leave a decision to one of the other branches or levels of government, that itself is a decision, one with possibly momentous consequences. The justices, then, cannot escape their responsibility by renouncing it.

On the Internet . . .

American Studies Web
This eclectic site provides links to a wealth of Internet resources for research in American studies, including agriculture and rural development, government, and race and ethnicity.
http://www.georgetown.edu/crossroads/asw/

The Written Word
This is an online journal of economic, political, and social commentary, primarily from a center or left-of-center viewpoint. The site provides links to governmental and political Web resources.
http://www.mdle.com/WrittenWord/

Policy Digest Archives
Through this site of the National Center for Policy Analysis, access discussions on an array of topics that are of major interest in the study of American government, from regulatory policy and privatization to economy and income.
http://www.public-policy.org/~ncpa/pd/pdindex.html

The Henry L. Stimson Center
The Henry L. Stimson Center, a nonprofit and (self-described) nonpartisan organization, focuses on issues where policy, technology, and politics intersect. Use this site to find assessments of U.S. foreign and domestic policy and other topics. *http://www.stimson.org/*

RAND
RAND is a nonprofit institution that works to improve public policy through research and analysis. Links offered on this home page provide for keyword searches of certain topics and descriptions of RAND activities and major research areas. *http://www.rand.org/*

PART 3

Social Change and Public Policy

Few topics are more emotional and divisive than those that involve social morality. Whatever consensus once existed on such issues as capital punishment, abortion, and equality of opportunity, that consensus has been shattered in recent years as Americans have lined up very clearly on opposing sides—and what is more important, they have taken those competing views into Congress, state legislatures, and the courts.

The issues in this section generate intense emotions because they ask us to clarify our values on a number of very personal concerns.

■ Will Mandatory Sentencing Reduce Crime?

■ Is Capital Punishment Justified?

■ Do We Need Tougher Gun Control Laws?

■ Is Affirmative Action Reverse Discrimination?

■ Should Hate Speech Be Punished?

■ Is Welfare Reform Succeeding?

■ Is Socioeconomic Inequality Increasing in America?

■ Should Abortion Be Restricted?

■ Should Gay Marriage Be Legalized?

ISSUE 8

Will Mandatory Sentencing Reduce Crime?

YES: James Wootton, from "Truth in Sentencing: Why States Should Make Violent Criminals Do Their Time," *State Backgrounder* (December 30, 1993)

NO: Lois G. Forer, from *A Rage to Punish: The Unintended Consequences of Mandatory Sentencing* (W. W. Norton, 1994)

ISSUE SUMMARY

YES: James Wootton, president of Safe Streets Alliance in Washington, D.C., argues that mandatory sentencing effectively keeps hardened criminals off the streets and sends a signal to would-be felons that they will pay heavily if they commit a crime.

NO: Judge Lois G. Forer contends that mandatory sentencing not only fails to deter crime, which is more a result of impulse than of calculation, but it disrupts families, increases welfare costs, and hurts the poor and minorities.

Few issues are of deeper concern to Americans than crime, and with good reason. America has higher rates of violent crime—homicide, rape, robbery, and assault—than other industrial democracies. The good news at the century's end is that violent crime rates have reversed their climb; the bad news is that violent crime is increasing among children and young adults. Particularly in cities, people increasingly live behind double- and triple-locked doors, afraid to walk the streets of their own neighborhoods.

The perennial question is what to do about this plague of crime. A generation ago, the most popular view among social scientists was that crime was the result of poverty, ignorance, lack of opportunity, and racial discrimination. In a sense, criminals are themselves victims—victims of a pathological social environment. If that diseased environment can be properly treated through social programs, the experts believed, then we can eliminate the underlying causes of crime, and we no longer need to be obsessed with punishing it. More recently, however, some criminologists, along with most of the public at large, have taken a more hard-nosed view of crime and criminals. As far back as 1975, criminologist James Q. Wilson concluded his book *Thinking About Crime* on this note:

> Wicked people exist. Nothing avails except to set them apart from innocent people. And many people, neither wicked nor innocent, but watchful, dissembling,

and calculating of their opportunities ponder our reaction to wickedness as a cue to what they might profitably do.

If criminals and would-be criminals are not so much victims as they are "calculating" individuals weighing costs against benefits, it follows that society ought to make the costs prohibitive and certain. A new era of "toughness" on crime thus began in the late 1970s. Several states enacted "determinate" sentencing laws, which limited the discretion of judges in handing down penalties. Touted as a kind of "truth in sentencing," the offender was now required to serve the entire sentence. This was followed by mandatory sentencing, the requirement of minimum prison terms for certain offenses that could not be reduced by parole or good behavior. Often this took the form of "sentencing guidelines." As set forth in Minnesota and some other states, a "grid" was developed specifying the length of prison stay for particular crimes committed under particular conditions. Many states also passed mandatory sentences for drug offenders.

In 1984 the federal government weighed in with its own versions of these laws. The Comprehensive Crime Control Act of 1984 prescribes stiff mandatory sentences for drug possession, and the Sentencing Reform Act, passed in the same year, took an approach similar to Minnesota's by drawing up detailed guidelines for sentencing. The federal Anti-Drug Abuse Acts of 1986 and 1988 and the 1990 federal crime bill added more layers of mandatory sentencing. Most recently, the much-debated crime bill passed by Congress in the summer of 1994 includes a "three strikes and you're out" provision requiring life imprisonment for those convicted of three violent crimes.

Under California's "three strikes" law, criminals convicted of violent crimes have been released prematurely to make room for criminals convicted three times for nonviolent crimes. Also, criminals increasingly demand expensive, time-consuming jury trials because they are reluctant to accept a plea bargain that would lead to a "three strikes" conviction. In Los Angeles County, this has led to defendants spending an average of 177 days in jail awaiting trial, which has contributed to overcrowding, early release, and higher security costs.

By the end of 1995 getting tough on criminals resulted in 411 out of every 100,000—1 of every 250—Americans being in prison. Some critics argue that we have used the wrong approach, and they urge us to further limit firearms, expand drug treatment facilities (some recommend legalizing drugs), require nonviolent criminals to perform community service, create innovative sentencing, and employ more community police and probation officers to correct the situation.

In the following selections, James Wootton maintains that mandatory sentencing not only keeps criminals off the streets but it also signals would-be criminals that the crime is not worth the price they will pay for it. Lois G. Forer argues that mandatory sentencing is neither just nor efficient and that it has undesirable and costly social consequences.

YES

TRUTH IN SENTENCING: WHY STATES SHOULD MAKE VIOLENT CRIMINALS DO THEIR TIME

Not surprisingly, Americans are increasingly alarmed at news stories of violent crimes committed by individuals who had received long sentences for other crimes and yet were released after serving only a small fraction of their time. This alarm is legitimate, because a high proportion of such early-release prisoners commit serious crimes after being released. If crime is to be reduced in America, this trend needs to be reversed. Experience shows clearly that the first step in fighting crime is to keep violent criminals off the street. Keeping violent criminals incarcerated for at least 85 percent of their sentences would be the quickest, surest route to safer streets, schools, and homes.[1]

Government statistics on release practices in 36 states and the District of Columbia in 1988 show that although violent offenders received an average sentence of seven years and eleven months imprisonment, they actually served an average of only two years and eleven months in prison—or only 37 percent of their imposed sentences.[2] The statistics also show that, typically, 51 percent of violent criminals were discharged from prison in two years or less, and 76 percent were back on the streets in four years or less.

Consider the median sentence and time served in prison for those released for the first time in 1988:[3]

Murder: Median sentence = 15 years/Median time served = 5.5 years
Rape: Median sentence = 8 years/Median time served = 3 years
Robbery: Median sentence = 6 years/Median time served = 2.25 years
Assault: Median sentence = 4 years/Median time served = 1.25 years

When these prisoners are released early, a high percentage commit more violent crimes. A three-year follow up of 108,850 state prisoners released in 1983 from institutions in eleven states found that within three years 60 percent of violent offenders were rearrested for a felony or serious misdemeanor, 42 percent were reconvicted, and 37 percent were reincarcerated. Of the

From James Wootton, "Truth in Sentencing: Why States Should Make Violent Criminals Do Their Time," *State Backgrounder* (December 30, 1993). Copyright © 1993 by The Heritage Foundation. Reprinted by permission.

violent offenders, 35 percent were rearrested for a new violent crime. Among nonviolent prisoners released, 19 percent were rearrested within three years for a new violent crime.

As a result of these lenient early-release practices and the high percentage of crimes committed by criminals released early, Americans are suffering a fearful epidemic of violent crime. Studies indicate that over 25 percent of all males admitted to prison were being reincarcerated after a new trial for a new offense before the prison term for the first offense had expired. Since 1960, the compounding effect of these crimes by prisoners or early-release prisoners has driven the violent crime rate up by over 500 percent. Now eight out of ten Americans are likely to be victims of violent crime at least once in their lives,[4] at a total cost of $140 billion.[5]

Not surprisingly, the fear of violent crime is intensifying. Polls indicate a growing loss of public confidence in their personal safety and the safety of their streets and neighborhoods. Some 90 percent of Americans think the crime problem is growing, and 43 percent say there is more crime in their neighborhood than there was a year ago.[6] The reason: despite rising arrest rates and prison overcrowding, 3.2 million convicted felons are out on parole or probation rather than in prison. Studies show that within three years, 62 percent of all prisoners released from prison are rearrested,[7] and 43 percent of felons on probation are rearrested for a felony.[8]

HIGH RECIDIVISM: THE FAILURE OF PAROLE

Releasing violent criminals from prison before they have completed their sentences is justified by proponents for one of three reasons: first, prisons are overcrowded and it is too costly to build more prisons; second, "good time" credits, which have the effect of reducing sentences, are and should be given to well-behaved prisoners; and third, prisoners sometimes can be rehabilitated, and so should be paroled.

The problem is that the evidence seriously questions the second and third rationales, and shows the first to be very short-sighted.

Recidivism among violent criminals is high. Consider a three-year follow-up of 108,850 state prisoners released in 1983 from institutions in eleven states, conducted by the Bureau of Justice Statistics.[9] The study, the conclusions of which are consistent with those of other such studies, found that within three years some 60 percent of violent offenders were rearrested for a felony or serious misdemeanor; 42 percent of all violent offenders released were reincarcerated. Of all the violent offenders released, 36 percent were rearrested for a violent crime. Among nonviolent prisoners released, 19 percent were rearrested within three years for a violent crime.

The prisoners in the study accounted for over 1.6 million arrest charges for the time before they had entered prison and for the three years afterwards. These included nearly 215,000 arrests for violent crimes before going to prison and 50,000 violent crimes within three years after release. Altogether they were arrested for:

- 14,467 homicides
- 7,073 kidnappings
- 23,174 rapes or sexual assaults
- 101,226 robberies
- 107,130 assaults

The U.S. Parole Board uses a sophisticated Salient Factor Score (SFS) to guide it in deciding who will be paroled. Unfortunately for law-abiding Americans, the Parole Board turns out to be over-optimistic. Of those classified by the Parole Board staff as "good risks" for parole, the Parole Board assumes that 18 percent will be rearrested and again sentenced to prison for over one year within five years of release. In addition, the Parole Board expects that 29 percent of "fair risks" who are paroled will be resentenced to over a year in prison within five years of release.[10]

Considering the government's—and the American people's—anxiety about risk, this parole policy is remarkable. Where else would such a high failure rate be tolerated, when it results in the death, rape, or injury of ordinary Americans? The Federal Aviation Administration certainly does not allow airplanes to fly with critical parts that fail 29 percent of the time. And the Food and Drug Administration does not allow drugs on the market that have dangerous side effects 18 percent of the time.

Twenty years ago, James Q. Wilson, then a professor of government at Harvard University, asked a basic question about rehabilitation:

If rehabilitation is the object, and if there is little or no evidence that available correctional systems will produce much rehabilitation, why should any offender be sent to any institution? But to turn them free on the grounds that society does not know how to make them better is to fail to protect society from those crimes they may commit again and to violate society's moral concern for criminality and thus to undermine society's conception of what constitutes proper conduct. [Because the correctional system had not re-

duced recidivism], we would view the correctional system as having a very different function—namely, to isolate and to punish. It is a measure of our confusion that such a statement will strike many enlightened readers today as cruel, even barbaric. It is not. It is merely a recognition that society at a minimum must be able to protect itself from dangerous offenders and to impose some costs (other than the stigma and inconvenience of an arrest and court appearance) on criminal acts; it is also frank admission that society really does not know how to do much else.[11]

Until there are dramatic improvements in the techniques of rehabilitation and identifying those who can safely be paroled, state legislators would be wise to follow Professor Wilson's admonition: society must protect itself from dangerous offenders and impose real costs on criminal acts. Or, as Douglas Jeffrey, executive vice president of the Claremont Institute says, "We need to put justice back into the criminal justice system by putting convicted criminals behind bars and keeping them there for appropriate periods of time."[12] If state legislators were to adopt that simple mission, today's unacceptable risks to law-abiding Americans would be reduced.

INCARCERATION SAVES MONEY

While full sentences may mean more spending on prison, lawmakers and taxpayers need to understand that early-release programs cost dollars rather than save them. A 1982 Rand Corporation study of prison inmates found that the average inmate had committed 187 crimes the year before being incarcerated.[13] When criminals are released early, many

commit a similar volume of crimes when back on the streets.

The cost of crime committed by these early-release criminals is both direct and indirect. Taxpayers must finance the criminal justice system. Householders and businesses must buy private protection such as lighting, locks, dogs, fences, and alarm systems. They must buy insurance. The victims lose property and wages, and often incur heavy hospitalization costs.

In addition to the direct costs, there is the hidden cost of crime. Businesses, for instance, pass on to customers some of their costs for security and stolen merchandise. Households also must "pay" for crime by altering their behavior and life style.[14] It has been estimated that crime increases in the early 1980s caused "150,000 more New Yorkers to take taxis instead of public transportation; some 140,000 more New York City households sacrificed trips rather than leave their apartments unprotected. 50,000 put bars on their windows and 40,000 bought weapons. Even more difficult to assess are the costs of 'urban blight' such as abandoned buildings, unsafe schools, and inner city unemployment. Quite possibly the costs we can't count exceed the ones we can."[15] ...

INVESTING IN SAFETY

The imprisonment rate is higher in the United States than it is in other Western democracies mainly because Americans commit crime at a higher rate. The homicide rate in the United States is five times as high as in Europe; the rape rate is more than six times as high; and the robbery rate is four times as high.[16]

Given the higher crime rates in the United States, and the benefits to society

Table 1
Crimes Committed by Felons Not Incarcerated

One Criminal	Crimes Per Year
Burglar	76–118 burglaries
Robber	41–61 robberies
Thief	135–202 thefts
Auto Thief	76–100 auto thefts
Forger	62–98 frauds
Conman	127–283 frauds
Drug Dealer	880–1,299 drug deals

of incarcerating criminals, state and federal officials have underinvested in public safety. According to one estimate, more than 120,000 additional prison beds were needed across the nation at the close of 1990.[17] Some might argue that some inmates do not belong in prison, and should be replaced with hardened criminals. But 95 percent of Americans in prison are repeat or violent offenders.[18] Despite this enormous need for additional prison space, spending on corrections remains a very small percentage of state and local budgets. In fiscal year 1990, only 2.5 percent of the $975.9 billion in total expenditures by state and local governments went for corrections (about $24.7 billion). Investment in new prison construction is only a small fraction of that figure.[19] ...

WHY TRUTH IN SENTENCING HELPS

Truth in sentencing will increase the length of time convicted violent criminals are incarcerated. Currently violent criminals are serving 37 percent of the sentence that has been imposed. If required to serve at least 85 percent of their sentences, violent criminals would serve 2.3 times longer than they do now.

If the 55 percent of the estimated 800,000 current state and federal prisoners who are violent offenders were subject to serving 85 percent of their sentence, and assuming that those violent offenders would have committed ten violent crimes a year while on the street, then the number of crimes prevented each year by truth in sentencing would be 4,400,000.[20] That would be over two-thirds of the 6,000,000 violent crimes reported in the National Criminal Victims Survey for 1990.[21]

Targeting Hardened Criminals

Truth-in-sentencing laws would require state prison officials to retain more prisoners, at a higher cost to the state. But research shows that these prisoners are generally society's most dangerous predators.[22] In a landmark study, University of Pennsylvania criminologist Marvin Wolfgang compiled arrest records up to their 30th birthday for every male born and raised in Philadelphia in 1945 and 1958. He found that just 7 percent of each age group committed two-thirds of all violent crime, including three-fourths of the rapes and robberies and virtually all of the murders. Moreover, this 7 percent not only had five or more arrests by age 18 but went on committing felonies. Wolfgang and his colleagues estimate these criminals got away with about a dozen crimes.[23] Their studies suggest that about 75,000 new, young, persistent criminal predators are added to the population every year. They hit their peak rate of offenses at about age 16.[24]

In response to these findings, Alfred Regnery, who was Administrator of the Office of Juvenile Justice and Delinquency Prevention at the Justice Department from 1982 to 1986, funded projects in cities in which police, prosecutors, schools, and welfare and probation workers pooled information to focus on the "serious habitual offender." The program had a significant effect in many cities. Thanks to this Justice Department program, for example, Oxnard, California, was able to place the city's thirty most active serious habitual offenders behind bars, and violent crimes dropped 38 percent in 1987, more than double the drop in any other California city. By 1989, when all thirty of the active serious habitual offenders were behind bars, murders declined 60 percent compared with 1980, robberies 41 percent and burglaries 29 percent.[25]

Thus in conjunction with a criminal justice system that convicts and incarcerates the hardened criminals, a truth-in-sentencing policy will reduce crime by keeping these serious and habitual offenders in prison longer.

How Truth in Sentencing Deters Criminals

Incarceration incapacitates violent criminals, and directly benefits law-abiding Americans, by protecting families and also by yielding greater financial savings from reduced crime than the cost of incarceration itself. But stepped-up imprisonment also deters crime. Criminologist Isaac Ehrlich of the University of Chicago estimated that a one percent increase in arrest rates produces a one point decrease in crime rates, and a one percent increase in sentence length produces a one percent decrease in crime rates, for a combined deterrent and incapacitation effect of 1.1 percent.[26] Observed trends seem to support Ehrlich's broad conclusion and hence the claim of deterrence. When the rate of imprisonment per 100 crimes began dropping in the early 1960s, for in-

stance, the rate of crime per 100 population began to climb steeply.

A recent report by the Dallas-based National Center for Policy Analysis, written by Texas A&M economist Morgan Reynolds, makes a strong case for the deterrence value of longer sentences. According to Reynolds:

> Crime has increased as the expected costs of committing crimes has fallen. Today, for a burglary, for example, the chance of arrest is 7 percent. If you are unlucky enough to be one of the 7 percent arrested, relax; only 87 percent of arrestees are prosecuted. Of those, only 79 percent are convicted. Then only 25 percent of those convicted actually go to prison. Multiplying out all these probabilities gives your would-be burglar a 1.2 percent chance of going to jail.[27]

So, too many criminals do not go to jail for the crimes they commit. Reynolds points out that "once in prison, a burglar will stay there for about 13 months, but since more than 98 percent of burglaries never result in a prison sentence, the average expected sentence for each act of burglary is only 4.8 days. Similar calculations yield an expected punishment in 1990 of 1.8 years for murder, 60.5 days for rape, and 6.7 days for arson. Thus, for every crime, the expected punishment has declined over the decades. The decline continues between 1988 and 1990. When punishments rise, crime falls."[28] In short, Reynolds's argument is that raising expected punishment deters crime. Expected punishment is a function of the risk of being caught and convicted multiplied by the median time served. Therefore, everything being equal, increasing the length of sentence increases expected punishment, and hence a criminal is more likely to be deterred when the sentence is longer.

Reynolds also finds that since 1960, the expected punishment for committing a serious crime in Texas has dropped by more than two-thirds, while the number of serious crimes per 100,000 population in Texas has increased more than sixfold.[29]

While these data do not separate out the deterrent effect of longer sentences from the incapacitation effect, it is clear that longer sentences can generally be expected to reduce crime rates.

OBJECTIONS TO TRUTH-IN-SENTENCING LAWS

State truth-in-sentencing laws have great potential to combat violent crime. While academics and legislators in Washington and the states often focus on long-term solutions to the crime problem, such as social or economic conditions or the "root causes" of crime, the special merit of the truth-in-sentencing approach is simply that it keeps violent criminals off the streets while citizens, legislators, and professionals debate the merits of differing approaches in relative safety. In spite of its appeal to common sense, opponents of truth-in-sentencing legislation often make invalid objections. Some argue that truth in sentencing simply costs too much. But such an objection overlooks the opportunity cost of not keeping dangerous offenders in prison. For example, the cost of incarcerating a criminal is approximately $23,000 per year, but the cost of that criminal on the street is $452,000 per year. Some financial estimates are much higher. And, of course, for the families and victims of violent crime . . . , the human cost is beyond calculation. Others argue that the already large

numbers of persons in American jails is an international scandal. While there are indeed more criminals in America who serve more time than criminals in other countries, the fact remains that the violent crime rate in America is proportionately higher than in virtually all other countries. And if there is any scandal, it is the perpetuation of a failing criminal justice system that allows convicted rapists, kidnappers, and armed robbers back on the streets, ignoring the concerns of an American public that desperately needs security from predatory, violent criminals.

Beyond the questions of cost and the higher percentage of individuals being incarcerated, another objection to the enactment of truth-in-sentencing laws is that they ignore the "root causes" of crime. These root causes are often discussed in terms of persistent poverty, poor education, and deteriorating families. Liberal academics, of course, are not alone in addressing these maladies; and conservative social criticism, including recent analyses by scholars from The Heritage Foundation, have enriched the growing national debate on America's failing criminal justice system.[30] But an academic focus on "root causes," whatever its long-term impact on public policy, should not ignore the fact that violent crime itself immediately aggravates these social problems.

Beyond these general reservations, there are several other objections to truth in sentencing laws:

Objection #1: Truth in sentencing interferes with other policies.

Truth in-sentencing does not. For instance, it does not affect *habeas corpus*, mandatory minimum sentences, the exclusionary rule, the death penalty, or gun control. Moreover, truth in sentencing is no threat to existing programs designed to divert criminals from jail or prison, such as community-based corrections, intensive probation, house arrest, restitution, or boot camps for first-time offenders. A judge or jury sentencing a convicted criminal to any of these alternatives would not be in conflict with truth in sentencing. But if a judge or jury imposes a prison sentence on a criminal with such a law on the books, another government official cannot later amend the sentence and send that person to an alternative program not involving incarceration. If a judge or jury feels comfortable permitting alternatives to prison for a criminal after listening to the evidence, learning the criminal's background, and hearing from the victim, then truth-in-sentencing requirements would be satisfied.

Objection #2: Truth in sentencing discriminates against minorities.

Some critics argue that the criminal justice system discriminates against black Americans, and so truth-in-sentencing rules will unfairly hit those inmates. On their face, the raw statistics are indeed disturbing. Blacks comprise only 12 percent of the population, but constitute 48.9 percent of state prisoners and 31.4 percent of federal prisoners. The impact of truth-in-sentencing law would depend on whether blacks or whites are disproportionately convicted of the crimes covered by the laws, and whether parole currently favors blacks or whites. However, these laws would be even-handed. All convicted offenders, regardless of race, would have to serve 85 percent of their sentences before being eligible for parole. A more signif-

icant question is whether the higher percentages of blacks in prison are the result of racial bias or of higher rates of crime. A number of studies have been conducted to answer that question and appear to demonstrate that it is higher rates of crime among blacks, and not bias, that accounts for their disproportionate representation in America's prisons.

CONCLUSION

The time has come for states to enact truth-in-sentencing laws. There are few viable alternatives that protect citizens from the immediate threat of violent crime. Parole, for example, is a failed experiment. The American people deserve better.

The task before America's state legislators and governors is to pass truth-in-sentencing legislation that would require violent criminals to serve the bulk of their sentences—85 percent is a good benchmark—and to provide the resources it will take to implement such laws. The federal government can encourage this commonsense approach. One such initiative is the Truth in Sentencing Act of 1993, H.R. 3584, introduced by Representatives Jim Chapman and Don Young. This bill would encourage each state to adopt truth-in-sentencing laws and would fund assistance to the states, amounting to $10.5 billion over five years, to help them implement such laws, including the building and operating of prisons. Trimming the federal bureaucracy, not tax increases, is the financing mechanism for these efforts.

The cost of doing nothing is unacceptably high. Crime is a leading concern for Americans. Political leaders and state legislators who can focus the public's attention on a common sense reform like truth in sentencing will be setting the terms of the national debate.

NOTES

1. See Bureau of Justice Statistics, U.S. Department of Justice, *National Corrections Reporting Program, 1988*, table 2–7 (1992).

2. See Bureau of Justice Statistics, *National Corrections Reporting Program, 1988*, table 2–4.

3. See Bureau of Justice Statistics, *National Corrections Reporting Program, 1988*, table 2–7.

4. See Bureau of Justice Statistics, U.S. Department of Justice, *Lifetime Likelihood of Victimization*, technical report, March 1987.

5. See U.S. Department of Justice, "The Case for More Incarceration," 1992, p. 16.

6. See CNN/Gallup Poll, cited in *USA Today*, October 28, 1993, p. 1A.

7. See Bureau of Justice Statistics, U.S. Department of Justice, Special Report, *Recidivism of Prisoners Released in 1983*, April 1989.

8. See Bureau of Justice Statistics, U.S. Department of Justice, Special Report, *Recidivism of Felons on Probation*, February 1992.

9. See Bureau of Justice Statistics, *Recidivism of Prisoners Released in 1983*. See also, Bureau of Justice Statistics, U.S. Department of Justice, Special Report, *Examining Recidivism*, February 1985.

10. See Peter B. Hoffman and James L. Beck, "Recidivism Among Released Federal Prisoners: Salient Factor Score and Five Year Follow-Up," *Criminal Justice and Behavior*, Vol. 12, No. 4 (December 1985), pp. 501–507.

11. See J. Q. Wilson, "If Every Criminal Knew He Would Be Punished If Caught," *The New York Times Magazine*, January 28, 1973, pp. 52–56.

12. Editor's note in Joseph M. and Anne Nutter Bissette, *Ten Myths About Crime and Justice* (Claremont, CA: The Claremont Institute, March 1992).

13. See generally Peter Greenwood et al., *Selective Incapacitation*, Report R-2815-NIJ, The Rand Corporation, Santa Monica, CA, 1982.

14. Edward Zedlewski, *Costs and Benefits of Sanction: A Synthesis of Recent Research*. Unpublished paper, National Institute of Justice, June 1992.

15. William W. Greer, "What Is The Cost of Rising Crime?" *New York Affairs*, January 1984, pp. 6–16.

16. "International Crime Rates," May 1988, NCJ-110776.

17. See Bureau of Justice Statistics, U.S. Department of Justice, *Prisoners in 1990*, table 9 (1991).

18. See Bureau of Justice Statistics, U.S. Department of Justice, *Prisons and Prisoners in the United States* (1992), p. 16.

19. See Bureau of the Census, U.S. Department of Commerce, *Government Finances: 1989–90* (1991), p. 2.

20. The median number of crimes reported in Rand Study was 15. See Greenwood et al., *op. cit.*

21. See U.S. Department of Justice, *Criminal Victimization in the United States, 1990*, p. 4.

22. Methvyn, *op. cit.*

23. See P. E. Tracy, M. E. Wolfgang, and R. M. Figlio, *Delinquency Careers in Two Birth Cohorts* (New York: Plenum Press, 1990), pp. 279–280.

24. *Ibid.*

25. Methvyn, *op. cit.*

26. See Isaac Ehrlich, "Participation in Illegitimate Activities: A Theoretical and Empirical Investigation," *Journal of Political Economy*, May/June 1973, pp. 521–564.

27. See Morgan O. Reynolds, "Why Does Crime Pay?" National Center for Policy Analysis *Backgrounder* No. 110 (1990), p.5.

28. *Ibid.*

29. See Morgan O. Reynolds, *Crime in Texas*, National Center for Policy Analysis Report No. 102 (1991), p. 4.

30. For an excellent summary of the relationship between crime and the deterioration of family life, particularly in urban areas, see Robert Rector, "A Comprehensive Urban Policy: How to Fix Welfare and Revitalize America's Inner Cities," Heritage Foundation *Memo to President-Elect Clinton* No. 12, January 18, 1993; see also Carl F. Horowitz, "An Empowerment Strategy For Eliminating Neighborhood Crime," Heritage Foundation *Backgrounder* No. 814, March 5, 1991.

NO

Lois G. Forer

THE COUNTER REFORMATION

The movement in American criminal law which is referred to here as the "counter reformation" was initiated to counteract the reforms of the criminal law begun in the 1950s. Its proponents sought to block and undo the decisions of the Warren Court, particularly those enforcing the constitutional rights of persons accused of crime.

The Counter-Reformation from which this term is derived was a movement within the Catholic Church to . . . reform the abuses of the Church, particularly corruption of the clergy, simony, and the selling of indulgences. Almost three centuries were required to achieve its goals.

The counter reform movement in American criminal law succeeded in barely four decades. Indeed, the death penalty which had been abolished in 1972 was restored four years later.

The dismantling of the reforms of the criminal law continues. The goal of the counter reformers is to transmogrify the criminal justice system of the United States to a system of crime control through the use of severe penalties: capital punishments and laws mandating long periods of incarceration. It has been accomplished in large part by decisions limiting the procedural rights of those accused of crime, and by the enactment of mandatory sentencing laws, sentencing guideline laws, and death penalty laws. The most striking and disruptive effects of these changes have been the massive overcrowding of jails and prisons at a cost of billions of dollars and loss of public confidence in the fairness of the law.

A comparable movement occurred simultaneously in the United Kingdom. In both nations prison populations rose alarmingly, commencing in the 1970s and 1980s. In England in 1986, the prison population was the highest of any of the member states of the Council of Europe: 95.3 per 100,000 of the population. Only Turkey's, with a rate of imprisonment of 102.3, was higher.

In the United States the rate of imprisonment . . . is even higher and increasing year by year, although the number of crimes has declined since 1991. . . .

*   *   *

A century and a half ago that perceptive observer of the American scene Alexis de Tocqueville noted, after visiting many prisons, "There are similar

punishments and crimes called by the same name, but there are no two beings equal in regard to their morals." These obvious differences in morals and culpability have been deliberately eliminated from judicial consideration in sentencing.

Many lawyers, judges, and criminologists have ... taken issue with the choice of crimes covered under mandatory sentencing laws and the classifications of crimes under sentencing guidelines. One example is incest. In most guidelines, it is included in the category of child abuse and given a less severe rating than robbery. Robbery on public transportation is penalized more severely than robbery on a street or in a school room. The result is a greater disparity in sentences for similar crimes.

In a recent case in Minnesota, one of the first states to adopt guidelines, a judge departed from the guideline in sentencing an ex-priest convicted of sexual abuse of a child. This man was wanted for similar crimes in three states. The guideline sentence for this offense was two and a half years probation. The judge in imposing a prison sentence stated that he departed from the guidelines because the defendant showed no remorse, a permitted aggravating factor. The dangerous behavior of this man over a long period of time was not a factor that could be considered under the guidelines.

The classification of crimes under most mandatory laws and most guidelines is conceptual, based on the structure of crime codes that classify offenses as felonies of different grades and misdemeanors. Many of these codes were enacted decades ago and fail to take into account present conditions of life and new findings in the fields of psychology and psychiatry as to the nature of of-fenders and the lasting harm done to victims of sexual assault. Nor do they reflect the widespread harm done to individuals and communities from violations of environmental laws and pure food and drug laws. The commissions that created the guidelines pursuant to these laws did not consider dangerousness in establishing presumptive sentences. They were bemused by the theory of just deserts.

A more sensible method of calculating crime severity would be to structure the law to reflect public perceptions of harm and dangerousness in fixing penalties. Public opinion studies by criminologists of crime severity based not on the names of crimes but on factual situations describing the offender, the victim and the circumstances of the crime yield very different results.

Mandatory sentencing laws and guideline sentencing laws preclude judicial consideration of factors that most people consider highly relevant. The federal sentencing guidelines specifically exclude from consideration race, gender, age, education, vocational skills, and mental and emotional conditions, as well as physical conditions of the offender. Such a neutral sentencing scheme sounds fair. In operation it bears most heavily on women, minorities, the young, and the disadvantaged. Since blacks are disproportionately poorer and many have lower levels of education and job skills than most whites, the result has been to exacerbate the disproportionate racial composition of the prison population. Nonetheless, these statutes have been upheld by the United States Supreme Court.

During the Reagan-Bush years the composition of state legislatures and the Congress changed. The new legislators reflected the philosophy of the counter reformation and the theory of just deserts.

The membership of the United States Supreme Court also changed dramatically during this period. The minority views soon became the majority. Ignoring the doctrine of *stare decisis*, that prior decisions should be followed, and flouting their own much-professed strictures against "judicial activism," the majority of the Burger/Rehnquist Court promptly proceeded to erode, if not reverse, the decisions of the previous two decades. Rights of women, children, racial minorities, homosexuals, and those accused of crime were sharply curtailed. The rights of prisoners were also restricted. Despite vigorous challenges, guideline sentencing laws were upheld.

Whether these changes in pretrial and trial procedures and the limitations on appeals and habeas corpus brought about more convictions of those accused of crime probably cannot be accurately determined. There is no way of knowing whether these decisions contributed to prison overcrowding.

There can be no doubt, however, that legislation enacted embracing the theory of just deserts and fair and certain punishment is responsible in large part for the massive burgeoning of the prison population. Violent and property crime rates fell from 24 percent to 23 percent in 1992, down from 32 percent in 1975, while the prison population soared.

The United States Sentencing Commission in its Sentencing and Guidelines and Policy Statement, issued in April 1987, acknowledged not only that the prison population would increase as a result of the drug laws and the career offenders provision of the sentencing law but also that "The guidelines themselves, insofar as they reflect policy decisions made by the Commission . . . will lead to an increase in the prison population."

This was most probably not the intent of the legislators. Lawmakers in the states and in the Congress were frustrated by the rising incidence of street crime. Abetted by political rhetoric demanding stern punishment for criminals, they embraced the new penology to the plaudits of their constituents.

Lawmakers did not ask what the results of these laws would be. Indeed, vehement proponents of the new penology of just deserts and long prison sentences admitted they did not know what effect these changes in the law would bring about. Professor James Q. Wilson of Harvard, in proposing long prison sentences and severely limiting judicial discretion, wrote in 1977: "No one can know what effect any of these changes in sentencing policy will have on offenders or on society and its institutions."

Judges in criminal courts, probation officers, and prison officials were acutely aware that these laws would drastically increase the number of prisoners, that they would disrupt families, and place additional strains on the welfare system. But they were not consulted.

When judges in my court sought to discuss the practicalities of a proposed sentencing guideline law, they were told that if this law was not passed, a mandatory sentencing law would be enacted. So the judges remained silent. The legislature then enacted both a sentencing guideline statute and mandatory sentencing laws.

The theory behind these laws was that if potential felons knew in advance that the penalty for certain crimes was a long prison sentence or death, they would think carefully and refrain from violating the law. This was patently fallacious. Most street criminals act impulsively, without forethought. Even white-collar felons and professional criminals who

carefully plot and plan their misdeeds are not deterred by knowledge of the severe penalties under the Racketeering Influence and Corrupt Organizations Act, popularly known as RICO. They think they can beat the law. Many do. Poor, ignorant offenders are far more likely to be caught and punished. Even when a long prison sentence is imposed on a white-collar offender "to send a message," it is usually revised and the offender is released after a relatively short time in prison. For example, Michael Milken served only twenty-two months of a ten-year sentence.

Proponents of just deserts also believed that if punishment was swift and certain, it would be an effective deterrent. Because American law requires that after a crime has been committed a suspect must be arrested, given a preliminary hearing, and a jury trial if he or she so desires, punishment cannot be swift. Because the law requires proof beyond a reasonable doubt, evidence must be presented, witnesses must testify; there is many a slip between arrest and conviction. Punishment cannot be certain. The Supreme Court has eroded the requirement of proof beyond a reasonable doubt with respect to the elements of a crime necessary for sentencing. But even this abandonment of constitutional rights does not ensure swift and certain punishment.

The United States Sentencing Commission explicitly adopted the new theory of just deserts rather than rehabilitation, stating: "Most observers of the criminal law agree that the ultimate aim of the law itself, and of punishment in particular, is the control of crime." This new policy has not succeeded. Crime has not been substantially reduced.

Even if the United States dispensed with constitutional requirements and adopted a penal system like that of Iran, where accusation is tantamount to conviction, and punishment—death or mutilation—follows inexorably without possibility of appeals or clemency, one must doubt whether impulsive street felons would stop to calculate the consequences....

These sentencing laws also wrought a drastic transformation in the practice of entering guilty pleas, often called plea bargaining. The United States Sentencing Commission has pointed out that 90 percent of all accused persons plead guilty. Since the adoption of guidelines and mandatory sentences, fewer defendants are willing to plead guilty knowing in advance the harsh sentences that will be imposed. Many prosecutors now oppose these laws because of the added burdens such trials impose.

Before the counter reformation, judges had the authority to fix sentences within the maximum limits set by statute, taking into account the circumstances of the crime and the characteristics of the offender. Guilty pleas were entered in open court. Judges imposed sentences on the basis of the facts placed on the record, presentence investigations, psychiatric evaluations if they were deemed appropriate, and any evidence defendants wished to offer. Guilty pleas are disparaged by many critics. I, however, believe that there is no reason to compel an accused who acknowledges guilt to plead not guilty and undergo a trial. When a guilty plea takes place in open court the defendant and the public are protected because an account of the facts is placed on the record, the judge explains the reason for the sentence, and the victims of the crime can be heard.

Under mandatory sentences and guidelines, plea bargaining takes place in secret, in the offices of the prosecutors. Because judges have no discretion in imposing sentence under mandatory laws and little discretion, if any, under guidelines, there is no incentive for an accused to plead guilty and hope for a lenient sentence based on extenuating circumstances or good character. The only official who has authority under these laws to decide what the penalty will be is the prosecutor, who can drop more serious charges and proceed on the less serious ones.

Sensible prosecutors charge all possible crimes for which there is reasonable evidence. Under prior practice at trial, the judge or jury would decide which charges had been proved. When a guilty plea was entered, the prosecutor was not under pressure to drop charges because the judge would impose the sentence. Now it is the prosecutor who, in effect, sets the sentence. Because the sentence for the crime is fixed by statute or guidelines, discretion has been transferred from the judge to the prosecutor. The public does not know what "deal" has been made or the basis for the decision. It is a secret process not unlike that of the hated Star Chamber* that was abolished in England in 1641.

The philosophy of just deserts gave new impetus and respectability to the rage to punish. Prior to the counter reformation, the emphasis was on rehabilitation, education, and crime prevention. Retribution or vengeance is now recognized as a legitimate motivation in sen-

*[The Star Chamber refers to a fifteenth-century court in England that was characterized by secrecy and often irresponsible arbitrariness and oppressiveness.—Eds.]

tencing. The criminal sanction and punishment are the preferred mode of dealing with difficult social, medical, and economic conditions.

Drug laws offer a telling example of the folly of relying on the criminal law to deal with what are essentially social and health problems. The government appears to have suffered a case of collective amnesia in forgetting the unsuccessful effort to deal with drinking through criminal laws.

More than three quarters of a century ago alcohol abuse was viewed as a moral issue to be controlled by the criminal law. Drinkers were treated as sinners who must be punished severely. In the grip of moral outrage the Congress passed the Volstead Act (1919) and the Eighteenth Amendment was adopted. The "demon rum" was pursued as a public menace, whether the beverage was wine or bathtub gin. These laws were expected to eliminate 75 percent of crime, poverty, and broken homes in the United States. When it became clear that these ends had not been fulfilled, barely a decade and a half later, common sense prevailed and the Twenty-First Amendment was enacted repealing the Eighteenth Amendment.

In New York, a similar fervor resulted in the Rockefeller laws, mandating prison sentences of from five to twenty years for possession of various quantities of drugs. These laws were not restricted to cocaine, heroin, and angel dust but also included marijuana. Alcohol and tobacco cause many more deaths than drugs. But punishment of sin, not public danger, was the motivation. The prison population of New York rose alarmingly.

The same moral fervor prevailed in the Reagan-Bush era. Drugs were considered the cause of violent crime and drug

users, dealers, and producers in foreign countries were pursued with costly frenzy. Statistics reveal that 80 percent of drug offenders are non-violent.

Like the other laws of the counter reformation, drug laws have taken a heavy toll on poor black youth. The poor, ethnic minorities, and women are the three categories most seriously prejudiced by drug laws that prevent judges in sentencing from taking into account risk to the public and the social and medical problems of the offender. The result has been that one of every four black men is under some form of correctional control prison, probation, or parole. Women are prosecuted for using illegal drugs during pregnancy, imprisoned, and/or deprived of custody of their children.

A total of 220,000 persons were incarcerated for drug offenses in 1993. Seventy-five percent of new federal prisoners since 1987 are drug offenders; the length of their sentences has increased by 22 percent. The number of black inmates has increased by 55 percent, while white inmates increased by only 31 percent. The effect on the black communities in many cities has been devastating: 56 percent of all black males between the ages of eighteen and thirty-five in Baltimore and 40 percent of those in Washington, D.C., are either in prison or jail or on probation or parole or on arrest warrants, according to Jerome Miller, president of the National Center on Institutions and Alternatives. Only 26.4 percent of black drug offenders and 12.8 percent of white drug offenders had histories of violence. While the greatest burden of this misguided war on drugs has fallen on the black community, the burden on the taxpayers is very heavy.

As with alcohol laws, drug laws bear little relation to the nature of the substance or the danger to the public. Prohibited drugs include marijuana as well as crack cocaine and angel dust. All are punished harshly, even though by 1992 there were no reported cases of death from marijuana. All are considered illegal and all users are deemed sinners.

John Walters, former deputy director for supply reduction in the Office of National Drug Control Policy, maintained, "It's a moral question—the question of right and wrong." William P. Barr, former U.S. Attorney General, stated that building more prisons is "the morally right thing to do."

The cost to the taxpayers has been enormous. During the Bush administration, federal, state, and local governments spent $100 billion in the war on drugs. The federal drug budget was almost $1 billion, most of it spent on agents, prosecutors, and prisons. The courts are overwhelmed, attempting to process 1 million drug arrests a year; the incarceration of 75,000 drug offenders costs $3 billion a year. But cocaine use actually increased in 1991.

Belatedly, after the government has spent billions of dollars on drug enforcement with little appreciable success, knowledgeable persons are now recommending education rather than the heavy hand of the criminal law. But a similar understanding of other problems now confided solely to the criminal law is impeded by the conflation of crime and sin and the rage to punish.

The counter reformation, driven by the belief that punishment is the solution to all violations of law and all aberrant behavior, was remarkably effective in changing the criminal law during its short span of less than four decades. It succeeded in punishing with long terms of imprisonment more than 1.3

million persons at a cost of billions of dollars. More than 2,600 persons, some of whom are arguably innocent, have been condemned to death.

But the counter reformation did not reduce crime, eliminate unfairnesses in sentencing, or improve the quality of justice. Criminal law has a necessary but limited role in American life. It cannot solve all social and economic problems. Prison and the electric chair or lethal injection are not substitutes for families, homes, jobs, schools, health care, and other institutions and services. The theory of just deserts impedes a rational analysis of both offenses and offenders. It prevents judges from imposing appropriate penalties on offenders that treat them humanely, protect society, and are cost-effective.

The criminal justice system in the United States never achieved the goal of equal justice under law. It was always weighted heavily against the poor, the ignorant, and the disadvantaged. The reform movement that began in the 1950s mitigated many injustices. The counter reformation has exacerbated them. It has also filled the jails and prisons beyond capacity, placed hundreds on death row, and overwhelmed the courts with appeals from Draconian sentences.

POSTSCRIPT

Will Mandatory Sentencing Reduce Crime?

It may be said of crime—as Mark Twain said of the weather—that everyone talks about it but nobody does anything about it. Perhaps that is because the easy solutions only sound easy. If authorities are to "lock'em all up," where are they going to put them? The public applauds tough talk but seems unwilling to pay for new prison space. On the other hand, getting at the so-called root causes of crime—which supposedly include poverty and discrimination —is no easier. This approach assumes that these phenomena *are* the basic causes of crime. Yet the rate of violent crime was much lower during the poverty-ridden, racist decade of the 1930s than it was during the affluent and enlightened 1960s.

In Seattle, Washington, a man was convicted of a third felony under that state's three-strikes law. He had stolen $100 from a pizza parlor, $390 from his grandfather, and $100 from a sandwich shop. At very great expense to the state, he will die in prison.

As states have more experience with three-strikes laws, more studies and analyses are likely to produce different reactions. Daniel Franklin, in "The Right Three Strikes," *The Washington Monthly* (September 1994), argues that we must make a clear distinction between violent and nonviolent offenders in the application of such laws. An analysis of how this has worked in California can be found in Peter W. Greenwood, ed., *Three Strikes and You're Out: Estimated Benefits and Costs of California's New Mandatory-Sentencing Law* (Rand Corporation, 1994).

Forty-two state prison systems are under court order to relieve prison overcrowding. The federal prison system is operating at approximately 40 percent over capacity. With more than 1 million Americans in prison in the late 1990s, the prison rate has risen 10 times faster than the rate of crime since 1980. Although some of this increase is attributable to more arrests and longer sentences, most has resulted from people being imprisoned for nonviolent drug crimes.

Dramatic increases in prison population and the rising cost of imprisonment have been accompanied by revelations of appalling conditions that cannot contribute to rehabilitation. Larry E. Sullivan, in *The Prison Reform Movement: Forlorn Hope* (Twayne, 1990), explores the possibilities of reforming prisons.

Many of the writings about crime and punishment in the last decade examine the possibility of alternatives to prison, particularly for people guilty of so-called victimless crimes, such as marijuana smoking, curfew violations, or

public drunkenness. Restitution, community work service, monitored home confinement, and other sanctions are considered in Andrew R. Klein's *Alternative Sentencing: A Practitioner's Guide* (Anderson, 1988).

Various approaches to sentencing reform are examined in Tamasak Wicharaya, *Simple Theory, Hard Reality: The Impact of Sentencing Reforms on Courts, Prisons, and Crime* (State University of New York, 1995). Wicharaya argues that policymakers tend to reduce complex reality to a simplistic form. The author also develops a theory of criminal sentencing as applied to the criminal data of 47 states over almost 30 years.

In addition to sentencing reform, Michael Tonry and Franklin E. Zimring, the editors of *Reform and Punishment: Essays on Criminal Sentencing* (University of Chicago Press, 1983), look at how the criminal justice system deals with the mentally ill, and they examine sentencing in European countries. Lawrence M. Friedman's *Crime and Punishment in American History* (Basic Books, 1993) is a popular history of the American justice system, although it concludes sadly that crime is "the price we pay" for living in a free society.

Some critics argue that the wrong approaches have been used to reduce crime in America. They urge limiting firearms, expanding drug treatment facilities (some recommend legalizing drugs), creative sentencing for non-violent offenders (community service, for example, and the tack taken by a Memphis judge who allowed the victims of a burglary to enter the perpetrator's home and take anything they wanted), and increasing community policing and the number of probation officers.

No matter what solutions to the crime problem are attempted, Forer and Wootton have helped to set the terms of the debate. Wootton adopts the position set forth by criminologist James Q. Wilson 20 years ago with his famous observation that "wicked people exist." Forer, who characterizes this approach as "the counter-reformation," wants to recapture the spirit of the original reformation, which sought to combat crime by making American society more just and humane. The two goals, punishment and prevention, need not exclude each other, but today's limited resources may force us to decide where to place the emphasis.

ISSUE 9

Is Capital Punishment Justified?

YES: Robert W. Lee, from "Deserving to Die," *The New American* (August 13, 1990)

NO: Matthew L. Stephens, from "Instrument of Justice or Tool of Vengeance?" *Christian Social Action* (November 1990)

ISSUE SUMMARY

YES: Essayist Robert W. Lee argues that capital punishment is the only fair way for society to respond to certain heinous crimes.

NO: Matthew L. Stephens, a prison chaplain, contends that the death penalty is motivated by revenge, is arbitrary in its application, and is racist in its result.

Although capital punishment (the death penalty) is ancient, both the definition of a capital crime and the methods used to put convicted persons to death have changed dramatically. In eighteenth-century Massachusetts, for example, capital crimes included blasphemy and the worship of false gods. Slave states often imposed the death penalty upon blacks for crimes that were punished by only two or three years' imprisonment when committed by whites. It has been estimated that in the twentieth century approximately 10 percent of all legal executions have been for the crime of rape, 1 percent for all other crimes except murder (robbery, burglary, attempted murder, etc.), and nearly 90 percent for the commission of murder.

Long before the Supreme Court severely limited the use of the death penalty, executions in the United States were becoming increasingly rare. In the 1930s there were 1,667; the total for the 1950s was 717. In the 1960s the numbers fell even more dramatically. For example, seven persons were executed in 1965, one in 1966, and two in 1967. Put another way, in the 1930s and 1940s, there was 1 execution for every 60 or 70 homicides committed in states that had the death penalty; in the first half of the 1960s, there was 1 execution for every 200 homicides; and by 1966 and 1967, there were only 3 executions for approximately 20,000 homicides.

Then came the Supreme Court case of *Furman v. Georgia* (1972), which many thought—mistakenly—"abolished" capital punishment in America. Actually, only two members of the *Furman* majority thought that capital punishment *per se* violates the Eighth Amendment's injunction against "cruel and unusual punishment." The other three members of the majority took the view that

capital punishment is unconstitutional only when applied in an arbitrary or racially discriminatory manner, as they believed it was in this case. The four dissenters in the *Furman* case were prepared to uphold capital punishment both in general and in this particular instance. Not surprisingly, then, with a slight change of Court personnel—and with a different case before the Court —a few years later, the majority vote went the other way.

In the latter case, *Gregg v. Georgia* (1976), the majority upheld capital punishment under certain circumstances. In his majority opinion in the case, Justice Potter Stewart noted that the law in question (a new Georgia capital punishment statute) went to some lengths to avoid arbitrary procedures in capital cases. For example, Georgia courts were not given complete discretion in handing out death sentences to convicted murderers but had to consult a series of guidelines spelling out "aggravating circumstances," such as if the murder had been committed by someone already convicted of murder, if the murder endangered the lives of bystanders, and if the murder was committed in the course of a major felony. These guidelines, Stewart said, together with other safeguards against arbitrariness included in the new statute, preserved it against Eighth Amendment challenges.

Although the Court has upheld the constitutionality of the death penalty, it can always be abolished by state legislatures. However, that seems unlikely to happen in many states. If anything, the opposite is occurring. Almost immediately after the *Furman* decision of 1972, state legislatures began enacting new death penalty statutes designed to meet the objections raised in the case. By the time of the *Gregg* decision, 35 new death penalty statutes had been enacted.

In response to the public mood, Congress has put its own death penalty provisions into federal legislation. In 1988 Congress sanctioned the death penalty for drug kingpins convicted of intentionally killing or ordering anyone's death. More recently, in the 1994 crime bill, Congress authorized the death penalty for dozens of existing or new federal crimes, such as treason, kidnapping that results in death, or the murder of a federal law enforcement agent.

In the following selections, Robert W. Lee argues that capital punishment is an appropriate form of retribution for certain types of heinous offenses, while Matthew L. Stephens asserts that capital punishment is nothing but vengeance that falls disproportionately upon the poor and minorities.

YES

Robert W. Lee

DESERVING TO DIE

A key issue in the debate over capital punishment is whether or not it is an effective deterrent to violent crime. In at least one important respect, it unquestionably is: It simply cannot be contested that a killer, once executed, is forever deterred from killing again. The deterrent effect on others, however, depends largely on how swiftly and surely the penalty is applied. Since capital punishment has not been used with any consistency over the years, it is virtually impossible to evaluate its deterrent effect accurately. Abolitionists claim that a lack of significant difference between the murder rates for states with and without capital punishment proves that the death penalty does not deter. But the states with the death penalty on their books have used it so little over the years as to preclude any meaningful comparison between states. Through July 18, 1990 there had been 134 executions since 1976. Only 14 states (less than 40 percent of those that authorize the death penalty) were involved. Any punishment, including death, will cease to be an effective deterrent if it is recognized as mostly bluff. Due to costly delays and endless appeals, the death penalty has been largely turned into a paper tiger by the same crowd that calls for its abolition on the grounds that it is not an effective deterrent!

To allege that capital punishment, if imposed consistently and without undue delay, would not be a deterrent to crime is, in essence, to say that people are not afraid of dying. If so, as columnist Jenkin Lloyd Jones once observed, then warning signs reading "Slow Down," "Bridge Out," and "Danger— 40,000 Volts" are futile relics of an age gone by when men feared death. To be sure, the death penalty could never become a 100-percent deterrent to heinous crime, because the fear of death varies among individuals. Some race automobiles, climb mountains, parachute jump, walk circus high-wires, ride Brahma bulls in rodeos, and otherwise engage in endeavors that are more than normally hazardous. But, as author Bernard Cohen notes in his book *Law and Order*, "there are even more people who refrain from participating in these activities mainly because risking their lives is not to their taste."

From Robert W. Lee, "Deserving to Die," *The New American* (August 13, 1990). Copyright © 1990 by *The New American*. Reprinted by permission.

MERIT SYSTEM

On occasion, circumstances *have* led to meaningful statistical evaluations of the death penalty's deterrent effect. In Utah, for instance, there have been three executions since the Supreme Court's 1976 ruling:

- Gary Gilmore faced a firing squad at the Utah State Prison on January 17, 1977. There had been 55 murders in the Beehive State during 1976 (4.5 per 100,000 population). During 1977, in the wake of the Gilmore execution, there were 44 murders (3.5 per 100,000), a 20 percent decrease.

- More than a decade later, on August 28, 1987, Pierre Dale Selby (one of the two infamous "hi-fi killers" who in 1974 forced five persons in an Ogden hi-fi shop to drink liquid drain cleaner, kicked a ballpoint pen into the ear of one, then killed three) was executed. During all of 1987, there were 54 murders (3.2 per 100,000). The count for January through August was 38 (a monthly average of 4.75). For September–December (in the aftermath of the Selby execution) there were 16 (4.0 per month, a nearly 16 percent decrease). For July and August there were six and seven murders, respectively. In September (the first month following Selby's demise) there were three.

- Arthur Gary Bishop, who sodomized and killed a number of young boys, was executed on June 10, 1988. For all of 1988 there were 47 murders (2.7 per 100,000, the fewest since 1977). During January–June, there were 26; for July–December (after the Bishop execution) the tally was 21 (a 19 percent difference).

In the wake of all three Utah executions, there have been notable decreases in both the number and the rate of murders within the state. To be sure, there are other variables that could have influenced the results, but the figures are there and abolitionists to date have tended simply to ignore them.

Deterrence should never be considered the *primary* reason for administering the death penalty. It would be both immoral and unjust to punish one man merely as an example to others. The basic consideration should be: Is the punishment deserved? If not, it should not be administered regardless of what its deterrent impact might be. After all, once deterrence supersedes justice as the basis for a criminal sanction, the guilt or innocence of the accused becomes largely irrelevant. Deterrence can be achieved as effectively by executing an innocent person as a guilty one (something that communists and other totalitarians discovered long ago). If a punishment administered to one person deters someone else from committing a crime, fine. But that result should be viewed as a bonus of justice properly applied, not as a reason for the punishment. The decisive consideration should be: Has the accused *earned* the penalty?

THE COST OF EXECUTION

The exorbitant financial expense of death penalty cases is regularly cited by abolitionists as a reason for abolishing capital punishment altogether. They prefer to ignore, however, the extent to which they themselves are responsible for the interminable legal maneuvers that run up the costs....

As presently pursued, death-penalty prosecutions *are* outrageously expensive. But, again, the cost is primarily due

to redundant appeals, time-consuming delays, bizarre court rulings, and legal histrionics by defense attorneys:

Willie Darden, who had already survived three death warrants, was scheduled to die in Florida's electric chair on September 4, 1985 for a murder he had committed in 1973. Darden's lawyer made a last-minute emergency appeal to the Supreme Court, which voted against postponing the execution until a formal appeal could be filed. So the attorney (in what he later described as "last-minute ingenuity") then requested that the emergency appeal be technically transformed into a formal appeal. Four Justices agreed (enough to force the full court to review the appeal) and the execution was stayed. After additional years of delay and expense, Darden was eventually put out of our misery on March 15, 1988.

Ronald Gene Simmons killed 14 members of his family during Christmas week in 1987. He was sentenced to death, said he was willing to die, and refused to appeal. But his scheduled March 16, 1989 execution was delayed when a fellow inmate, also on death row, persuaded the Supreme Court to block it (while Simmons was having what he expected to be his last meal) on the grounds that the execution could have repercussions for other death-row inmates. It took the Court until April 24th of [1990] to reject that challenge. Simmons was executed on June 25th.

Robert Alton Harris was convicted in California of the 1978 murders of two San Diego teenagers whose car he wanted for a bank robbery. Following a seemingly interminable series of appeals, he was at last sentenced to die on April 3rd of [1990]. Four days earlier, a 9th U.S. Circuit Court of Appeals judge stayed the execution, largely on the claim that Harris was brain-damaged and therefore may possibly have been unable to "premeditate" the murders (as required under California law for the death penalty). On April 10th, the *Washington Times* reported that the series of tests used to evaluate Harris's condition had been described by some experts as inaccurate and "a hoax."

The psychiatric game is being played for all it is worth. On May 14th, Harris's attorneys argued before the 9th Circuit Court that he should be spared the death penalty because he received "inadequate" psychiatric advice during his original trial. In 1985, the Supreme Court had ruled that a defendant has a constitutional right to "a competent psychiatrist who will conduct an appropriate examination." Harris had access to a licensed psychiatrist, but now argues that—since the recent (highly questionable) evaluations indicated brain damage and other alleged disorders that the original psychiatrist failed to detect (and which may have influenced the jury not to impose the death sentence)—a new trial (or at least a re-sentencing) is in order. If the courts buy this argument, hundreds (perhaps thousands) of cases could be reopened for psychiatric challenge.

On April 2, 1974 William Neal Moore shot and killed a man in Georgia. Following his arrest, he pleaded guilty to armed robbery and murder and was convicted and sentenced to death. On July 20, 1975 the Georgia Supreme Court denied his petition for review. On July 16, 1976 the U.S. Supreme

Court denied his petition for review. On May 13, 1977 the Jefferson County Superior Court turned down a petition for a new sentencing hearing (the state Supreme Court affirmed the denial, and the U.S. Supreme Court again denied a review). On March 30, 1978 a Tattnall County Superior Court judge held a hearing on a petition alleging sundry grounds for a writ of *habeas corpus,* but declined on July 13, 1978 to issue a writ. On October 17, 1978 the state Supreme Court declined to review that ruling. Moore petitioned the U.S. District Court for Southern Georgia. After a delay of more than two years, a U.S. District Court judge granted the writ on April 29, 1981. After another two-year delay, the 11th U.S. Circuit Court of Appeals upheld the writ on June 23, 1983. On September 30, 1983 the Circuit Court reversed itself and ruled that the writ should be denied. On March 5, 1984 the Supreme Court rejected the case for the third time.

Moore's execution was set for May 24, 1984. On May 11, 1984 his attorneys filed a petition in Butts County Superior Court, but a writ was denied. The same petition was filed in the U.S. District Court for Georgia's Southern District on May 18th, but both a writ and a stay of execution were denied. Then, on May 23rd (the day before the scheduled execution) the 11th Circuit Court of Appeals granted a stay. On June 4, 1984 a three-judge panel of the Circuit Court voted to deny a writ. After another delay of more than three years, the Circuit Court voted 7 to 4 to override its three-judge panel and rule in Moore's favor. On April 18, 1988, the Supreme Court accepted the case. On April 17, 1989 it sent the case back to

the 11th Circuit Court for review in light of new restrictions that the High Court had placed on *habeas corpus.* On September 28, 1989 the Circuit Court ruled 6 to 5 that Moore had abused the writ process. On December 18, 1989 Moore's attorneys again appealed to the Supreme Court.

Moore's case was described in detail in *Insight* magazine for February 12, 1990. By the end of [1989] his case had gone through 20 separate court reviews, involving some 118 state and federal judges. It had been to the Supreme Court and back four times. There had been a substantial turnover of his attorneys, creating an excuse for one team of lawyers to file a petition claiming that all of the prior attorneys had given ineffective representation. No wonder capital cases cost so much!

Meanwhile, the American Bar Association proposes to make matters even worse by requiring states (as summarized by *Insight*) "to appoint two lawyers for every stage of the proceeding, require them to have past death penalty experience and pay them at 'reasonable' rates to be set by the court."

During an address to the American Law Institute on May 16, 1990, Chief Justice Rehnquist asserted that the "system at present verges on the chaotic" and "cries out for reform." The time expended between sentencing and execution, he declared, "is consumed not by structured review ... but in fits of frantic action followed by periods of inaction." He urged that death row inmates be given one chance to challenge their sentences in state courts, and one challenge in federal courts, period.

LIFETIME TO ESCAPE

Is life imprisonment an adequate substitute for the death penalty? Presently, according to the polls, approximately three-fourths of the American people favor capital punishment. But abolitionists try to discount that figure by claiming that support for the death penalty weakens when life imprisonment without the possibility of parole is offered as an alternative. (At other times, abolitionists argue that parole is imperative to give "lifers" some hope for the future and deter their violent acts in prison.)

Life imprisonment is a flawed alternative to the death penalty, if for no other reason than that so many "lifers" escape. Many innocent persons have died at the hands of men previously convicted and imprisoned for murder, supposedly for "life." The ways in which flaws in our justice system, combined with criminal ingenuity, have worked to allow "lifers" to escape include these recent examples:

- On June 10, 1977, James Earl Ray, who was serving a 99-year term for killing Dr. Martin Luther King Jr., escaped with six other inmates from the Brushy Mountain State Prison in Tennessee (he was captured three days later).
- Brothers Linwood and James Briley were executed in Virginia on October 12, 1984 and April 18, 1985, respectively. Linwood had murdered a disc jockey in 1979 during a crime spree. During the same spree, James raped and killed a woman (who was eight months pregnant) and killed her five-year-old son. On May 31, 1984, the Briley brothers organized and led an escape of five death-row inmates (the largest death-row breakout in U.S. history). They were at large for 19 days.

- On August 1, 1984 convicted murderers Wesley Allen Tuttle and Walter Wood, along with another inmate, escaped from the Utah State Prison. All were eventually apprehended. Wood subsequently sued the state for $2 million for violating his rights by allowing him to escape. In his complaint, he charged that, by allowing him to escape, prison officials had subjected him to several life-threatening situations: "Because of extreme fear of being shot to death, I was forced to swim several irrigation canals, attempt to swim a 'raging' Jordan River and expose myself to innumerable bites by many insects. At one point I heard a volley of shotgun blasts and this completed my anxiety."
- On April 3, 1988 three murderers serving life sentences without the chance of parole escaped from the maximum-security West Virginia Penitentiary. One, Bobby Stacy, had killed a Huntington police officer in 1981. At the time, he had been free on bail after having been arrested for shooting an Ohio patrolman.
- On November 21, 1988 Gonzalo Marrero, who had been convicted of two murders and sentenced to two life terms, escaped from New Jersey's Trenton state prison by burrowing through a three-foot-thick cell wall, then scaling a 20-foot outer wall with a makeshift ladder.
- In August 1989 Arthur Carroll, a self-proclaimed enforcer for an East Oakland street gang, was convicted of murdering a man. On September 28th, he was sentenced to serve 27-years-to-life in prison. On October 10th he was transferred to San Quentin prison. On October 25th he was set free after a paperwork snafu led officials to believe

that he had served enough time. An all-points bulletin was promptly issued.

- On February 11, 1990 six convicts, including three murderers, escaped from their segregation cells in the maximum security Joliet Correctional Center in Illinois by cutting through bars on their cells, breaking a window, and crossing a fence. In what may be the understatement of the year, a prison spokesman told reporters: "Obviously, this is a breach of security."

Clearly, life sentences do not adequately protect society, whereas the death penalty properly applied does so with certainty.

EQUAL OPPORTUNITY EXECUTION

Abolitionists often cite statistics indicating that capital punishment has been administered in a discriminatory manner, so that the poor, the black, the friendless, etc., have suffered a disproportionate share of executions. Even if true, such discrimination would not be a valid reason for abandoning the death penalty unless it could be shown that it was responsible for the execution of *innocent* persons (which it has not been, to date). Most attempts to pin the "discrimination" label on capital convictions are similar to one conducted at Stanford University a few years ago, which found that murderers of white people (whether white or black) are more likely to be punished with death than are killers of black people (whether white or black). But the study also concluded that blacks who murdered whites were somewhat *less* likely to receive death sentences than were whites who killed whites.

Using such data, the ACLU attempted to halt the execution of Chester Lee Wicker in Texas on August 26, 1986. Wicker, who was white, had killed a white person. The ACLU contended that Texas unfairly imposes the death penalty because a white is more likely than a black to be sentenced to death for killing a white. The Supreme Court rejected the argument. On the other hand, the execution of Willie Darden in Florida attracted worldwide pleas for amnesty from sundry abolitionists who, ignoring the Stanford study, claimed that Darden had been "railroaded" because he was black and his victim was white.

All criminal laws—in all countries, throughout all human history—have tended to be administered in an imperfect and uneven manner. As a result, some elements in society have been able to evade justice more consistently than others. But why should the imperfect administration of justice persuade us to abandon any attempt to attain it?

The most flagrant example of discrimination in the administration of the death penalty does not involve race, income, or social status, but gender. Women commit around 13 percent of the murders in America, yet, from 1930 to June 30, 1990, only 33 of the 3991 executions (less than 1 percent) involved women. Only one of the 134 persons executed since 1976 (through July 18th [1990]) has been a woman (Velma Barfield in North Carolina on November 2, 1984). One state governor commuted the death sentence of a woman because "humanity does not apply to women the inexorable law that it does to men."

According to L. Kay Gillespie, professor of sociology at Weber State College in Utah, evidence indicates that women who cried during their trials had a better chance of getting away with murder and avoiding the death penalty. Perhaps the

National Organization for Women can do something about this glaring example of sexist "inequality" and "injustice." In the meantime, we shall continue to support the death penalty despite the disproportionate number of men who have been required to pay a just penalty for their heinous crimes.

FORGIVE AND FORGET?

Another aspect of the death penalty debate is the extent to which justice should be tempered by mercy in the case of killers. After all, abolitionists argue, is it not the duty of Christians to forgive those who trespass against them? In Biblical terms, the most responsible sources to extend mercy and forgiveness are (1) God and (2) the victim of the injustice. In the case of murder, so far as *this* world is concerned, the victim is no longer here to extend mercy and forgiveness. Does the state or any other earthly party have the right or authority to intervene and tender mercy on behalf of a murder victim? In the anthology *Essays on the Death Penalty*, the Reverend E. L. H. Taylor clarifies the answer this way: "Now it is quite natural and proper for a man to forgive something you do to *him*. Thus if somebody cheats me out of $20.00 it is quite possible and reasonable for me to say, 'Well, I forgive him, we will say no more about it.' But what would you say if somebody had done you out of $20.00 and I said, 'That's all right. I forgive him on your behalf'?"

The point is simply that there is no way, in *this* life, for a murderer to be reconciled to his victim, and secure the victim's forgiveness. This leaves the civil authority with no other responsible alternative but to adopt *justice* as the standard for assigning punishment in such cases.

Author Bernard Cohen raises an interesting point: "... if it is allowable to deprive a would-be murderer of his life, in order to forestall his attack, why is it wrong to take away his life after he has successfully carried out his dastardly business?" Does anyone question the right of an individual to kill an assailant should it be necessary to preserve his or her life or that of a loved one?

Happily, however, both scripture and our legal system uphold the morality and legality of taking the life of an assailant, if necessary, *before* he kills us. How, then, can it be deemed immoral for civil authority to take his life *after* he kills us?

INTOLERANT VICTIMS?

Sometimes those who defend the death penalty are portrayed as being "intolerant." But isn't one of our real problems today that Americans are *too tolerant* of evil? Are we not accepting acts of violence, cruelty, lying, and immorality with all too little righteous indignation? Such indignation is not, as some would have us believe, a form of "hatred." In *Reflections on the Psalms*, C. S. Lewis discussed the supposed spirit of "hatred" that some critics claimed to see in parts of the Psalms: "Such hatreds are the kind of thing that cruelty and injustice, by a sort of natural law, produce.... Not to perceive it at all—not even to be tempted to resentment—to accept it as the most ordinary thing in the world—argues a terrifying insensibility. Thus the absence of anger, especially that sort of anger which we call indignation, can, in my opinion, be a most alarming symptom."

When mass murderer Ted Bundy was executed in Florida on January 24, 1989, a crowd of some 2000 spectators gathered across from the prison to cheer and celebrate. Many liberal commentators were appalled. Some contended that it was a spectacle on a par with Bundy's own callous disrespect for human life. One headline read: "Exhibition witnessed outside prison was more revolting than execution." What nonsense! As C. S. Lewis observed in his commentary on the Psalms: "If the Jews cursed more bitterly than the Pagans this was, I think, at least in part because they took right and wrong more seriously." It is long past time for us all to being taking right and wrong more seriously....

SEEDS OF ANARCHY

As we have seen, most discussions of the death penalty tend to focus on whether it should exist for murder or be abolished altogether. The issue should be reframed so that the question instead becomes whether or not it should be imposed for certain terrible crimes in addition to murder (such as habitual law-breaking, clearly proven cases of rape, and monstrous child abuse).

In 1953 the renowned British jurist Lord Denning asserted: "Punishment is the way in which society expresses its denunciation of wrongdoing; and in order to maintain respect for law, it is essential that the punishment for grave crimes shall adequately reflect the revulsion felt by a great majority of citizens for them." Nineteen years later, U.S. Supreme Court Justice Potter Stewart noted (while nevertheless concurring in the Court's 1972 opinion that temporarily banned capital punishment) that the "instinct for retribution is part of the nature of man and channeling that instinct in the administration of criminal justice serves an important purpose in promoting the stability of a society governed by law. When people begin to believe that organized society is unwilling or unable to impose upon criminal offenders the punishment they 'deserve,' then there are sown the seeds of anarchy—of self-help, vigilante justice, and lynch law."

To protect the innocent and transfer the fear and burden of crime to the criminal element where it belongs, we must demand that capital punishment be imposed when justified and expanded to cover terrible crimes in addition to murder.

NO

Matthew L. Stephens

INSTRUMENT OF JUSTICE OR
TOOL OF VENGEANCE?

When we look at capital punishment as an instrument of the administration of justice, we must ask: 1) Is capital punishment evenly applied to all cases of murder? 2) Will those charged in a capital punishment case have both the best lawyers and defense available to them? 3) Is the cost of carrying out the death penalty worth the money spent to execute one person? and, 4) Is capital punishment a deterrent to murder? After all, the latter is ultimately the question our society must answer. If it works, we must carry it out; if it doesn't, it is a ghastly and irrevocable error.

APPLYING THE DEATH PENALTY

In the United States, we experience the tragedy of over 20,000 homicides each year. These statistics are constantly increasing due to the devastating effects of drugs, racism and poverty. Yet, we choose, as a society, only 200, (or 1 percent of all murderers) to receive the ultimate punishment of death. When one looks at the criteria for selecting this nominal fraction of all murderers, the real issues come to light. Who are these people? What is their economic and racial background? What are their legal resources and representation? What is their intellectual capacity?

The facts are clear. Those on death row are the poorest of the poor. They are disproportionately "people of color": African American (40.7 percent), Hispanic (5.72 percent), Native American (1.49 percent) and Asian (0.61 percent), as compared to European/Caucasian. This means approximately 50 percent of all death row inmates are people of color in a society in which all of these populations constitute significant minorities.

Additionally, it is estimated that over one-third of all death row inmates are mentally retarded (with IQ's of less than 70), and that nearly half are functionally illiterate.

It is these poor and oppressed children of God who become the victims of our society's anger and need for revenge. The death penalty is clearly

not equally applied under the law, or under the more significant mandate of moral, ethical and spiritual values of a nation founded on these principles.

In a society that champions human rights and individual dignity in all of our creeds, we are far behind the rest of the so-called "civilized" western world in showing compassion to the poor and oppressed of our country. There are only two countries that still engage the death penalty as justice: South Africa and the United States. Recently, the South African government officially put a "hold" on death sentences and executions.*

There is overwhelming evidence that race is the single most important factor in choosing those who will be sentenced to death. Of the more than 3,000 people executed since 1930, nearly half were people of color. Eighty-five percent of those executed since 1977, when new death penalty statutes were passed, were punished for crimes against white victims. This is true despite the fact that the homicide rate for people of color is roughly 50 percent higher than that of the majority community.

Take, for example, the state of Ohio where 842 people have been executed since 1884. Of this number, only one white man was executed for killing a black person. In 1989, there were 100 people on death row in Ohio: 51 black men, 45 white men and 4 black women. Ohio has not executed anyone since the state reinstituted the death penalty, but the first execution will probably take place soon. Keep in mind that the minimum age for death sentencing in Ohio is 18.

[Since this article was written, South Africa has abolished the death penalty.—Eds.]

Consider the historic case of Willie Jasper Darden, executed March 15, 1988 in Florida's electric chair. He was 54 years old. Willie Darden was sentenced to death for the murder of a furniture store owner in Lakeland, Florida. Darden proclaimed his innocence from the moment of his arrest until the moment of his execution, over 14 years later. Significant doubt of Darden's guilt remains.

Willie Darden was tried by an all-white jury in Inverness, Florida, a county with a history of racial segregation and oppression. The prosecutor's opening remarks in the trial demonstrate the racial implications of this case:

> "... The testimony is going to show, I think very shortly, when the trial starts, that the victims in this case were white. And of course, Mr. Darden, the defendant, is black. Can each of you tell me you can try Mr. Darden as if he was white?"

Throughout the trial, the prosecutor characterized Darden as subhuman, saying such things as, "Willie Darden is an animal who should be placed on a leash." The US Supreme Court sharply criticized this misconduct, but refused to find that it unfairly influenced the trial.

In the face of evidence that those who kill whites in Florida are nearly five times more likely to be sentenced to death than those who kill blacks, the prosecution of Willie Darden becomes the story of a man who may well have been innocent, but whose protestations were overshadowed by the color of his victim and himself.

Finally, consider the case of Delbert Tibbs who went from Chicago Theological Seminary to Florida's death row. Luckily, he did not "graduate" from either. Deciding to take some time off from his studies, he hitchhiked across country.

"White boys could drop out to 'find themselves,'" says Tibbs, "but nobody ever heard of a black man needing to do the same thing." His journey ended abruptly when, being in the wrong place at the wrong time, he was arrested and later convicted for the rape of a 16-year-old girl and the murder of her boyfriend in 1974. He was sentenced to death.

It was only with the assistance of the National Council of Churches Defense Fund attorneys that on appeal, his conviction was overturned on the grounds that it was not supported by the weight of the evidence. However, he was never said to be innocent of the crime. In spite of a US Supreme Court decision that he could be retried, the state decided not to reopen the case on the grounds that the police investigation of the crime was tainted from the start. The original prosecutor said, "If there is a retrial, I will appear as a witness for Mr. Tibbs." Today, Delbert Tibbs devotes his life to his family and to anti-death penalty work across the nation and around the world.

It is more than clear that race is the single-most contributing factor to one being dealt the death penalty. In combination with poverty, lack of adequate legal representation and the drive of society for vengeance, people of color are the common victims of this catharsis of hate and cycle of violence.

QUALITY OF LEGAL REPRESENTATION

The quality of legal representation of indigent defendants in capital cases is of widespread concern. Most capital defendants cannot afford to pay for their own counsel and are represented by court-appointed lawyers in private practice, or by public defenders. Many

times they are given inexperienced counsel, ill-equipped to handle such cases and working with severely limited resources. Many public defenders' offices are overextended with caseloads and cannot devote the time necessary to defend a capital case.

In rural areas, lawyers handling capital cases have little or no experience in criminal law; many are ignorant of the special issues relating to capital punishment. A recent study found that capital defendants in Texas with court-appointed lawyers were more than twice as likely to receive death sentences than those who retained counsel. The trial lawyers of a number of executed prisoners were found to have spent very little time preparing the case for trial. Often, they failed to interview potentially important witnesses or to raise mitigating factors at the proper times.

A good example of this problem is the case of John Young, a black man executed in Georgia. He was convicted in 1976 of murdering three elderly people while under the influence of drugs. He was 18-years-old. His trial lawyer was disbarred from legal practice within days after the trial and left the state of Georgia.

When the lawyer learned of the execution, he came forward and submitted an affidavit to the court in which he admitted spending hardly any time preparing for the case, due to personal problems. He admitted he did not investigate his client's background or raise any mitigating circumstances at the sentencing stage of the trial that might have influenced the jury's decision. These circumstances included the fact that at the age of three, John Young had seen his mother murdered while he was lying in bed with her. He later was placed with an alcoholic rel-

ative who turned him out on the street to survive at an early age.

The US District Court and the Court of Appeals ruled that they could not consider the lawyer's affidavit as new evidence because it should have been presented earlier. John Young died because of inadequate defense counsel. (Reference: Amnesty International "USA: The Death Penalty Briefing.")

THE COST OF CAPITAL PUNISHMENT

Certainly there is the moral cost of taking a life, to make up for the taking of another life. There is no real way to replace one life with the death of another. Yet when capital punishment is the choice of the courts, this is exactly what has been decided.

The moral issue here is: Do we have the right to kill, or is that the right of God only? This does not excuse one who takes the life of another. That is clearly wrong. They will have to answer to the vengeance of their God. We do have the right to demand restitution and protection in the form of taking away the freedom of that individual found guilty of taking a life.

Taking freedom from individuals who kill others has also been shown to be less costly than executing them through our court system. The current debate on side-stepping a lengthy appeal process is nothing more than a rationale to expedite the death sentence while saving money.

In 1972, the Supreme Court of the United States, in *Furman vs. Georgia* held that "arbitrary and capricious" application of capital punishment violated the Eighth Amendment prohibition against cruel and unusual punishment. This means that a defendant has to be prosecuted and convicted in a way that is extraordinarily righteous and free of any kind of prejudice.

This "super" due process requirement has made the prosecutions of capital cases enormously expensive. In a recent University of California at Davis Law Review article, Margaret Garey calculated that it costs a minimum of $500,000 to complete a capital case in California. It costs approximately $30,000 per year to house an inmate in the California system.

Between August of 1977 and December of 1985, only 10 percent (190 of 1,847 cases) resulted in the death sentence. Data from New York State suggests that if it adapted capital punishment, the cost would be $1,828,000 per capital trial. Assuming even a 0.75 percent failure rate, it would cost about $7.3 million to sentence one person to death in New York, compared with $4.5 million ($500,000 × 0.90 percent failure rate) to sentence one person to death in California. (Reference: "Price of Executions Is Just Too High," Richard Moran and Joseph Ellis, *Wall Street Journal*, 1986.)

Cost effectiveness is a weak argument when talking about the value of human life. However, even when put on such a shallow rationale as cost-analysis, the death penalty does not hold up.

It has cost the state of Florida $57 million to execute 18 men. It is estimated that this is six times the cost of life imprisonment. A report from the *Miami Herald* said that keeping a prisoner in jail for life would cost the state $515,964 based on a 40-year life span in prison. It would cost $3.17 million for each execution. The newspaper broke the cost of execution down to show $36,000 to

$116,700 for trial and sentencing; $69,480 to $160,000 for mandatory state review, which is not required in non-capital trials; $274,820 to $1 million for additional appeals; $37,600 to $312,000 for jail costs, and $845,000 for the actual execution.

These figures should make us ask ourselves: Is the need for our vengeance worth all this money when the possibility that we still convict and execute the wrong person exists? What really guides our conscience—the money or the moral issue of state murder and street murder? Whatever side moves us, we must see that the cost of capital punishment is too high. (Reference: "The Cost of the Death Penalty," Illinois Coalition Against the Death Penalty.)

A DETERRENT TO MURDER?

Since capital punishment has been reinstated as a legal sentence of the law, there is no proof that shows murder has declined in any of the states in which it is being used. In fact, some states show an increase in violent crimes.

People who favor the death penalty often believe it helps reduce the number of violent crimes. This may be true if the person who considers homicide would make a rational decision in anticipation of the consequences. This rarely happens because most homicides happen in the "heat of passion," anger, and under the influence of drugs or alcohol.

Studies show that murder rates in states with capital punishment, such as Illinois, differ little from the states that do not have capital punishment, such as Michigan. In 1975, the year before Canada abolished the death penalty, the homicide rate was 3.09 per 100,000 persons. In 1986, that rate was down to 2.19 per 100,000 persons, the lowest in 15 years. In some states, the use of capital punishment increased the crime rate. In New York, between 1903 and 1963, executions were followed by a slight rise in the state's homicide rate.

The recent cry for the death penalty in our country comes more from the need for revenge than for justice.... Could it be that violence begets violence? Could it be that as long as the state is killing, we are sending a message that killing is the way to solve problems?

With all of the various factors we have considered, it is clear, even to the casual observer, that the death penalty does not work. It cannot be taken back, and it is arbitrary in its application and racist in its result. People of faith must take a stand. We must choose the day when we will transform instead of kill, when we will "do justice and love mercy and walk humbly with our God" instead of perpetuating a system that is evil, barbaric, costly and ineffective.

POSTSCRIPT

Is Capital Punishment Justified?

In their arguments, Lee and Stephens cite some of the same facts and figures but draw opposite conclusions. Both, for example, note how expensive it is to keep prisoners on death row for so many years while appeals continue. Lee, however, draws from this the conclusion that appeals should be limited, while Stephens uses it to show that it costs taxpayers less to keep a felon in prison for life than to try to kill him.

Note that Lee does not rest his case for capital punishment on deterrence. He calls deterrence a "bonus" but not a primary justification. What really counts, he says, is whether or not the accused has "earned" the death penalty. For a similar argument developed at greater length, see Walter Berns, *For Capital Punishment: Crime and the Morality of the Death Penalty* (Basic Books, 1979). Directly opposed to the contention that capital punishment is moral is the view of the late judge Lois G. Forer: "Killing human beings when carried out by government as a matter of policy is, I believe, no less abhorrent than any other homicide." Forer's case against capital punishment is presented in her book *A Rage to Punish: The Unintended Consequences of Mandatory Sentencing* (W. W. Norton, 1994). For a moving account of how one condemned man was put into the electric chair *twice* (the first time the jolt was not enough to kill him) after losing a Supreme Court appeal based on "double jeopardy" and "cruel and unusual punishment," see chapter 10 of Fred W. Friendly and Martha Elliott, *The Constitution: That Delicate Balance* (Random House, 1984). *Dead Man Walking: An Eyewitness Account of the Death Penalty in the United States* by Helen Prejean (Vintage Books, 1994) is an impassioned account by a Catholic nun of her friendship with two death row inmates and her pleas for the abolition of capital punishment. Prejean makes all the expected arguments against capital punishment, but the book's power lies in her account of executions. (This story has been made into a motion picture of the same name.)

How often are innocent people convicted of crimes punishable by death? How often are these innocent people executed? In *In Spite of Innocence: Erroneous Convictions in Capital Cases* (Northeastern University Press, 1992), Michael L. Radelet, Hugo Adam Bedau, and Constance E. Putnam describe more than 400 incidents in which they claim that such wrongful convictions occurred as a result of confused eyewitness testimony, perjury, coerced confessions, or police conspiracy.

For further exploration, Bryan Vila and Cynthis Morris, eds., *Capital Punishment in the United States: A Documentary History* (Greenwood Press, 1997) contains hearings, decisions, news stories, and other relevant material.

ISSUE 10

Do We Need Tougher Gun Control Laws?

YES: Carl T. Bogus, from "The Strong Case for Gun Control," *The American Prospect* (Summer 1992)

NO: Daniel D. Polsby, from "The False Promise of Gun Control," *The Atlantic Monthly* (March 1994)

ISSUE SUMMARY

YES: Writer Carl T. Bogus argues that even local gun control laws will reduce the number of gun-related crimes.

NO: Professor of law Daniel D. Polsby contends that not only does gun control not work, it may actually increase the incidence of robbery and other gun-related crimes.

During evening rush hour one day in December 1993, a man named Colin Ferguson boarded a Long Island Railroad train in New York City. When the train reached Long Island, Ferguson pulled out a 9-millimeter pistol and walked down the aisle methodically shooting people in the head. Six people died and 19 others were seriously wounded.

Ferguson's pistol had a 15-round magazine, meaning that he could fire 15 shots before he had to reload his gun. After finishing one magazine, he punched in a new clip and began firing again. (He was finally tackled and subdued by passengers.) He had purchased the pistol, a Ruger P-89, nine months earlier in a hunting-and-fishing store in California. California has a 15-day waiting period before anyone can buy a gun, during which time a background check is run on the purchaser; in Ferguson's case, the gun store added an extra day for good measure. Ferguson supplied all the information requested, then waited. Nothing suspicious showed up during the check, so he walked away with his Ruger after 16 days.

California's gun control law is one of the toughest state laws in America, much tougher than the federal law passed just one month before Ferguson's shooting spree. In November 1993, after seven years of wrangling, Congress finally passed the Brady Bill. For several years, James Brady, a press secretary to President Ronald Reagan who was partially paralyzed by a bullet intended for Reagan in 1981, had been heading a campaign to regulate handguns. The National Rifle Association (NRA) and other opponents of gun control had fought hard against any such legislation, and Republican presidents had

largely agreed with the NRA position that the best way to curb gun violence is not to ban guns but to stiffen penalties against those who use them illegally. But President Bill Clinton threw his support behind the Brady Bill, and during a signing ceremony he and Brady congratulated each other on finally making a breakthrough into meaningful federal gun control.

Brady and his wife, Sarah, who is chair of Handgun Control, Inc., spoke at the 1996 Democratic Convention to endorse Clinton's reelection. On the same day, the president urged extension of the law to forbid the sale of firearms to persons convicted of violent domestic abuse.

The Brady Act, requiring a background check on potential gun purchasers, has resulted in the rejection of 100,000 prospective gun buyers, but criminals can buy weapons on the black market or abroad, obtain them in informal transactions, and steal them.

The year following passage of the Brady Act, Congress confirmed the fears of those who argued that it would be the opening wedge for more gun control. The 1994 crime act included a ban on assault weapons. An assault weapon has a magazine capable of holding many rounds that can be fired each time the trigger is pulled. The 1994 law places a 10-year ban on the manufacture and sale of 19 types of assault weapons as well as copycat models and certain other guns with features similar to assault weapons.

Is it too late to curb gun possession in the United States? There are at least 200 million guns in private hands in the United States, and approximately one-half of all American households contain at least one gun. This has not changed much over the past 40 years, which means that most people who buy guns already own guns. In some rural areas, it is unusual for a household not to have a gun.

Advocates and opponents differ in their assessments of the consequences of gun control laws. Those supporting gun control point to Great Britain and Japan, which have very tough firearm laws and very low murder rates. Opponents respond that low murder rates in these countries result from their cultures. They point to countries like Switzerland, New Zealand, and Israel, where firearms are prevalent and murder rates are very low. Opponents also echo the National Rifle Association's argument that "guns do not kill people; people do." Supporters of gun control point out that it is harder to kill (especially large numbers of) people without guns.

Beyond the practical and factual issues, there is the constitutional question of what the Second Amendment permits or requires. In the following selections, Carl T. Bogus and Daniel D. Polsby focus on the consequences of gun control and reach opposed conclusions. Bogus presents evidence suggesting that, even with other demographic factors held nearly constant, there is less gun-related crime in areas that have gun control. Polsby argues that gun control, by keeping guns out of the hands of law-abiding citizens, may tempt criminals to a more indiscriminate use of firearms.

YES

Carl T. Bogus

THE STRONG CASE FOR GUN CONTROL

While abhorring violence, Americans generally believe that gun control cannot do much to reduce it. A majority of Americans questioned in a 1992 CBS–*New York Times* poll responded that banning handguns would only keep them away from law-abiding citizens rather than reduce the amount of violent crime. Many serious scholars have accepted the argument that the huge number of guns already in circulation would make any gun control laws ineffective. Until recently, it has been difficult to answer these objections. But in the past few years, new research has demonstrated that some gun control laws do work, dramatically reducing murder rates.

Gun violence is a plague of such major proportions that its destructive power is rivaled only by wars and epidemics. During the Vietnam War, more than twice as many Americans were shot to death in the United States as died in combat in Vietnam. Besides the 34,000 Americans killed by guns each year, more than 60,000 are injured—many seriously—and about a quarter of a million Americans are held up at gunpoint.

Measures that demonstrably reduce gun violence would gain wide public support. But that has been exactly the problem: A public that approves of gun control by wide margins also is skeptical about its effectiveness and even its constitutionality. Both of these sources of doubt can now be put to rest.

A TALE OF TWO CITIES

Perhaps the most dramatic findings about the efficacy of gun control laws come from a study comparing two cities that have followed different policies for regulating handguns: Seattle, Washington and Vancouver, British Columbia.[1] Only 140 miles apart, the two cities are remarkably alike despite being located on opposite sides of an international border. They have populations nearly identical in size and, during the study period (1980–86), had similar socioeconomic profiles. Seattle, for example, had a 5.8 percent unemployment rate while Vancouver's was 6.0 percent. The median household income in Seattle was $16,254; in Vancouver, adjusted in U.S. dollars, it was $16,681. In racial and ethnic makeup, the two cities are also similar. Whites

From Carl T. Bogus, "The Strong Case for Gun Control," *The American Prospect* (Summer 1992). Copyright © 1992 by New Prospect, Inc. Reprinted by permission.

represent 79 percent of Seattle's inhabitants and 76 percent of Vancouver's. The principal racial difference is that Asians make up a larger share of Vancouver's population (22 percent versus 7 percent). The two cities share not only a common frontier history but a current culture as well. Most of the top ten television shows in one city, for example, also rank among the top ten in the other.

As one might expect from twin cities, burglary rates in Seattle and Vancouver were nearly identical. The aggravated assault rate was, however, slightly higher in Seattle. On examining the data more closely, the Sloan study found "a striking pattern." There were almost identical rates of assaults with knives, clubs and fists, but there was a far greater rate of assault with firearms in Seattle. Indeed, the firearm assault rate in Seattle was nearly eight times higher than in Vancouver [see Figure 1].

The homicide rate was also markedly different in the two cities. During the seven years of the study, there were 204 homicides in Vancouver and 388 in Seattle—an enormous difference for two cities with comparable populations. Further analysis led to a startling finding: the entire difference was due to gun-related homicides. The murder rates with knives—and all other weapons excluding firearms—were virtually identical, but the rate of murders involving guns was five times greater in Seattle [see Figure 2]. That alone accounted for Seattle having nearly twice as many homicides as Vancouver.

People in Seattle may purchase a handgun for any reason after a five-day waiting period; 41 percent of all households have handguns. Vancouver on the other hand, requires a permit for handgun purchases and issues them

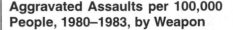

Figure 1

Aggravated Assaults per 100,000 People, 1980–1983, by Weapon

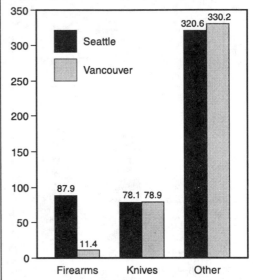

Source: John Henry Sloan, et al., "Handgun Regulations, Crime, Assaults, and Homicide," *The New England Journal of Medicine*, Nov. 10, 1988, pp. 1256–62. Reprinted by permission.

only to applicants who have a lawful reason to own a handgun and who, after a careful investigation, are found to have no criminal record and to be sane. Self-defense is not a valid reason to own a handgun, and recreational uses of handguns are strictly regulated. The penalty for illegal possession is severe—two years' imprisonment. Handguns are present in only 12 percent of Vancouver's homes.

The Seattle-Vancouver study provides strong evidence for the efficacy of gun control. Sloan and his colleagues concluded that the wider proliferation of handguns in Seattle was the sole cause of the higher rate of murders and assaults. The study answered other important questions as well.

Figure 2

Murders per 100,000 People, 1980–1986, by Weapon

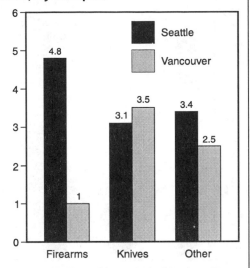

Source: John Henry Sloan, et al., "Handgun Regulations, Crime, Assaults, and Homicide," *The New England Journal of Medicine*, Nov. 10, 1988, pp. 1256–62. Reprinted by permission.

- *Do handguns deter crime?* If handguns deter burglary, the burglary rate in Seattle—where so many more homes have handguns—should have been lower than the burglary rate in Vancouver. But it was not.
- *How often are handguns used for self-defense?* Less than 4 percent of the homicides in both cities resulted from acts of self-defense.
- Perhaps most important: *If handguns are unavailable, will people merely use other weapons instead?* The answer must be "no." Otherwise, the cities would have had similar total murder rates and Vancouver would have had higher rates of homicide with other weapons.

* * *

A more recent study measured gun control legislation more directly.[2] In 1976 the District of Columbia enacted a new gun control law. Residents who lawfully owned firearms had sixty days to reregister them. After the sixty-day period, newly acquired handguns became illegal. Residents could continue to register rifles and shotguns, provided they purchased them from licensed dealers and complied with other regulations.

The researchers compared gun-related violence in the nine years prior to the law's enactment with the following nine years. They also compared the experience within the District with that of the immediately surrounding metropolitan area. The law was, of course, only in force within the boundaries of the District itself and not in contiguous areas of Maryland and Virginia that belong to the same metropolitan area, as the Census Bureau defines it.

The results of the study were surprising even to the most ardent gun control advocates. Within the District, gun-related homicides fell by more than 25 percent and gun-related suicides declined by 23 percent. Meanwhile, there was no statistically significant change in either gun-related homicides or suicides in the adjacent areas. Here again the data demonstrated that people did not switch to other weapons: within the District there was no statistically significant change in either homicides or suicides with other weapons.

Perhaps most surprising of all was the suddenness of the change. Any decline in murders and suicides was expected to be gradual, as the number of weapons in the district slowly shrank. Yet homicides and suicides abruptly declined when the law went into effect. The D.C. law, therefore, had a significant and virtually immediate benefit.

The D.C. study demonstrates that gun control can work in the United States. Despite the similarities between Seattle and Vancouver, some critics of the Sloan study have suggested that Canada and the United States are sufficiently different to make extrapolations questionable. The D.C. study shows that even local gun control laws can be effective in the U.S. Previously, the prevailing opinion was that only national legislation could be effective. Critics said that if local laws blocked handgun purchases, buyers would simply import one from a nearby area. Many people probably do just that, and there is little doubt that national legislation would be far more effective.

Washington D.C.'s gun control law has not transformed the city into a utopia. It has remained a violent city and—along with many other large cities—its murder rate rose sharply in the last few years of the study (1986–88), when the use of "crack" cocaine was increasing. Yet the fact remains that for the full nine-year period after the gun control law was enacted, the mean D.C. murder rate was more than 25 percent lower and its mean suicide rate was 23 percent lower than in the preceding nine years. The effect of the law was not only immediate but sustained as well.

WHY GUN CONTROL WORKS

The gun lobby is fond of saying, "If guns are outlawed, only outlaws will have guns." What's wrong with this picture?

The National Rifle Association (NRA) slogan leads us to envision two groups —solid citizens and hardened criminals —but the real world cannot be neatly divided into good guys and bad guys. Many people are law-abiding citizens until they become inflamed in a domestic dispute, a drunken argument in a bar, even a fender-bender on the highway. Murder is usually an act of rage; it is more often impulsive than premeditated. In fact, 80 percent of all murders occur during altercations and 71 percent involve acquaintances, including lovers, family members, and neighbors. Only 29 percent of those arrested for murder are previously convicted felons.

Rage can pass quickly, but if there is a gun available, even a few seconds may not be soon enough. Of course, enraged lovers and brawlers use other weapons, but it is better to be attacked with anything other than a gun. Guns are, by far, the most lethal weapons. The second deadliest is the knife, but knife attacks result in death only one-fifth as often as those with guns.

For the same reason that it is better to face a knife than a gun in a lover's quarrel, it is better to be robbed at knife point rather than gunpoint. There are good reasons to believe that reducing the number of guns in the general population will reduce them in the hands of muggers and robbers. Prison inmates report that they acquired one-third of their guns by stealing them, typically in home burglaries. There are also people at the margin—not yet career criminals but drifting in that direction—who are more inclined to have guns if they are cheap and readily available. And since handguns are lawful almost everywhere, these people do not even have to cross a psychological Rubicon to get a gun.

* * *

Many of the people at the margin are youngsters. Nearly 70 percent of all serious crimes are committed by boys and young men, ages fourteen to twenty-four. Many of them are not yet

career criminals. They are the children of despair, kids from dysfunctional families and impoverished communities who thirst for a feeling of importance. They are angry, immature, and unstable. In the 1950s, they carried switchblades, but since the early 1960s they have increasingly been carrying handguns. Packing a gun makes them feel like men, and it just takes a little alcohol or drugs, a buddy's dare, or a moment of bravado to propel them into their first mugging or holdup of a convenience store. Many juvenile robbers say that they did not intend to commit a robbery when they went out. The nation will be a less dangerous place if these kids go out without guns.

There is a frightening increase in the number of youngsters carrying guns. The National Adolescent Student Health Survey discovered that by 1987, nearly 2 percent of all eighth and tenth graders across the nation said that they carried a gun to school within the past year. A third of those said they took a gun to school with them every day, which translates into more than 100,000 students packing a pistol all the time. In just the first two months of 1992, more than a hundred firearms were confiscated in New York City schools.

And kids are not just carrying guns, they are using them. New York City was shaken earlier this year when, moments before Mayor David Dinkins was to give a speech to the students at Brooklyn's Thomas Jefferson High School, a fifteen-year-old pulled out a Smith & Wesson .38 and killed two other students. Had it not been for the mayor's presence at the school, the shootings might not have been front-page news.

It is somewhat disingenuous to be shocked about youths with handguns.

Kids emulate adults. They live in a society that has not attached a sense of gravity to owning handguns. In half of the fifty states, handguns are completely unregulated; anyone may walk into a gun shop and buy a handgun just as easily as a quart of milk at a grocery. Most of the other states have only modest handgun regulations; four states, for example, have forty-eight hour waiting periods. Except in a very few locales, automobiles are regulated far more rigorously than handguns.

There are 35 million handguns in the United States; a quarter of all homes have at least one handgun in them. We can tell a teenage boy that he is really safer if he does not pack a gun. But why should he believe adults who keep handguns in their nightstand drawers, even though they have been told that a gun in the home is six times more likely to be used to shoot a family member than an intruder?

For more than a decade some observers, such as Charles Silberman, have noted a rising tide of savagery. Today, for example, my morning newspaper carries a report about a robbery at a local McDonald's restaurant. A man with a pistol demanded the restaurant's cash, which the manager immediately gave him. The robber then told the manager and two other employees to lie down, and proceeded to shoot two to death while one of the three ran away. Not long ago it would have been extraordinarily rare for a robber—with the money in his hand—to kill his victims gratuitously; now it seems commonplace. We may wonder what impels someone to top off a robbery with a double murder, but whatever the motive, the handgun makes that act possible.

* * *

We are also witnessing a bewildering escalation in suicides. In 1960 there were about 19,000 suicides in the United States; now there are more than 30,000 each year. (This represents a rise in the suicide rate from 10.6 per 100,000 in 1960 to 12.4 per 100,000 in 1988.) Nearly two-thirds of all suicides in the United States are committed with firearms, more than 80 percent of those with handguns. The rising number of suicides is due almost completely to firearm suicides. While the number of suicides with other weapons has remained relatively stable (even slightly declining over the past two decades), the number of firearm suicides has more than doubled since 1960.

Why should that be so? If someone really wants to kill himself, is he not going to find a way to do so regardless of whether a handgun is available? This is something of a trick question. The rabbit in the hat is the phrase "really wants to kill himself" because suicide, like murder, is often an impulsive act, particularly among the 2,000 to 3,000 American teenagers who commit suicide each year. If an individual contemplating suicide can get through the moment of dark despair, he may reconsider. And if a gun is not available, many potential suicides will resort to a less lethal method, survive, and never attempt suicide again. Nothing is as quick and certain as a gun. The desire to die need only last as long as it takes to pull a trigger, and the decision is irrevocable.

In the Seattle-Vancouver study, the researchers found a 40-percent higher suicide rate among the fifteen- to twenty-five-year-olds in Seattle, a difference they discovered was due to a firearm suicide rate that is ten times higher among Seattle

adolescents. Other research reveals that a potentially suicidal adolescent is *seventy-five times* as likely to kill himself when there is a gun in the house.[3]

This is the one area, however where the type of gun may not matter. While more than 80 percent of all gun-related suicides are with handguns, research suggests that when handguns are not available, people attempting suicide may just as readily use long guns. But many homes only have a handgun, and reducing the number of homes with handguns will therefore reduce the number of suicides.

WHAT KIND OF GUN CONTROL WORKS?

No one suggests that gun control legislation will be a panacea. Nevertheless, the strong evidence is that the right kind of gun control legislation can reduce murders, suicides, and accidents substantially in the United States.

First and foremost, gun control means controlling handguns. Handguns account for only about one-third of all firearms in general circulation, but they are used in more than 75 percent of all gun-related homicides and more than 80 percent of all gun-related robberies. No other weapon is used nearly so often to murder: While handguns are used in half of all murders in America, knives are used in 18 percent, shotguns in 6 percent, rifles in 4 percent.

Two basic approaches are available to regulate handguns. One is to allow anyone to have a handgun, except for individuals in certain prohibited categories such as convicted felons, the mentally ill, drunkards, and the like. This approach is fatally flawed. The vast majority of people who end up abusing handguns do not have records that place

them in a high-risk category. Whenever someone commits a murder, we can in retrospect always say that the murderer was mentally unstable, but it is not easy to check potential handgun purchasers for signs of instability or smoldering rage. There is no test to give. Many mentally unstable individuals have no record of psychiatric treatment and, even if they do, their records are confidential. Because we want to encourage people who need psychological help to seek treatment, legislation that would open psychiatric records to the government or place them in some national data bank would be counterproductive. Moreover, even someone who clearly falls into a prohibited category, such as a convicted felon, can easily circumvent this system by sending a surrogate to purchase a handgun for him.

* * *

The second approach, known as a need-based or a restrictive permitting system, allows only people who fall within certain categories to own handguns. Handgun permits are, of course, issued to law enforcement personnel, but among the general population someone who wants a handgun permit must demonstrate a special need. Simply wanting a handgun for self-defense is not enough, but someone who can provide a sufficiently concrete reason to fear attack would be granted a handgun permit. Sportsmen can obtain special permits, but their handguns must be kept under lock and key at a gun club. It may inconvenience them, but when public safety is balanced against recreation, public safety must win out.

Many states have similar systems for permits to carry a concealed weapon in public, but in the United States only New Jersey and a few cities have true need-

base permitting systems for handgun possession. Canada adopted this system nationally in 1978....

Handgun registration should be part of a restrictive permitting system. Owners should be required to register their handguns, and a permanent identification number should be engraved on every handgun. All transfers should be recorded. Everyone who has a driver's license or owns a car understands such a system, and even 78 percent of gun owners in America favor the registration of handguns, according to a 1991 Gallup poll.

* * *

With one exception, long guns do not present the same kind of threat to public safety as handguns. The exception, of course, is assault weapons. We remember how Patrick Purdy fired his AK-47 into a schoolyard in Stockton, California. In less than two minutes, he fired 106 rounds at children and teachers, killing five and wounding twenty-nine.

The NRA argues that it is impossible to differentiate an assault weapon from a standard hunting rifle—and to some extent it is right. Both hunting rifles and the assault weapons that are sold to the general public are semi-automatic. With a semi-automatic, firing repeat rounds requires pulling the trigger back for each one; with an automatic weapon, one must only pull the trigger back once and keep it depressed. This, however, is an inconsequential difference. A thirty-round magazine can be emptied in two seconds with a fully automatic weapon and in five seconds with a semi-automatic.

The way to regulate long guns, therefore, is to limit the size of magazines. Civilians should not be permitted to

have magazines that hold more than five rounds. This simply means that after firing five rounds one must stop, remove the empty magazine and either reload it or insert another full magazine. No hunter worth his salt blasts away at a deer as if he were storming the beach at Guadalcanal, and therefore this is no real inconvenience for hunters. But as Patrick Purdy demonstrated with his seventy-five-round magazine in Stockton, large-capacity magazines pose an unreasonable danger to public safety and should not be available to civilians.

The gun lobby urges that instead of regulating handguns (or assault weapons), severe and mandatory penalties should be imposed on persons who violate firearm laws. The weight of the evidence, however, suggests that these laws are not as effective. In 1987, for example, Detroit enacted an ordinance that imposed mandatory jail sentences on persons convicted of unlawfully concealing a handgun or carrying a firearm within the city. The strategy was to allow the general population to keep guns in their homes and offices but to reduce the number of people carrying guns on the streets. After evaluating the law, researchers concluded that, at best, "the ordinance had a relatively small preventive effect on the incidence of homicides in Detroit."[4] The researchers were, in fact, dubious that there was any effect. An analysis of the case histories of more than a thousand persons charged under the ordinance revealed that only 3 percent spent time in prison. With overcrowded jails, judges choose instead to incarcerate people convicted of more serious crimes. This is consistent with other studies of mandatory sentencing laws.[5] . . .

* * *

Blame for the failure of gun control is generally laid at the feet of the NRA, but the problem is not so much a zealous minority as it is a quiescent majority. There has not been a sufficiently clear understanding of why the majority of Americans want gun control but do not want it enough to make it a priority in the voting booth. Much effort has been wasted describing the magnitude and horror of gun violence in America. The gun lobby has taken one broadside after another—from television network specials and newsweekly cover stories—all to no avail.

In talking about the horror of gun violence however, the news media are preaching to the converted. Americans are aware of the level of gun violence, and they detest it. But news specials decrying gun violence may unwittingly have the same effect as the entertainment media's glorification of gun violence. They only reinforce a sense of hopelessness. If things could be different, Americans think, they would be. Otherwise, the carnage would not be tolerated. The media portrayals may also have a numbing effect. Research shows that if people are frightened but believe there is no way to escape or to improve conditions, the fear becomes debilitating.

Majority passivity is rooted in the belief that the status quo is immutable. It is this attitude that gun control advocates must try to change, by communicating the evidence that gun control laws do work. Americans know how bad gun violence is; they must now hear the evidence that reducing the violence is possible.

NOTES

1. John Henry Sloan, et al., "Handgun Regulations, Crime, Assaults, and Homicide," *The New England Journal of Medicine*, Nov. 10, 1988, pp. 1256–62.

2. Colin Liftin, et al., "Effects of Restrictive Licensing of Handguns on Homicide and Suicide in the District of Columbia," *The New England Journal of Medicine*, Dec. 5, 1991, pp. 1615–1649.

3. David A. Brent, et al., "The Presence and Accessibility of Firearms in the Homes of Adolescent Suicides," *Journal of the American Medical Association*, Dec. 4, 1991, pp. 2989–93.

4. Patrick W. O'Carroll, "Preventing Homicide: An Evaluation of the Efficacy of a Detroit Gun Ordinance," *American Journal of Public Health*, May 1991, pp. 576–81.

5. Alan Lizotte and Marjorie A. Zatz, "The Use and Abuse of Sentence Enhancement for Firearms Offenses in California," *Law and Contemporary Problems* (1986), pp. 199–221.

NO

Daniel D. Polsby

THE FALSE PROMISE OF GUN CONTROL

During the 1960s and 1970s the robbery rate in the United States increased sixfold, and the murder rate doubled; the rate of handgun ownership nearly doubled in that period as well. Handguns and criminal violence grew together apace, and national opinion leaders did not fail to remark on the coincidence.

It has become a bipartisan article of faith that more handguns cause more violence. Such was the unequivocal conclusion of the National Commission on the Causes and Prevention of Violence in 1969, and such is now the editorial opinion of virtually every influential newspaper and magazine, from *The Washington Post* to *The Economist* to the *Chicago Tribune*. Members of the House and Senate who have not dared to confront the gun lobby concede the connection privately. Even if the National Rifle Association [NRA] can produce blizzards of angry calls and letters to the Capitol virtually overnight, House members one by one have been going public, often after some new firearms atrocity at a fast-food restaurant or the like. And last November they passed the Brady bill.

Alas, however well accepted, the conventional wisdom about guns and violence is mistaken. Guns don't increase national rates of crime and violence —but the continued proliferation of gun-control laws almost certainly does. Current rates of crime and violence are a bit below the peaks of the late 1970s, but because of a slight oncoming bulge in the at-risk population of males aged fifteen to thirty-four, the crime rate will soon worsen. The rising generation of criminals will have no more difficulty than their elders did in obtaining the tools of their trade. Growing violence will lead to calls for laws still more severe. Each fresh round of legislation will be followed by renewed frustration.

Gun-control laws don't work. What is worse, they act perversely. While legitimate users of firearms encounter intense regulation, scrutiny, and bureaucratic control, illicit markets easily adapt to whatever difficulties a free society throws in their way. Also, efforts to curtail the supply of firearms inflict collateral damage on freedom and privacy interests that have long been considered central to American public life. Thanks to the seemingly never-

ending war on drugs and long experience attempting to suppress prostitution and pornography, we know a great deal about how illicit markets function and how costly to the public attempts to control them can be. It is essential that we make use of this experience in coming to grips with gun control.

The thousands of gun-control laws in the United States are of two general types. The older kind sought to regulate how, where, and by whom firearms could be carried. More recent laws have sought to make it more costly to buy, sell, or use firearms (or certain classes of firearms, such as assault rifles, Saturday-night specials, and so on) by imposing fees, special taxes, or surtaxes on them. The Brady bill is of both types: it has a background-check provision, and its five-day waiting period amounts to a "time tax" on acquiring handguns. All such laws can be called scarcity-inducing, because they seek to raise the cost of buying firearms, as figured in terms of money, time, nuisance, or stigmatization.

Despite the mounting number of scarcity-inducing laws, no one is very satisfied with them. Hobbyists want to get rid of them, and gun-control proponents don't think they go nearly far enough. Everyone seems to agree that gun-control laws have some effect on the distribution of firearms. But it has not been the dramatic and measurable effect their proponents desired.

Opponents of gun control have traditionally wrapped their arguments in the Second Amendment to the Constitution. Indeed, most modern scholarship affirms that so far as the drafters of the Bill of Rights were concerned the right to bear arms was to be enjoyed by everyone, not just a militia, and that one of the principal justifications for an armed populace was to secure the tranquillity and good order of the community. But most people are not dedicated antiquitarians, and would not be impressed by the argument "I admit that my behavior is very dangerous to public safety, but the Second Amendment says I have a right to do it anyway." That would be a case for repealing the Second Amendment, not respecting it.

FIGHTING THE DEMAND CURVE

Everyone knows that possessing a handgun makes it easier to intimidate, wound, or kill someone. But the implication of this point for social policy has not been so well understood. It is easy to count the bodies of those who have been killed or wounded with guns, but not easy to count the people who have avoided harm because they had access to weapons. Think about uniformed police officers, who carry handguns in plain view not in order to kill people but simply to daunt potential attackers. And it works. Criminals generally do not single out police officers for opportunistic attack. Though officers can expect to draw their guns from time to time, few even in big-city departments will actually fire a shot (except in target practice) in the course of a year. This observation points to an important truth: people who are armed make comparatively unattractive victims. A criminal might not know if any one civilian is armed, but if it becomes known that a large number of civilians do carry weapons, criminals will become warier.

Which weapons laws are the right kinds can be decided only after considering two related questions. First, what is the connection between civilian possession of firearms and social violence? Second, how can we expect gun-control laws to alter people's behavior? Most

recent scholarship raises serious questions about the "weapons increase violence" hypothesis. The second question is emphasized here, because it is routinely overlooked and often mocked when noticed; yet it is crucial. Rational gun control requires understanding not only the relationship between weapons and violence but also the relationship between laws and people's behavior. Some things are very hard to accomplish with laws. The purpose of a law and its likely effects are not always the same thing. Many statutes are notorious for the way in which their unintended effects have swamped their intended ones.

In order to predict who will comply with gun-control laws, we should remember that guns are economic goods that are traded in markets. Consumers' interest in them varies. For religious, moral, aesthetic, or practical reasons, some people would refuse to buy firearms at any price. Other people willingly pay very high prices for them.

Handguns, so often the subject of gun-control laws, are desirable for one purpose—to allow a person tactically to dominate a hostile transaction with another person. The value of a weapon to a given person is a function of two factors: how much he or she wants to dominate a confrontation if one occurs, and how likely it is that he or she will actually be in a situation calling for a gun.

Dominating a transaction simply means getting what one wants without being hurt. Where people differ is in how likely it is that they will be involved in a situation in which a gun will be valuable. Someone who *intends* to engage in a transaction involving a gun—a criminal, for example—is obviously in the best possible position to predict that likelihood. Criminals should therefore be willing to pay more for a weapon than most other people would. Professors, politicians, and newspaper editors are, as a group, at very low risk of being involved in such transactions, and they thus systematically underrate the value of defensive handguns. (Correlative, perhaps, is their uncritical readiness to accept studies that debunk the utility of firearms for self-defense.) The class of people we wish to deprive of guns, then, is the very class with the most inelastic demand for them —criminals—whereas the people most likely to comply with gun-control laws don't value guns in the first place.

DO GUNS DRIVE UP CRIME RATES?

Which premise is true—that guns increase crime or that the fear of crime causes people to obtain guns? Most of the country's major newspapers apparently take this problem to have been solved by an article published by Arthur Kellermann and several associates in the October 7, 1993, *New England Journal of Medicine*. Kellermann is an emergency-room physician who has published a number of influential papers that he believes discredit the thesis that private ownership of firearms is a useful means of self-protection. (An indication of his wide influence is that within two months the study received almost 100 mentions in publications and broadcast transcripts indexed in the Nexis data base.) For this study Kellermann and his associates identified fifteen behavioral and fifteen environmental variables that applied to a 388-member set of homicide victims, found a "matching" control group of 388 nonhomicide victims, and then ascertained how the two groups differed in gun ownership. In interviews Kellermann made clear his belief that owning

a handgun markedly increases a person's risk of being murdered.

But the study does not prove that point at all. Indeed, as Kellermann explicitly conceded in the text of the article, the causal arrow may very well point in the other direction: the threat of being killed may make people more likely to arm themselves. Many people at risk of being killed, especially people involved in the drug trade or other illegal ventures, might well rationally buy a gun as a precaution, and be willing to pay a price driven up by gun-control laws. Crime, after all, is a dangerous business. Peter Reuter and Mark Kleiman, drug-policy researchers, calculated in 1987 that the average crack dealer's risk of being killed was far greater than his risk of being sent to prison. (Their data cannot, however, support the implication that ownership of a firearm causes or exacerbates the risk of being killed.)

Defending the validity of his work, Kellermann has emphasized that the link between lung cancer and smoking was initially established by studies methodologically no different from his. Gary Kleck, a criminology professor at Florida State University, has pointed out the flaw in this comparison. No one ever thought that lung cancer causes smoking, so when the association between the two was established the direction of the causal arrow was not in doubt. Kleck wrote that it is as though Kellermann, trying to discover how diabetics differ from other people, found that they are much more likely to possess insulin than nondiabetics, and concluded that insulin is a risk factor for diabetes.

The New York Times, the Los Angeles Times, The Washington Post, The Boston Globe, and the Chicago Tribune all gave prominent coverage to Kellermann's study as soon as it appeared, but none saw fit to discuss the study's limitations. A few, in order to introduce a hint of balance, mentioned that the NRA, or some member of its staff, disagreed with the study. But readers had no way of knowing that Kellermann himself had registered a disclaimer in his text. "It is possible," he conceded. "that reverse causation accounted for some of the association we observed between gun ownership and homicide." Indeed, the point is stronger than that: "reverse causation" may account for most of the association between gun ownership and homicide. Kellermann's data simply do not allow one to draw any conclusion.

If firearms increased violence and crime, then rates of spousal homicide would have skyrocketed, because the stock of privately owned handguns has increased rapidly since the mid-1960s. But according to an authoritative study of spousal homicide in the American Journal of Public Health, by James Mercy and Linda Saltzman, rates of spousal homicide in the years 1976 to 1985 fell. If firearms increased violence and crime, the crime rate should have increased throughout the 1980s, while the national stock of privately owned handguns increased by more than a million units in every year of the decade. It did not. Nor should the rates of violence and crime in Switzerland, New Zealand, and Israel be as low as they are, since the number of firearms per civilian household is comparable to that in the United States. Conversely, gun-controlled Mexico and South Africa should be islands of peace instead of having murder rates more than twice as high as those [in the United States]. The determinants of crime and law-abidingness are, of course, complex matters, which are not fully understood

and certainly not explicable in terms of a country's laws. But gun-control enthusiasts, who have made capital out of the low murder rate in England, which is largely disarmed, simply ignore the counterexamples that don't fit their theory.

If firearms increased violence and crime, Florida's murder rate should not have been falling since the introduction, seven years ago, of a law that makes it easier for ordinary citizens to get permits to carry concealed handguns. Yet the murder rate has remained the same or fallen every year since the law was enacted, and it is now lower than the national murder rate (which has been rising). As of last November 183,561 permits had been issued, and only seventeen of the permits had been revoked because the holder was involved in a firearms offense. It would be precipitate to claim that the new law has "caused" the murder rate to subside. Yet here is a situation that doesn't fit the hypothesis that weapons increase violence.

If firearms increased violence and crime, programs of induced scarcity would suppress violence and crime. But —another anomaly—they don't. Why not? A theorem, which we could call the futility theorem, explains why gun-control laws must either be ineffectual or in the long term actually provoke more violence and crime. Any theorem depends on both observable fact and assumption. An assumption that can be made with confidence is that the higher the number of victims a criminal assumes to be armed, the higher will be the risk—the price—of assaulting them. By definition, gun-control laws should make weapons scarcer and thus more expensive. By our prior reasoning about

demand among various types of consumers, after the laws are enacted criminals should be better armed, compared with noncriminals, than they were before. Of course, plenty of noncriminals will remain armed. But even if many noncriminals will pay as high a price as criminals will to obtain firearms, a larger number will not.

Criminals will thus still take the same gamble they already take in assaulting a victim who might or might not be armed. But they may appreciate that the laws have given them a freer field, and that crime still pays—pays even better, in fact, than before. What will happen to the rate of violence? Only a relatively few gun-mediated transactions —currently, five percent of armed robberies committed with firearms—result in someone's actually being shot (the statistics are not broken down into encounters between armed assailants and unarmed victims, and encounters in which both parties are armed). It seems reasonable to fear that if the number of such transactions were to increase because criminals thought they faced fewer deterrents, there would be a corresponding increase in shootings. Conversely, if gun-mediated transactions declined—if criminals initiated fewer of them because they feared encountering an armed victim or an armed good Samaritan—the number of shootings would go down. The magnitude of these effects is, admittedly, uncertain. Yet it is hard to doubt the general tendency of a change in the law that imposes legal burdens on buying guns. The futility theorem suggests that gun-control laws, if effective at all, would unfavorably affect the rate of violent crime.

The futility theorem provides a lens through which to see much of the

debate. It is undeniable that gun-control laws work—to an extent. Consider, for example, California's background-check law, which in the past two years has prevented about 12,000 people with a criminal record or a history of mental illness or drug abuse from buying handguns. In the same period Illinois's background-check law prevented the delivery of firearms to more than 2,000 people. Surely some of these people simply turned to an illegal market, but just as surely not all of them did. The laws of large numbers allow us to say that among the foiled thousands, some potential killers were prevented from getting a gun. We do not know whether the number is large or small, but it is implausible to think it is zero. And, as gun-control proponents are inclined to say, "If only one life is saved..."

The hypothesis that firearms increase violence does predict that if we can slow down the diffusion of guns, there will be less violence; one life, or more, *will* be saved. But the futility theorem asks that we look not simply at the gross number of bad actors prevented from getting guns but at the effect the law has on *all* the people who want to buy a gun. Suppose we succeed in piling tax burdens on the acquisition of firearms. We can safely assume that a number of people who might use guns to kill will be sufficiently discouraged not to buy them. But we cannot assume this about people who feel that they must have guns in order to survive financially and physically. A few lives might indeed be saved. But the overall rate of violent crime might not go down at all. And if guns are owned predominantly by people who have good reason to think they will use them, the rate might even go up.

Are there empirical studies that can serve to help us choose between the futility theorem and the hypothesis that guns increase violence? Unfortunately, no: the best studies of the effects of gun-control laws are quite inconclusive. Our statistical tools are too weak to allow us to identify an effect clearly enough to persuade an open-minded skeptic. But it is precisely when we are dealing with undetectable statistical effects that we have to be certain we are using the best models available of human behavior....

ADMINISTERING PROHIBITION

Assume for the sake of argument that to a reasonable degree of criminological certainty, guns are every bit the public-health hazard they are said to be. It follows, and many journalists and a few public officials have already said, that we ought to treat guns the same way we do smallpox viruses or other critical vectors of morbidity and mortality—namely, isolate them from potential hosts and destroy them as speedily as possible. Clearly, firearms have at least one characteristic that distinguishes them from smallpox viruses: nobody wants to keep smallpox viruses in the nightstand drawer. Amazingly enough, gun-control literature seems never to have explored the problem of getting weapons away from people who very much want to keep them in the nightstand drawer.

Our existing gun-control laws are not uniformly permissive, and, indeed, in certain places are tough even by international standards. Advocacy groups seldom stress the considerable differences among American jurisdictions, and media reports regularly assert that firearms are readily available to anybody anywhere in the country. This is

not the case. For example,... in Chicago and the District of Columbia, excepting peace officers and the like, only grandfathered registrants may legally possess handguns. Of course, tens or hundreds of thousands of people in both those cities—nobody can be sure how many—do in fact possess them illegally.

Although there is, undoubtedly, illegal handgun ownership in the United Kingdom, especially in Northern Ireland (where considerations of personal security and public safety are decidedly unlike those elsewhere in the British Isles), it is probable that Americans and Britons differ in their disposition to obey gun-control laws: there is reputed to be a marked national disparity in compliance behavior. This difference, if it exists, may have something to do with the comparatively marginal value of firearms to British consumers. Even before it had strict firearms regulation, Britain had very low rates of crimes involving guns; British criminals, unlike their American counterparts, prefer burglary (a crime of stealth) to robbery (a crime of intimidation).

Unless people are prepared to surrender their guns voluntarily, how can the U.S. government confiscate an appreciable fraction of our country's nearly 200 million privately owned firearms? We know that it is possible to set up weapons-free zones in certain locations —commercial airports and many court-houses and, lately, some troubled big-city high schools and housing projects. The sacrifices of privacy and convenience, and the costs of paying guards, have been thought worth the (perceived) gain in security. No doubt it would be possible, though it would probably not be easy, to make weapons-free zones of shopping centers, department stores, movie theaters, ball parks. But it is not obvious how one would cordon off the whole of an open society.

Voluntary programs have been ineffectual. From time to time community-action groups or police departments have sponsored "turn in your gun" days, which are nearly always disappointing. Sometimes the government offers to buy guns at some price. This approach has been endorsed by Senator Chafee and the Los Angeles Times. Jonathan Alter, of Newsweek, has suggested a variation on this theme: youngsters could exchange their guns for a handshake with Michael Jordan or some other sports hero. If the price offered exceeds that at which a gun can be bought on the street, one can expect to see plans of this kind yield some sort of harvest—as indeed they have. But it is implausible that these schemes will actually result in a less-dangerous population. Government programs to buy up surplus cheese cause more cheese to be produced without affecting the availability of cheese to people who want to buy it. So it is with guns....

The solution to the problem of crime lies in improving the chances of young men. Easier said than done, to be sure. No one has yet proposed a convincing program for checking all the dislocating forces that government assistance can set in motion. One relatively straightforward change would be reform of the educational system. Nothing guarantees prudent behavior like a sense of the future, and with average skills in reading, writing, and math, young people can realistically look forward to constructive employment and the straight life that steady work makes possible.

But firearms are nowhere near the root of the problem of violence. As long

as people come in unlike sizes, shapes, ages, and temperaments, as long as they diverge in their taste for risk and their willingness and capacity to prey on other people or to defend themselves from predation, and above all as long as some people have little or nothing to lose by spending their lives in crime, dispositions to violence will persist.

This is what makes the case for the right to bear arms, not the Second Amendment. It is foolish to let anything ride on hopes for effective gun control. As long as crime pays as well as it does, we will have plenty of it, and honest folk must choose between being victims and defending themselves.

POSTSCRIPT

Do We Need Tougher Gun Control Laws?

What does the Second Amendment mean? In its entirety it reads, "A well regulated Militia, being necessary to the security of a free State, the right of the people to keep and bear Arms, shall not be infringed." Does this confer an unqualified right to bear arms? Or is it a right conditioned by the clause preceding the statement of right? Does the militia refer to the people generally, or does it specifically relate to the organized ("well regulated") military bodies of state and national guards and the armed forces?

Wayne LaPierre, chief executive officer and spokesman for the National Rifle Association (NRA), has written *Guns, Crime, and Freedom* (Regnery, 1994), which may be the most authoritative defense of the NRA's unqualified opposition to gun control. Gary Willsin, in "To Keep and Bear Arms," *The New York Review of Books* (September 21, 1995), argues that the constitutional right to bear arms is limited to its military usage.

As far back as 1976, Barry Bruce-Briggs anticipated some of the arguments made by Polsby. See "The Great American Gun War," *The Public Interest* (Fall 1976). For a similar view, see Don B. Kates, Jr., *Restricting Handguns: The Liberal Skeptics Speak Out* (North River Press, 1979). Neal Bernards, *Gun Control* (Lucent Books, 1991) and David E. Newton, *Gun Control: An Issue for the Nineties* (Enslow Publications, 1992) are both attempts to summarize fairly the chief arguments for and against gun control. To put the issue of guns in a larger historical perspective, readers may wish to examine the impact of the American frontier, with its gun-slinging heroes and villains, on modern American culture. Richard Slotkin's *Gunfighter Nation* (Atheneum, 1992) is an illuminating study of this enduring American myth.

In *More Guns, Less Crime: Understanding Crime and Gun-Control Laws* (University of Chicago Press, 1998), John R. Lott argues that weapons in the possession of law-abiding people deter crime. A related defense of gun ownership is examined in the editorial "Gun Availability and Violent Death," *American Journal of Public Health* (June 1997). In a 1993 survey gun owners indicated that in an incident during the previous year, someone "almost certainly would have" died if a gun had not been used for protection. By contrast, 38,000 people died in that year because of injuries due to firearms. The result would appear to be that guns took far fewer lives than they saved. But how exaggerated are the estimates of certain death? How many of the deaths by firearms might have taken place by other means if guns had not been available? The public debate continues.

ISSUE 11

Is Affirmative Action Reverse Discrimination?

YES: Shelby Steele, from *The Content of Our Character: A New Vision of Race in America* (St. Martin's Press, 1990)

NO: Clarence Page, from *Showing My Color* (HarperCollins, 1996)

ISSUE SUMMARY

YES: Associate professor of English Shelby Steele argues that affirmative action demoralizes both blacks and whites and that racial preferences do not empower blacks.

NO: Journalist Clarence Page argues that although affirmative action is not a perfect remedy, it has benefited minorities and, in some cases, increased opportunities for whites as well.

"We didn't land on Plymouth Rock, my brothers and sisters—Plymouth Rock landed on *us!*" Malcolm X's observation is borne out by the facts of American history. Snatched from their native land, transported thousands of miles—in a nightmare of disease and death—and sold into slavery, blacks were reduced to the legal status of farm animals. Even after emancipation, blacks were segregated from whites—in some states by law, and by social practice almost everywhere. American apartheid continued for another century.

In 1954 the Supreme Court declared state-compelled segregation in schools unconstitutional, and it followed up that decision with others that struck down many forms of official segregation. Still, discrimination survived, and in most southern states blacks were either discouraged or prohibited from exercising their right to vote. Not until the 1960s was compulsory segregation finally and effectively challenged. Between 1964 and 1968 Congress passed the most sweeping civil rights legislation since the end of the Civil War. It banned discrimination in employment, public accommodations (hotels, motels, restaurants, etc.), and housing; it also guaranteed voting rights for blacks and even authorized federal officials to take over the job of voter registration in areas suspected of disenfranchising blacks. Today, several agencies in the federal government exercise sweeping powers to enforce these civil rights measures.

But is that enough? Equality of condition between blacks and whites seems as elusive as ever. The black unemployment rate is double that of whites, and the percentage of black families living in poverty is nearly four times that of

whites. Only a small percentage of blacks ever make it into medical school or law school.

Advocates of affirmative action have focused upon these *de facto* differences to bolster their argument that it is no longer enough just to stop discrimination. The damage done by three centuries of racism now has to be remedied, they argue, and effective remediation requires a policy of "affirmative action." At the heart of affirmative action is the use of "numerical goals." Opponents call them "racial quotas." Whatever the name, what they imply is the setting aside of a certain number of jobs or positions for blacks or other historically oppressed groups. Opponents charge that affirmative action really amounts to reverse discrimination, that it penalizes innocent people simply because they are white, that it often results in unqualified appointments, and that it ends up harming instead of helping blacks.

Affirmative action has had an uneven history in U.S. federal courts. In *Regents of the University of California v. Allan Bakke* (1978), which marked the first time the Supreme Court directly dealt with the merits of affirmative action, a 5–4 majority ruled that a white applicant to a medical school had been wrongly excluded due to the school's affirmative action policy; yet the majority also agreed that "race-conscious" policies may be used in admitting candidates—as long as they do not amount to fixed quotas. Since Bakke, Supreme Court decisions have gone one way or the other depending on the precise circumstances of the case (such as whether it was a federal or state policy, whether or not it was mandated by a congressional statute, and whether quotas were required or simply permitted). In recent years, however, most of the Court's decisions seem to have run against affirmative action programs. For example, the Court has ruled against federal "set-aside" programs, which offer fixed percentages of federal contracts to minority-owned firms, although in the past it has permitted them.

The most radical popular challenge to affirmative action was the ballot initiative endorsed by California voters in 1996. Proposition 209 banned any state program based upon racial or gender "preferences." Among the effects of this ban was a sharp decline in the numbers of non-Asian minorities admitted to the elite campuses of the state's university system, especially Berkeley and U.C.L.A. (Asian admissions to the elite campuses either stayed the same or increased, and non-Asian minority admissions to some of the less-prestigious branches increased.)

In the following selections, Shelby Steele contends that affirmative action has not solved the problem of inequality but has simply resulted in a kind of reverse racism, while Clarence Page contends that such programs are necessary to undo the damage caused by centuries of slavery and segregation.

YES

Shelby Steele

AFFIRMATIVE ACTION: THE PRICE OF PREFERENCE

[I]n theory, affirmative action certainly has all the moral symmetry that fairness requires—the injustice of historical and even contemporary white advantage is offset with black advantage; preference replaces prejudice, inclusion answers exclusion. It is reformist and corrective, even repentant and redemptive. And I would never sneer at these good intentions. Born in the late forties in Chicago, I started my education (a charitable term in this case) in a segregated school and suffered all the indignities that come to blacks in a segregated society. My father, born in the South, only made it to the third grade before the white man's fields took permanent priority over his formal education. And though he educated himself into an advanced reader with an almost professorial authority, he could only drive a truck for a living and never earned more than ninety dollars a week in his entire life. So yes, it is crucial to my sense of citizenship, to my ability to identify with the spirit and the interests of America, to know that this country, however imperfectly, recognizes its past sins and wishes to correct them.

Yet good intentions, because of the opportunity for innocence they offer us, are very seductive and can blind us to the effects they generate when implemented. In our society, affirmative action is, among other things, a testament to white goodwill and to black power, and in the midst of these heavy investments, its effects can be hard to see. But after twenty years of implementation, I think affirmative action has shown itself to be more bad than good and that blacks—whom I will focus on in this essay—now stand to lose more from it than they gain.

In talking with affirmative action administrators and with blacks and whites in general, it is clear that supporters of affirmative action focus on its good intentions while detractors emphasize its negative effects. Proponents talk about "diversity" and "pluralism"; opponents speak of "reverse discrimination," the unfairness of quotas and set-asides. It was virtually impossible to find people outside either camp. The closest I came was a white male manager at a large computer company who said, "I think it amounts to reverse discrimination, but I'll put up with a little of that for a little more

diversity." I'll live with a little of the effect to gain a little of the intention, he seemed to be saying. But this only makes him a halfhearted supporter of affirmative action. I think many people who don't really like affirmative action support it to one degree or another anyway.

I believe they do this because of what happened to white and black Americans in the crucible of the sixties when whites were confronted with their racial guilt and blacks tasted their first real power. In this stormy time white absolution and black power coalesced into virtual mandates for society. Affirmative action became a meeting ground for these mandates in the law, and in the late sixties and early seventies it underwent a remarkable escalation of its mission from simple anti-discrimination enforcement to social engineering by means of quotas, goals, timetables, set-asides and other forms of preferential treatment.

Legally, this was achieved through a series of executive orders and EEOC [Equal Employment Opportunity Commission] guidelines that allowed racial imbalances in the workplace to stand as proof of racial discrimination. Once it could be assumed that discrimination explained racial imbalances, it became easy to justify group remedies to presumed discrimination, rather than the normal case-by-case redress for proven discrimination. Preferential treatment through quotas, goals, and so on is designed to correct imbalances based on the assumption that they always indicate discrimination. This expansion of what constitutes discrimination allowed affirmative action to escalate into the business of social engineering in the name of anti-discrimination, to push society toward statistically proportionate racial repre-

sentation, without any obligation of proving actual discrimination.

What accounted for this shift, I believe, was the white mandate to achieve a new racial innocence and the black mandate to gain power. Even though blacks had made great advances during the sixties without quotas, these mandates, which came to a head in the very late sixties, could no longer be satisfied by anything less than racial preferences. I don't think these mandates in themselves were wrong, since whites clearly needed to do better by blacks and blacks needed more real power in society. But, as they came together in affirmative action, their effect was to distort our understanding of racial discrimination in a way that allowed us to offer the remediation of preference on the basis of mere color rather than actual injury. By making black the color of preference, these mandates have reburdened society with the very marriage of color and preference (in reverse) that we set out to eradicate. The old sin is reaffirmed in a new guise.

But the essential problem with this form of affirmative action is the way it leaps over the hard business of developing a formerly oppressed people to the point where they can achieve proportionate representation on their own (given equal opportunity) and goes straight for the proportionate representation. This may satisfy some whites of their innocence and some blacks of their power, but it does very little to truly uplift blacks.

A white female affirmative action officer at an Ivy League university told me what many supporters of affirmative action now say: "We're after diversity. We ideally want a student body where racial and ethnic groups are represented according to their proportion in society." When affirmative action escalated into

social engineering, diversity became a golden word. It grants whites an egalitarian fairness (innocence) and blacks an entitlement to proportionate representation (power). *Diversity* is a term that applies democratic principles to races and cultures rather than to citizens, despite the fact that there is nothing to indicate that real diversity is the same thing as proportionate representation. Too often the result of this on campuses (for example) has been a democracy of colors rather than of people, an artificial diversity that gives the appearance of an educational parity between black and white students that has not yet been achieved in reality. Here again, racial preferences allow society to leapfrog over the difficult problem of developing blacks to parity with whites and into a cosmetic diversity that covers the blemish of disparity—a full six years after admission, only about 26 percent of black students graduate from college.

Racial representation is not the same thing as racial development, yet affirmative action fosters a confusion of these very different needs. Representation can be manufactured; development is always hard-earned. However, it is the music of innocence and power that we hear in affirmative action that causes us to cling to it and to its distracting emphasis on representation. The fact is that after twenty years of racial preferences, the gap between white and black median income is greater than it was in the seventies. None of this is to say that blacks don't need policies that ensure our right to equal opportunity, but what we need more is the development that will let us take advantage of society's efforts to include us.

I think that one of the most troubling effects of racial preferences for blacks is a kind of demoralization, or put another way, an enlargement of self-doubt. Under affirmative action the quality that earns us preferential treatment is an implied inferiority. However this inferiority is explained—and it is easily enough explained by the myriad deprivations that grew out of our oppression—it is still inferiority. There are explanations, and then there is the fact. And the fact must be borne by the individual as a condition apart from the explanation, apart even from the fact that others like himself also bear this condition. In integrated situations where blacks must compete with whites who may be better prepared, these explanations may quickly wear thin and expose the individual to racial as well as personal self-doubt.

All of this is compounded by the cultural myth of black inferiority that blacks have always lived with. What this means in practical terms is that when blacks deliver themselves into integrated situations, they encounter a nasty little reflex in whites, a mindless, atavistic reflex that responds to the color black with alarm. Attributions may follow this alarm if the white cares to indulge them, and if they do, they will most likely be negative—one such attribution is intellectual ineptness. I think this reflex and the attributions that may follow it embarrass most whites today, therefore, it is usually quickly repressed. Nevertheless, on an equally atavistic level, the black will be aware of the reflex his color triggers and will feel a stab of horror at seeing himself reflected in this way. He, too, will do a quick repression, but a lifetime of such stabbings is what constitutes his inner realm of racial doubt.

The effects of this may be a subject for another essay. The point here is that the implication of inferiority that racial preferences engender in both

the white and black mind expands rather than contracts this doubt. Even when the black sees no implication of inferiority in racial preferences, he knows that whites do, so that—consciously or unconsciously—the result is virtually the same. The effect of preferential treatment —the lowering of normal standards to increase black representation—puts blacks at war with an expanded realm of debilitating doubt, so that the doubt itself becomes an unrecognized preoccupation that undermines their ability to perform, especially in integrated situations. On largely white campuses, blacks are five times more likely to drop out than whites. Preferential treatment, no matter how it is justified in the light of day, subjects blacks to a midnight of self-doubt, and so often transforms their advantage into a revolving door.

Another liability of affirmative action comes from the fact that it indirectly encourages blacks to exploit their own past victimization as a source of power and privilege. Victimization, like implied inferiority, is what justifies preference, so that to receive the benefits of preferential treatment one must, to some extent, become invested in the view of one's self as a victim. In this way, affirmative action nurtures a victim-focused identity in blacks. The obvious irony here is that we become inadvertently invested in the very condition we are trying to overcome. Racial preferences send us the message that there is more power in our past suffering than our present achievements —none of which could bring us a *preference* over others.

When power itself grows out of suffering, then blacks are encouraged to expand the boundaries of what qualifies as racial oppression, a situation that can lead us to paint our victimization in vivid colors, even as we receive the benefits of preference. The same corporations and institutions that give us preference are also seen as our oppressors. At Stanford University minority students— some of whom enjoy as much as $15,000 a year in financial aid—recently took over the president's office demanding, among other things, more financial aid. The power to be found in victimization, like any power, is intoxicating and can lend itself to the creation of a new class of super-victims who can feel the pea of victimization under twenty mattresses. Preferential treatment rewards us for being underdogs rather than for moving beyond that status—a misplacement of incentives that, along with its deepening of our doubt, is more a yoke than a spur.

But, I think, one of the worst prices that blacks pay for preference has to do with an illusion. I saw this illusion at work recently in the mother of a middle-class black student who was going off to his first semester of college. "They owe us this, so don't think for a minute that you don't belong there." This is the logic by which many blacks, and some whites, justify affirmative action —it is something "owed," a form of reparation. But this logic overlooks a much harder and less digestible reality, that it is impossible to repay blacks living today for the historic suffering of the race. If all blacks were given a million dollars tomorrow morning it would not amount to a dime on the dollar of three centuries of oppression, nor would it obviate the residues of that oppression that we still carry today. The concept of historic reparation grows out of man's need to impose a degree of justice on the world that simply does not exist. Suffering can be endured and overcome, it cannot be repaid. Blacks cannot be

repaid for the injustice done to the race, but we can be corrupted by society's guilty gestures of repayment.

Affirmative action is such a gesture. It tells us that racial preferences can do for us what we cannot do for ourselves. The corruption here is in the hidden incentive *not* to do what we believe preferences will do. This is an incentive to be reliant on others just as we are struggling for self-reliance. And it keeps alive the illusion that we can find some deliverance in repayment. The hardest thing for any sufferer to accept is that his suffering excuses him from very little and never has enough currency to restore him. To think otherwise is to prolong the suffering.

Several blacks I spoke with said they were still in favor of affirmative action because of the "subtle" discrimination blacks were subject to once on the job. One photojournalist said, "They have ways of ignoring you." A black female television producer said, "You can't file a lawsuit when your boss doesn't invite you to the insider meetings without ruining your career. So we still need affirmative action." Others mentioned the infamous "glass ceiling" through which blacks can see the top positions of authority but never reach them. But I don't think racial preferences are a protection against this subtle discrimination; I think they contribute to it.

In any workplace, racial preferences will always create two-tiered populations composed of preferreds and unpreferreds. This division makes automatic a perception of enhanced competence for the unpreferreds and of questionable competence for the preferreds—the former earned his way, even though others were given preference, while the latter made it by color as much as by competence. Racial preferences implicitly mark whites with an exaggerated superiority just as they mark blacks with an exaggerated inferiority. They not only reinforce America's oldest racial myth but, for blacks, they have the effect of stigmatizing the already stigmatized.

I think that much of the "subtle" discrimination that blacks talk about is often (not always) discrimination against the stigma of questionable competence that affirmative action delivers to blacks. In this sense, preferences scapegoat the very people they seek to help. And it may be that at a certain level employers impose a glass ceiling, but this may not be against the race so much as against the race's reputation for having advanced by color as much as by competence. Affirmative action makes a glass ceiling virtually necessary as a protection against the corruptions of preferential treatment. This ceiling is the point at which corporations shift the emphasis from color to competency and stop playing the affirmative action game. Here preference backfires for blacks and becomes a taint that holds them back. Of course, one could argue that this taint, which is, after all, in the minds of whites, becomes nothing more than an excuse to discriminate against blacks. And certainly the result is the same in either case—blacks don't get past the glass ceiling. But this argument does not get around the fact that racial preferences now taint this color with a new theme of suspicion that makes it even more vulnerable to the impulse in others to discriminate. In this crucial yet gray area of perceived competence, preferences make whites look better than they are and blacks worse, while doing nothing whatever to stop the

very real discrimination that blacks may encounter. I don't wish to justify the glass ceiling here, but only to suggest the very subtle ways that affirmative action revives rather than extinguishes the old rationalizations for racial discrimination.

In education, a revolving door; in employment, a glass ceiling.

I believe affirmative action is problematic in our society because it tries to function like a social program. Rather than ask it to ensure equal opportunity we have demanded that it create parity between the races. But preferential treatment does not teach skills, or educate, or instill motivation. It only passes out entitlement by color, a situation that in my profession has created an unrealistically high demand for black professors. The social engineer's assumption is that this high demand will inspire more blacks to earn Ph.D.'s and join the profession. In fact, the number of blacks earning Ph.D.'s has declined in recent years. A Ph.D. must be developed from preschool on. He requires family and community support. He must acquire an entire system of values that enables him to work hard while delaying gratification. There are social programs, I believe, that can (and should) help blacks *develop* in all these areas, but entitlement by color is not a social program; it is a dubious reward for being black....

Preferences are inexpensive and carry the glamour of good intentions—change the numbers and the good deed is done. To be against them is to be unkind. But I think the unkindest cut is to bestow on children like my own an undeserved advantage while neglecting the development of those disadvantaged children on the East Side of my city who will likely never be in a position to benefit from a preference. Give my children fairness; give disadvantaged children a better shot at development— better elementary and secondary schools, job training, safer neighborhoods, better financial assistance for college, and so on. Fewer blacks go to college today than ten years ago; more black males of college age are in prison or under the control of the criminal justice system than in college. This despite racial preferences.

The mandates of black power and white absolution out of which preferences emerged were not wrong in themselves. What was wrong was that both races focused more on the goals of these mandates than on the means of the goals. Blacks can have no real power without taking responsibility for their own educational and economic development. Whites can have no racial innocence without earning it by eradicating discrimination and helping the disadvantaged to develop. Because we ignored the means, the goals have not been reached, and the real work remains to be done.

NO

Clarence Page

SUPPLY-SIDE AFFIRMATIVE ACTION

Occasionally I have been asked whether I ever benefited from affirmative action in my career. Yes, I respond. You might say that my first jobs in newspapers came as a result of an affirmative action program called "urban riots."

Most newspapers and broadcast news operations in America were not much interested in hiring black reporters or photographers when I graduated from high school in 1965. Nevertheless, I asked the editor of the local daily if he had any summer jobs in his newsroom. I knew I was good. I was an honors graduate and feature editor at the local high school's student newspaper. I had a regional award already glistening on my short resume. Still, I was not picky. I would be delighted to mop floors just to get a job in a real newsroom.

And it was not as if I did not have connections. The editor had known me since I had been one of his newspaper's carriers at age twelve. Still, it was not to be. He told me the budget would not allow any summer jobs for any young folks that year. Then the very next day I found out through a friend that the newspaper did have an opening after all. The editors had hired a white girl a year younger than I, who also happened to be a reporter under my supervision at the student newspaper, to fill it.

Don't get mad, my dad advised me, just get smart. Get your education, he said. "Then someday you can get even!"

My saintly, interminably patient schoolteacher grandmother, dear old Mother Page, also helped ease my tension. "Son," she said, "just prepare yourself, for someday the doors of opportunity will open up. When they do, you must be ready to step inside."

Little did she know that that very summer, riots would erupt in the Watts section of Los Angeles. More than four hundred riots would explode across the nation over the next three years. Suddenly editors and news directors across the country were actively looking to hire at least a few reporters and photographers who could be sent into the "ghetto" without looking too conspicuous.

Many of the black journalists hired in that talent raid, much of it waged on the staffs of black publications and radio stations, would bring Pulitzers and other honors to their new bosses, dispelling the notion that they were mere

"tokens" and confirming the depth of talent that had been passed over for so long. Women soon followed. So did Hispanics, some of whom had worked for years with Anglo pseudonyms to get past anti-Latino prejudices; Asians; and Native Americans.

Times have changed. Twenty-two years after it became the first newspaper to turn me down for a job, my hometown daily became the first to purchase my newly syndicated column. The advice of my elders ("Just prepare yourself") had come to fruition.

You might say that it took me only twenty years to become an "overnight success."

Yet it is significant that I and other "first blacks" hired in the nation's newsrooms felt pretty lonely through several years of "tokenism" before affirmative hiring—or, if you prefer, "diversity hiring"—policies began to take hold at the dawn of the 1970s. The message to us journalists of color was clear: White managers did not mind hiring a few of us now and then, but they didn't want to make a habit of it, not until policies came down from the top stating in military fashion that "you *will* hire more women and minorities."

So, of all the arguments I have heard various people make against affirmative action, I find the least persuasive to be the charge that it makes its recipients feel bad. Stanford law professor Barbara Babcock had the proper response to that notion when President Jimmy Carter appointed her to head the civil rights division of the Justice Department. When she was asked in a press conference how it felt to think that she had gotten the job because she was a woman, she replied that it felt a lot better than thinking that she had *not* gotten the job because she was a woman.

True enough. Most white males have not felt particularly bad about the special preferences they have received because of their race and gender for thousands of years. Why should we? Believe me, compared to the alternative, preferential treatment feels better.

Nor have I heard many express a nagging doubt about their ability to "hack it" in fair competition with others. Quite the opposite, privileged groups tend to look upon their privilege as an entitlement. Whatever guilt or misgivings they may have are assuaged by the cottage industry that has grown up around bolstering the self-esteem of white people. Books like Charles Murray and Richard J. Herrnstein's *Bell Curve* are intended, at bottom, to answer this deep yearning. Much is made in the book about how whites perform fifteen percentage points higher on average than blacks do on standardized tests and that this may easily explain why whites earn more money than blacks. Little is made of how Asian Americans perform fifteen percentage points higher than whites, yet they have hardly taken over management or ownership of American corporations.

Or, as one of my black professional friends put it, "Since we all know that hardly any of us is really all-black, I want to know how come we only got all the dumb white folks' genes?"

The notion that Babcock should feel bad about her appointment is based on the pernicious presumption that, simply and solely because she is a woman, she must be less qualified than the man who normally would be preferred simply because he was a man.

Charles Sykes, in *A Nation of Victims: The Decay of the American Character* (1993), says that those who insist on affirmative action really are arguing that "minorities"

(he speaks little of women) cannot meet existing standards, and that ultimately affirmative action forces all minorities to "deal with the nagging doubt that its policies stigmatize all successful minority individuals."

Another critic of affirmative action, Dinesh D'Souza, resident scholar at the American Enterprise Institute, goes so far as to say in his inflammatory *The End of Racism: Principles for a Multiracial Society* (1995) that most of us middle-class blacks should be stigmatized because we owe our prosperity, such as it is, to affirmative action. He then speculates that middle-class blacks must suffer "intense feelings of guilt" because "they have abandoned their poor brothers and sisters, and realize that their present circumstances became possible solely because of the heart-wrenching sufferings of the underclass."

Yet nothing in affirmative action law calls for the unqualified to be hired regardless of merit. Even "special admissions" minority students are selected from among those who already have met the standards required to do the college's work.

Affirmative action calls only for "merit" standards to be more inclusive. Affirmative action, properly implemented, *widens the pool* of qualified candidates who will be considered. This often benefits qualified white males, too, who would otherwise have been bypassed because of nepotism, favoritism, and other unnecessarily narrow criteria. My favorite example is the University of Indiana Law School's decision in 1969 to broaden its acceptance criteria to open doors to bright, promising applicants who showed high potential but, for the present, had not scored as well as other applicants in a highly competitive field. The goal of the program was to offer a second chance to disadvantaged students like those who could be found in abundance in Gary and other urban centers, but the program was not limited to them. Several white students got in, too. One was a well-heeled De Pauw University graduate named J. Danforth Quayle. He later became vice president of the United States. He apparently had not scored well enough to qualify for the law school under existing criteria, but, like him or not, he did have potential. Some people are late bloomers....

Arguments against affirmative action fall under the following general categories:

"We don't need it anymore." The work of early feminists and the civil rights movement did their job, but now it is time to move on. The nation has outgrown employment and educational discrimination. Nonwhite skin may actually be an advantage in many businesses and schools. The market is ultimately color-blind and would be fair, if only those infernal lawyers and government regulators would get out of the way.

Comment: Americans hate intrusions into their marketplace, unless the intrusions benefit them. I would argue that bias is as natural as xenophobia and as common as apple pie. Until opportunities are equalized enough to encourage women and minorities to have more trust in the free marketplace, there will be a glaring demand for extraordinary measures to target what is actually only a quite modest amount of jobs, scholarships, and contracts to minorities.

"Racism has reversed." This is David Duke's claim. Whites, particularly white males, now suffer a distinct disadvan-

tage in the workplace and in college applications. Affirmative action sets racial "quotas" that only reinforce prejudices. Besides, two wrongs do not make a right.

Comment: Not anymore, Conservative court decisions in the 1990s actually have shifted the burden of proof in hiring, promotions, publicly funded scholarships, and contract set-aside cases from whites and males to minorities and women. If women and minorities ever had a time of supremacy under the law, it is gone. Conservative court opinions have worked hastily to restore white male primacy.

"It cheats those who need help most." The biggest beneficiaries of affirmative action have been, first, middle-class women and, second, advantaged minorities. It misses the less qualified "underclass."

Comment: It is easy to criticize a program that fails to reach goals it never was intended to achieve. The argument that affirmative action benefits those who need help the least falsely presumes affirmative action to be (1) an anti-poverty program and (2) a program that forces employers and colleges to accept the unqualified. It is neither. It is an equal opportunity process that, by that definition, helps most those who are best equipped to take advantage of opportunities once they are opened. I find it ironic that many of the same critics who argue that affirmative action is anti-competitive and bad for business can so quickly spin on a dime to complain that it also is uncharitable.

For example, the biggest black beneficiaries of affirmative action have been working-class blacks who had skills but were shut out of slots for which they were fully qualified in higher-paying blue-collar semiskilled, service, craft, police, and firefighter jobs because of restrictive unions and other discriminatory policies. Before President Nixon signed an executive order in 1972 calling for vigorous affirmative action among federal contractors, few black carpenters, plumbers, and other skilled building tradesmen were allowed to receive union cards. Only when construction boomed high enough to hire all available whites were skilled black tradesmen given union cards, and then only temporary cards, on a last-hired, first-fired basis. Significantly, within months of signing the executive order, Nixon was campaigning for reelection against racial "quotas." His executive order had come not so much out of his best intentions for blacks as out of a keen desire to drive a political wedge between minorities and labor-union whites.

Other examples can be found in the southern textile industry, which, under government pressure in the middle and late 1960s, finally hired blacks into their predominantly female workforce as laborers, operatives, and service and craft workers. "As a result, these black women—many of whom had spent their working lives cleaning other people's homes for a few dollars a day—tripled their wages, an enormous improvement in the quality of their lives," Gertrude Ezorsky, a Brooklyn College philosophy professor, wrote in *Racism & Justice: The Case for Affirmative Action* (1991). "I conclude that affirmative action has not merely helped a 'few fortunate' blacks."

"Be like the model minorities." Behave more like Asians and, for that matter, hardworking immigrant African and West Indian blacks who appear to get along just fine despite racism and without

affirmative action. In one notable screed, backlash journalist Jared Taylor's *Paved with Good Intentions: The Failure of Race Relations in America*, asks the question: Why do blacks continue in spite of civil rights reforms and outright preferential treatment to bring so much trouble on themselves and others with family failures, violent crimes, and drug abuse? Black leaders are no help, says Taylor, for they have become "shakedown artists" who encourage excuses, handouts, and self-pity that generate a "denial of individual responsibility." Why, oh why, asks Taylor, don't blacks simply behave more like Asian immigrants in "taking possession of their own lives"?

Comment: Opponents of affirmative action invented the "model minority" myth to stereotype Asian-American success in misleading ways that don't benefit Asians or anyone else. According to the myth, Asians succeed better academically and earn higher household income than whites despite racial discrimination and without the benefit of affirmative action. Quite the contrary, goes the myth, affirmative action sets quota ceilings on Asian participation, much like those that once limited enrollment of Jews in the Ivy League. So, therefore, affirmative action actually is harmful, both to minority initiative and to Asian success.

It's an attractive myth, but reality is a bit more complicated. There is a significant difference, for example, between *household* income and *individual* income. Asian household income, like the household income of immigrant blacks from the West Indies, exceeds white household income because more individuals in the house are likely to be working. Asian individual income still lags behind whites at every income level, from the bottom,

where low-income Hmongs and many Filipinos, in particular, suffer poverty not unlike that of poor blacks and Hispanics, to the upper levels of corporate management, where a new set of myths continue to stereotype Asians as "not quite American" or "good at rational skills, but not 'people skills.'" Asian-American friends whose families have been here for several generations speak of being asked routinely, "You speak such good English; how long have you been in this country?" More ominous to many Asians are the horror stories like that of Vincent Chin, a Chinese-American who was beaten to death one night in the early 1980s by two disgruntled Detroit auto workers who were angry at competition by Japanese automakers....

"Give meritocracy a chance." Free market zealots like University of Chicago law professor Richard Epstein, who believes all "irrational discrimination" would disappear in an unfettered marketplace, have called for the elimination of anti-discrimination laws, saying the market will punish those who turn aside talented workers or customers with money in their pockets just because of race or ethnicity. D'Souza agrees with Epstein's bold assertion that anti-discrimination laws actually get in the way of women and minorities who would prefer to hire family members. He calls for an end to all anti-discrimination laws except those that apply solely to government.

Comment: "Merit" by whose standard? Market forces do count, but so do culture and personal prejudices. Segregation cost white businesses valuable consumer business, yet, even in the North, where it was required only by local cus-

tom, not by government, many refused to serve blacks anyway.

Any intrusions into the marketplace trouble free-market conservatives like Epstein and D'Souza, but the larger question we Americans must ask ourselves is this: What kind of country do we want? There is no neutral "color-blind" approach to the law that has for centuries been tilted against women and minorities. It either defends the status quo, which is imbalanced by race and gender, it shifts some benefits to certain groups, or it shifts benefits away from those groups. Do we want rampant irrational completely unfair discrimination reminiscent of the Jim Crow days that dehumanizes large numbers of Americans while we wait for the vagaries of the marketplace to catch up? Or do we want to shape law and social practice to encourage people to mix, get to know each other better, and ultimately reduce tensions?

"It encourages balkanization." Affirmative action opens social wedges that threatens to replace the basic American melting pot creed with a new "balkanization."

Comment: Anyone who thinks American society was *less* balkanized in the 1950s and 1960s was not only color-blind but also quite deaf to the complaints of people of color. If there were less racial or gender friction in major newsrooms, campuses, and other workplaces, it is only because there was no race or gender in them except white men.

Racism and sexism have not disappeared, it is widely agreed, they have only become more subtle—"gone underground"—making them less easy to detect, harder to root out. Most of us tend to ignore our own prejudices un-

less someone points them out. If individuals wish to discriminate in their private social world, that's their business. But discrimination in hiring and promotional practices is everyone's business. With the courts already jammed and the complaint mechanisms of the Equal Employment Opportunity Commission suffering backlogs of two years or worse, especially after Americans with Disabilities Act cases were layered onto its already overtaxed, underfunded enforcement mechanisms, promises of enforcement of individual complaints were simply not enough to make up for cruel realities. Even when the courts do reach guilty verdicts, they often impose racial or gender quotas onto the plaintiffs as part of the penalty and remedies. Such court-ordered mandates are, by the way, the only real "quotas" that are allowed under civil rights law and only as a last resort to remedy particularly egregious cases of historic discrimination, such as the police and fire department hiring and promotion practices in cities like Chicago, Memphis, and Birmingham. Yet even these quotas have been quite modest, used sparingly, and, beginning in the 1980s, steadily rolled back by the courts, even while the numbers showed modest progress in the face of the enormous problem.

What most people call rigid "quotas" are actually quite flexible goals and timetables, a distinction that has diminished in the public mind in recent years as conservative politicians have, with remarkable success, attacked flexible goals and timetables with as much vigor as they once reserved for attacking rigid quotas.

"Focus on class not race." In attempts to salvage some rudiments of affirmative action in the face of a conservative on-

slaught, some centrists have argued for programs that reach out to the most needy, regardless of race or gender. If such programs are conducted equitably, a preponderance of minorities will be brought in anyway, without the dubious air of unfairness.

The ghetto "underclass" has not benefited from affirmative action, University of Chicago sociology professor William Julius Wilson writes in *The Truly Disadvantaged* (1987) because this group is "outside the mainstream of the American occupational system." For this group, Wilson advocates macroeconomic policies aimed at promoting economic growth to replace inner-city manufacturing jobs lost since the 1950s and on-the-job training programs.

Each of these arguments has some merit and much myth. Left to our own devices, most of us unfortunately will discriminate, often in ways too subtle for us to notice even when we do it. Either way, such irrational discrimination occurs and is not healthy for a diverse society....

America will not have racial equality until opportunities are equalized, beginning at the preschool level, to build up the supply of qualified applicants for the new jobs emerging in information-age America. The American ideal of equal opportunity still produces rewards, when it is given a real try. It needs to be tried more often. Affirmative action is not a perfect remedy, but it beats the alternative, if the only alternative is to do nothing.

POSTSCRIPT

Is Affirmative Action Reverse Discrimination?

Much of the argument between Steele and Page turns on the question of "color blindness." To what extent should our laws be color-blind? During the 1950s and early 1960s, civil rights leaders were virtually unanimous on this point. Martin Luther King, Jr., in a speech given at a civil rights march on Washington, said, "I have a dream that my four little children will one day live in a nation where they will not be judged by the color of their skin but by the content of their character." This was the consensus view in 1963, but today it may need to be qualified: In order to *bring about* color blindness, it may be necessary to become temporarily color-conscious. But for how long? And is there a danger that this temporary color consciousness may become a permanent policy?

Clint Bolick, in *The Affirmative Action Fraud: Can We Restore the Civil Rights Vision?* (Cato Institute, 1996), argues that racial and gender preferences deepen racial hostilities and undermine individual freedom without doing minorities much good. This argument is also advanced by Paul Craig Roberts and Lawrence M. Stratton in *The New Color Line: How Quotas and Privilege Destroy Democracy* (Regnery, 1995). In *The Color Bind* (University of California Press, 1998), Linda Chavez recounts the battles over California's Proposition 209, a ballot initiative opposed by the author. Columnist Jim Sleeper's *Liberal Racism* (Viking, 1997) is critical of affirmative action and other race-based programs, as is a book by *ABC News* reporter Bob Zelnick, *Backfire: A Reporter's Look at Affirmative Action* (Regnery, 1996). Barbara Bergmann supports affirmative action in *In Defense of Affirmative Action* (Basic Books, 1996), while Stephan Thernstrom and Abigail Thernstrom, in their comprehensive survey of racial progress in America entitled *America in Black and White: One Nation, Indivisible* (Simon & Schuster, 1997), argue that it is counterproductive. Without taking sides in the debate, John David Skrentny, in *The Ironies of Affirmative Action: Politics, Culture, and Justice in America* (University of Chicago Press, 1996), provides an extensive historical account of how affirmative action developed.

Affirmative action is one of those issues, like abortion, in which the opposing sides seem utterly intransigent. But there may be a large middle sector of opinion that is simply weary of the whole controversy and may be willing to support any expedient solution worked out by pragmatists in the executive and legislative branches of the government.

ISSUE 12

Should Hate Speech Be Punished?

YES: Charles R. Lawrence III, from "Crossburning and the Sound of Silence: Antisubordination Theory and the First Amendment," *Villanova Law Review* (vol. 37, no. 4, 1992)

NO: Jonathan Rauch, from "In Defense of Prejudice: Why Incendiary Speech Must Be Protected," *Harper's Magazine* (May 1995)

ISSUE SUMMARY

YES: Law professor Charles R. Lawrence III asserts that speech should be impermissible when, going beyond insult, it inflicts injury on its victims.

NO: Author Jonathan Rauch maintains that there can be no genuine freedom of expression unless it includes the freedom to offend those who oppose the expressed opinion.

In 1942, on a busy public street in Rochester, New Hampshire, a man named Walter Chaplinsky was passing out literature promoting the Jehovah's Witnesses, which would have been all right except that the literature denounced all other religions as "rackets." As might be expected, Chaplinsky's activities caused a stir. The city marshall warned Chaplinsky that he was on the verge of creating a riot and told him that he ought to leave, whereupon Chaplinsky answered him in these words: "You are a Goddamned racketeer ... a damned Fascist, and the whole government of Rochester are Fascists or agents of Fascists." Chaplinsky was arrested for disturbing the peace, and he appealed on the grounds that his First Amendment right to free speech had been violated. The Supreme Court of the United States ruled unanimously against him. In *Chaplinsky v. New Hampshire* (1942) the Court said that his words were "fighting words," not deserving of First Amendment protection because they were "likely to provoke the average person to retaliation."

In 1984 a Texan named Gregory Lee Johnson stood in front of Dallas City Hall, doused an American flag in kerosene, and set it on fire while chanting, "Red, white, and blue, we spit on you." When he was arrested for flag desecration, he appealed to the Supreme Court on grounds of free speech—and won. In *Texas v. Johnson* (1989) the Court ruled that flag burning was a form of "symbolic speech" protected by the First Amendment.

So Chaplinsky used his mouth and was punished for it, and Johnson burned a flag and was not. How do we square these decisions, or should we? If a state can punish a person for calling someone a "Goddamned racketeer," can it also punish someone for shouting racial epithets?

Some municipalities have enacted laws that punish "hate speech" directed at women and minorities. The intention of these codes and laws is to ensure at least a minimum of civility in places where people of very diverse backgrounds must live and work together. But do they infringe upon essential freedoms?

In 1992 the Supreme Court confronted this issue in a case testing the constitutionality of a St. Paul, Minnesota, statute punishing anyone who displays symbols attacking people because of their "race, color, creed, religion, or gender." A group of St. Paul teenagers had burned a cross in the yard of a black family. Prosecutors used this newly enacted law, which raised the essential issues in the case: Did the statute violate freedoms guaranteed by the First Amendment? If so, why? In its decision of *R. A. V. v. St. Paul* (1992), the Court gave a unanimous answer to the first question. All nine justices agreed that the statute was indeed a violation of the First Amendment. But on the second question—*why* was it a violation?—the Court was deeply divided. Four members thought that it was unconstitutional because it was "overbroad," that is, worded in such general language that it would reach beyond the narrow bounds of speech activities that the Court has deemed punishable. But the majority, in an opinion by Justice Antonin Scalia, struck down the statute for a very different reason: because it contained "content discrimination." By punishing speech that attacks people because of their "race, color, creed, religion, or gender," it was prohibiting speech "solely on the basis of the subjects the speech addresses." A statute punishing speech may not single out specific categories like race or creed for protection, for to do so is to involve the state in deciding which sorts of people deserve protection against "hate speech."

In response to increasing incidents of highly derogatory racial, religious, and sexual remarks and writing on college campuses, a number of colleges adopted speech codes that went beyond what the Supreme Court had characterized as "fighting words" in *Chaplinsky.* These restrictions prompted outcries that "political correctness" was stifling the expression of unpopular ideas. Lower federal courts voided antidiscrimination codes at the Universities of Michigan and Wisconsin as overbroad and vague, calling into question similar codes at other public and private institutions.

Against this tendency of the federal courts to define more narrowly the extent to which governments may punish offensive expression in the areas of political advocacy, obscenity, libel, or group hatred, the Supreme Court in *Wisconsin v. Mitchell* (1993) unanimously upheld a hate crimes law. This case was distinguished from hate speech cases in that the speech per se was not punished, but the determination that hatred inspired the commission of a crime could be the basis for increasing the penalty for that crime.

In the following selections, Charles R. Lawrence III argues that speech has the power to inflict injury and curtail the freedom of the victims of hate. Jonathan Rauch defends incendiary speech on the ground that the rights of all are better protected by pluralism than purism, which would curtail all dissenting expression.

YES

Charles R. Lawrence III

CROSSBURNING AND THE SOUND OF SILENCE: ANTISUBORDINATION THEORY AND THE FIRST AMENDMENT

In the early morning hours of June 21, 1990, long after they had put their five children to bed, Russ and Laura Jones were awakened by voices outside their house. Russ got up, went to his bedroom window and peered into the dark. "I saw a glow," he recalled. There, in the middle of his yard, was a burning cross. The Joneses are black. In the spring of 1990 they had moved into their four-bedroom, three-bathroom dream house on 290 Earl Street in St. Paul, Minnesota. They were the only black family on the block. Two weeks after they had settled into their predominantly white neighborhood, the tires on both their cars were slashed. A few weeks later, one of their cars' windows was shattered, and a group of teenagers had walked past their house and shouted "nigger" at their nine-year-old son. And now this burning cross. Russ Jones did not have to guess at the meaning of this symbol of racial hatred. There is not a black person in America who has not been taught the significance of this instrument of persecution and intimidation, who has not had emblazoned on his mind the image of black men's scorched bodies hanging from trees, and who does not know the story of Emmett Till.[1] One can only imagine the terror which Russell Jones must have felt as he watched the flames and thought of the vulnerability of his family and of the hateful, cowardly viciousness of those who would attack him and those he loved under cover of darkness.

This assault on Russ Jones and his family begins the story of *R.A.V. v. City of St. Paul*, the "hate speech" case recently decided by the United States Supreme Court. The Joneses, however, are not the subject of the Court's opinion. The constitutional injury addressed in *R.A.V.* was not this black family's right to live where they pleased, or their right to associate with their neighbors. The Court was not concerned with how this attack might impede the exercise of the Joneses' constitutional right to be full and valued participants in the political community, for it did not view *R.A.V.* as a case about the Joneses' injury. Instead, the Court was concerned primarily with

From Charles R. Lawrence III, "Crossburning and the Sound of Silence: Antisubordination Theory and the First Amendment," *Villanova Law Review*, vol. 37, no. 4 (1992), pp. 787–804. Copyright © 1992 by Villanova University. Reprinted by permission. Some notes omitted.

the alleged constitutional injury to those who assaulted the Joneses, that is, the First Amendment rights of the crossburners.

There is much that is deeply troubling about Justice Scalia's majority opinion in *R.A.V.* But it is the utter disregard for the silenced voice of the victims that is most frightening. Nowhere in the opinion is any mention made of the Jones family or of their constitutional rights. Nowhere are we told of the history of the Ku Klux Klan or of its use of the burning cross as a tool for the suppression of speech. Justice Scalia turns the First Amendment on its head, transforming an act intended to silence through terror and intimidation into an invitation to join a public discussion. In so doing, he clothes the crossburner's terroristic act in the legitimacy of protected political speech and invites him to burn again.

"Let there be no mistake about our belief that burning a cross in someone's front yard is reprehensible" writes Justice Scalia at the close of his opinion. I am skeptical about his concern for the victims. These words seem little more than an obligatory genuflection to decency. For even in this attempt to assure the reader of his good intentions, Justice Scalia's words betray his inability to see the Joneses or hear their voices. "Burning a cross in *someone's* front yard is *reprehensible*," he says. It is reprehensible but not injurious, or immoral, or violative of the Joneses' rights. For Justice Scalia, the identity of the "someone" is irrelevant. As is the fact that it is a *cross* that is burned.

When I first read Justice Scalia's opinion it felt as if another cross had just been set ablaze. This cross was burning on the pages of U.S. Reports. It was a cross like the cross that Justice Taney had burned in 1857,[2] and that which Justice

Brown had burned in 1896.[3] Its message: "You have no rights which a white man is bound to respect (or protect).[4] If you are injured by this assaultive act, the injury is a figment of your imagination that is not constitutionally cognizable."[5]

For the past couple of years I have been struggling to find a way to talk to my friends in the civil liberties community about the injures which are ignored in the *R.A.V.* case. I have tried to articulate the ways in which hate speech harms its victims and the ways in which it harms us all by undermining core values in our Constitution.

The first of these values is full and equal citizenship expressed in the Fourteenth Amendment's Equal Protection Clause. When hate speech is employed with the purpose and effect of maintaining established systems of caste and subordination, it violates that core value. Hate speech often prevents its victims from exercising legal rights guaranteed by the Constitution and civil rights statutes. The second constitutional value threatened by hate speech is the value of free expression itself. Hate speech frequently silences its victims, who, more often than not, are those who are already heard from least. An understanding of both of these injuries is aided by the methodologies of feminism and critical race theory that give special attention to the structures of subordination and the voices of the subordinated.

My own understanding of the need to inform the First Amendment discourse with the insights of an antisubordination theory began in the context of the debate over the regulation of hate speech on campus. As I lectured at universities throughout the United States, I learned of serious racist and anti-Semitic hate incidents. Students who had been victimized

told me of swastikas appearing on Jewish holy days. Stories of cross burnings, racist slurs and vicious verbal assaults made me cringe even as I heard them secondhand. Universities, long the home of institutional and euphemistic racism, were witnessing the worst forms of gutter racism. In 1990, the Chronicle of Higher Education reported that approximately 250 colleges and universities had experienced serious racist incidents since 1986, and the National Institute Against Prejudice and Violence estimated that 25% of all minority students are victimized at least once during an academic year.

I urged my colleagues to hear these students' voices and argued that *Brown v. Board of Education* and its antidiscrimination principle identified an injury of constitutional dimension done to these students that must be recognized and remedied. We do not normally think of *Brown* as being a case about speech. Most narrowly read, it is a case about the rights of black children to equal educational opportunity. But *Brown* teaches us another very important lesson: that the harm of segregation is achieved by the meaning of the message it conveys. The Court's opinion in *Brown* stated that racial segregation is unconstitutional not because the "physical separation of black and white children is bad or because resources were distributed unequally among black and white schools. *Brown* held that segregated schools were unconstitutional primarily because of the message segregation conveys—the message that black children are an untouchable caste, unfit to be educated with white children." Segregation stamps a badge of inferiority upon blacks. This badge communicates a message to others that signals their exclusion from the community of citizens.

The "Whites Only" signs on the lunch counter, swimming pool and drinking fountain convey the same message. The antidiscrimination principle articulated in *Brown* presumptively entitles every individual to be treated by the organized society as a respected, responsible and participating member. This is the principle upon which all our civil rights laws rest. It is the guiding principle of the Equal Protection Clause's requirement of nondiscriminatory government action. In addition, it has been applied in regulating private discrimination.

The words "Women Need Not Apply" in a job announcement, the racially exclusionary clause in a restrictive covenant and the racial epithet scrawled on the locker of the new black employee at a previously all-white job site all convey a political message. But we treat these messages as "discriminatory practices" and outlaw them under federal and state civil rights legislation because they are more than speech. In the context of social inequality, these verbal and symbolic acts form integral links in historically ingrained systems of social discrimination. They work to keep traditionally victimized groups in socially isolated, stigmatized and disadvantaged positions through the promotion of fear, intolerance, degradation and violence. The Equal Protection Clause of the Fourteenth Amendment requires the disestablishment of these practices and systems. Likewise, the First Amendment does *not* prohibit our accomplishment of this compelling constitutional interest simply because those discriminatory practices are achieved through the use of words and symbols.

The primary intent of the cross burner in *R.A.V.* was not to enter into a dialogue with the Joneses, or even with the

larger community, as it arguably was in *Brandenburg v. Ohio*. His purpose was to intimidate—to cast fear in the hearts of his victims, to drive them out of the community, to enforce the practice of residential segregation, and to encourage others to join him in the enforcement of that practice. The discriminatory impact of this speech is of even more importance than the speaker's intent. In protecting victims of discrimination, it is the presence of this discriminatory impact, which is a compelling government interest unrelated to the suppression of the speaker's political message, that requires a balancing of interests rather than a presumption against constitutionality. This is especially true when the interests that compete with speech are also interests of constitutional dimension.

One such interest is in enforcing the antidiscrimination principle. Those opposed to the regulation of hate speech often view the interest involved as the maintenance of civility, the protection of sensibilities from offense, or the prohibition of group defamation. But this analysis misconstrues the nature of the injury. "Defamation—injury to group reputation—is not the same as discrimination—injury to group status and treatment." The former "is more ideational and less material" than the latter, "which recognizes the harm of second-class citizenship and inferior social standing with the attendant deprivation of access to resources, voice, and power."

The Title VII paradigm of "hostile environment" discrimination best describes the injury to which victims of racist, sexist and homophobic hate speech are subjected. When plaintiffs in employment discrimination suits have been subjected to racist or sexist verbal harassment in the workplace, courts have recognized that such assaultive speech denies the targeted individual equal access to employment. These verbal assaults most often occur in settings where the relatively recent and token integration of the workplace makes the victim particularly vulnerable and where the privately voiced message of denigration and exclusion echoes the whites-only and males-only practices that were all-too-recently official policy.

Robinson v. Jacksonville Shipyards, Inc., a Title VII case that appears to be headed for review in the Supreme Court, presents a clear example of the tension between the law's commitment to free speech and its commitment to equality. Lois Robinson, a welder, was one of a very small number of female skilled craftworkers employed by Jacksonville Shipyards. She brought suit under Title VII of the Civil Rights Act of 1964, alleging that her employer had created and encouraged a sexually hostile, intimidating work environment. A U.S. District Court ruled in her favor, finding that the presence in the workplace of pictures of women in various stages of undress and in sexually suggestive or submissive poses, as well as remarks made by male employees and supervisors which demeaned women, constituted a violation of Title VII "through the maintenance of a sexually hostile work environment." Much of District Court Judge Howell Melton's opinion is a recounting of the indignities that Ms. Robinson and five other women experienced almost daily while working with 850 men over the course of ten years. In addition to the omnipresent display of sexually explicit drawings, graffiti, calendars, centerfold-style pictures, magazines and cartoons, the trial record contains a number of incidents in which

sexually suggestive pictures and comments were directed at Robinson. Male employees admitted that the shipyard was "a boys' club" and "more or less a man's world."

The local chapter of the American Civil Liberties Union (ACLU) appealed the District Court's decision, arguing that "even sexists have a right to free speech." However, anyone who has read the trial record cannot help but wonder about these civil libertarians' lack of concern for Lois Robinson's right to do her work without being subjected to assault.

The trial record makes clear that Lois Robinson's male colleagues had little concern for advancing the cause of erotic speech when they made her the target of pornographic comments and graffiti. They wanted to put the usurper of their previously all-male domain in her place, to remind her of her sexual vulnerability and to send her back home where she belonged. This speech, like the burning cross in *R.A.V.*, does more than communicate an idea. It interferes with the victim's right to work at a job where she is free from degradation because of her gender.

But it is not sufficient to describe the injury occasioned by hate speech only in terms of the countervailing value of equality. There is also an injury to the First Amendment. When Russ Jones looked out his window and saw that burning cross, he heard a message that said, "*Shut up, black man, or risk harm to you and your family.*" It may be that Russ Jones is especially brave, or especially foolhardy, and that he may speak even more loudly in the face of this threat. But it is more likely that he will be silenced, and that *we* will lose the benefit of his voice.

Professor Laurence H. Tribe has identified two values protected by the First Amendment. The first is the intrinsic value of speech, which is the value of individual self expression. Speech is intrinsically valuable as a manifestation of our humanity and our individuality. The second is the instrumental value of speech. The First Amendment protects dissent to maximize public discourse, and to achieve the great flowering of debate and ideas that we need to make our democracy work. Both of these values are implicated in the silencing of Russ Jones by his nocturnal attacker.

For African-Americans, the intrinsic value of speech as self-expression and self-definition has been particularly important. The absence of a "black voice" was central to the ideology of European-American racism, an ideology that denied Africans their humanity and thereby justified their enslavement. African-American slaves were prevented from learning to read and write, and they were prohibited from engaging in forms of self-expression that might instill in them a sense of self-worth and pride. Their silence and submission was then interpreted as evidence of their subhuman status. The use of the burning cross as a method of disempowerment originates, in part, in the perpetrators' understanding of how, in the context of their ideology, their victims are rendered subhuman when they are silenced. When, in the face of threat and intimidation, the oppressors' victims are afraid to give full expression to their individuality, the oppressors achieve their purpose of denying the victims the liberty guaranteed to them by the Constitution.

When the Joneses moved to Earl Street in St. Paul, they were expressing their individuality. When they chose their house and their neighbors, they were saying, "This is who we are.

We are a proud black family and we want to live here." This self-expression and self-definition is the intrinsic value of speech. The instrumental value of speech is likewise threatened by this terrorist attack on the Joneses. Russ and Laura Jones also brought new voices to the political discourse in this St. Paul community. Ideally, they will vote and talk politics with their neighbors. They will bring new experiences and new perspectives to their neighborhood. A burning cross not only silences people like the Joneses, it impoverishes the democratic process and renders our collective conversation less informed.

First Amendment doctrine and theory have no words for the injuries of silence imposed by private actors. There is no language for the damage that is done to the First Amendment when the hateful speech of the crossburner or the sexual harasser silences its victims. In antidiscrimination law, we recognize the necessity of regulating private behavior that threatens the values of equal citizenship. Fair housing laws, public accommodations provisions and employment discrimination laws all regulate the behavior of private actors. We recognize that much of the discrimination in our society occurs without the active participation of the state. We know that we could not hope to realize the constitutional ideal of equal citizenship if we pretended that the government was the only discriminator.

But there is no recognition in First Amendment law of the systematic private suppression of speech. Courts and scholars have worried about the heckler's veto, and, where there is limited access to speech fora, we have given attention to questions of equal time and the right to reply. But for the most part, we act as if the government is the only regulator of speech, the only censor. We treat the marketplace of ideas as if all voices are equal, as if there are no silencing voices or voices that are silenced. In the discourse of the First Amendment, there is no way to talk about how those who are silenced are always less powerful than those who do the silencing. First Amendment law ignores the ways in which patriarchy silences women, and racism silences people of color. When a woman's husband threatens to beat her the next time she contradicts him, a First Amendment injury has occurred. "Gay-bashing" keeps gays and lesbians "in the closet." It silences them. They are denied the humanizing experience of self-expression. We *all* are denied the insight and beauty of their voices.

Professor Mari Matsuda has spoken compellingly of this problem in a telling personal story about the publication of her own thoughtful and controversial *Michigan Law Review* article on hate speech, "Public Response to Racist Speech: Considering the Victim's Story." When she began working on the article, a mentor at Harvard Law School warned her not to use this topic for her tenure piece. "It's a lightning rod," he told her. She followed his advice, publishing the article years later, only after receiving her university tenure and when visiting offers from prestigious schools were in hand.

"What is the sound of a paper unpublished?" writes Professor Matsuda. "What don't we hear when some young scholar chooses tenure over controversial speech? Every fall, students return from summer jobs and tell me of the times they didn't speak out against racist or anti-Semitic comments, in protest over unfairness or ethical dilemmas. They tell of the times they were invited to discrimi-

natory clubs and went along in silence. What is the sound of all those silenced because they need a job? These silences, these things that go unsaid, aren't seen as First Amendment issues. The absences are characterized as private and voluntary, beyond collective cure."

In the rush to protect the "speech" of crossburners, would-be champions of the First Amendment must not forget the voices of their victims. If First Amendment doctrine and theory is to truly serve First Amendment ideals, it must recognize the injury done by the private suppression of speech; it must take into account the historical reality that some members of our community are less powerful than others and that those persons continue to be systematically silenced by those who are more powerful. If we are truly committed to free speech, First Amendment doctrine and theory must be guided by the principle of antisubordination. There can be no free speech where there are still masters and slaves.

NOTES

1. Emmett Till, a 14-year-old boy from Chicago, was killed while visiting relatives in Mississippi in 1955. His alleged "wolf whistle" at a white woman provoked his murderer. CONRAD LYNN, THERE IS A FOUNTAIN: THE AUTOBIOGRAPHY OF A CIVIL RIGHTS LAWYER 155 (1979); see also STEPHEN J. WHITFIELD, A DEATH IN THE DELTA; THE STORY OF EMMETT TILL (1988) (recounting story of black teenager murdered for allegedly whistling at white woman).

2. Dred Scott v. Sanford, 60 U.S. (19 How.) 393 (1856).

3. Plessy v. Ferguson, 163 U.S. 537 (1896).

4. Justice Taney, in holding that African Americans were not included and were not intended to be included under the word "citizen" in the Constitution, and could therefore claim none of the rights and privileges which that instrument provides for and secures opined, "[the colored race] had for more than a century before been regarded as being of an inferior order, and altogether unfit to associate with the white race, either in social or political relations; and so far inferior, that they had no rights which the white man was bound to respect." *Dred Scott*, 60 U.S. at 407.

5. In rejecting plaintiff's argument in *Plessy v. Ferguson* that enforced separation of the races constituted a badge of inferiority Judge Brown stated, "[i]f this be so, it is not by reason of anything found in the act, but solely because the colored race chooses to put that construction upon it." *Plessy*, 163 U.S. at 551....

NO
Jonathan Rauch

IN DEFENSE OF PREJUDICE: WHY INCENDIARY SPEECH MUST BE PROTECTED

The war on prejudice is now, in all likelihood, the most uncontroversial social movement in America. Opposition to "hate speech," formerly identified with the liberal left, has become a bipartisan piety. In the past year, groups and factions that agree on nothing else have agreed that the public expression of any and all prejudices must be forbidden. On the left, protesters and editorialists have insisted that Francis L. Lawrence resign as president of Rutgers University for describing blacks as "a disadvantaged population that doesn't have that genetic, hereditary background to have a higher average." On the other side of the ideological divide, Ralph Reed, the executive director of the Christian Coalition, responded to criticism of the religious right by calling a press conference to denounce a supposed outbreak of "name-calling, scapegoating, and religious bigotry." Craig Rogers, an evangelical Christian student at California State University, recently filed a $2.5 million sexual-harassment suit against a lesbian professor of psychology, claiming that anti-male bias in one of her lectures violated campus rules and left him feeling "raped and trapped."

In universities and on Capitol Hill, in workplaces and newsrooms, authorities are declaring that there is no place for racism, sexism, homophobia, Christian-bashing, and other forms of prejudice in public debate or even in private thought. "Only when racism and other forms of prejudice are expunged," say the crusaders for sweetness and light, "can minorities be safe and society be fair." So sweet, this dream of a world without prejudice. But the very last thing society should do is seek to utterly eradicate racism and other forms of prejudice....

Indeed, "eradicating prejudice" is so vague a proposition as to be meaningless. Distinguishing prejudice reliably and nonpolitically from non-prejudice, or even defining it crisply, is quite hopeless. We all feel we know prejudice when we see it. But do we? At the University of Michigan, a student said in a classroom discussion that he considered homosexuality a disease treat-

able with therapy. He was summoned to a formal disciplinary hearing for violating the school's policy against speech that "victimizes" people based on "sexual orientation." Now, the evidence is abundant that this particular hypothesis is wrong, and any American homosexual can attest to the harm that the student's hypothesis has inflicted on many real people. But was it a statement of prejudice or of misguided belief? Hate speech or hypothesis? Many Americans who do not regard themselves as bigots or haters believe that homosexuality is a treatable disease. They may be wrong, but are they all bigots? I am unwilling to say so, and if you are willing, beware. The line between a prejudiced belief and a merely controversial one is elusive, and the harder you look the more elusive it becomes. "God hates homosexuals" is a statement of fact, not of bias, to those who believe it; "American criminals are disproportionately black" is a statement of bias, not of fact, to those who disbelieve it. . . .

Pluralism is the principle that protects and makes a place in human company for that loneliest and most vulnerable of all minorities, the minority who is hounded and despised among blacks and whites, gays and straights, who is suspect or criminal among every tribe and in every nation of the world, and yet on whom progress depends: the dissident. I am not saying that dissent is always or even usually enlightened. Most of the time it is foolish and self-serving. No dissident has the right to be taken seriously, and the fact that Aryan Nation racists or Nation of Islam anti-Semites are unorthodox does not entitle them to respect. But what goes around comes around. As a supporter of gay marriage, for example, I reject the majority's view

of family, and as a Jew I reject its view of God. I try to be civil, but the fact is that most Americans regard my views on marriage as a reckless assault on the most fundamental of all institutions, and many people are more than a little discomfited by the statement "Jesus Christ was no more divine than anybody else" (which is why so few people ever say it). Trap the racists and anti-Semites, and you lay a trap for me too. Hunt for them with eradication in your mind, and you have brought dissent itself within your sights.

The new crusade against prejudice waves aside such warnings. Like earlier crusades against antisocial ideas, the mission is fueled by good (if cocksure) intentions and a genuine sense of urgency. Some kinds of error are held to be intolerable, like pollutants that even in small traces poison the water for a whole town. Some errors are so pernicious as to damage real people's lives, so wrongheaded that no person of right mind or goodwill could support them. Like their forebears of other stripe—the Church in its campaigns against heretics, the McCarthyites in their campaigns against Communists —the modern anti-racist and anti-sexist and anti-homophobic campaigners are totalists, demanding not that misguided ideas and ugly expressions be corrected or criticized but that they be eradicated. They make war not on errors but on error, and like other totalists they act in the name of public safety—the safety, especially, of minorities.

* * *

The sweeping implications of this challenge to pluralism are not, I think, well enough understood by the public at large. Indeed, the new brand of totalism has yet even to be properly named. "Multiculturalism," for instance, is much too broad

"Political correctness" comes closer but is too trendy and snide. For lack of anything else, I will call the new anti-pluralism "purism," since its major tenet is that society cannot be just until the last traces of invidious prejudice have been scrubbed away. Whatever you call it, the purists' way of seeing things has spread through American intellectual life with remarkable speed, so much so that many people will blink at you uncomprehendingly or even call you a racist (or sexist or homophobe, etc.) if you suggest that expressions of racism should be tolerated or that prejudice has its part to play. . . .

* * *

What is especially dismaying is that the purists pursue prejudice in the name of protecting minorities. In order to protect people like me (homosexual), they must pursue people like me (dissident). In order to bolster minority self-esteem, they suppress minority opinion. There are, of course, all kinds of practical and legal problems with the purists' campaign: the incursions against the First Amendment; the inevitable abuses by prosecutors and activists who define as "hateful" or "violent" whatever speech they dislike or can score points off of; the lack of any evidence that repressing prejudice eliminates rather than inflames it. But minorities, of all people, ought to remember that by definition we cannot prevail by numbers, and we generally cannot prevail by force. Against the power of ignorant mass opinion and group prejudice and superstition, we have only our voices. If you doubt that minorities' voices are powerful weapons, think of the lengths to which Southern officials went to silence the Reverend Martin Luther King Jr. (recall that the city commissioner of Montgomery, Alabama, won a $500,000 libel suit, later

overturned in *New York Times v. Sullivan* [1964], regarding an advertisement in the *Times* placed by civil-rights leaders who denounced the Montgomery police). Think of how much gay people have improved their lot over twenty-five years simply by refusing to remain silent. Recall the Michigan student who was prosecuted for saying that homosexuality is a treatable disease, and notice that he was black. Under that Michigan speech code, more than twenty blacks were charged with racist speech, while no instance of racist speech by whites was punished. In Florida, the hate-speech law was invoked against a black man who called a policeman a "white cracker"; not so surprisingly, in the first hate-crimes case to reach the Supreme Court, the victim was white and the defendant black.

In the escalating war against "prejudice," the right is already learning to play by the rules that were pioneered by the purist activists of the left. Last year leading Democrats, including the President, criticized the Republican Party for being increasingly in the thrall of the Christian right. Some of the rhetoric was harsh ("fire-breathing Christian radical right"), but it wasn't vicious or even clearly wrong. Never mind: when Democratic Representative Vic Fazio said Republicans were "being forced to the fringes by the aggressive political tactics of the religious right," the chairman of the Republican National Committee, Haley Barbour, said, "Christian-bashing" was the "left's" preferred form of religious bigotry. Bigotry! Prejudice! "Christians active in politics are now on the receiving end of an extraordinary campaign of bias and prejudice," said the conservative leader William J. Bennett. One discerns, here, where the new purism leads. Eventually,

any criticism of any group will be "prejudice."

Here is the ultimate irony of the new purism: words, which pluralists hope can be substituted for violence, are redefined by purists *as* violence. "The experience of being called 'nigger,' 'spic,' 'Jap,' or 'kike' is like receiving a slap in the face," Charles Lawrence wrote in 1990. "Psychic injury is no less an injury than being struck in the face, and it often is far more severe." This kind of talk is commonplace today. Epithets, insults, often even polite expressions of what's taken to be prejudice are called by purists "assaultive speech," "words that wound," "verbal violence." "To me, racial epithets are not speech," one University of Michigan law professor said. "They are bullets." In her speech accepting the 1993 Nobel Prize for Literature in Stockholm, Sweden, the author Toni Morrison said this: "Oppressive language does more than represent violence; it is violence."

It is not violence. I am thinking back to a moment on the subway in Washington, a little thing. I was riding home late one night and a squad of noisy kids, maybe seventeen or eighteen years old, noisily piled into the car. They yelled across the car and a girl said, "Where do we get off?"

A boy said, "Farragut North."

The girl: "*Faggot* North!"

The boy: "Yeah! Faggot North!"

General hilarity.

First, before the intellect resumes control, there is a moment of fear, an animal moment. Who are they? How many of them? How dangerous? Where is the way out? All of these things are noted preverbally and assessed by the gut. Then the brain begins an assessment: they are sober, this is probably too public a place for them to do it, there are more girls than

boys, they were just talking, it is probably nothing.

They didn't notice me and there was no incident. The teenage babble flowed on, leaving me to think. I became interested in my own reaction: the jump of fear out of nowhere like an alert animal, the sense for a brief time that one is naked and alone and should hide or run away. For a time, one ceases to be a human being and becomes instead a faggot.

* * *

The fear engendered by these words is real. The remedy is as clear and as imperfect as ever: protect citizens against violence. This, I grant, is something that American society has never done very well and now does quite poorly. It is no solution to define words as violence or prejudice as oppression, and then by cracking down on words or thoughts pretend that we are doing something about violence and oppression. No doubt it is easier to pass a speech code or hate-crimes law and proclaim the streets safer than actually to make the streets safer, but the one must never be confused with the other. Every cop or prosecutor chasing words is one fewer chasing criminals. In a world rife with real violence and oppression, full of Rwandas and Bosnias and eleven-year-olds spraying bullets at children in Chicago and in turn being executed by gang lords, it is odious of Toni Morrison to say that words are violence.

Indeed, equating "verbal violence" with physical violence is a treacherous, mischievous business. Not long ago a writer was charged with viciously and gratuitously wounding the feelings and dignity of millions of people. He was charged, in effect, with exhibiting flagrant prejudice against Muslims and out

rageously slandering their beliefs. "What is freedom of expression?" mused Salman Rushdie a year after the ayatollahs sentenced him to death and put a price on his head. "Without the freedom to offend, it ceases to exist." I can think of nothing sadder than that minority activists, in their haste to make the world better, should be the ones to forget the lesson of Rushdie's plight: for minorities, pluralism, not purism, is the answer. The campaigns to eradicate prejudice—all of them, the speech codes and workplace restrictions and mandatory therapy for accused bigots and all the rest—should stop, now. The whole objective of eradicating prejudice, as opposed to correcting and criticizing it, should be repudiated as a fool's errand. Salman Rushdie is right, Toni Morrison wrong, and minorities belong at his side, not hers.

POSTSCRIPT

Should Hate Speech Be Punished?

Many forms of hate speech are punished in countries other than the United States, but other democracies do not have the American tradition of freedom of opinion and expression. At the same time, the United States has more races, religions, and nationalities than other countries, giving rise to suspicion, prejudice, and hostility.

On one hand, this diversity has given rise to sharp political disagreement on issues relating to race, religion, women, homosexuals, and others. On the other hand, this diversity has stimulated greater sensitivity to the claims of these groups for equal treatment and social justice. Free speech on controversial issues risks giving offense. At what point, if any, does giving offense curtail the liberty of the offended group? Should such speech be punished?

Nowhere have these questions provoked greater controversy than on college campuses. Do college codes inhibiting or punishing racist, sexist, or other biased speech protect the liberty of the victims of these insults or injuries? Or do they prevent the examination of disapproved beliefs and threaten the suppression of other unpopular ideas?

When the U.S. Supreme Court unanimously upheld the Wisconsin hate crimes law, it was reversing an opinion of the Wisconsin Supreme Court. The American Civil Liberties Union concluded that the law did not inhibit free expression, but the Ohio Civil Liberties Union believed that it did. Edward J. Cleary's *Beyond the Burning Cross: The First Amendment and the Landmark R. A. V. Case* (Random House, 1994) is an account of the attorney who represented the accused youth in *R. A. V. v. St. Paul*. Robert J. Kelly, ed., *Bias Crime: American Law Enforcement and Legal Responses*, rev. ed. (Office of International Criminal Justice, 1993) includes essays on a variety of issues, including religious and gay bias, bias on college campuses, and the Rodney King case, in which four white Los Angeles police officers were filmed beating a black suspect.

Arguing for absolute freedom of expression is Nat Hentoff, *Free Speech for Me—But Not for Thee: How the American Left and Right Relentlessly Censor Each Other* (HarperCollins, 1992). Less absolutist in defending all speech is Cass R. Sunstein, in *Democracy and the Problem of Free Speech* (Free Press, 1993), who attempts to define a distinction between protected and unprotected speech. A case for suppressing speech based on what the authors call "critical race theory" can be found in the essays in Mari J. Matsuda et al., *Words That Wound: Critical Race Theory, Assaultive Speech, and the First Amendment* (Westview Press, 1993).

A somewhat similar argument is developed by Richard Delgado and Jean Stefancic in *Must We Defend Nazis? Hate Speech, Pornography, and the First Amendment* (New York University Press, 1996). The authors insist that free speech must always be weighed against the sometimes-competing values of human dignity and equality. Judith Butler, in *Excitable Speech: A Politics of the Performance* (Routledge, 1997), examines the linguistics of hate and reflects on the implications of speech as a form of conduct. Milton Heumann et al., eds., *Hate Speech on Campus: Cases, Case Studies, and Commentary* (Northeastern University Press, 1997) reprints some classic Supreme Court opinions on free speech as well as excerpts from essays by John Stuart Mill, Herbert Marcuse, and others who have struggled with the question of whether or not freedom should be allowed for "words that wound."

ISSUE 13

Is Welfare Reform Succeeding?

YES: Daniel Casse, from "Why Welfare Reform Is Working," *Commentary* (September 1997)

NO: Peter Edelman, from "The Worst Thing Bill Clinton Has Done," *The Atlantic Monthly* (March 1997)

ISSUE SUMMARY

YES: Policy analyst Daniel Casse argues that the 1996 overhaul of welfare has encouraged long-term welfare clients to find meaningful jobs and to better their lives.

NO: Peter Edelman, a former adviser for the Clinton administration, maintains that the 1996 welfare overhaul will have a multitude of adverse consequences, including an increase in malnutrition, crime, drug and alcohol abuse, and family violence.

No social problem seems more intractable than poverty. Even in America's current upbeat economy, more than 36 million Americans live below the official poverty line (about $15,000 for a family of four). Most are white (though one-third are black), and the largest single age group is children; more than 15 million poor people are under the age of 18, living in families headed by single mothers.

Traditionally, poor families were helped largely through private charities or, at most, by local and state government programs. But in the 1930s the Roosevelt administration established a variety of national antipoverty programs, including public employment projects, old-age pensions, and help for single mothers and their children. This latter aid category has generated much of the controversy over "welfare." The Social Security Act of 1935 contained a provision, later called Aid to Families with Dependent Children (AFDC), that provided grants to needy families who lacked a breadwinner.

AFDC grants were based on the principle of *entitlement*, which meant that there would be a federally defined guarantee of assistance to families with children who met a state's statutory definition of need. It would also guarantee to the state matching grants to help the state pay for assistance to these families. Little was made of AFDC at the time because divorce was rare and the illegitimacy rate was only about 4 percent. The typical AFDC family in 1935 was not that of a "welfare mother" but a "widow lady" struggling to feed her family after the death of her husband. It was also assumed that the

assistance would be of short duration, sufficient to tide things over until the mother remarried, found a job, or moved in with relatives.

Within 30 years, however, the whole context of the program was radically transformed: by the mid-1960s the major category of AFDC recipients consisted of unmarried women and their children, and a substantial portion of them stayed on welfare for many years.

Criticism of AFDC had been building for many years. The main criticism was that it was fostering dependency by handing out money without requiring any work for it. It was the frequent target of Republican politicians, and even many Democrats conceded that the program needed reform. When he first ran for president in 1992, Bill Clinton promised to "end welfare as we know it." He proposed a strict, two-year time limit for people to get off welfare and into productive work. When the Republicans took over Congress in 1995 they decided to put this pledge to the test. During the next year they passed two different versions of welfare reform, both of which Clinton vetoed. But in August 1996 Clinton signed a third version, called the Personal Responsibility Act, which is now part of U.S. public law. The following are among its key provisions:

- It abolishes AFDC, the federally guaranteed program of cash assistance to poor children. Instead, states will get lump sums of federal money to run their own welfare and work-training programs.
- It requires the head of every family to go to work within two years or lose benefits.
- It limits lifetime benefits to five years in most cases.
- It limits the amount of food stamps available to adults who are not raising children.

The signing of this act set off a furious debate on what the effects of the new law would be. Supporters heralded it as a liberation of the poor from the Washington bureaucracy; opponents decried it as a shameful abdication of responsibility that will cause social misery.

In the selections that follow, policy analyst Daniel Casse argues that the 1996 overhaul of welfare has encouraged long-term welfare clients to find meaningful jobs and to better their lives. Peter Edelman, a former Clinton administration official who resigned after Clinton signed the bill, argues that it will produce catastrophic consequences, including an increase in malnutrition, crime, drug and alcohol abuse, and family violence.

YES

Daniel Casse

WHY WELFARE REFORM IS WORKING

On July 1, [1997], the "end of welfare as we know it," began in earnest. On that day, the federal legislation that President Clinton had signed nearly a year earlier went into effect, terminating a 62-year-old federal entitlement and creating, for the first time, a limit on how long one can receive federal welfare assistance.

In Washington, however, it seems impossible to leave well enough alone. Clinton himself had promised last year to "fix" troublesome portions of the welfare law, and by the end of July, as Congress passed a balanced-budget plan, it became apparent that the law's implementation was still susceptible of political manipulation. In the final days of negotiation over the budget, a passive Republican Congress and a politically alert White House began diluting the potent formula conceived and signed a year earlier and in effect for all of three weeks.

These eleventh-hour changes are not insignificant. But they should not obscure the larger achievement. The welfare-reform legislation that went into effect on July 1 is the most far-reaching policy move of the Clinton presidency —and also, to date, the most successful. Not surprisingly, the President used his July 4 national radio address to crow about it. Since he took office in January 1993, he announced, three million fewer people were on the welfare rolls. Even more impressive was the fact that an astonishing 1.2 million had come off the rolls in the first nine months since the welfare-reform legislation passed Congress and before it formally went into effect. Using rhetoric that was once the preserve of conservative polemicists, the President told the nation on July 4 that "we have begun to put an end to the culture of dependency, and to elevate our values of family, work, and responsibility."

In truth, the legislation itself deserves only part of the credit. Earlier this year, the President's own Council of Economic Advisers concluded that the drop in the number of people on welfare was due in some measure to the healthy economy and also to the wide variety of initiatives that had emerged over the last few years at the state level. We have, indeed, never witnessed such a fertile period of experimentation, with dozens of state legislatures trying new ways to move people off government assistance and onto a path

of self-sufficiency. Most of these former recipients have gone successfully into full- or part-time jobs, while others, recognizing the new demands the local welfare office will soon place on them, have voluntarily dropped out of the system. With the more comprehensive measures of the federal law now taking effect—and notwithstanding the deleterious changes introduced in the balanced-budget negotiations—we have every reason to expect that these trends will continue.

Not everyone is rejoicing, to be sure. The hand-wringing among some conservatives over the last-minute changes smuggled in by the White House in late July is one thing; but it pales in comparison to the deep distress which the legislation, amended or unamended, has brought to liberal policy circles, not to mention the real rifts which the President's support for welfare reform has caused within his own party. For those who have not wanted to hear that the era of big government is over, the welfare-reform bill has been, indeed, a bitter pill to swallow.

That may explain why, from the beginning, those opposed to the plan repeatedly resorted to a kind of demagoguery that was shameless even by Washington standards. Thus, when the first round of legislation began moving through the Republican-controlled Congress in 1994, Senator Daniel Patrick Moynihan boldly predicted that the result would be "scenes of social trauma such as we haven't known since the cholera epidemics." Not to be outdone, Senator Edward M. Kennedy called an early version of the reform bill "legislative child-abuse."

By the summer of 1996, when it was clear that a bipartisan coalition existed for replacing the federal welfare entitlement with state block grants, time limits, and work requirements, still more alarms were set off. The Urban Institute warned that one million children would fall into poverty, the *New York Times* condemned the bill as "atrocious," and Moynihan pronounced it "an obscene act of social regression." Finally, days after the President signed the legislation, two of his top policy appointees at the Department of Health and Human Services resigned in protest. One of them, Peter Edelman, waited less than six months before publishing an article in the *Atlantic* calling the welfare-reform plan "the worst thing Bill Clinton has done." As Edelman saw it, the new legislation offered a grim future for America's poor:

> [T]here will be suffering.... There will be more malnutrition and more crime, increased infant mortality and increased drug and alcohol abuse. There will be increased family violence and abuse against children and women, and a consequent significant spillover of the problem into the already overloaded child-welfare system and battered-women's shelters.

* * *

... The Personal Responsibility and Work Opportunity Reconciliation Act of 1996 passed both Houses of Congress with considerable bipartisan support. Like all such sweeping pieces of legislation, it makes changes to numerous federal laws and regulations. But the bulk of the legislation is directed at Aid to Families with Dependent Children (AFDC), the Roosevelt-era assistance program that was the target of most of the growing public dissatisfaction with welfare. The new law effectively repeals AFDC and replaces it with a new program known as Temporary Assistance for Needy

Families (TANF). In addition, the law introduces four fundamental changes that distinguish it from every attempt at welfare reform that has come before.

First, it ends the federal entitlement to cash assistance. In the past, eligibility for this assistance was means-tested: anyone meeting the income requirements was automatically qualified. Under the new law, each state determines eligibility. Second, the new law gives a block grant to each of the 50 states, permitting it to design a cash-assistance program as it sees fit. Third, the law establishes a five-year lifetime limit on cash assistance and a two-year limit on receiving assistance without working, thus ensuring that welfare cannot become a way of life. Finally, the law requires each state to craft work requirements as part of its welfare program. By the year 2002, states will need to show that at least 50 percent of those receiving welfare are involved in some form of work or training in exchange for benefits.

These changes all come with a catalogue of exemptions, qualifications, and alternative requirements in special cases —a flexibility that guarantees that the actual programs will vary considerably from state to state. The law will not, for example, "throw a million children into poverty." States can exempt 20 percent of their caseload from the time limit, and also convert block-grant money into vouchers for children after their families have reached the limit. Even when the federal limits are triggered, states can continue to spend their own money helping poor families (as they do now). And states may exempt parents of infants from all work requirements, while single parents with children under six will be asked to work only part-time.

Although one would never know it from the critics, left untouched by this reform are a host of poverty-assistance programs. Medicaid, a program still in need of reform, continues to provide health coverage to all poor families under the new welfare law. Public-housing programs remain in effect, as do child-nutrition programs and the Earned Income Tax Credit. The food-stamp program will continue to grow, if at a slower rate. Again contrary to what has been charged, children with serious long-term medical conditions and disabilities will *not* lose their Supplemental Security Income aid; the new law merely narrows the definition of "disability" to exclude some purely behavioral problems.

Most of the bill's critics have also misunderstood the financing behind it. According to the *Washington Post*, the new law "hands the problem to the states and fails to equip them with the resources to solve" it. In fact, the bill represents a giant windfall for state welfare spending. The block grants replacing the old, formula-driven AFDC payments have been fixed at 1994 spending levels—but in the meantime, as the President reminded us in his July 4 radio address, the welfare caseload across the nation has been dropping dramatically. (In Maryland, Oregon, Massachusetts, Oklahoma, and Michigan, the AFDC caseload has shrunk by 20 to 30 percent in the past two years alone.) For many states, then, the new block grants, financed on the basis of the more crowded welfare rolls of two years ago, represent a significant hike in funding— hardly the outcome one would anticipate from a Republican Congress routinely described as mean-spirited, heartless, and insensitive to the needs of the poor.

* * *

But most confounding of all to critics of the bill, and most heartening to its supporters, is the fact that welfare reform, in its embryonic stages, has wildly surpassed expectations. In April of [1997], eleven million people were on welfare, the lowest share of the U.S. population since 1970. Nor have any of the widely predicted nightmare scenarios materialized. Even in cities like Milwaukee, where thousands of welfare recipients have dropped off the rolls in the last two years, local shelters and food banks have reported no new surges in demand for their services.

What accounts for these early signs of success? Following the lead of the Council of Economic Advisers, some have suggested that the drop in caseloads is traceable entirely to the current strength of the economy. But this cannot be right. The economy has indeed been strong; yet previous cycles of prosperity have failed to produce anything close to the reductions we see today.

What is different, clearly, is that the *rules* governing welfare dependence have started to change. Indeed, they started to change well before the federal law was passed last year. Impatient with Washington's habitual inaction, both Democratic and Republican governors began introducing time limits, work requirements, and rules designed to promote responsibility in their own state systems. The burgeoning economy has made their work easier, but there is no denying that in states where the rules have changed, the lives and behavior of welfare recipients have also changed, and for the better.

Wisconsin's much-touted reforms are a case in point. In a detailed study published in *Policy Review,* Robert Rector has shown how two new programs in that state, Self-Sufficiency First and Pay for Performance, fundamentally altered the relationship between welfare recipients and government. Implemented in April 1996, the programs required recipients to work in the private sector or perform community service, attend remedial-education classes, or participate in a supervised job search in exchange for AFDC payments or food stamps. Those who did not want to work, take classes, or look for a job were no longer eligible for payments. Seven months after the programs began, the AFDC caseload had dropped 33 percent.

Recent experience in Tennessee, though less widely reported, is no less impressive. As it happens, Tennessee is not subject to the provisions of the new federal law, having won prior approval for an equally comprehensive program of its own. Like the federal law, the Tennessee plan, known as Families First, replaces AFDC with a cash-assistance program that requires recipients to work, go to school, or train while working part-time. Tennessee exempts almost a third of its welfare recipients from the time limits (and from some of the work requirements), and in that respect its plan is even more flexible than the federal law. On the other hand, Tennessee imposes a tighter restriction on the number of consecutive months welfare recipients can receive cash benefits. Finally, everyone eligible for benefits, even if exempt from the work requirements and the time limits, must sign a "personal-responsibility contract" outlining the steps to be taken toward self-sufficiency.

In the first six months of the program, 19,000 Tennesseans left the welfare rolls —a 21-percent drop, unprecedented in

the state's history. What makes this reduction more remarkable still is that during these early months no one was being forcibly removed from the rolls by an arbitrary cutoff date. Instead, social-service officials in Tennessee discovered that the mere requirement to show up at a welfare office, sign a statement of personal responsibility, and participate in a work or educational program had a dramatic impact on the lives of people accustomed to receiving a government check without anything being asked of them at all.

Tennessee officials broke down the declining caseload to understand what was taking place. The results are revealing: 5,800 recipients asked that their cases be closed within the first month ("I don't want to be bothered," was a common response). Another 5,500 found work and earned enough money to make them ineligible. Almost a third either refused to sign the personal-responsibility contract, or failed to comply with its terms, or refused to attend classes or begin a job search. The rest moved out of the state. As for those still receiving cash assistance, many appear to be enthusiastically pursuing a route to independence. In the first six months of Families First, 18 percent of this group had found full-time employment; 22 percent were in training or were looking for a job; 19 percent were pursuing adult education; 6 percent had gotten some form of employment mixed with training.

Tennessee's record so far vividly contradicts the most prevalent and long-standing liberal criticism of a decentralized welfare system: that it will spur a "race to the bottom" among the states. Harvard's David Ellwood, who served as an assistant secretary of Health and Human Services and was a point man for the administration's welfare-reform plans before quitting in frustration, has made this criticism most explicitly:

> History is filled with examples of states choosing to ignore poor families or ignoring racial minorities, regions, or types of families. Moreover, if one state's rules differ markedly from those of another, there will be an incentive for migration. It is a lot easier to move poor people from welfare to the state border than from welfare to work. Needs and resources also differ widely across states. The states with the smallest tax base are usually the states with the greatest proportion of poor children and families. Fearful of becoming "welfare magnets," some states may cut benefits and impose more punitive measures than they would otherwise prefer.

On almost every point, the Tennessee example has disproved Ellwood and those who repeat his arguments. Tennessee, a relatively poor Southern state, is also no stranger to racial tensions. With no state income tax, a lean state budget, a recent history of political corruption, and a strong Republican tilt in recent elections, it would hardly seem an ideal candidate for meaningful welfare reform. Yet Tennessee's program *has* promoted work and independence without suddenly snatching away the safety net. Moreover, as part of its reform initiative, the state legislature has actually increased spending on welfare by 22 percent since 1994. Nor is Tennessee unique in this respect. The *New York Times* recently reported that, to the surprise of antipoverty advocates, state legislatures, flush with federal dollars from the welfare-reform bill, have been spending money on day-care services, emergency loans for car repairs, and free subway

passes, all designed to make it easier for welfare recipients to find work. . . .

* * *

It cannot be stressed enough that the current round of welfare reform is different from all that have preceded it. In the past, reform initiatives simply added a labyrinth of incentives to what remained, at heart, a system of entitlements. Work programs, counseling, job searches, child care, and transportation subsidies are surely limited tools if the recipient knows that at the end of the day, there will be no penalty for failing to respond to the rules and incentives. And the most able welfare recipients *always* knew how to "game" the system.

That is why a legal work requirement and a clear time limit for cash assistance are so crucial. Without the certainty of a fixed cutoff date, workfare programs of the past invariably devolved into another form of open-ended government job training that did little to move the trainee into a real job. The key to the current reform is that it promotes self-sufficiency by *removing* welfare as a long-term alternative.

And that, regrettably, is also where the changes introduced in [the July, 1997] budget agreement are likely to do the most damage. A number of state governors have reacted to these changes by charging that the President has effectively undermined the whole thrust of the legislation. "Even Democratic governors are screaming he's all but killed it," wrote the columnist Paul Gigot in the *Wall Street Journal*.

There is much justice in the governors' complaints. The administration's $3-billion Welfare-to-Work program, for example, was stuffed into the July budget agreement as a payoff to big-city mayors who had been left out of the welfare-reform process. Federal funding for yet another unproven job-preparedness initiative like this one runs counter to the main intent of welfare reform, which is (again) to require work, not training, in exchange for a government check. By permitting such alternatives to thrive, the administration has succeeded in creating yet more loopholes for welfare recipients —the very thing that has repeatedly undone past efforts at reform.

But the administration's attempt to roll back or qualify the progress that has been made has taken on an even more disturbing aspect. Both the President and his Department of Labor have begun to insist that all work performed by welfare recipients, even those in community-service jobs, must be treated as "employment" and therefore subject to the panoply of federal labor regulations. Such an interpretation not only runs contrary to 30 years of sensible precedent, but, by asserting a new and intrusive federal role, it has the very real potential to prevent every new state workfare program from getting off the ground. If the administration has its way, more than two dozen federal requirements would be placed on any workfare position, including the payment of minimum wages (and prevailing wages in construction jobs), payroll taxes for employers, workers'-compensation programs, and so on. It would be hard to conceive a greater obstacle in the path of programs that were intended, after all, to help those most unlikely to find work in the private sector.

* * *

As the Republican Congress was notably unenthusiastic about fighting off these rearguard actions against a bill it spent two years struggling to pass, it will now

be up to state governments to challenge ongoing efforts to exert federal control over workfare. Still, these legal and technical issues, and others like them, are *all* that remains of the welfare discussion. Which means that the larger debate that began in the early 1980's is finally over. . . .

[W]hat distinguishes the current reform is that it has forced both federal and state governments to take seriously the idea that welfare policy can deter, or encourage, behavior. The fact that Tennessee will increase welfare spending this year tells us nothing in itself. But the fact that Tennessee now holds parents accountable for their children's immunizations and school attendance; that it forces teen parents to stay in school and live at home or with a guardian; and that it provides no additional benefits for single mothers who have additional children while on welfare, means that government is no longer indifferent to the way welfare recipients live and raise their children. All this represents a stark departure from the liberalism that has dominated government policy toward the poor for the last three decades.

Changing the way the poor behave may not make them prosperous, and there will always be critics to insist that until poverty is eradicated, no program can claim success. But by eliminating the certainty that one will be paid whether or not one works or seeks work, we have already taken the most important step on the road toward the end of welfare—and of liberalism—as we have known them.

NO
Peter Edelman

THE WORST THING BILL CLINTON HAS DONE

I hate welfare. To be more precise, I hate the welfare system we had until [August of 1996,] when Bill Clinton signed a historic bill ending "welfare as we know it." It was a system that contributed to chronic dependency among large numbers of people who would be the first to say they would rather have a job than collect a welfare check every month—and its benefits were never enough to lift people out of poverty. In April of 1967 I helped Robert Kennedy with a speech in which he called the welfare system bankrupt and said it was hated universally, by payers and recipients alike. Criticism of welfare for not helping people to become self-supporting is nothing new.

But the bill that President Clinton signed is not welfare reform. It does not promote work effectively, and it will hurt millions of poor children by the time it is fully implemented. What's more, it bars hundreds of thousands of legal immigrants—including many who have worked in the United States for decades and paid a considerable amount in Social Security and income taxes—from receiving disability and old-age assistance and food stamps, and reduces food-stamp assistance for millions of children in working families. [Since this was written, Congress has restored assistance for legal immigrants who were already in the United States at the time the bill was signed.—Eds.]

When the President was campaigning for re-election . . . , he promised that if re-elected he would undertake to fix the flaws in the bill. We are now far enough into his second term to look at the validity of that promise, by assessing its initial credibility and examining what has happened since.

I resigned as the assistant secretary for planning and evaluation at the Department of Health and Human Services [in September, 1996], because of my profound disagreement with the welfare bill. At the time, I confined my public statement to two sentences, saying only that I had worked as hard as I could over the past thirty-plus years to reduce poverty and that in my opinion this bill moved in the opposite direction. My judgment was that it was important to make clear the reasons for my resignation but not helpful to politicize the issue further during an election campaign. And I did want to see President Clinton re-elected. Worse is not better, in my view, and Bob

From Peter Edelman, "The Worst Thing Bill Clinton Has Done," *The Atlantic Monthly* (March 1997). Copyright © 1997 by Peter Edelman. Reprinted by permission.

Dole would certainly have been worse on a wide range of issues, especially if coupled with a Republican Congress.

I feel free to speak out in more detail now, not to tell tales out of school but to clarify some of the history and especially to underscore the damage the bill will do and explain why the bill will be hard to fix in any fundamental way for a long time to come. It is also important to understand what is being done and could be done to minimize the damage in the short run, and what would be required for a real "fix": a strategy to prevent poverty and thus reduce the need for welfare in the first place.

Four questions are of interest now. Did the President have to sign the bill? How bad is it really, and how can the damage be minimized as the states move to implement it? Can it be fixed in this Congress? What would a real fix be, and what would it take to make that happen?

DID THE PRESIDENT HAVE TO SIGN THE BILL?

Was the President in a tight political box in late July, when he had to decide whether to sign or veto? At the time, there was polling data in front of him showing that very few people were likely to change their intended vote in either direction if he vetoed the bill. But even if he accurately foresaw a daily pounding from Bob Dole that would ultimately draw political blood, the real point is that the President's quandary was one of his own making. He had put himself there, quite deliberately and by a series of steps that he had taken over a long period of time.

Governor Clinton campaigned in 1992 on the promise to "end welfare as we know it" and the companion phrase "Two

years and you're off." He knew very well that a major piece of welfare-reform legislation, the Family Support Act, had already been passed, in 1988. As governor of Arkansas he had been deeply involved in the enactment of that law, which was based on extensive state experimentation with new welfare-to-work initiatives in the 1980s, especially GAIN in California. The 1988 law represented a major bipartisan compromise. The Democrats had given in on work requirements in return for Republican concessions on significant federal funding for job training, placement activities, and transitional child care and health coverage.

The Family Support Act had not been fully implemented, partly because not enough time had passed and partly because in the recession of the Bush years the states had been unable to provide the matching funds necessary to draw down their full share of job-related federal money. Candidate Clinton ought responsibly to have said that the Family Support Act was a major piece of legislation that needed more time to be fully implemented before anyone could say whether it was a success or a failure.

Instead Clinton promised to end welfare as we know it and to institute what sounded like a two-year time limit. This was bumper-sticker politics —oversimplification to win votes. Polls during the campaign showed that it was very popular, and a salient item in garnering votes. Clinton's slogans were also cleverly ambiguous. On the one hand, as President, Clinton could take a relatively liberal path that was nonetheless consistent with his campaign rhetoric. In 1994 he proposed legislation that required everyone to be working by the time he or she had been on the rolls for two years. But it also said, more or less in the fine

print, that people who played by the rules and couldn't find work could continue to get benefits within the same federal-state framework that had existed since 1935. The President didn't say so, but he was building—quite incrementally and on the whole responsibly—on the framework of the Family Support Act. On the other hand, candidate Clinton had let his listeners infer that he intended radical reform with real fall-off-the-cliff time limits. He never said so explicitly, though, so his liberal flank had nothing definitive to criticize. President Clinton's actual 1994 proposal was based on a responsible interpretation of what candidate Clinton had said.

Candidate Clinton, however, had let a powerful genie out of the bottle. During his first two years it mattered only insofar as his rhetoric promised far more than his legislative proposal actually offered. When the Republicans gained control of Congress in 1994, the bumper-sticker rhetoric began to matter. So you want time limits? the Republicans said in 1995. Good idea. We'll give you some serious time limits. We now propose an absolute lifetime limit of five years, cumulatively, that a family can be on welfare. End welfare as we know it? You bet. From now on we will have block grants. And what does that mean? First, that there will be no federal definition of who is eligible and therefore no guarantee of assistance to anyone; each state can decide whom to exclude in any way it wants, as long as it doesn't violate the Constitution (not much of a limitation when one reads the Supreme Court decisions on this subject). And second, that each state will get a fixed sum of federal money each year, even if a recession or a local calamity causes a state to run out of federal funds before the end of the year.

This was a truly radical proposal. For sixty years Aid to Families with Dependent Children had been premised on the idea of entitlement. "Entitlement" has become a dirty word, but it is actually a term of art. It meant two things in the AFDC program: a federally defined guarantee of assistance to families with children who met the statutory definition of need and complied with the other conditions of the law; and a federal guarantee to the states of a matching share of the money needed to help everyone in the state who qualified for help. (AFDC was never a guarantor of income at any particular level. States chose their own benefit levels, and no state's AFDC benefits, even when coupled with food stamps, currently lift families out of poverty.) The block grants will end the entitlement in both respects, and in addition the time limits say that federally supported help will end even if a family has done everything that was asked of it and even if it is still needy....

HOW BAD IS IT, REALLY?

... Why is the new law so bad? To begin with, it turned out that after all the noise and heat over the past two years about balancing the budget, the only deep, multi-year budget cuts actually enacted were those in this bill, affecting low-income people.

The magnitude of the impact is stunning. Its dimensions were estimated by the Urban Institute, using the same model that produced the Department of Health and Human Services study a year earlier. To ensure credibility for the study, its authors made optimistic assumptions: two thirds of long-term recipients would find jobs, and all states would maintain their current levels of financial support

for the benefit structure. Nonetheless, the study showed, the bill would move 2.6 million people, including 1.1 million children, into poverty. It also predicted some powerful effects not contained in the previous year's analysis, which had been constrained in what it could cover because it had been sponsored by the Administration. The new study showed that a total of 11 million families—10 percent of all American families—would lose income under the bill. This included more than eight million families with children, many of them working families affected by the food-stamp cuts, which would lose an average of about $1,300 per family. Many working families with income a little above what we call the poverty line (right now $12,158 for a family of three) would lose income without being made officially poor, and many families already poor would be made poorer.

The view expressed by the White House and by Hill Democrats, who wanted to put their votes for the bill in the best light, was that the parts of the bill affecting immigrants and food stamps were awful (and would be re-addressed in the future) but that the welfare-reform part of the bill was basically all right. The immigrant and food-stamp parts of the bill *are* awful, but so is the welfare part....

The food-stamp cuts are very troubling.... Exclusive of the food-stamp cuts for immigrants, they involve savings of about $24 billion. Almost half of that is in across-the-board cuts in the way benefits are calculated. About two thirds of the benefit reductions will be borne by families with children, many of them working families (thus reflecting a policy outcome wildly inconsistent with the stated purposes of the overall bill). Perhaps the most troubling cut is the one limiting food stamps to three months out of every

three years for unemployed adults under age fifty who are not raising children. The Center on Budget and Policy Priorities describes this as "probably the single harshest provision written into a major safety net program in at least 30 years" —although it turns out that more states than the drafters anticipated can ask for an exception that was written to accommodate places with disproportionate unemployment. One of the great strengths of food stamps until now has been that it was the one major program for the poor in which help was based only on need, with no reference to family status or age. It was the safety net under the safety net. That principle of pure need-based eligibility has now been breached.

Neither the cuts for immigrants nor the food-stamp cuts have anything to do with welfare reform. Many of them are just mean, with no good policy justification. The bill also contains other budget and benefit reductions unrelated to welfare. The definition of SSI eligibility for disabled children has been narrowed, which will result in removal from the rolls of 100,000 to 200,000 of the 965,000 children who currently receive SSI. Although there was broad agreement that some tightening in eligibility was warranted, the changes actually made will result in the loss of coverage for some children who if they were adults would be considered disabled. Particularly affected are children with multiple impairments no one of which is severe enough to meet the new, more stringent criteria. Child-nutrition programs have also been cut, by nearly $3 billion over six years, affecting meals for children in family day care and in the summer food program. Federal funding for social services has been cut by a six-year total of $2.5 billion. This is a 15 percent cut in an important area,

and will hamper the states in providing exactly the kind of counseling and support that families often need if a parent is going to succeed in the workplace.

So this is hardly just a welfare bill. In fact, most of its budget reductions come in programs for the poor other than welfare, and many of them affect working families. Many of them are just cuts, not reform. (The bill also contains an elaborate reform of federal child-support laws, which had broad bipartisan support and could easily have been enacted as separate legislation.)

* * *

This brings us to welfare itself. Basically, the block grants mean that the states can now do almost anything they want —even provide no cash benefits at all. There is no requirement in the new law that the assistance provided to needy families be in the form of cash. States may contract out any or all of what they do to charitable, religious, or private organizations, and provide certificates or vouchers to recipients of assistance which can be redeemed with a contract organization. So the whole system could be run by a corporation or a religious organization if a state so chooses (although the latter could raise constitutional questions, depending on how the arrangement is configured). Or a state could delegate everything to the counties, since the law explicitly says that the program need not be run "in a uniform manner" throughout a state, and the counties could have varying benefit and program frameworks. For good or for ill, the states are in the process of working their way through an enormous—indeed, a bewildering— array of choices, which many of them are ill equipped to make, and which outside

advocates are working hard to help them make well.

The change in the structure is total. Previously there was a national definition of eligibility. With some limitations regarding two-parent families, any needy family with children could get help. There were rules about participation in work and training, but anybody who played by the rules could continue to get assistance. If people were thrown off the rolls without justification, they could get a hearing to set things right, and could go to court if necessary. The system will no longer work that way.

The other major structural change is that federal money is now capped. The block grants total $16.4 billion annually for the country, with no new funding for jobs and training and placement efforts, which are in fact very expensive activities to carry out. For the first couple of years most of the states will get a little more money than they have been getting, because the formula gives them what they were spending a couple of years ago, and welfare rolls have actually decreased somewhat almost everywhere (a fact frequently touted by the President, although one might wonder why the new law was so urgently needed if the rolls had gone down by more than two million people without it).

Many governors are currently crowing about this "windfall" of new federal money. But what they are not telling their voters is that the federal funding will stay the same for the next six years, with no adjustment for inflation or population growth, so by 2002 states will have considerably less federal money to spend than they would have had under AFDC. The states will soon have to choose between benefits and job-related activities, with the very real

possibility that they will run out of federal money before the end of a given year. A small contingency fund exists for recessions, and an even smaller fund to compensate for disproportionate population increases, but it is easy to foresee a time when states will have to either tell applicants to wait for the next fiscal year or spend their own money to keep benefits flowing.

The bill closes its eyes to all the facts and complexities of the real world and essentially says to recipients, Find a job. That has a nice bumper-sticker ring to it. But as a one-size-fits-all recipe it is totally unrealistic.

Total cutoffs of help will be felt right away only by immigrants and disabled children—not insignificant exceptions. The big hit, which could be very big, will come when the time limits go into effect—in five years, or less if the state so chooses—or when a recession hits. State treasuries are relatively flush at the moment, with the nation in the midst of a modest boom period. When the time limits first take effect, a large group of people in each state will fall into the abyss all at once. Otherwise the effects will be fairly gradual. Calcutta will not break out instantly on American streets.

To the extent that there are any constraints on the states in the new law, they are negative. The two largest—and they are very large—are the time limit and the work-participation requirements.

There is a cumulative lifetime limit of five years on benefits paid for with federal money, and states are free to impose shorter time limits if they like. One exception is permitted, to be applied at the state's discretion: as much as 20 percent of the caseload at any particular time may be people who have already received assistance for five years. This sounds promising until one understands that about half the current caseload is composed of people who have been on the rolls longer than five years. A recent study sponsored by the Kaiser Foundation found that 30 percent of the caseload is composed of women who are caring for disabled children or are disabled themselves. The time limits will be especially tough in states that have large areas in chronic recession —for example, the coal-mining areas of Appalachia. And they will be even tougher when the country as a whole sinks into recession. It will make no difference if a recipient has played by all the rules and sought work faithfully, as required. When the limit is reached and the state is unable or unwilling to grant an exception, welfare will be over for that family forever.

Under the work-participation requirements, 25 percent of the caseload must be working or in training this year, and 50 percent by 2002. For two-parent families 75 percent of the caseload must be working or in training, and the number goes up to 90 percent in two years. The Congressional Budget Office estimates that the bill falls $12 billion short of providing enough funding over the next six years for the states to meet the work requirements. Even the highly advertised increased child-care funding falls more than $1 billion short of providing enough funding for all who would have to work in order for the work requirements to be satisfied. States that fail to meet the work requirements lose increasing percentages of their block grants.

The states are given a rather Machiavellian out. The law in effect assumes that any reduction in the rolls reflects people who have gone to work. So states have a de facto incentive to get people off the

rolls in any way they can, not necessarily by getting them into work activities.

The states can shift a big chunk of their own money out of the program if they want to. There is no matching requirement for the states, only a maintenance-of-effort requirement that each state keep spending at least 80 percent of what it was previously contributing. This will allow as much as $40 billion nationally to be withheld from paying benefits over the next six years, on top of the $55 billion cut by the bill itself. Moreover, the 80 percent requirement is a static number, so the funding base will immediately start being eroded by inflation.

Besides being able to transfer some of their own money out, the states are allowed to transfer up to 30 percent of their federal block grants to spending on child care or other social services. Among other things, this will encourage them to adopt time limits shorter than five years, because this would save federal money that could then be devoted to child care and other help that families need in order to be able to go to work. Hobson's choice will flourish.

The contingency fund to cushion against the impact of recessions or local economic crises is wholly inadequate— $2 billion over five years. Welfare costs rose by $6 billion in three years during the recession of the early nineties.

The federal AFDC law required the states to make decisions on applications within forty-five days and to pay, retroactively if necessary, from the thirtieth day after the application was put in. There is no such requirement in the new law. All we know from the new law is that the state has to tell the Secretary of Health and Human Services what its "objective criteria" will be for "the delivery of benefits," and how it will accord "fair and eq-uitable treatment" to recipients, including how it will give "adversely affected" recipients an opportunity to be heard. This is weak, to say the least.

FIFTY WELFARE POLICIES

Given this framework, what can we predict will happen? No state will want to be a magnet for people from other states by virtue of a relatively generous benefit structure. This is common sense, unfortunately. As states seek to ensure that they are not more generous than their neighbors, they will try to make their benefit structures less, not more, attractive. If states delegate decisions about benefit levels to their counties, the race to the bottom will develop within states as well.

I do not wish to imply that all states, or even most states, are going to take the opportunity to engage in punitive policy behavior. There will be a political dynamic in the process whereby each state implements the law. Advocates can organize and express themselves to good effect, and legislatures can frustrate or soften governors' intentions. There is another important ameliorating factor: many welfare administrators are concerned about the dangers that lie in the new law and will seek to implement it as constructively as they can, working to avoid some of the more radical negative possibilities.

Citizens can make a difference in what happens in their state. They can push to make sure that it doesn't adopt a time limit shorter than five years, doesn't reduce its own investment of funds, doesn't cut benefits, doesn't transfer money out of the block grant, doesn't dismantle procedural protections, and doesn't create bureaucratic hurdles that

will discourage recipients. They can press for state and local funds to help legal immigrants who have been cut off from SSI or food stamps and children who have been victimized by the time limits. They can advocate an energetic and realistic jobs and training strategy, with maximum involvement by the private sector. And they can begin organizing and putting together the elements of a real fix, which I will lay out shortly.

THE JOBS GAP

Even given effective advocacy, relatively responsive legislatures and welfare administrators, and serious efforts to find private-sector jobs, the deck is stacked against success, especially in states that have high concentrations of poverty and large welfare caseloads. The basic issue is jobs. *There simply are not enough jobs now.* Four million adults are receiving Aid to Families with Dependent Children. Half of them are long-term recipients. In city after city around America the number of people who will have to find jobs will quickly dwarf the number of new jobs created in recent years. Many cities have actually lost jobs over the past five to ten years. New York City, for example, has lost 227,000 jobs since 1990, and the New York metropolitan area overall has lost 260,000 over the same period. New York City had more than 300,000 adults in the AFDC caseload in 1995, to say nothing of the adults without dependent children who are receiving general assistance. Statistics aside, all one has to do is go to Chicago, or to Youngstown, Ohio, or to Newark, or peruse William Julius Wilson's powerful new book, *When Work Disappears,* to get the point. The fact is that there are not enough appropriate private-sector jobs in appropriate locations even

now, when unemployment is about as low as it ever gets in this country.

For some people, staying on welfare was dictated by economics, because it involved a choice between the "poor support" of welfare, to use the Harvard professor David Ellwood's term, and the even worse situation of a low-wage job, with its take-home pay reduced by the out-of-pocket costs of commuting and day care, and the potentially incalculable effects of losing health coverage. With time limits these people will no longer have that choice, unappetizing as it was, and will be forced to take a job that leaves them even deeper in poverty. How many people will be able to get and keep a job, even a lousy job, is impossible to say, but it is far from all of those who have been on welfare for an extended period of time.

The labor market, even in its current relatively heated state, is not friendly to people with little education and few marketable skills, poor work habits, and various personal and family problems that interfere with regular and punctual attendance. People spend long spells on welfare or are headed in that direction for reasons other than economic choice or, for that matter, laziness. If we are going to put long-term welfare recipients to work—and we should make every effort to do so—it will be difficult and it will cost money to train people, to place them, and to provide continuing support so that they can keep a job once they get it. If they are to have child care and health coverage, that will cost still more. Many of the jobs that people will get will not offer health coverage, so transitional Medicaid for a year or two will not suffice. People who have been on welfare for a long time will too often not make it in their first job and will need continuing help toward and into

a second job. Both because the private sector may well not produce enough jobs right away and because not all welfare recipients will be ready for immediate placement in a private-sector job, it will be appropriate also to use public jobs or jobs with nonprofit organizations at least as a transition if not as permanent positions. All of this costs real money.

For a lot of people it will not work at all. Kansas City's experience is sadly instructive here. In the past two years, in a very well-designed and well-implemented effort, a local program was able to put 1,409 out of 15,562 welfare recipients to work. As of last December only 730 were still at work. The efforts of Toby Herr and Project Match in Chicago's Cabrini-Green public-housing project are another case in point. Working individually and intensively with women and supporting them through succesive jobs until they found one they were able to keep, Herr had managed to place 54 percent of her clients in year-round jobs at the end of five years. This is a remarkable (and unusual) success rate, but it also shows how unrealistic is a structure that offers only a 20 percent exception to the five-year time limit.

I want to be very clear: I am not questioning the willingness of long-term welfare recipients to work. Their unemployment is significantly related to their capacity to work, whether for personal or family reasons, far more than to their willingness to work. Many long-term welfare recipients are functionally disabled even if they are not disabled in a legal sense. News coverage of what the new law will mean has been replete with heartbreaking stories of women who desperately want to work but have severe trouble learning how to operate a cash register or can't remember basic things they need to master. A study in the state of Washington shows that 36 percent of the caseload have learning disabilities that have never been remediated. Many others have disabled children or parents for whom they are the primary caretakers. Large numbers are victims of domestic violence and risk physical retaliation if they enter the workplace. These personal and family problems make such people poor candidates for work in the best of circumstances. Arbitrary time limits on their benefits will not make them likelier to gain and hold employment. When unemployment goes back up to six or seven or eight percent nationally, as it will at some point, the idea that the private sector will employ and continue to employ those who are the hardest to employ will be even more fanciful than it is at the current, relatively propitious moment.

When the time limits take effect, the realities occasioned by the meeting of a bottom-line-based labor market with so many of our society's last hired and first fired will come into focus. Of course, a considerable number will not fall off the cliff. An increased number will have obtained jobs along the way. The time limits will help some people to discipline themselves and ration their years of available assistance. Some will move in with family or friends when their benefits are exhausted. The 20 percent exception will help as well.

But there will be suffering. Some of the damage will be obvious—more homelessness, for example, with more demand on already strapped shelters and soup kitchens. The ensuing problems will also appear as increases in the incidence of other problems, directly but perhaps not provably owing to the impact of the wel-

fare bill. There will be more malnutrition and more crime, increased infant mortality, and increased drug and alcohol abuse. There will be increased family violence and abuse against children and women, and a consequent significant spillover of the problem into the already overloaded child-welfare system and battered-women's shelters....

WHAT WOULD A REAL FIX INVOLVE?

... We need to watch very carefully, and we need to document and publicize, the impact of the 1996 welfare legislation on children and families across America. We need to do everything we can to influence the choices the states have to make under the new law. We *can* ultimately come out in a better place. We should not want to go back to what we had. It was not good social policy. We want people to be able to hold up their heads and raise their children in dignity. The best that can be said about this terrible legislation is that perhaps we will learn from it and eventually arrive at a better approach. I am afraid, though, that along the way we will do some serious injury to American children, who should not have had to suffer from our national backlash.

POSTSCRIPT

Is Welfare Reform Succeeding?

"I hate welfare." The author of these words is not Casse, who defends the Republican welfare overhaul, but Edelman, who resigned in protest from the Clinton administration after the president signed it. Despite their obvious disagreements, then, both authors agree that the system needed changing and that the able-bodied poor needed to be gotten off welfare and into productive work. The question dividing them is how to go about it.

The evolution of welfare policies is traced in Michael B. Katz, *The Undeserving Poor: From the War on Poverty to the War on Welfare* (Pantheon Books, 1989). Lawrence M. Mead, in *The New Politics of Poverty* (Basic Books, 1992), presents a detailed criticism of the welfare system. Jonathan Kozol, in *Savage Inequalities: Children in America's Schools* (Harper Perennial, 1992), argues that the system fails because it does not deal with root causes, such as the inadequate education of poor children. In *When Work Disappears: The World of the New Urban Poor* (Alfred A. Knopf, 1996), sociologist William Julius Wilson argues that the real issue is not welfare but "the disappearance of work in the ghetto," a problem that he thinks has now reached "catastrophic proportions." Wilson's argument is similar to Edelman's in that both insist that it is cruel to demand that the poor work if there are no jobs they can handle. Edelman is thus ready to support work requirements but only if the law provides more leeway about deadlines and ensures job training, placement, child care, and health coverage. Casse would leave much of training and placement up to states and supports the strict time limits in the 1996 law. Which approach is better? Perhaps time will tell.

ISSUE 14

Is Socioeconomic Inequality Increasing in America?

YES: Paul Krugman, from "The Spiral of Inequality," *Mother Jones* (November/December 1996)

NO: Christopher C. DeMuth, from "The New Wealth of Nations," *Commentary* (October 1997)

ISSUE SUMMARY

YES: Economist Paul Krugman maintains that corporate greed, the decline of organized labor, and changes in production have contributed to a sharp increase in social and economic inequality in America.

NO: Christopher C. DeMuth, president of the American Enterprise Institute, asserts that Americans have achieved an impressive level of wealth and equality and that a changing economy ensures even more opportunities.

There has always been a wide range in real income in the United States. In the first three decades after the end of World War II, family incomes doubled, income inequality narrowed slightly, and poverty rates declined. Prosperity declined in the mid-1970s, when back-to-back recessions produced falling average incomes, greater inequality, and higher poverty levels. Between the mid-1980s and the late 1990s, sustained economic recovery resulted in a modest average growth in income, but high poverty rates continued.

Defenders of the social system maintain that, over the long run, poverty has declined. Many improvements in social conditions benefit virtually all people and, thus, make us more equal. The increase in longevity (attributable in large measure to advances in medicine, nutrition, and sanitation) affects all social classes. In a significant sense, the U.S. economy is far fairer now than at any time in the past. In the preindustrial era, when land was the primary measure of wealth, those without land had no way to improve their circumstances. In the industrial era, when people of modest means needed physical strength and stamina to engage in difficult and hazardous labor in mines, mills, and factories, those who were too weak, handicapped, or too old stood little chance of gaining or keeping reasonable jobs.

Now, as we enter an era in which most profitable employment will come from the information and service industries, what matters most for economic success is brainpower, the capacity to learn and perform complex mental

tasks. Fortunately, intelligence cuts across classes and, thus, creates new opportunities for those who would otherwise be disadvantaged.

Detractors of the social system do not share this sanguine view. They are alarmed that there is a continuing redistribution of income and wealth in the United States through which the rich are getting an increasingly larger share and the rest of the population is getting less. A quarter century ago the top 5 percent earned 11 times as much as the bottom 20 percent; in 1994, the top 5 percent received 20 times as much. The business pages repeatedly report staggering salaries and bonuses paid to executives. In May 1998, for example, three executives of a computer software company received $1.1 billion in bonuses, while the company's 9,850 other employees received no bonus. Multimillion-dollar salaries for major executives in large corporations are commonplace, and these are often augmented with lucrative stock bonuses.

By contrast, millions at the bottom cannot participate in or benefit from social, cultural, economic, and political life because they are too poor (unmarried teenage mothers and their offspring, the unemployed and underemployed, older people living on meager pensions), physically unable (handicapped individuals, drug addicts, AIDS victims, the seriously ill), or socially excluded (victims of racial prejudice, prisoners and parolees, illiterates).

Universal education created the promise of nearly equal opportunity for all children, but the reality falls short. The children of more-prosperous parents attend private schools in the cities and well-financed schools in the wealthy suburbs. The children of the poorest parents are likely to attend poorly financed schools where they live because poor school districts cannot afford to pay for better schools. In 1996 a national assessment of educational performance concluded that students in schools with large minority populations are unlikely to get a science or math teacher with a license and a degree in the field. The federal government's General Accounting Office reported in the same year that more than one-third of all school districts need extensive repair or replacement of one or more school buildings.

The issue of equality in the United States must always be considered in the context of a society that places a higher value on individual freedom than do other industrial nations. Nevertheless, there are notable instances of U.S. government intervention that have had the effect of reducing economic inequality. The Homestead Act of 1892, for instance, entitled any citizen to claim 160 acres of public land and to purchase it for a small fee after living on it for five years. The Morrill Act, also enacted in 1862, gave public land to every state to help finance the creation of public colleges. And the Social Security Act of 1935 established a contributory pension scheme for most workers in the private sector, unemployment compensation, and Aid to Families with Dependent Children, which became the cornerstone of the modern welfare system.

The contrasting assessment of American society in the following essays could not be sharper. Where Paul Krugman examines a variety of factors that sustain and increase inequality, Christopher C. DeMuth outlines a number of social forces that have greatly reduced inequality.

YES   Paul Krugman

THE SPIRAL OF INEQUALITY

Ever since the election of Ronald Reagan, right-wing radicals have insisted that they started a revolution in America. They are half right. If by a revolution we mean a change in politics, economics, and society that is so large as to transform the character of the nation, then there is indeed a revolution in progress. The radical right did not make this revolution, although it has done its best to help it along. If anything, we might say that the revolution created the new right. But whatever the cause, it has become urgent that we appreciate the depth and significance of this new American revolution—and try to stop it before it becomes irreversible.

The consequences of the revolution are obvious in cities across the nation. Since I know the area well, let me take you on a walk down University Avenue in Palo Alto, California.

Palo Alto is the de facto village green of Silicon Valley, a tree-lined refuge from the valley's freeways and shopping malls. People want to live here despite the cost—rumor has it that a modest three-bedroom house sold recently for $1.6 million—and walking along University you can see why. Attractive, casually dressed people stroll past trendy boutiques and restaurants; you can see a cooking class in progress at the fancy new kitchenware store. It's a cheerful scene, even if you have to detour around the people sleeping in doorways and have to avoid eye contact with the beggars. (The town council plans to crack down on street people, so they probably won't be here next year, anyway.)

If you tire of the shopping district and want to wander further afield, you might continue down University Avenue, past the houses with their well-tended lawns and flower beds—usually there are a couple of pickup trucks full of Hispanic gardeners in sight. But don't wander too far. When University crosses Highway 101, it enters the grim environs of East Palo Alto. Though it has progressed in the past few years, as recently as 1992 East Palo Alto was the murder capital of the nation and had an unemployment rate hovering around 40 percent. Luckily, near the boundary, where there is a cluster of liquor stores and check-cashing outlets, you can find two or three police

From Paul Krugman, "The Spiral of Inequality," *Mother Jones* (November/December 1996). Copyright © 1996 by The Foundation for National Progress. Reprinted by permission. Notes omitted.

cruisers keeping an eye on the scene—and, not incidentally, serving as a thin blue line protecting the nice neighborhood behind them.

Nor do you want to head down 101 to the south, to "Dilbert Country" with its ranks of low-rise apartments, the tenements of the modern proletariat—the places from which hordes of lower-level white-collar workers drive to sit in their cubicles by day and to which they return to watch their VCRs by night.

No. Better to head up into the hills. The "estates" brochure at Coldwell Banker real estate describes the mid-Peninsula as "an area of intense equestrian character," and when you ascend to Woodside-Atherton, which the *New York Times* has recently called one of "America's born-again Newports," there are indeed plenty of horses, as well as some pretty imposing houses. If you look hard enough, you might catch a glimpse of one of the new $10 million-plus mansions that are going up in growing numbers.

What few people realize is that this vast gap between the affluent few and the bulk of ordinary Americans is a relatively new fixture on our social landscape. People believe these scenes are nothing new, even that it is utopian to imagine it could be otherwise.

But it has not always been thus—at least not to the same extent. I didn't see Palo Alto in 1970, but longtime residents report that it was a mixed town in which not only executives and speculators but schoolteachers, mailmen, and sheet-metal workers could afford to live. At the time, I lived on Long Island, not far from the old *Great Gatsby* area on the North Shore. Few of the great mansions were still private homes then (who could afford the servants?); they had been converted into junior colleges

and nursing homes, or deeded to the state as historic monuments. Like Palo Alto, the towns contained a mix of occupations and education levels—no surprise, given that skilled blue-collar workers often made as much as, or more than, white-collar middle managers.

Now, of course, Gatsby is back. New mansions, grander than the old, are rising by the score; keeping servants, it seems, is no longer a problem. A couple of years ago I had dinner with a group of New York investment bankers. After the business was concluded, the talk turned to their weekend homes in the Hamptons. Naively, I asked whether that wasn't a long drive; after a moment of confused silence, the answer came back: "But the helicopter only takes half an hour."

You can confirm what your eyes see, in Palo Alto or in any American community, with dozens of statistics. The most straightforward are those on income shares supplied by the Bureau of the Census, whose statistics are among the most rigorously apolitical. In 1970, according to the bureau, the bottom 20 percent of U.S. families received only 5.4 percent of the income, while the top 5 percent received 15.6 percent. By 1994, the bottom fifth had only 4.2 percent, while the top 5 percent had increased its share to 20.1 percent. That means that in 1994, the average income among the top 5 percent of families was more than 19 times that of the bottom 20 percent of families. In 1970, it had been only about 11.5 times as much. (Incidentally, while the change in distribution is most visible at the top and bottom, families in the middle have also lost: The income share of the middle 20 percent of families has fallen from 17.6 to 15.7 percent.) These are not abstract numbers. They are the

statistical signature of a seismic shift in the character of our society.

The American notion of what constitutes the middle class has always been a bit strange, because both people who are quite poor and those who are objectively way up the scale tend to think of themselves as being in the middle. But if calling America a middle-class nation means anything, it means that we are a society in which most people live more or less the same kind of life.

In 1970 we were that kind of society. Today we are not, and we become less like one with each passing year. As politicians compete over who really stands for middle-class values, what the public should be asking them is, *What* middle class? How can we have common "middle-class" values if whole segments of society live in vastly different economic universes?

If this election was really about what the candidates claim, it would be devoted to two questions: Why has America ceased to be a middle-class nation? And, more important, what can be done to make it a middle-class nation again?

THE SOURCES OF INEQUALITY

Most economists who study wages and income in the United States agree about the radical increase in inequality—only the hired guns of the right still try to claim it is a statistical illusion. But not all agree about why it has happened.

Imports from low-wage countries—a popular villain—are part of the story, but only a fraction of it. The numbers just aren't big enough. We invest billions in low-wage countries—but we invest trillions at home. What we spend on manufactured goods from the Third World represents just 2 percent of our income. Even if we shut out imports from low-wage countries (cutting off the only source of hope for the people who work in those factories), most estimates suggest it would raise the wages of low-skill workers here by only 1 or 2 percent.

Information technology is a more plausible villain. Technological advance doesn't always favor elite workers, but since 1970 there has been clear evidence of a general "skill bias" toward technological change. Companies began to replace low-skill workers with smaller numbers of high-skills ones, and they continue to do so even though low-skill workers have gotten cheaper and high-skill workers more expensive.

These forces, while easily measurable, don't fully explain the disparity between the haves and the have-nots. Globalization and technology may explain why a college degree makes more difference now than it did 20 years ago. But schoolteachers and corporate CEOs typically have about the same amount of formal education. Why, then, have teachers' salaries remained flat while those of CEOs have increased fivefold? The impact of technology and of foreign trade do not answer why it is harder today for most people to make a living but easier for a few to make a killing. Something else is going on.

VALUES, POWER, AND WAGES

In 1970 the CEO of a typical Fortune 500 corporation earned about 35 times as much as the average manufacturing employee. It would have been unthinkable to pay him 150 times the average, as is now common, and downright outrageous to do so while announcing mass layoffs and cutting the real earnings of many of the company's workers, espe-

cially those who were paid the least to start with. So how did the unthinkable become first thinkable, then doable, and finally—if we believe the CEOs—unavoidable?

The answer is that values changed—not the middle-class values politicians keep talking about, but the kind of values that helped to sustain the middle-class society we have lost.

Twenty-five years ago, prosperous companies could have paid their janitors minimum wage and still could have found people to do the work. They didn't, because it would have been bad for company morale. Then, as now, CEOs were in a position to arrange for very high salaries for themselves, whatever their performance, but corporate boards restrained such excesses, knowing that too great a disparity between the top man and the ordinary worker would cause problems. In short, though America was a society with large disparities between economic classes, it had an egalitarian ethic that limited those disparities. That ethic is gone.

One reason for the change is a sort of herd behavior: When most companies hesitated to pay huge salaries at the top and minimum wage at the bottom, any company that did so would have stood out as an example of greed; when everyone does it, the stigma disappears.

There is also the matter of power. In 1970 a company that appeared too greedy risked real trouble with other powerful forces in society. It would have had problems with its union if it had one, or faced the threat of union organizers if it didn't. And its actions would have created difficulties with the government in a way that is now unthinkable. (Can anyone imagine a current president confronting a major industry over price increases, the way John F. Kennedy did the steel industry?)

Those restraining forces have largely disappeared. The union movement is a shadow of its former self, lucky to hold its ground in a defensive battle now and then. The idea that a company would be punished by the government for paying its CEO too much and its workers too little is laughable today: since the election of Ronald Reagan the CEO would more likely be invited to a White House dinner.

In brief, much of the polarization of American society can be explained in terms of power and politics. But why has the tide run so strongly in favor of the rich that it continues regardless of who is in the White House and who controls the Congress?

THE DECLINE OF LABOR

The decline of the labor movement in the United States is both a major cause of growing inequality and an illustration of the larger process under way in our society. Unions now represent less than 12 percent of the private workforce, and their power has declined dramatically. In 1970 some 2.5 million workers participated in some form of labor stoppage; in 1993, fewer than 200,000 did. Because unions are rarely able or willing to strike, being a union member no longer carries much of a payoff in higher wages.

There are a number of reasons for the decline of organized labor: the shift from manufacturing to services and from blue-collar to white-collar work, growing international competition, and deregulation. But these factors can't explain the extent or the suddenness of labor's decline.

The best explanation seems to be that the union movement fell below critical mass. Unions are good for unions: In a nation with a powerful labor movement, workers have a sense of solidarity, one union can support another during a strike, and politicians take union interests seriously. America's union movement just got too small, and it imploded.

We should not idealize the unions. When they played a powerful role in America, they often did so to bad effect. Occasionally they were corrupt, often they extracted higher wages at the consumer's expense, sometimes they opposed new technologies and enforced inefficient practices. But unions helped keep us a middle-class society—not only because they forced greater equality within companies, but because they provided a counterweight to the power of wealthy individuals and corporations. The loss of that counterweight is clearly bad for society.

The point is that a major force that kept America a more or less unified society went into a tailspin. Our whole society is now well into a similar downward spiral, in which growing inequality creates the political and economic conditions that lead to even more inequality.

THE POLARIZING SPIRAL

Textbook political science predicts that in a two-party democracy like the United States, the parties will compete to serve the interests of the median voter—the voter in the middle, richer than half the voters but poorer than the other half. And since ordinary workers are more likely to lose their jobs than strike it rich, the interests of the median voter should include protecting the poor. You might expect, then, the public to demand that

government work against the growing divide by taxing the rich more heavily and by increasing benefits for lower-paid workers and the unemployed.

In fact, we have done just the opposite. Tax rates on the wealthy—even with Clinton's modest increase of 1993—are far lower now than in the 1960s. We have allowed public schools and other services that are crucial for middle-income families to deteriorate. Despite the recent increase, the minimum wage has fallen steadily compared with both average wages and the cost of living. And programs for the poor have been savaged: Even before the recent bipartisan gutting of welfare, AFDC payments for a typical family had fallen by a third in real terms since the 1960s.

The reason why government policy has reinforced rather than opposed this growing inequality is obvious: Well-off people have disproportionate political weight. They are more likely to vote—the median voter has a much higher income than the median family—and far more likely to provide the campaign contributions that are so essential in a TV age.

The political center of gravity in this country is therefore not at the median family, with its annual income of $40,000, but way up the scale. With decreasing voter participation and with the decline both of unions and of traditional political machines, the focus of political attention is further up the income ladder than it has been for generations. So never mind what politicians say; political parties are competing to serve the interests of families near the 90th percentile or higher, families that mostly earn $100,000 or more per year.

Because the poles of our society have become so much more unequal, the interests of this political elite diverge

increasingly from those of the typical family. A family at the 95th percentile pays a lot more in taxes than a family at the 50th, but it does not receive a correspondingly higher benefit from public services, such as education. The greater the income gap, the greater the disparity in interests. This translates, because of the clout of the elite, into a constant pressure for lower taxes and reduced public services.

Consider the issue of school vouchers. Many conservatives and even a few liberals are in favor of issuing educational vouchers and allowing parents to choose among competing schools. Let's leave aside the question of what this might do to education and ask what its political implications might be.

Initially, we might imagine, the government would prohibit parents from "topping up" vouchers to buy higher-priced education. But once the program was established, conservatives would insist such a restriction is unfair, maybe even unconstitutional, arguing that parents should have the freedom to spend their money as they wish. Thus, a voucher would become a ticket you could supplement freely. Upper-income families would realize that a reduction in the voucher is to their benefit: They will save more in lowered taxes than they will lose in a decreased education subsidy. So they will press to reduce public spending on education, leading to ever-deteriorating quality for those who cannot afford to spend extra. In the end, the quintessential American tradition of public education for all could collapse.

School vouchers hold another potential that, doubtless, makes them attractive to the conservative elite: They offer a way to break the power of the American union movement in its last remaining stronghold, the public sector. Not by accident did Bob Dole, in his acceptance speech at the Republican National Convention, pause in his evocation of Norman Rockwell values to take a swipe at teachers' unions. The leaders of the radical right want privatization of schools, of public sanitation—of anything else they can think of—because they know such privatization undermines what remaining opposition exists to their program.

If public schools and other services are left to deteriorate, so will the skills and prospects of those who depend on them, reinforcing the growing inequality of incomes and creating an even greater disparity between the interests of the elite and those of the majority.

Does this sound like America in the '90s? Of course it does. And it doesn't take much imagination to envision what our society will be like if this process continues for another 15 or 20 years. We know all about it from TV, movies, and best-selling novels. While politicians speak of recapturing the virtues of small-town America (which never really existed), the public—extrapolating from the trends it already sees—imagines a *Blade Runner*-style dystopia, in which a few people live in luxury while the majority grovel in Third World living standards.

STRATEGIES FOR THE FUTURE

There is no purely economic reason why we cannot reduce inequality in America. If we were willing to spend even a few percent of national income on an enlarged version of the Earned Income Tax Credit, which supplements the earnings of low-wage workers, we could make a dramatic impact on both incomes and job opportunities for the poor and near-poor—bringing a greater

number of Americans into the middle class. Nor is the money for such policies lacking: America is by far the least heavily taxed of Western nations and could easily find the resources to pay for a major expansion of programs aimed at limiting inequality.

But of course neither party advanced such proposals during the electoral campaign. The Democrats sounded like Republicans, knowing that in a society with few counterweights to the power of money, any program that even hints at redistribution is political poison. It's no surprise that Bill Clinton's repudiation of his own tax increase took place in front of an audience of wealthy campaign contributors. In this political environment, what politician would talk of taxing the well-off to help the low-wage worker?

And so, while the agenda of the GOP would surely accelerate the polarizing trend, even Democratic programs now amount only to a delaying action. To get back to the kind of society we had, we need to rebuild the institutions and values that made a middle-class nation possible.

The relatively decent society we had a generation ago was largely the creation of a brief, crucial period in American history: the presidency of Franklin Roosevelt, during the New Deal and especially during the war. That created what economic historian Claudia Goldin called the Great Compression—an era in which a powerful government, reinforced by and in turn reinforcing a newly powerful labor movement, drastically narrowed the gap in income levels through taxes, benefits, minimum wages, and collective bargaining. In effect, Roosevelt created a new, middle-class America, which lasted for more than a generation. We have lost that America, and it will take another

Roosevelt, and perhaps the moral equivalent of another war, to get it back.

Until then, however, we can try to reverse some of the damage. To do so requires more than just supporting certain causes. It means thinking strategically—asking whether a policy is not only good in itself but how it will affect the political balance in the future. If a policy change promises to raise average income by a tenth of a percentage point, but will widen the wedge between the interests of the elite and those of the rest, it should be opposed. If a law reduces average income a bit but enhances the power of ordinary workers, it should be supported.

In particular, we also need to apply strategic thinking to the union movement. Union leaders and liberal intellectuals often don't like each other very much, and union victories are often of dubious value to the economy. Nonetheless, if you are worried about the cycle of polarization in this country, you should support policies that make unions stronger, and vociferously oppose those that weaken them. There are some stirrings of life in the union movement—a new, younger leadership with its roots in the service sector has replaced the manufacturing-based old guard, and has won a few political victories. They must be supported, almost regardless of the merits of their particular case. Unions are one of the few *political* counterweights to the power of wealth.

Of course, even to talk about such things causes the right to accuse us of fomenting "class warfare." They want us to believe we are all members of a broad, more or less homogeneous, middle class. But the notion of a middle-class nation was always a stretch. Unless we are prepared to fight the trend toward inequality, it will become a grim joke.

NO

Christopher C. DeMuth

THE NEW WEALTH OF NATIONS

The Nations of North America, Western Europe, Australia, and Japan are wealthier today than they have ever been, wealthier than any others on the planet, wealthier by far than any societies in human history. Yet their governments appear to be impoverished—saddled with large accumulated debts and facing annual deficits that will grow explosively over the coming decades. As a result, government spending programs, especially the big social-insurance programs like Social Security and Medicare in the United States, are facing drastic cuts in order to avert looming insolvency (and, in France and some other European nations, in order to meet the Maastricht treaty's criteria of fiscal rectitude). American politics has been dominated for several years now by contentious negotiations over deficit reduction between the Clinton administration and the Republican Congress. This past June, first at the European Community summit in Amsterdam and then at the Group of Eight meeting in Denver, most of the talk was of hardship and constraint and the need for governmental austerity ("Economic Unease Looms Over Talks at Denver Summit," read the *New York Times* headline).

These bloodless problems of governmental accounting are said, moreover, to reflect real social ills: growing economic inequality in the United States; high unemployment in Europe; an aging, burdensome, and medically needy population everywhere; and the globalization of commerce, which is destroying jobs and national autonomy and forcing bitter measures to keep up with the bruising demands of international competitiveness.

How can it be that societies so surpassingly wealthy have governments whose core domestic-welfare programs are on the verge of bankruptcy? The answer is as paradoxical as the question. We have become not only the richest but also the freest and most egalitarian societies that have ever existed, and it is our very wealth, freedom, and equality that are causing the welfare state to unravel.

* * *

That we have become very rich is clear enough in the aggregate. That we have become very equal in the enjoyment of our riches is an idea strongly resisted

From Christopher C. DeMuth, "The New Wealth of Nations," *Commentary* (October 1997). Copyright © 1997 by The American Jewish Committee. Reprinted by permission. Notes omitted.

by many. Certainly there has been a profusion of reports in the media and political speeches about increasing income inequality: the rich, it is said, are getting richer, the poor are getting poorer, and the middle and working classes are under the relentless pressure of disappearing jobs in manufacturing and middle management.

Although these claims have been greatly exaggerated, and some have been disproved by events, it is true that, by some measures, there has been a recent increase in income inequality in the United States. But it is a very small tick in the massive and unprecedented leveling of material circumstances that has been proceeding now for almost three centuries and in this century has accelerated dramatically. In fact, the much-noticed increase in measured-income inequality is in part a result of the increase in real social equality. Here are a few pieces of this important but neglected story.

• First, progress in agriculture, construction, manufacturing, and other key sectors of economic production has made the material necessities of life—food, shelter, and clothing—available to essentially everyone. To be sure, many people, including the seriously handicapped and the mentally incompetent, remain dependent on the public purse for their necessities. And many people continue to live in terrible squalor. But the problem of poverty, defined as material scarcity, has been solved. If poverty today remains a serious problem, it is a problem of individual behavior, social organization, and public policy. This was not so 50 years ago, or ever before.

• Second, progress in public health, in nutrition, and in the biological sciences and medical arts has produced dramatic improvements in longevity, health, and physical well-being. Many of these improvements—resulting, for example, from better public sanitation and water supplies, the conquest of dread diseases, and the abundance of nutritious food—have affected entire populations, producing an equalization of real personal welfare more powerful than any government redistribution of income.

The Nobel prize-winning economist Robert Fogel has focused on our improved mastery of the biological environment—leading over the past 300 years to a doubling of the average human life span and to large gains in physical stature, strength, and energy—as the key to what he calls "the egalitarian revolution of the 20th century." He considers this so profound an advance as to constitute a distinct new level of human evolution. Gains in stature, health, and longevity are continuing today and even accelerating. Their outward effects may be observed, in evolutionary fast-forward, in the booming nations of Asia (where, for example, the physical difference between older and younger South Koreans is strikingly evident on the streets of Seoul).

• Third, the critical *source* of social wealth has shifted over the last few hundred years from land (at the end of the 18th century) to physical capital (at the end of the 19th) to, today, human capital—education and cognitive ability. This development is not an unmixed gain from the standpoint of economic equality. The ability to acquire and deploy human capital is a function of intelligence, and intelligence is not only unequally distributed but also, to a significant degree, heritable. As Charles Murray and the late Richard J. Herrnstein argue in *The Bell Curve*, an economy that rewards sheer brainpower replaces one old source

of inequality, socioeconomic advantage, with a new one, cognitive advantage.

* * *

But an economy that rewards human capital also tears down far more artificial barriers than it erects. For most people who inhabit the vast middle range of the bell curve, intelligence is much more equally distributed than land or physical capital ever was. Most people, that is, possess ample intelligence to pursue all but a handful of specialized callings. If in the past many were held back by lack of education and closed social institutions, the opportunities to use one's human capital have blossomed with the advent of universal education and the erosion of social barriers.

Furthermore, the material benefits of the knowledge-based economy are by no means limited to those whom Murray and Herrnstein call the cognitive elite. Many of the newest industries, from fast food to finance to communications, have succeeded in part by opening up employment opportunities for those of modest ability and training—occupations much less arduous and physically much less risky than those they have replaced. And these new industries have created enormous, widely shared economic benefits in consumption; I will return to this subject below.

• Fourth, recent decades have seen a dramatic reduction in one of the greatest historical sources of inequality: the social and economic inequality of the sexes. Today, younger cohorts of working men and women with comparable education and job tenure earn essentially the same incomes. The popular view would have it that the entry of women into the workforce has been driven by falling male earnings and the need "to make ends meet" in middle-class families. But the popular view is largely mistaken. Among married women (as the economist Chinhui Juhn has demonstrated), it is wives of men with high incomes who have been responsible for most of the recent growth in employment.

• Fifth, in the wealthy Western democracies, material needs and desires have been so thoroughly fulfilled for so many people that, for the first time in history, we are seeing large-scale voluntary reductions in the amount of time spent at paid employment. This development manifests itself in different forms: longer periods of education and training for the young; earlier retirement despite longer life spans; and, in between, many more hours devoted to leisure, recreation, entertainment, family, community and religious activities, charitable and other nonremunerative pursuits, and so forth. The dramatic growth of the sports, entertainment, and travel industries captures only a small slice of what has happened. In Fogel's estimation, the time devoted to nonwork activities by the average male head of household has grown from 10.5 hours per week in 1880 to 40 hours today, while time per week at work has fallen from 61.6 hours to 33.6 hours. Among women, the reduction in work (including not only outside employment but also household work, food preparation, childbearing and attendant health problems, and child rearing) and the growth in nonwork have been still greater.

There is a tendency to overlook these momentous developments because of the often frenetic pace of modern life. But our busy-ness actually demonstrates the point: time, and not material things, has become the scarce and valued commodity in modern society.

* * *

One implication of these trends is that in very wealthy societies, income has become a less useful gauge of economic welfare and hence of economic equality. When income becomes to some degree discretionary, and when many peoples' incomes change from year to year for reasons unrelated to their life circumstances, *consumption* becomes a better measure of material welfare. And by this measure, welfare appears much more evenly distributed: people of higher income spend progressively smaller shares on consumption, while in the bottom ranges, annual consumption often exceeds income. (In fact, government statistics suggest that in the bottom 20 percent of the income scale, average annual consumption is about twice annual income—probably a reflection of a substantial underreporting of earnings in this group.) According to the economist Daniel Slesnick, the distribution of consumption, unlike the distribution of reported income, has become measurably *more* equal in recent decades.

If we include leisure-time pursuits as a form of consumption, the distribution of material welfare appears flatter still. Many such activities, being informal by definition, are difficult to track, but Dora Costa of MIT has recently studied one measurable aspect—expenditures on recreation—and found that these have become strikingly more equal as people of lower income have increased the amount of time and money they devote to entertainment, reading, sports, and related enjoyments.

Television, videocassettes, CD's, and home computers have brought musical, theatrical, and other entertainments (both high and low) to everyone, and have enormously narrowed the differences in cultural opportunities between wealthy urban centers and everywhere else. Formerly upper-crust sports like golf, tennis, skiing, and boating have become mass pursuits (boosted by increased public spending on parks and other recreational facilities as well as on environmental quality), and health clubs and full-line book stores have become as plentiful as gas stations. As some of the best things in life become free or nearly so, the price of pursuing them becomes, to that extent, the "opportunity cost" of time itself.

The substitution of leisure activities for income-producing work even appears to have become significant enough to be contributing to the recently much-lamented increase in inequality in measured income. In a new AEI study, Robert Haveman finds that most of the increase in earnings inequality among U.S. males since the mid-1970's can be attributed not to changing labor-market opportunities but to voluntary choice—to the free pursuit of nonwork activities at the expense of income-producing work.

Most of us can see this trend in our own families and communities. A major factor in income inequality in a wealthy knowledge economy is age—many people whose earnings put them at the top of the income curve in their late fifties were well down the curve in their twenties, when they were just getting out of school and beginning their working careers. Fogel again: today the average household in the top 10 percent might consist of a professor or accountant married to a nurse or secretary, both in their peak years of earning. As for the stratospheric top 1 percent, it includes not only very rich people like Bill Cosby but also people like Cosby's

fictional Huxtable family: an obstetrician married to a corporate lawyer. All these individuals would have appeared well down the income distribution as young singles, and that is where their young counterparts appear today.

That more young people are spending more time in college or graduate school, taking time off for travel and "finding themselves," and pursuing interesting but low- or non-paying jobs or apprenticeships before knuckling down to lifelong careers is a significant factor in "income inequality" measured in the aggregate. But this form of economic inequality is in fact the social equality of the modern age. It is progress, not regress, to be cherished and celebrated, not feared and fretted over.

* * *

Which brings me back to my contention that it is our very wealth and equality that are the undoing of the welfare state. Western government today largely consists of two functions. One is income transfers from the wages of those who are working to those who are not working: mainly social-security payments to older people who have chosen to retire rather than go on working and education subsidies for younger people who have chosen to extend their schooling before beginning work. The other is direct and indirect expenditures on medical care, also financed by levies on the wages of those who are working. It is precisely these aspects of life—nonwork and expenditures on medical care and physical well-being —that are the booming sectors of modern, wealthy, technologically advanced society.

When the Social Security program began in America in the 1930's, retirement was still a novel idea: most men worked until they dropped, and they dropped much earlier than they do today. Even in the face of our approaching demographic crunch, produced by the baby boom followed by the baby bust, we could solve the financial problems of the Social Security program in a flash by returning to the days when people worked longer and died younger. Similarly, a world without elaborate diagnostic techniques, replaceable body parts, and potent pharmaceutical and other means of curing or ameliorating disease—a world where medical care consisted largely of bed rest and hand-holding—would present scant fiscal challenge to government as a provider of health insurance.

Our big government-entitlement programs truly are, as conservatives like to call them, obsolete. They are obsolete not because they were terrible ideas to begin with, though some of them were, but because of the astounding growth in social wealth and equality and because of the technological and economic developments which have propelled that growth. When Social Security was introduced, not only was retirement a tiny part of most people's lives but people of modest means had limited ability to save and invest for the future. Today, anyone can mail off a few hundred dollars to a good mutual fund and hire the best investment management American finance has to offer.

In these circumstances it is preposterous to argue, as President Clinton has done, that privatizing Social Security (replacing the current system of income transfers from workers to retirees with one of individually invested retirement savings) would be good for Warren Buffett but bad for the little guy. Private savings—through pension plans, mutual funds, and personal investments

in housing and other durables—are *already* a larger source of retirement income than Social Security transfers. Moreover, although there is much talk nowadays about the riskiness of tying retirement income to the performance of financial markets, the social developments I have described suggest that the greater risk lies in the opposite direction. The current Social Security program ties retirement income to the growth of wage earners' payrolls; that growth is bound to be less than the growth of the economy as a whole, as reflected in the financial markets.

Similarly, Medicare is today a backwater of old-fashioned fee-for-service medicine, hopelessly distorted by a profusion of inefficient and self-defeating price-and-service controls. Over the past dozen years, a revolution has been carried out in the private financing and organization of medical care. The changes have not been unmixed blessings; nor could they be, so long as the tax code encourages people to overinsure for routine medical care. Yet substantial improvements in cost control and quality of service are now evident throughout the health-care sector—except under Medicare. These innovations have not been greeted by riots or strikes at the thousands of private organizations that have introduced them. Nor will there be riots in the streets if, in place of the lamebrained proposals for Medicare "spending cuts" and still more ineffective price controls currently in fashion in Washington, similar market-based innovations are introduced to Medicare.

* * *

In sum, George Bush's famous statement in his inaugural address that "we have more will than wallet" was exactly backward. Our wallets are bulging; the problems we face are increasingly problems not of necessity, but of will. The political class in Washington is still marching to the tune of economic redistribution and, to a degree, "class warfare." But Washington is a lagging indicator of social change. In time, the progress of technology and the growth of private markets and private wealth will generate the political will to transform radically the redistributive welfare state we have inherited from an earlier and more socially balkanized age.

There are signs, indeed, that the Progressive-era and New Deal programs of social insurance, economic regulation, and subsidies and protections for farming, banking, labor organization, and other activities are already crumbling, with salutary effects along every point of the economic spectrum. Anyone who has been a business traveler since the late 1970's, for example, has seen firsthand how deregulation has democratized air travel. Low fares and mass marketing have brought such luxuries as foreign travel, weekend getaways to remote locales, and reunions of far-flung families —just twenty years ago, pursuits of the wealthy—to people of relatively modest means. Coming reforms, including the privatization of Social Security and, most of all, the dismantling of the public-school monopoly in elementary and secondary education, will similarly benefit the less well-off disproportionately, providing them with opportunities enjoyed today primarily by those with high incomes.

I venture a prediction: just as airline deregulation was championed by Edward Kennedy and Jimmy Carter before Ronald Reagan finished the job, so the coming reforms will be a bipartisan enterprise. When the political class catches on

(as Prime Minister Tony Blair has already done in England), the Left will compete vigorously and often successfully with the Right for the allegiance of the vast new privileged middle class. This may sound implausible at a moment when the Clinton administration has become an energetic agent of traditional unionism and has secured the enactment of several new redistributive tax provisions and spending programs. But the watershed event of the Clinton years will almost certainly be seen to be not any of these things but rather the defeat of the President's national health-insurance plan in the face of widespread popular opposition.

The lesson of that episode is that Americans no longer wish to have the things they care about socialized. What has traditionally attracted voters to government as a provider of insurance and other services is not that government does the job better or more efficiently or at a lower cost than private markets; it is the prospect of securing those services through taxes paid by others. That is why today's advocates of expanding the welfare state are still trying to convince voters to think of themselves as members of distinct groups that are net beneficiaries of government: students, teachers, women, racial minorities, union members, struggling young families, retirees, and so forth. But as the material circumstances of the majority become more equal, and as the proficiency and social reach of private markets increasingly outstrip what government can provide, the possibilities for effective redistribution diminish. The members of an egalitarian, middle-class electorate cannot improve their lot by subsidizing one another, and they know it.

With the prospects dimming for further, broad-based socialization along the lines of the Clinton health-care plan, the private supply of important social services will continue to exist and, in general, to flourish alongside government programs. Defenders of the welfare state will thus likely be reduced to asserting that private markets and personal choice may be fine for the well-off, but government services are more appropriate for those of modest means. This is the essence of President Clinton's objection to privatizing Social Security and of the arguments against school choice for parents of students in public elementary and high schools. But "capitalism for the rich, socialism for the poor" is a highly unpromising banner for liberals to be marching under in an era in which capitalism has itself become a profound egalitarian force.

* * *

Where, then, will the battlegrounds be for the political allegiance of the new middle class? Increasingly, that allegiance will turn on policies involving little or no redistributive cachet but rather society-wide benefits in the form of personal amenity, autonomy, and safety: environmental quality and parks, medical and other scientific research, transportation and communications infrastructure, defense against terrorism, and the like. The old welfare-state debates between Left and Right will be transformed into debates over piecemeal incursions into private markets that compete with or replace government services. Should private insurers be required to cover annual mammograms for women in their forties? Should retirement accounts be permitted to invest in tobacco companies? Should parents be permitted to use vouchers to send their children to religious schools? Thus transformed, these debates, too, will

tend to turn on considerations of general social advantage rather than on the considerations of social justice and economic desert that animated the growth of the welfare state.

Political allegiance will also turn increasingly on issues that are entirely nonmaterial. I recently bumped into a colleague, a noted political analyst, just after I had read the morning papers, and asked him to confirm my impression that at least half the major political stories of the past few years had something to do with sex. He smiled and replied, "Peace and prosperity."

What my colleague may have had in mind is that grave crises make all other issues secondary: President Roosevelt's private life received less scrutiny than has President Clinton's, and General Eisenhower's private life received less scrutiny than did that of General Ralston (whose nomination to become chairman of the Joint Chiefs of Staff was torpedoed by allegations of an extramarital affair). There is, however, another, deeper truth in his observation. The stupendous wealth, technological mastery, and autonomy of modern life have freed man not just for worthy, admirable, and self-improving pursuits but also for idleness and unworthy and self-destructive pursuits that are no less a part of his nature.

And so we live in an age of astounding rates of divorce and family break-up, of illegitimacy, of single teenage motherhood, of drug use and crime, of violent and degrading popular entertainments, and of the "culture of narcissism"—and also in an age of vibrant religiosity, of elite universities where madrigal singing and ballroom dancing are all the rage and rampant student careerism is a major faculty concern, and of the Promise Keepers, over a million men of all incomes and races who have packed sports stadiums around the United States to declare their determination to be better husbands, fathers, citizens, and Christians. Ours is an age in which obesity has become a serious public-health problem—and in which dieting, fitness, environmentalism, and self-improvement have become major industries.

It is true, of course, that the heartening developments are in part responses to the disheartening ones. But it is also true that *both* are the results of the economic trends I have described here. In a society as rich and therefore as free as ours has become, the big question, in our personal lives and also in our politics, is: what is our freedom for?

POSTSCRIPT

Is Socioeconomic Inequality Increasing in America?

Social Darwinists have long held that a free-enterprise system results in the survival of the fittest. We are not equal in intellect, ambition, energy, or any other critical faculty, and nothing that the government does can make us equal. In their influential and controversial work *The Bell Curve: Intelligence and Class Structure in American Life* (Free Press, 1994), Charles Murray and Richard J. Herrnstein conclude that social factors have only a minor influence on intelligence. Murray returns to this subject in his short book *Income Inequality and IA* (AEI Press, 1998), in which he concludes, "It is time for policy analysts to stop avoiding the reality of human inequality, a reality that neither equalization of opportunity nor a freer market will circumvent."

Michael J. Sandel, in *Democracy's Discontent: America in Search of a Public Philosophy* (Harvard University Press, 1998), calls for a reinterpretation of American values and the role of government in promoting them. Sandel maintains that Americans have abandoned the sense of common interest for politics based on personal choice and that this has led to undesirable trends in court decisions and public policy. The consequences of a widening gulf between the haves and have-nots has been the creation of professional and managerial elites that, according to Christopher Lash, in *The Revolt of the Elites: And the Betrayal of Democracy* (W. W. Norton, 1996), abandon the middle class and betray the idea of democracy for all Americans.

One striking element regarding economic rewards in modern society is the fact that in many markets, a huge disproportion in income exists between the best or near-best and everyone else. Superstars, whether athletes, actors, or CEOs, earn vastly more than those just below them in achievement. This phenomenon is studied in Robert H. Frank and Philip J. Cook, *The Winner-Take-All Society* (Free Press, 1995).

Specific proposals to redistribute income more equally are made by Sheldon Danziger and Peter Gottschalk in *America Unequal* (Harvard University Press, 1995). The reasons why American blacks and whites differ in wealth accumulation are considered by Melvin L. Oliver and Thomas M. Shapiro, in *Black Wealth/White Wealth: A New Perpsective on Racial Inequality* (Routledge, 1995). Women and racial minorities are not the only significant groups that believe that they are victims of socioeconomic inequality. *White Trash: Race and Class in America* edited by Matt Wray and Annalee Newitz (Routledge, 1996) is a collection of essays examining the economic, social, and cultural conditions of poor whites.

ISSUE 15

Should Abortion Be Restricted?

YES: Robert H. Bork, from "Inconvenient Lives," *First Things* (December 1996)

NO: Mary Gordon, from "A Moral Choice," *The Atlantic Monthly* (March 1990)

ISSUE SUMMARY

YES: Legal scholar Robert H. Bork concludes that the semantics of "pro-choice" cannot hide the fact that aborting a fetus is killing an unborn child and that most abortions are performed for the woman's convenience.

NO: Writer Mary Gordon maintains that having an abortion is a moral choice that women are capable of making for themselves, that aborting a fetus is not killing a person, and that antiabortionists fail to understand female sexuality.

Until 1973 the laws governing abortion were set by the states, most of which barred legal abortion except where pregnancy imperiled the life of the pregnant woman. In that year, the U.S. Supreme Court decided the controversial case *Roe v. Wade.* The *Roe* decision acknowledged both a woman's "fundamental right" to terminate a pregnancy before fetal viability and the state's legitimate interest in protecting both the woman's health and the "potential life" of the fetus. It prohibited states from banning abortion to protect the fetus before the third trimester of a pregnancy, and it ruled that even during that final trimester, a woman could obtain an abortion if she could prove that her life or health would be endangered by carrying to term. (In a companion case to *Roe*, decided on the same day, the Court defined *health* broadly enough to include "all factors—physical, emotional, psychological, familial, and the woman's age—relevant to the well-being of the patient.") These holdings, together with the requirement that state regulation of abortion had to survive "strict scrutiny" and demonstrate a "compelling state interest," resulted in later decisions striking down mandatory 24-hour waiting periods, requirements that abortions be performed in hospitals, and so-called informed consent laws.

The Supreme Court did uphold state laws requiring parental notification and consent for minors (though it provided that minors could seek permission from a judge if they feared notifying their parents). And federal courts have affirmed the right of Congress not to pay for abortions. Proabortion groups, proclaiming the "right to choose," have charged that this and similar action at

the state level discriminates against poor women because it does not inhibit the ability of women who are able to pay for abortions to obtain them. Efforts to adopt a constitutional amendment or federal law barring abortion have failed, but antiabortion forces have influenced legislation in many states.

Can legislatures and courts establish the existence of a scientific fact? Opponents of abortion believe that it is a fact that life begins at conception and that the law must therefore uphold and enforce this concept. They argue that the human fetus is a live human being, and they note all the familiar signs of life displayed by the fetus: a beating heart, brain waves, thumb sucking, and so on. Those who defend abortion maintain that human life does not begin before the development of specifically human characteristics and possibly not until the birth of a child. As Justice Harry A. Blackmun put it in 1973, "There has always been strong support for the view that life does not begin until live birth."

Antiabortion forces sought a court case that might lead to the overturning of *Roe v. Wade*. Proabortion forces rallied to oppose new state laws limiting or prohibiting abortion. In *Webster v. Reproductive Health Services* (1989), with four new justices, the Supreme Court pulled back from its proabortion stance. In a 5–4 decision, the Court upheld a Missouri law that banned abortions in public hospitals and abortions that were performed by public employees (except to save a woman's life). The law also required that tests be performed on any fetus more than 20 weeks old to determine its viability—that is, its ability to survive outside the womb.

In the later decision of *Planned Parenthood v. Casey* (1992), however, the Court affirmed what it called the "essence" of the constitutional right to abortion while permitting some state restrictions, such as a 24-hour waiting period and parental notification in the case of minors.

During the Clinton presidency, opponents of abortion focused on what they identified as "partial-birth" abortions; that is, where a fetus is destroyed during the process of birth. President Clinton twice vetoed partial-birth bans that allowed such abortions to save a woman's life but not her health. By early 1998, 22 states adopted such bans, but in 11 of these states challenges to the law's constitutionality were upheld in federal or state courts. In 1998, in the first of these cases to reach the U.S. Supreme Court, the Court let stand without a written opinion (but with three dissenters) a federal court of appeals decision declaring Ohio's law unconstitutional. The Supreme Court did not confront the question of how it would decide a law that narrowly defined the procedure and provided a maternal health exception.

In the following selections, Robert H. Bork argues that even the most embryonic human fetus must inescapably be defined as human life and that most abortions are performed merely to suit the convenience of the pregnant women. Mary Gordon asserts that the fetus removed in most abortions may not be considered a person and that women must retain the right to make decisions regarding their sexual lives.

YES

Robert H. Bork

INCONVENIENT LIVES

Judging from the evidence, Americans do not view human life as sacrosanct. We engage in a variety of activities, from driving automobiles to constructing buildings, that we know will cause deaths. But the deliberate taking of the life of an individual has never been regarded as a matter of moral indifference. We debate the death penalty, for example, endlessly. It seems an anomaly, therefore, that we have so easily accepted practices that are the deliberate taking of identifiable individual lives. We have turned abortion into a constitutional right; one state has made assisted suicide a statutory right and two federal circuit courts, not to be outdone, have made it a constitutional right; campaigns to legalize euthanasia are underway. It is entirely predictable that many of the elderly, ill, and infirm will be killed, and often without their consent. This is where radical individualism has taken us.

When a society revises its attitude toward life and death, we can see the direction of its moral movement. The revision of American thought and practice about life questions began with abortion, and examination of the moral confusion attending that issue helps us understand more general developments in public morality.

The necessity for reflection about abortion does not depend on, but is certainly made dramatic by, the fact that there are approximately a million and a half abortions annually in the United States. To put it another way, since the Supreme Court's 1973 decision in *Roe v. Wade*, there have been perhaps over thirty million abortions in the United States. Three out of ten conceptions today end in the destruction of the fetus. These facts, standing alone, do not decide the issue of morality, but they do mean that this issue is hugely significant.

The issue is also heated, polarizing, and often debated on both sides in angry, moralistic terms. I will refrain from such rhetoric because for most of my life I held a position on the subject very different from the one I now take. For years I adopted, without bothering to think, the attitude common among secular, affluent, university-educated people who took the propriety of abortion for granted, even when it was illegal. The practice's illegality, like that of drinking alcohol during Prohibition, was thought to reflect merely

From Robert H. Bork, "Inconvenient Lives," *First Things* (December 1996). Adapted from *Slouching Towards Gomorrah* by Robert H. Bork. Copyright © 1996 by Robert H. Bork. Reprinted by permission of HarperCollins Publishers, Inc.

unenlightened prejudice or religious conviction, the two being regarded as much the same. From time to time, someone would say that it was a difficult moral problem, but there was rarely any doubt how the problem should be resolved. I remember a woman at Yale saying, without any disagreement from those around her, that "The fetus isn't nothing, but I am for the mother's right to abort it." I probably nodded. Most of us had a vague and unexamined notion that while the fetus wasn't nothing, it was also not fully human.[1] The slightest reflection would have suggested that non-human or semi-human blobs of tissue do not magically turn into human beings.

Qualms about abortion began to arise when I first read about fetal pain. There is no doubt that, after its nervous system has developed to a degree, the fetus being dismembered or poisoned in the womb feels excruciating pain. For that reason, many people would confine abortion to the early stages of pregnancy but have no objection to it then. There are, on the other hand, people who oppose abortion at any stage and those who regard it as a right at any stage up to the moment of birth. But in thinking about abortion —especially abortion at any stage—it is necessary to address two questions. Is abortion always the killing of a human being? If it is, is that killing done simply for convenience? I think there can be no doubt that the answer to the first questions is, yes; and the answer to the second is, almost always.[2]

*   *   *

The question of whether abortion is the termination of a human life is a relatively simple one. It has been described as a question requiring no more than a knowledge of high school biology. There may be doubt that high school biology courses are clear on the subject these days, but consider what we know. The male sperm and the female egg each contains twenty-three chromosomes. Upon fertilization, a single cell results containing forty-six chromosomes, which is what all humans have, including, of course, the mother and the father. But the new organism's forty-six chromosomes are in a different combination from those of either parent; the new organism is unique. It is not an organ of the mother's body but a different individual. This cell produces specifically human proteins and enzymes from the beginning. Its chromosomes will heavily influence its destiny until the day of its death, whether that death is at the age of ninety or one month after conception.

The cell will multiply and develop, in accordance with its individual chromosomes, and, when it enters the world, will be recognizably a human baby. From single-cell fertilized egg to baby to teenager to adult to old age to death is a single process of one individual, not a series of different individuals replacing each other. It is impossible to draw a line anywhere after the moment of fertilization and say before this point the creature is not human but after this point it is. It has all the attributes of a human from the beginning, and those attributes were in the forty-six chromosomes with which it began. Francis Crick, the Nobel laureate and biophysicist, is quoted as having estimated that "the amount of information contained in the chromosomes of a single fertilized human egg is equivalent to about a thousand printed volumes of books, each as large as a volume of the Encyclopedia Britannica." Such a creature is not a blob of tissue or, as the *Roe* opinion so felicitously put it, a "potential life." As

someone has said, it is a life with potential.

It is impossible to say that the killing of the organism at any moment after it originated is not the killing of a human being. Yet there are those who say just that by redefining what a human being is. Redefining what it means to be a human being will prove dangerous in contexts other than abortion. One of the more primitive arguments put forward is that in the embryonic stage, which lasts about two months after conception, the creature does not look human. One man said to me, "Have you ever seen an embryo? It looks like a guppy." A writer whose work I greatly respect refers to "the patently inhuman fetus of four weeks." A cartoonist made fun of a well-known anti-abortion doctor by showing him pointing to the microscopic dot that is the zygote and saying, "We'll call him Timmy." It is difficult to know what the appearance of Timmy has to do with the humanity of the fetus. I suspect appearance is made an issue because the more recognizably a baby the fetus becomes, the more our emotions reject the idea of destroying it. But those are uninstructed emotions, not emotions based on a recognition of what the fetus is from the beginning.

* * *

Other common arguments are that the embryo or fetus is not fully sentient, or that it cannot live outside the mother's womb, or that the fetus is not fully a person unless it is valued by its mother. These seem utterly insubstantial arguments. A newborn is not fully sentient, nor is a person in an advanced state of Alzheimer's disease. There are people who would allow the killing of the newborn and the senile, but I doubt that is a view with general acceptance. At least not yet. Equally irrelevant to the discussion is the fact that the fetus cannot survive outside the womb. Neither can a baby survive without the nurture of others, usually the parents. Why dependency, which lasts for years after birth, should justify terminating life is inexplicable. No more apparent is the logic of the statement that a fetus is a person only if the mother values its life. That is a tautology: an abortion is justified if the mother wants an abortion.

In discussing abortion, James Q. Wilson wrote, "The moral debate over abortion centers on the point in the development of the fertilized ovum when it has acquired those characteristics that entitle it to moral respect." He did not, apparently, think the cell resulting from conception was so entitled. Wilson gave an example of moral respect persisting in difficult circumstances: "An elderly man who has been a devoted husband and father but who now lies comatose in a vegetative state barely seems to be alive, . . . yet we experience great moral anguish in deciding whether to withdraw his life support." In response, my wife was moved to observe, "But suppose the doctor told us that in eight months the man would recover, be fully human, and live a normal life as a unique individual. It is even conceivable that we would remove his life-support system on the ground that his existence, like that of the fetus, is highly inconvenient to us and that he does not look human at the moment? There would be no moral anguish but instead a certainty that such an act would be a grave moral wrong."

It is certainly more likely that we would refuse to countenance an abortion if a sonogram showed a recognizable human being than if only a tiny, guppy-like

being appeared. But that is an instinctive reaction and instinctive reactions are not always the best guide to moral choice. Intellect must play a role as well. What if biology convinces us that the guppy-like creature or the microscopic fertilized egg has exactly the same future, the same capacity to live a full human life, as does the fetus at three months or at seven months or the infant at birth? "It is difficult to see," my wife added, "that the decision in the imagined case of the comatose elderly man who in time will recover is different from the abortion decision." In both cases, it is only a matter of time. The difference is that the death of the elderly man would deprive him of a few years of life while the aborted embryo or fetus loses an entire lifetime.

The issue is not, I think, one of appearance, sentience, or anything other than prospective life that is denied the individual by abortion. In introductory ethics courses, there used to be a question put: If you could obtain a hundred million dollars by pressing a button that would kill an elderly Chinese mandarin whom you had never seen, and if nobody would know what you had done, would you press the button? That seems to me the same issue as the abortion decision, except that the unborn child has a great deal longer to live if you don't press that particular button. Most of us, I suspect, would like to think we would not kill the mandarin. The characteristics of appearance, sentience, ability to live without assistance, and being valued by others cannot be the characteristics that entitle you to sufficient moral respect to be allowed to go on living. What characteristic does, then? It must lie in the fact that you are alive with the prospect of years of life ahead. That characteristic the unborn child has.

That seems to me an adequate ground to reject the argument made by Peter Singer last year in the London *Spectator* that supports not only abortion but infanticide. He writes that is doubtful that a fetus becomes conscious until well after the time most abortions are performed and even if it is conscious, that would not put the fetus at a level of awareness comparable to that of "a dog, let alone a chimpanzee. If on the other hand it is self-awareness, rather than mere consciousness, that grounds a right to life, that does not arise in a human being until some time after birth."

Aware that this line leaves out of account the potential of the child for a full human life, Singer responds that "in a world that is already over-populated, and in which the regulation of fertility is universally accepted, the argument that we should bring all potential people into existence is not persuasive." That is disingenuous. If overpopulation were a fact, that would hardly justify killing humans. If overpopulation were taken to be a justification, it would allow the killing of any helpless population, preferably without the infliction of pain.

Most contraceptive methods of regulating fertility do not raise the same moral issue as abortion because they do not permit the joining of the sperm and the egg. Until the sperm and the egg unite, there is no human being. Singer goes on to make the unsubstantiated claim that "just as the human being develops gradually in a physical sense, so too does its moral significance gradually increase." That contention is closely allied to the physical appearance argument and is subject to the same rebuttal. One wonders at measuring moral significance by physique. If a person gradually degenerated physically,

would his moral significance gradually decline?

* * *

Many who favor the abortion right understand that humans are being killed. Certainly the doctors who perform and nurses who assist at abortions know that. So do nonprofessionals. Otherwise, abortion would not be smothered in euphemisms. Thus, we hear the language of "choice," "reproductive rights," and "medical procedures." Those are oddly inadequate terms to describe the right to end the life of a human being. It has been remarked that "pro-choice" is an odd term since the individual whose life is at stake has no choice in the matter. These are ways of talking around the point that hide the truth from others and, perhaps, from one's self. President Clinton speaks of keeping abortion "safe, legal, and rare." Why rare, if it is merely a choice, a medical procedure without moral problems?

That there are severe moral problems is becoming clear even to many who favor abortion. That is probably why, as Candace C. Crandall observed last year in the *Women's Quarterly*, "the morale of the pro-choice side of the abortion stalemate has visibly collapsed." The reason: "Proponents of abortion rights overcame Americans' qualms about the procedure with a long series of claims about the benefits of unrestricted abortion on demand. Without exception, those claims have proved false." The proponents claimed that *Roe v. Wade* rescued women from death during unsafe, back-alley abortions, but it was the availability of antibiotics beginning in the 1940s and improved medical techniques that made abortion safe well before *Roe*. It was argued that abortion on demand would guarantee that every child was a wanted child, would keep children from being born into poverty, reduce illegitimacy rates, and help end child abuse. Child poverty rates, illegitimacy rates, and child abuse have all soared. We heard that abortion should be a decision between a woman and her doctor. The idea of a woman and her personal physician deliberating about the choice is a fantasy: women are going to specialized abortion clinics that offer little support or counseling. (Crandall does not address the point, but it is difficult to see that bringing a doctor in for consultation would change the nature of the decision about taking human life.) She does note, however, that many women use abortion for birth control.

Crandall says she sympathizes with abortion-rights advocates. But on her own showing, it is difficult to see why. No anti-abortion advocate could make it clearer that human lives are being destroyed at the rate of 1.5 million a year for convenience.

The author Naomi Wolf, who favors the right to abort, has challenged the feminists whose rhetoric seeks to disguise the truth that a human being is killed by abortion. In a 1995 article in the *New Republic*, she asks for "an abortion-rights movement willing publicly to mourn the evil —necessary evil though it may be—that is abortion." But she asks a question and gives an answer about her support for abortion rights that is troublesome: "But how, one might ask, can I square a recognition of the humanity of the fetus, and the moral gravity of destroying it, with a pro-choice position? The answer can only be found in the context of a paradigm abandoned by the left and misused by the right: the paradigm of sin and redemption."

* * *

That seems an odd paradigm for this problem. It is one thing to have sinned, atoned, and sought redemption. It seems quite another to justify planning to sin on the ground that you also plan to seek redemption afterward. That justification seems even stranger for repeat abortions, which Wolf says are at least 43 percent of the total. Sin plus redemption falls short as a resolution of her dilemma. If that were an adequate resolution, it would seem to follow, given the humanity of the fetus, that infanticide, the killing of the elderly, indeed any killing for convenience, would be licensed if atonement and redemption were planned in advance.

Nor is it clear why the evil is necessary. It is undeniable that bearing and rearing a child sometimes places a great burden on a woman or a family. That fact does not, however, answer the question whether the burden justifies destroying a human life. In most other contexts, we would say such a burden is not sufficient justification. The fact is, in any event, that the burden need not be borne. Putting the child up for adoption is an alternative. The only drawback is that others will know the woman is pregnant. If that is the reason to choose abortion, then the killing really is for convenience.

But it is clear, in any event, that the vast majority of all abortions are for convenience. In those cases, abortion is used as merely one more technique of birth control. A 1987 survey of the reasons given by women for having abortions made by researchers with the Alan Guttmacher Institute, which is very much pro-abortion, demonstrated this fact. [Table 1] shows the percentage of women who gave the listed reasons.

Table 1

Reason	Total Percentage
Woman is concerned about how having a baby could change her life	76
Woman can't afford baby now	68
Woman has problems with relationship or wants to avoid single parenthood	51
Woman is unready for responsibility	31
Woman doesn't want others to know she has had sex or is pregnant	31
Woman is not mature enough or is too young to have a child	30
Woman has all the children she wanted, or has all grown-up children	26
Husband or partner wants woman to have abortion	23
Fetus has possible health problem	13
Woman has health problem	7
Woman's parents want her to have abortion	7
Woman was victim of rape or incest	1
Other	6

It is clear that the overwhelming number of abortions were for birth control unrelated to the health of the fetus or the woman. Moreover, of those who were concerned about a possible health problem of the fetus, only 8 percent said that a physician had told them that the fetus had a defect or was abnormal. The rest were worried because they had taken medication, drugs, or alcohol before realizing they were pregnant, but did not apparently obtain a medical confirmation of any problem. Of those aborting because of their own health, 53 percent said a doctor had told them their condition would be made worse by being pregnant. Some of the rest cited physical problems, and 11 percent gave a mental or emotional problem as the reason. Only 1 percent cited rape or incest.

The survey noted that "some 77 percent of women with incomes under 100 percent or between 100 and 149 percent of the poverty level said they were having

an abortion because they could not afford to have a child, compared with 69 percent of those with incomes between 150 and 199 percent and 60 percent of those with incomes at or above 200 percent of the poverty level." The can't afford category thus included a great many women who, by most reckonings, could afford to have a baby and certainly could have put the baby up for adoption.

This demonstration that abortion is almost always a birth control technique rather than a response to a serious problem with the mother's or the fetus' health must have been a considerable embarrassment to the pro-abortion forces. Perhaps for that reason no survey by them seems to have been reported since. More recent statistics by anti-abortion groups, however, bear out the conclusions to be drawn from the Guttmacher Institute study. The reasons most women give for having an abortion are "social": a baby would affect their education, jobs, lives, or they felt unable to handle it economically, their partners did not want babies, etc.

* * *

Perhaps the most instructive episode demonstrating the brutalization of our culture by abortion was the fight over "partial-birth abortions." These abortions are usually performed late in the pregnancy. The baby is delivered feet first until only the head remains within the mother. The aborting physician inserts scissors into the back of the infant's skull and opens the blades to produce a hole. The child's brains are then vacuumed out, the skull collapses, and the rest of the newly made corpse is removed. If the head had been allowed to come out of the mother, killing the baby then would be the criminal act of infanticide.

When it was proposed to outlaw this hideous procedure, which obviously causes extreme pain to the baby, the pro-abortion forces in Congress and elsewhere made false statements to fend off the legislation or to justify an anticipated presidential veto. Planned Parenthood and the National Abortion and Reproductive Rights Action League stated that the general anesthesia given the mother killed the fetus so that there is no such thing as a partial-birth abortion. Physicians promptly rebutted the claim. Local anesthesia, which is most often used in these abortions, has no effect on the baby and general anesthesia not only does not kill the baby, it provides little or no painkilling effect to the baby. The vice president of the Society for Obstetric Anesthesia and Perinatology said the claim was "crazy," noting that "anesthesia does not kill an infant if you don't kill the mother." Two doctors who perform partial-birth abortions stated that the majority of fetuses aborted in this fashion are alive until the end of the procedure.

Other opponents of a ban on partial-birth abortions claimed that it was used only when necessary to protect the mother's life. Unfortunately for that argument, the physician who is the best-known practitioner of these abortions stated in 1993 that 80 percent of them are "purely elective," not necessary to save the mother's life or health. Partial-birth understates the matter. The baby is outside the mother, except for its head, which is kept in the mother only to avoid a charge of infanticide. Full birth is inches away and could easily be accomplished.

No amount of discussion, no citation of evidence, can alter the opinions of radical feminists about abortion. One evening I naively remarked in a talk

that those who favor the right to abort would likely change their minds if they could be convinced that a human being was being killed. I was startled at the anger that statement provoked in several women present. One of them informed me in no uncertain terms that the issue had nothing to do with the humanity of the fetus but was entirely about the woman's freedom. It is here that radical egalitarianism reinforces radical individualism in supporting the abortion right. Justice Harry Blackmun, who wrote *Roe* and who never offered the slightest constitutional defense of it, simply remarked that the decision was a landmark on women's march to equality. Equality, in this view, means that if men do not bear children, women should not have to either. Abortion is seen as women's escape from the idea that biology is destiny, to escape from the tyranny of the family role.

* * *

Discussions about life and death in one area influence such decisions in others. Despite assurances that the abortion decision did not start us down a slippery and very steep slope, that is clearly where we are, and gathering speed. The systematic killing of unborn children in huge numbers is part of a general disregard for human life that has been growing for some time. Abortion by itself did not cause that disregard, but it certainly deepens and legitimates the nihilism that is spreading in our culture and finds killing for convenience acceptable. We are crossing lines, at first slowly and now with ra-

pidity: killing unborn children for convenience; removing tissue from live fetuses; contemplating creating embryos for destruction in research; considering taking organs from living anencephalic babies; experimenting with assisted suicide; and contemplating euthanasia. Abortion has coarsened us. If it is permissible to kill the unborn human for convenience, it is surely permissible to kill those thought to be soon to die for the same reason. And it is inevitable that many who are not in danger of imminent death will be killed to relieve their families of burdens. Convenience is becoming the theme of our culture. Humans tend to be inconvenient at both ends of their lives.

NOTES

1. I objected to *Roe v. Wade* the moment it was decided, not because of any doubts about abortion, but because the decision was a radical deformation of the Constitution. The Constitution has nothing to say about abortion, leaving it, like most subjects, to the judgment and moral sense of the American people and their elected representatives. *Roe* and the decisions reaffirming it are equal in their audacity and abuse of judicial office to *Dred Scott v. Sandford.* Just as *Dred Scott* forced a southern proslavery position on the nation, *Roe* is nothing more than the Supreme Court's imposition of the morality of our cultural elites.

2. In discussing abortion I will not address instances where most people, however they might ultimately decide the issue, would feel genuine moral anguish, cases, for example, where it is known that the child will be born with severe deformities. My purpose is not to solve all moral issues but simply to address the major ones. Abortions in cases of deformity, etc., are a very small fraction of the total and, because they introduce special factors, do not cast light on the direction of our culture as do abortions of healthy pre-borns performed for convenience.

NO   Mary Gordon

A MORAL CHOICE

I am having lunch with six women. What is unusual is that four of them are in their seventies, two of them widowed, the other two living with husbands beside whom they've lived for decades. All of them have had children. Had they been men, they would have published books and hung their paintings on the walls of important galleries. But they are women of a certain generation, and their lives were shaped around their families and personal relations. They are women you go to for help and support. We begin talking about the latest legislative act that makes abortion more difficult for poor women to obtain. An extraordinary thing happens. Each of them talks about the illegal abortions she had during her young womanhood. Not one of them was spared the experience. Any of them could have died on the table of whatever person (not a doctor in any case) she was forced to approach, in secrecy and in terror, to end a pregnancy that she felt would blight her life.

I mention this incident for two reasons: first as a reminder that all kinds of women have always had abortions; second because it is essential that we remember that an abortion is performed on a living woman who has a life in which a terminated pregnancy is only a small part. Morally speaking, the decision to have an abortion doesn't take place in a vacuum. It is connected to other choices that a woman makes in the course of an adult life.

Anti-choice propagandists paint pictures of women who choose to have abortions as types of moral callousness, selfishness, or irresponsibility. The woman choosing to abort is the dressed-for-success yuppie who gets rid of her baby so that she won't miss her Caribbean vacation or her chance for promotion. Or she is the feckless, promiscuous ghetto teenager who couldn't bring herself to just say no to sex. A third, purportedly kinder, gentler picture has recently begun to be drawn. The woman in the abortion clinic is there because she is misinformed about the nature of the world. She is having an abortion because society does not provide for mothers and their children, and she mistakenly thinks that another mouth to feed will be the ruin of her family, not understanding that the temporary truth of family unhappiness doesn't stack up beside the eternal verity that abortion is murder. Or she is the dupe of her husband or boyfriend, who talks her into having an abortion because

From Mary Gordon, "A Moral Choice," *The Atlantic Monthly* (March 1990). Copyright © 1990 by Mary Gordon. Reprinted by permission of Sterling Lord Literistic, Inc.

a child will be a drag on his life-style. None of these pictures created by the anti-choice movement assumes that the decision to have an abortion is made responsibly, in the context of a morally lived life, by a free and responsible moral agent.

THE ONTOLOGY* OF THE FETUS

How would a woman who habitually makes choices in moral terms come to the decision to have an abortion? The moral discussion of abortion centers on the issue of whether or not abortion is an act of murder. At first glance it would seem that the answer should follow directly upon two questions: Is the fetus human? and Is it alive? It would be absurd to deny that a fetus is alive or that it is human. What would our other options be—to say that it is inanimate or belongs to another species? But we habitually use the terms "human" and "live" to refer to parts of our body—"human hair," for example, or "live red-blood cells"—and we are clear in our understanding that the nature of these objects does not rank equally with an entire personal existence. It then seems important to consider whether the fetus, this alive human thing, is a *person*, to whom the term "murder" could sensibly be applied. How would anyone come to a decision about something so impalpable as personhood? Philosophers have struggled with the issue of personhood, but in language that is so abstract that it is unhelpful to ordinary people making decisions in the course of their lives. It might be more productive to begin thinking about the status of the fetus by examining the language and customs that

*[*Ontology* refers to the nature of being or existing. —Eds.]

surround it. This approach will encourage us to focus on the choosing, acting woman, rather than the act of abortion—as if the act were performed by abstract forces without bodies, histories, attachments.

This focus on the acting woman is useful because a pregnant woman has an identifiable, consistent ontology, and a fetus takes on different ontological identities over time. But common sense, experience, and linguistic usage point clearly to the fact that we habitually consider, for example, a seven-week-old fetus to be different from a seven-month-old one. We can tell this by the way we respond to the involuntary loss of one as against the other. We have different language for the experience of the involuntary expulsion of the fetus from the womb depending upon the point of gestation at which the experience occurs. If it occurs early in the pregnancy, we call it a miscarriage; if late, we call it a stillbirth.

We would have an extreme reaction to the reversal of those terms. If a woman referred to a miscarriage at seven weeks as a stillbirth, we would be alarmed. It would shock our sense of propriety; it would make us uneasy; we would find it disturbing, misplaced—as we do when a bag lady sits down in a restaurant and starts shouting, or an octogenarian arrives at our door in a sailor suit. In short, we would suspect that the speaker was mad. Similarly, if a doctor or a nurse referred to the loss of a seven-month-old fetus as a miscarriage, we would be shocked by that person's insensitivity: could she or he not understand that a fetus that age is not what it was months before?

Our ritual and religious practices underscore the fact that we make distinc-

tions among fetuses. If a woman took the bloody matter—indistinguishable from a heavy period—of an early miscarriage and insisted upon putting it in a tiny coffin and marking its grave, we would have serious concerns about her mental health. By the same token, we would feel squeamish about flushing a seven-month-old fetus down the toilet—something we would quite normally do with an early miscarriage. There are no prayers for the matter of a miscarriage, nor do we feel there should be. Even a Catholic priest would not baptize the issue of an early miscarriage.

The difficulties stem, of course, from the odd situation of a fetus's ontology: a complicated, differentiated, and nuanced response is required when we are dealing with an entity that changes over time. Yet we are in the habit of making distinctions like this. At one point we know that a child is no longer a child but an adult. That this question is vexed and problematic is clear from our difficulty in determining who is a juvenile offender and who is an adult criminal and at what age sexual intercourse ceases to be known as statutory rape. So at what point, if any, do we on the pro-choice side say that the developing fetus is a person, with rights equal to its mother's?

The anti-choice people have one advantage over us; their monolithic position gives them unity on this question. For myself, I am made uneasy by third-trimester abortions, which take place when the fetus could live outside the mother's body, but I also know that these are extremely rare and often performed on very young girls who have had difficulty comprehending the realities of pregnancy. It seems to me that the question of late abortions should be decided case by case, and that fixation on this issue is a deflection from what is most important: keeping early abortions, which are in the majority by far, safe and legal. I am also politically realistic enough to suspect that bills restricting late abortions are not good-faith attempts to make distinctions about the nature of fetal life. They are, rather, the cynical embodiments of the hope among anti-choice partisans that technology will be on their side and that medical science's ability to create situations in which younger fetuses are viable outside their mothers' bodies will increase dramatically in the next few years. Ironically, medical science will probably make the issue of abortion a minor one in the near future. The RU-486 pill, which can induce abortion early on, exists, and whether or not it is legally available (it is not on the market here, because of pressure from anti-choice groups), women will begin to obtain it. If abortion can occur through chemical rather than physical means, in the privacy of one's home, most people not directly involved will lose interest in it. As abortion is transformed from a public into a private issue, it will cease to be perceived as political; it will be called personal instead.

AN EQUIVOCAL GOOD

But because abortion will always deal with what it is to create and sustain life, it will always be a moral issue. And whether we like it or not, our moral thinking about abortion is rooted in the shifting soil of perception. In an age in which much of our perception is manipulated by media that specialize in the sound bite and the photo op, the anti-choice partisans have a twofold advantage over us on the pro-choice side. The pro-choice moral position is more complex, and the experience

we defend is physically repellent to contemplate. None of us in the pro-choice movement would suggest that abortion is not a regrettable occurrence. Anti-choice proponents can offer pastel photographs of babies in buntings, their eyes peaceful in the camera's gaze. In answer, we can't offer the material of an early abortion, bloody, amorphous in a paper cup, to prove that what has just been removed from the woman's body is not a child, not in the same category of being as the adorable bundle in an adoptive mother's arms. It is not a pleasure to look at the physical evidence of abortion, and most of us don't get the opportunity to do so.

The theologian Daniel Maguire, uncomfortable with the fact that most theological arguments about the nature of abortion are made by men who have never been anywhere near an actual abortion, decided to visit a clinic and observe abortions being performed. He didn't find the experience easy, but he knew that before he could in good conscience make a moral judgment on abortion, he needed to experience through his senses what an aborted fetus is like: he needed to look at and touch the controversial entity. He held in his hand the bloody fetal stuff; the eight-week-old fetus fit in the palm of his hand, and it certainly bore no resemblance to either of his two children when he had held them moments after their birth. He knew at that point what women who have experienced early abortions and miscarriages know: that some event occurred, possibly even a dramatic one, but it was not the death of a child.

Because issues of pregnancy and birth are both physical and metaphorical, we must constantly step back and forth between ways of perceiving the world. When we speak of gestation, we are often talking in terms of potential, about events and objects to which we attach our hopes, fears, dreams, and ideals. A mother can speak to the fetus in her uterus and name it; she and her mate may decorate a nursery according to their vision of the good life; they may choose for an embryo a college, a profession, a dwelling. But those of us who are trying to think morally about pregnancy and birth must remember that these feelings are our own projections onto what is in reality an inappropriate object. However charmed we may be by an expectant father's buying a little football for something inside his wife's belly, we shouldn't make public policy based on such actions, nor should we force others to live their lives conforming to our fantasies.

As a society, we are making decisions that pit the complicated future of a complex adult against the fate of a mass of cells lacking cortical development. The moral pressure should be on distinguishing the true from the false, the real suffering of living persons from our individual and often idiosyncratic dreams and fears. We must make decisions on abortion based on an understanding of how people really do live. We must be able to say that poverty is worse than not being poor, that having dignified and meaningful work is better than working in conditions of degradation, that raising a child one loves and has desired is better than raising a child in resentment and rage, that it is better for a twelve-year-old not to endure the trauma of having a child when she is herself a child.

When we put these ideas against the ideas of "child" or "baby," we seem to be making a horrifying choice of life-style over life. But in fact we are telling the truth of what it means to bear a child, and what the experience of abortion really is.

This is extremely difficult, for the object of the discussion is hidden, changing, potential. We make our decisions on the basis of approximate and inadequate language, often on the basis of fantasies and fears. It will always be crucial to try to separate genuine moral concern from phobia, punitiveness, superstition, anxiety, a desperate search for certainty in an uncertain world.

One of the certainties that is removed if we accept the consequences of the pro-choice position is the belief that the birth of a child is an unequivocal good. In real life we act knowing that the birth of a child is not always a good thing: people are sometimes depressed, angry, rejecting, at the birth of a child. But this is a difficult truth to tell; we don't like to say it, and one of the fears preyed on by anti-choice proponents is that if we cannot look at the birth of a child as an unequivocal good, then there is nothing to look toward. The desire for security of the imagination, for typological fixity, particularly in the area of "the good," is an understandable desire. It must seem to some anti-choice people that we on the pro-choice side are not only murdering innocent children but also murdering hope. Those of us who have experienced the birth of a desired child and felt the joy of that moment can be tempted into believing that it was the physical experience of the birth itself that was the joy. But it is crucial to remember that the birth of a child itself is a neutral occurrence emotionally: the charge it takes on is invested in it by the people experiencing or observing it.

THE FEAR OF SEXUAL AUTONOMY

These uncertainties can lead to another set of fears, not only about abortion but about its implications. Many anti-choice people fear that to support abortion is to cast one's lot with the cold and technological rather than with the warm and natural, to head down the slippery slope toward a brave new world where handicapped children are left on mountains to starve and the old are put out in the snow. But if we look at the history of abortion, we don't see the embodiment of what the anti-choice proponents fear. On the contrary, excepting the grotesque counterexample of the People's Republic of China (which practices forced abortion), there seems to be a real link between repressive anti-abortion stances and repressive governments. Abortion was banned in Fascist Italy and Nazi Germany; it is illegal in South Africa and in Chile. It is paid for by the governments of Denmark, England, and the Netherlands, which have national health and welfare systems that foster the health and well-being of mothers, children, the old, and the handicapped.

Advocates of outlawing abortion often refer to women seeking abortion as self-indulgent and materialistic. In fact these accusations mask a discomfort with female sexuality, sexual pleasure, and sexual autonomy. It is possible for a woman to have a sexual life unriddled by fear only if she can be confident that she need not pay for a failure of technology or judgment (and who among us has never once been swept away in the heat of a sexual moment?) by taking upon herself the crushing burden of unchosen motherhood.

It is no accident, therefore, that the increased appeal of measures to restrict maternal conduct during pregnancy—and a new focus on the physical autonomy of the pregnant woman—have come into public discourse at precisely

the time when women are achieving un-precedented levels of economic and po-litical autonomy. What has surprised me is that some of this new anti-autonomy talk comes to us from the left. An ex-ample of this new discourse is an ar-ticle by Christopher Hitchens that ap-peared in *The Nation* last April, in which the author asserts his discomfort with abortion. Hitchens's tone is impeccably British: arch, light, we're men of the left.

> Anyone who has ever seen a sonogram or has spent even an hour with a textbook on embryology knows that the emotions are not the deciding factor. In order to terminate a pregnancy, you have to still a heartbeat, switch off a developing brain, and whatever the method, break some bones and rupture some organs. As to whether this involves pain on the "Silent Scream" scale, I have no idea. The "right to life" leadership, again, has cheapened everything it touches. ["Silent Scream" refers to Dr. Bernard Nathanson's widely debated antiabortion film *The Silent Scream,* in which an abortion on a 12-week-old fetus is shown from inside the uterus.—Eds.]

"It is a pity," Hitchens goes on to say, "that... the majority of feminists and their allies have stuck to the dead ground of 'Me Decade' possessive individualism, an ideology that has more in common than it admits with the prehistoric right, which it claims to oppose but has in fact encouraged." Hitchens proposes, as an alternative, a program of social reform that would make contraception free and support a national adoption service. In his opinion, it would seem, women have abortions for only two reasons: because they are selfish or because they are poor. If the state will take care of the economic problems and the bureaucratic messiness around adoption, it remains only for

the possessive individualists to get their act together and walk with their babies into the communal utopia of the future. Hitchens would allow victims of rape or incest to have free abortions, on the grounds that since they didn't choose to have sex, the women should not be forced to have the babies. This would seem to put the issue of volition in a wrong and telling place. To Hitchens's mind, it would appear, if a woman chooses to have sex, she can't choose whether or not to have a baby. The implications of this are clear. If a woman is consciously and volitionally sexual, she should be prepared to take her medicine. And what medicine must the consciously sexual male take? Does Hitchens really believe, or want us to believe, that every male who has unintentionally impregnated a woman will be involved in the lifelong responsibility for the upbringing of the engendered child? Can he honestly say that he has observed this behavior—or, indeed, would want to see it observed—in the world in which he lives?

REAL CHOICES

It is essential for a moral decision about abortion to be made in an atmosphere of open, critical thinking. We on the pro-choice side must accept that there are in-deed anti-choice activists who take their position in good faith. I believe, however, that they are people for whom childbirth is an emotionally overladen topic, peo-ple who are susceptible to unclear think-ing because of their unrealistic hopes and fears. It is important for us in the pro-choice movement to be open in dis-cussing those areas involving abortion which are nebulous and unclear. But we must not forget that there are some things that we know to be undeniably true.

There are some undeniable bad consequences of a woman's being forced to bear a child against her will. First is the trauma of going through a pregnancy and giving birth to a child who is not desired, a trauma more long-lasting than that experienced by some (only some) women who experience an early abortion. The grief of giving up a child at its birth—and at nine months it is a child whom one has felt move inside one's body—is underestimated both by anti-choice partisans and by those for whom access to adoptable children is important. This grief should not be forced on any woman—or, indeed, encouraged by public policy.

We must be realistic about the impact on society of millions of unwanted children in an overpopulated world. Most of the time, human beings have sex not because they want to make babies. Yet throughout history sex has resulted in unwanted pregnancies. And women have always aborted. One thing that is not hidden, mysterious, or debatable is that making abortion illegal will result in the deaths of women, as it has always done. Is our historical memory so short that none of us remember aunts, sisters, friends, or mothers who were killed or rendered sterile by septic abortions? Does no one in the anti-choice movement remember stories or actual experiences of midnight drives to filthy rooms from which aborted women were sent out, bleeding, to their fate? Can anyone genuinely say that it would be a moral good for us as a society to return to those conditions?

Thinking about abortion, then, forces us to take moral positions as adults who understand the complexities of the world and the realities of human suffering, to make decisions based on how people actually live and choose, and not on our fears, prejudices, and anxieties about sex and society, life and death.

POSTSCRIPT

Should Abortion Be Restricted?

Bork and Gordon come to different conclusions in considering the question, When does human life begin and have the right to be protected by the state? At the moment of conception? At a defined stage of fetal development? When a live child could be delivered? At the moment of biological birth?

Antiabortionists ask, Do abortions cause pain to fetuses? Are pregnant women psychologically scarred by abortion? Does legalized abortion produce insensitivity to human life? Pro-abortionists, in turn, ask, What harm is done to an unmarried teenage girl in bearing a baby? Who will raise and care for all the unwanted children? Will prohibition produce, as it always has, countless unsafe back-alley abortions?

Dozens of books have dealt with these questions since the Supreme Court's decision in *Roe v. Wade* in 1973. A comprehensive selection ranging from the proabortion views of Dr. Alan Guttmacher to the antiabortion position of Daniel Callahan can be found in J. Douglas Butler and David F. Walbert, eds., *Abortion, Medicine, and the Law*, 3rd ed. (Facts on File, 1986).

More briefly, most of the legal, ethical, and medical issues are considered in Hyman Rodman, Betty Sarvis, and Joy Walker Bonar, *The Abortion Question* (Columbia University Press, 1987). In *Real Choices* (Multnomah Press, 1994), Frederica Mathewes-Green argues the case against abortion from the standpoint of the harm (physical and psychological) that it inflicts on women. A similar approach is taken by David C. Reardon in *Making Abortion Rare* (Acorn Books, 1996).

Robert M. Baird and Stuart E. Rosenbaum, eds., *The Ethics of Abortion: Pro-Life vs. Pro-Choice*, rev. ed. (Prometheus Books, 1993), contains a wide variety of views, including those of Robert H. Bork, Ronald Dworkin, Anna Quindlen, and Richard Selzer. An unbiased history of abortion as an American political issue can be found in Barbara Hinkson Craig and David M. O'Brien, *Abortion and American Politics* (Chatham House Publishers, 1993).

Books that purport to establish a common ground include Elizabeth Mensch and Alan Freeman, *The Politics of Virtue: Is Abortion Debatable?* (Duke University Press, 1993); Lawrence Tribe, *Abortion: The Clash of Absolutes* (W. W. Norton, 1990); and Roger Rosenblatt, *Life Itself: Abortion in the American Mind* (Random House, 1992).

The passion that these authors express in articulating their thoughtful analyses makes clear that no other moral issue that has become the subject of political debate in modern America arouses such deep and irreconcilable feelings.

ISSUE 16

Should Gay Marriage Be Legalized?

YES: Andrew Sullivan, from *Virtually Normal: An Argument About Homosexuality* (Alfred A. Knopf, 1995)

NO: James Q. Wilson, from "Against Homosexual Marriage," *Commentary* (March 1996)

ISSUE SUMMARY

YES: Essayist and editor Andrew Sullivan contends that legalizing gay marriage would be a profoundly humanizing step because such marriages, with their honesty, their flexibility, and their equality, could nourish the broader society as well.

NO: Social scientist James Q. Wilson asserts that to legalize homosexual marriage would be to enter an untested area that could profoundly damage the already-fragile institutions of marriage and family.

On May 12, 1979, in Sioux Falls, South Dakota, Randy Rohl and Grady Quinn made history of a sort. They were the first acknowledged homosexual couple ever to receive permission from their high school principal to attend the prom together. The National Gay Task force hailed the event as a milestone in the history of human rights. What the voters of Sioux Falls thought of it cannot be determined (they weren't asked), but if their reactions were similar to those of people who voted on various state and local referenda since that time, they probably were not pleased. In several county and municipal elections, voters were asked to approve resolutions specifically banning discrimination based on "sexual preference," but the voters rejected these resolutions by large majorities. More recently, voters in Colorado approved a resolution denying local jurisdictions the authority to grant homosexuals any rights beyond those granted by the U.S. Constitution. The U.S. Supreme Court struck this down as unconstitutional in 1996, but the passage of the initiative showed that Colorado voters were not ready to include homosexuals among those groups that are entitled to state civil rights protection, such as blacks and women.

Despite these popular rebuffs to "gay rights," the attitude of most Americans toward homosexuals appears to be rather complex and nuanced. A 1995 public opinion poll showed that only 41 percent of the public believed that the homosexual lifestyle should be accepted, a result consistent with those of several earlier polls showing that the majority consider homosexuality "abnormal" and homosexual behavior "immoral." At the same time, however,

American voters have defeated resolutions (such as one in California in 1978) that would ban the hiring of homosexuals to teach in public schools, and they have elected public officials who have pledged to uphold "gay rights," including some who have openly declared their own homosexuality.

If there is a thread of consistency here, it is this: Americans believe in fair play and equal treatment for people of equal merit; they also, as a rule, believe in minding their own business. Most Americans would agree that what people do in their bedrooms has no place in the public realm. But it is precisely here that the conflict arises, for as many Americans see it, what organized homosexual groups are attempting to do is to bring their private behavior *into* the public realm by making homosexuality a "civil right." American social mores are deeply rooted in Judeo-Christian tradition, which unambiguously condemns homosexual behavior. Although they are willing to tolerate such behavior in private, most Americans are reluctant to support any measure that appears to give it official recognition.

The raw nerve of this conflict was touched in 1996 when Hawaii's highest state court ruled that the state must present compelling public reason for prohibiting same-sex marriages. The state failed to do so, and it is now anticipated that "gay marriage" will be permissible in Hawaii. Because of the U.S. Constitution, this controversy has national dimensions. Article IV, Section 1, of the Constitution stipulates that "Full Faith and Credit shall be given in each state to the public Acts, Records, and judicial Proceedings of every other State." What that means is that every state of the union must honor the Hawaiian court's legalization of same-sex marriage. Therefore, gay couples will be able to fly to Hawaii to get married, then come back home and enjoy all the legal benefits of marriage in their home state: inheritance, housing, tax benefits, adoption rights, and so forth. (This is what happened in the past in cases of divorce, when states like Nevada, which adopted liberal divorce laws, in effect forced other states to adopt similar practices.) In an effort to head off this eventuality, the House of Representatives in the summer of 1996 passed the Defense of Marriage Act, which would allow each state to ignore same-sex marriages sanctioned by another state. President Bill Clinton signed the bill on September 20, 1996.

In the following selections, former *New Republic* editor Andrew Sullivan, who is gay, defends the concept of same-sex marriage, which he sees as not only a civil right but as the kind of idea that might add needed flexibility to the institution of marriage. Social scientist James Q. Wilson expresses concern that legalizing such unions can only weaken the already-fragile framework of marriage.

YES

Andrew Sullivan

VIRTUALLY NORMAL

In everyone there sleeps
  A Sense of life lived according to love.
To some it means the difference they could make
By loving others, but across most it sweeps
As all they might have been had they been loved.
That nothing cures.

—PHILIP LARKIN

If there were no alternative to today's conflicted politics of homosexuality, we might be condemned to see the proponents of the four major positions fight noisily while society stumbles from one awkward compromise to another. But there is an alternative: a politics that can reconcile the best arguments of liberals and conservatives, and find a way to marry the two. In accord with liberalism, this politics respects the law, its limits, and its austerity. It places a high premium on liberty, and on a strict limit to the regulation of people's minds and actions. And in sympathy with conservatism, this politics acknowledges that in order to create a world of equality, broader arguments may often be needed to persuade people of the need for change, apart from those of rights and government neutrality. It sees that beneath politics, human beings exist whose private lives may indeed be shaped by a shift in public mores.

This politics begins with the view that for a small minority of people, from a young age, homosexuality is an essentially involuntary condition that can neither be denied nor permanently repressed. It is a function of both nature and nurture, but the forces of nurture are formed so early and are so complex that they amount to an involuntary condition. It is *as if* it were a function of nature. Moreover, so long as homosexual adults as citizens insist on the involuntary nature of their condition, it becomes politically impossible simply to deny or ignore the fact of homosexuality.

This politics adheres to an understanding that there is a limit to what politics can achieve in such a fraught area as homosexuality, and trains its focus not on the behavior of citizens in civil society but on the actions of

From Andrew Sullivan, *Virtually Normal: An Argument About Homosexuality* (Alfred A. Knopf, 1995). Copyright © 1995 by Andrew Sullivan. Reprinted by permission of Alfred A. Knopf, Inc.

the public and allegedly neutral state. While it eschews the use of law to legislate culture, it strongly believes that law can affect culture indirectly by its insistence on the equality of all citizens. Its goal in the area of homosexuality is simply to ensure that the liberal state live up to its promises for all its citizens. It would seek full public equality for those who, through no fault of their own, happen to be homosexual; and it would not deny homosexuals, as the other four politics do, their existence, integrity, dignity, or distinctness. It would attempt neither to patronize nor to exclude.

This politics affirms a simple and limited principle: that all *public* (as opposed to private) discrimination against homosexuals be ended and that every right and responsibility that heterosexuals enjoy as public citizens be extended to those who grow up and find themselves emotionally different. *And that is all.* No cures or re-educations, no wrenching private litigation, no political imposition of tolerance; merely a political attempt to enshrine formal public equality, whatever happens in the culture and society at large. For these reasons, it is the only politics that actually tackles the *political* problem of homosexuality; the only one that fully respects liberalism's public-private distinction; and, ironically, as we shall see, the only one that cuts the Gordian knot of the shame and despair and isolation that many homosexuals feel. For these reasons, perhaps, it has the least chance of being adopted by homosexuals and heterosexuals alike.

What would it mean in practice? Quite simply, an end to all proactive discrimination by the state against homosexuals. That means an end to sodomy laws that apply only to homosexuals; a recourse to the courts if there is not equal protection of heterosexuals and homosexuals in law enforcement; an equal legal age of consent to sexual activity for heterosexuals and homosexuals, where such regulations apply; inclusion of the facts about homosexuality in the curriculum of every government-funded school, in terms no more and no less clear than those applied to heterosexuality (although almost certainly with far less emphasis, because of homosexuality's relative rareness when compared with heterosexuality); recourse to the courts if any government body or agency can be proven to be engaged in discrimination against homosexual employees; equal opportunity and inclusion in the military; and legal homosexual marriage and divorce. . . .

Its most powerful and important elements are equal access to the military and marriage. The military ban is by far the most egregious example of proactive public discrimination in the Western democracies. By conceding the excellent service that many gay and lesbian soldiers have given to their country, the U.S. military in recent years has elegantly clarified the specificity of the government's unfairness. By focusing on the mere public admission of homosexuality in its 1993 "don't ask, don't tell" compromise, the military isolated the core issue at the heart of the equality of homosexual persons. It argued that homosexuals could serve in the military; that others could know they were homosexuals; that *they* could know they were homosexuals; but that if they ever so much as mentioned this fact, they were to be discharged. The prohibition was not against homosexual acts as such—occasional lapses by heterosexuals were not to be grounds for expulsion. The prohibition was not even against homosexuality. The prohibition was against

homosexuals' being honest about their sexuality, because that honesty allegedly lowered the morale of others.

Once the debate has been constructed this way, it will eventually, surely, be won by those advocating the admission of open homosexuals in the military. When this is the sole argument advanced by the military—it became the crux of the debate on Capitol Hill—it has the intellectual solidity of a pack of cards. One group is arbitrarily silenced to protect not the rights but the sensibilities of the others. To be sure, it won the political battle; but it clearly lost the moral and intellectual war, as subsequent court tests demonstrated. It required one of the most respected institutions in American society to impose upon its members a rule of fundamental dishonesty in order for them to perform their duties. It formally introduced hypocrisy as a rule of combat....

If this politics is feasible, both liberal and conservative dead ends become new beginnings. The liberal can campaign for formal public equality—for the abolition of sodomy laws, equal protection in public employment and institutions, the end of the ban on openly gay men and lesbians in the military—and rightly claim that he is merely seeing that all citizens in their public capacity are treated equally. But he can also argue fervently for freedom of expression—for those on both sides of the cultural war —and for freedom of economic contract. And he can concentrate his efforts on the work of transforming civil society, the place where every liberal longs to be.

And the conservative, while opposing "special rights," is able to formulate a vision of what values the society wants to inculcate. He can point to the virtues of a loyal and dedicated soldier, homosexual or heterosexual, and celebrate his patriotism; he can involve another minority group in the collective social good. He can talk about relations between heterosexuals and homosexuals not under the rubric of a minority group seeking preferences from a majority group, but as equal citizens, each prepared and willing to contribute to the common good, so long as they are treated equally by the state.

But the centerpiece of this new politics goes further than this. The critical measure for this politics of public equality–private freedom is something deeper and more emotional, perhaps, than the military.

It is equal access to civil marriage.

As with the military, this is a question of formal public discrimination, since only the state can grant and recognize marriage. If the military ban deals with the heart of what it means to be a citizen, marriage does even more so, since, in peace and war, it affects everyone. Marriage is not simply a private contract; it is a social and public recognition of a private commitment. As such, it is the highest public recognition of personal integrity. Denying it to homosexuals is the most public affront possible to their public equality.

This point may be the hardest for many heterosexuals to accept. Even those tolerant of homosexuals may find this institution so wedded to the notion of heterosexual commitment that to extend it would be to undo its very essence. And there may be religious reasons for resisting this that, within certain traditions, are unanswerable. But I am not here discussing what churches do in their private affairs. I am discussing what the allegedly neutral liberal state should do in public matters. For liberals, the case for

homosexual marriage is overwhelming. As a classic public institution, it should be available to any two citizens.

Some might argue that marriage is by definition between a man and a woman; and it is difficult to argue with a definition. But if marriage is articulated beyond this circular fiat, then the argument for its exclusivity to one man and one woman disappears. The center of the public contract is an emotional, financial, and psychological bond between two people; in this respect, heterosexuals and homosexuals are identical. The heterosexuality of marriage is intrinsic only if it is understood to be intrinsically procreative; but that definition has long been abandoned in Western society. No civil marriage license is granted on the condition that the couple bear children; and the marriage is no less legal and no less defensible if it remains childless. In the contemporary West, marriage has become a way in which the state recognizes an emotional commitment by two people to each other for life. And within that definition, there is no public way, if one believes in equal rights under the law, in which it should legally be denied homosexuals....

But perhaps surprisingly ... one of the strongest arguments for gay marriage is a conservative one. It's perhaps best illustrated by a comparison with the alternative often offered by liberals and liberationists to legal gay marriage, the concept of "domestic partnership." Several cities in the United States have domestic partnership laws, which allow relationships that do not fit into the category of heterosexual marriage to be registered with the city and qualify for benefits that had previously been reserved for heterosexual married couples. In these cities, a variety of interpersonal arrangements qualify for health insurance, bereavement leave, insurance, annuity and pension rights, housing rights (such as rent-control apartments), adoption and inheritance rights. Eventually, the aim is to include federal income tax and veterans' benefits as well. Homosexuals are not the only beneficiaries; heterosexual "live-togethers" also qualify.

The conservative's worries start with the ease of the relationship. To be sure, potential domestic partners have to prove financial interdependence, shared living arrangements, and a commitment to mutual caring. But they don't need to have a sexual relationship or even closely mirror old-style marriage. In principle, an elderly woman and her live-in nurse could qualify, or a pair of frat buddies. Left as it is, the concept of domestic partnership could open a Pandora's box of litigation and subjective judicial decision making about who qualifies. You either are or you're not married; it's not a complex question. Whether you are in a domestic partnership is not so clear.

More important for conservatives, the concept of domestic partnership chips away at the prestige of traditional relationships and undermines the priority we give them. Society, after all, has good reasons to extend legal advantages to heterosexuals who choose the formal sanction of marriage over simply living together. They make a deeper commitment to one another and to society; in exchange, society extends certain benefits to them. Marriage provides an anchor, if an arbitrary and often weak one, in the maelstrom of sex and relationships to which we are all prone. It provides a mechanism for emotional stability and economic security. We rig the law in its favor not because we disparage all forms of relationship other than the nuclear family, but because we recognize that not to promote

marriage would be to ask too much of human virtue . . .

Any heterosexual man who takes a few moments to consider what his life would be like if he were never allowed a formal institution to cement his relationships will see the truth of what I am saying. Imagine life without a recognized family; imagine dating without even the possibility of marriage. Any heterosexual woman who can imagine being told at a young age that her attraction to men was wrong, that her loves and crushes were illicit, that her destiny was single-hood and shame, will also appreciate the point. Gay marriage is not a radical step; it is a profoundly humanizing, traditionalizing step. It is the first step in any resolution of the homosexual question—more important than any other institution, since it is the most central institution to the nature of the problem, which is to say, the emotional and sexual bond between one human being and another. If nothing else were done at all, and gay marriage were legalized, ninety percent of the political work necessary to achieve gay and lesbian equality would have been achieved. It is ultimately the only reform that truly matters.

. . . It has become a truism that in the field of emotional development, homosexuals have much to learn from the heterosexual culture. The values of commitment, of monogamy, of marriage, of stability are all posited as models for homosexual existence. And, indeed, of course, they are. Without an architectonic institution like that of marriage, it is difficult to create the conditions for nurturing such virtues, but that doesn't belie their importance.

It is also true, however, that homosexual relationships, even in their current, somewhat eclectic form, may contain features that could nourish the broader society as well. Precisely because there is no institutional model, gay relationships are often sustained more powerfully by genuine commitment. The mutual nurturing and sexual expressiveness of many lesbian relationships, the solidity and space of many adult gay male relationships, are qualities sometimes lacking in more rote, heterosexual couplings. Same-sex unions often incorporate the virtues of friendship more effectively than traditional marriages; and at times, among gay male relationships, the openness of the contract makes it more likely to survive than many heterosexual bonds. Some of this is unavailable to the male-female union: there is more likely to be greater understanding of the need for extramarital outlets between two men than between a man and a woman; and again, the lack of children gives gay couples greater freedom. Their failures entail fewer consequences for others. But something of the gay relationship's necessary honesty, its flexibility, and its equality could undoubtedly help strengthen and inform many heterosexual bonds. . . .

As I've just argued, I believe strongly that marriage should be made available to everyone, in a politics of strict public neutrality. But within this model, there is plenty of scope for cultural difference. There is something baleful about the attempt of some gay conservatives to educate homosexuals and lesbians into an uncritical acceptance of a stifling model of heterosexual normality. The truth is, homosexuals are not entirely normal; and to flatten their varied and complicated lives into a single, moralistic model is to miss what is essential and exhilarating about their otherness.

NO James Q. Wilson

AGAINST HOMOSEXUAL MARRIAGE

Our courts, which have mishandled abortion, may be on the verge of mishandling homosexuality. As a consequence of two pending decisions, we may be about to accept homosexual marriage.

In 1993 the supreme court of Hawaii ruled that, under the equal-protection clause of that state's constitution, any law based on distinctions of sex was suspect, and thus subject to strict judicial scrutiny. Accordingly, it reversed the denial of a marriage permit to a same-sex couple, unless the state could first demonstrate a "compelling state interest" that would justify limiting marriages to men and women.... [I]n the meantime, the executive branch of Hawaii appointed a commission to examine the question of same-sex marriages; its report, by a vote of five to two, supports them. The legislature, for its part, holds a different view of the matter, having responded to the court's decision by passing a law unambiguously reaffirming the limitation of marriage to male-female couples.

... [S]ince the United States Constitution has a clause requiring that "full faith and credit shall be given to the public acts, records, and judicial proceedings of every other state," a homosexual couple in a state like Texas, where the population is overwhelmingly opposed to such unions, may soon be able to fly to Hawaii, get married, and then return to live in Texas as lawfully wedded....

Contemporaneous with these events, an important book has appeared under the title *Virtually Normal*. In it, Andrew Sullivan, the editor of the *New Republic*, makes a strong case for a new policy toward homosexuals. He argues that "all *public* (as opposed to private) discrimination against homosexuals be ended.... *And that is all*." The two key areas where this change is necessary are the military and marriage law. Lifting bans in those areas, while also disallowing antisodomy laws and providing information about homosexuality in publicly supported schools, would put an end to the harm that gays have endured. Beyond these changes, Sullivan writes, American society would need no "cures [of homophobia] or reeducations, no wrenching private litigation, no political imposition of tolerance."

It is hard to imagine how Sullivan's proposals would, in fact, end efforts to change private behavior toward homosexuals, or why the next, inevitable, step would not involve attempts to accomplish just that purpose by using cures and reeducations, private litigation, and the political imposition of tolerance. But apart from this, Sullivan—an English Catholic, a homosexual, and someone who has on occasion referred to himself as a conservative—has given us the most sensible and coherent view of a program to put homosexuals and heterosexuals on the same public footing....

* * *

Sullivan recounts three main arguments concerning homosexual marriage, two against and one for. He labels them prohibitionist, conservative, and liberal. (A fourth camp, the "liberationist," which advocates abolishing all distinctions between heterosexuals and homosexuals, is also described—and scorched for its "strange confluence of political abdication and psychological violence.") I think it easier to grasp the origins of the three main arguments by referring to the principles on which they are based.

The prohibitionist argument is in fact a biblical one; the heart of it was stated by Dennis Prager in an essay in the *Public Interest* ("Homosexuality, the Bible, and Us," Summer 1993). When the first books of the Bible were written, and for a long time thereafter, heterosexual love is what seemed at risk. In many cultures—not only in Egypt or among the Canaanite tribes surrounding ancient Israel but later in Greece, Rome, and the Arab world, to say nothing of large parts of China, Japan, and elsewhere—homosexual practices were common and widely tolerated or even exalted. The

Torah reversed this, making the family the central unit of life, the obligation to marry one of the first responsibilities of man, and the linkage of sex to procreation the highest standard by which to judge sexual relations. Leviticus puts the matter sharply and apparently beyond quibble:

> Thou shalt not live with mankind as with womankind; it is an abomination.... If a man also lie with mankind, as he lieth with a woman, both of them have committed an abomination; they shall surely be put to death; their blood shall be upon them.

Sullivan acknowledges the power of Leviticus but deals with it by placing it in a relative context. What is the nature of this "abomination"? Is it like killing your mother or stealing a neighbor's bread, or is it more like refusing to eat shellfish or having sex during menstruation? Sullivan suggests that all of these injunctions were written on the same moral level and hence can be accepted or ignored *as a whole*. He does not fully sustain this view, and in fact a refutation of it can be found in Prager's essay. In Prager's opinion and mine, people at the time of Moses, and for centuries before him, understood that there was a fundamental difference between whom you killed and what you ate, and in all likelihood people then and for centuries earlier linked whom you could marry closer to the principles that defined life than they did to the rules that defined diets.

The New Testament contains an equally vigorous attack on homosexuality by St. Paul. Sullivan partially deflects it by noting Paul's conviction that the earth was about to end and the Second Coming was near; under these conditions, all forms of sex were suspect. But Sullivan

annot deny that Paul singled out homosexuality as deserving of special criticism. He seems to pass over this obstacle without effective retort.

Instead, he takes up a different theme, namely, that on grounds of consistency many heterosexual practices—adultery, sodomy, premarital sex, and divorce, among others—should be outlawed equally with homosexual acts of the same character. The difficulty with this is that it mistakes the distinction alive in most people's minds between marriage as an institution and marriage as a practice. As an institution, it deserves unqualified support; as a practice, we recognize that married people are as imperfect as anyone else. Sullivan's understanding of the prohibitionist argument suffers from his unwillingness to acknowledge this distinction.

* * *

The second argument against homosexual marriage—Sullivan's conservative category—is based on natural law as originally set forth by Aristotle and Thomas Aquinas and more recently restated by Hadley Arkes, John Finnis, Robert George, Harry V. Jaffa, and others. How is it phrased varies a bit, but in general its advocates support a position like the following: man cannot live without the care and support of other people; natural law is the distillation of what thoughtful people have learned about the conditions of that care. The first thing they have learned is the supreme importance of marriage, for without it the newborn infant is unlikely to survive or, if he survives, to prosper. The necessary conditions of a decent family life are the acknowledgement by its members that a man will not sleep with his daughter or a woman with her son and that neither will openly choose sex outside marriage.

Now, some of these conditions are violated, but there is a penalty in each case that is supported by the moral convictions of almost all who witness the violation. On simple utilitarian grounds it may be hard to object to incest or adultery; if both parties to such an act welcome it and if it is secret, what differences does it make? But very few people, and then only ones among the overeducated, seem to care much about mounting a utilitarian assault on the family. To this assault, natural-law theorists respond much as would the average citizen—never mind "utility," what counts is what is right. In particular, homosexual uses of the reproductive organs violate the condition that sex serve solely as the basis of heterosexual marriage.

To Sullivan, what is defective about the natural-law thesis is that it assumes different purposes in heterosexual and homosexual love: moral consummation in the first case and pure utility or pleasure alone in the second. But in fact, Sullivan suggests, homosexual love can be as consummatory as heterosexual. He notes that as the Roman Catholic Church has deepened its understanding of the involuntary—that is, in some sense genetic—basis of homosexuality, it has attempted to keep homosexuals in the church as objects of affection and nurture, while banning homosexual acts as perverse.

But this, though better than nothing, will not work, Sullivan writes. To show why, he adduces an analogy to a sterile person. Such a person is permitted to serve in the military or enter an unproductive marriage; why not homosexuals? If homosexuals marry without pro-

creation, they are no different (he suggests) from a sterile man or woman who marries without hope of procreation. Yet people, I think, want the form observed even when the practice varies; a sterile marriage, whether from choice or necessity, remains a marriage of a man and a woman. To this Sullivan offers essentially an aesthetic response. Just as albinos remind us of the brilliance of color and genius teaches us about moderation, homosexuals are a "natural foil" to the heterosexual union, "a variation that does not eclipse the theme." Moreover, the threat posed by the foil to the theme is slight as compared to the threats posed by adultery, divorce, and prostitution. To be consistent, Sullivan once again reminds us, society would have to ban adulterers from the military as it now bans confessed homosexuals.

But again this misses the point. It would make more sense to ask why an alternative to marriage should be invented and praised when we are having enough trouble maintaining the institution at all. Suppose that gay or lesbian marriage were authorized; rather than producing a "natural foil" that would "not eclipse the theme," I suspect such a move would call even more seriously into question the role of marriage at a time when the threats to it, ranging from single-parent families to common divorces, have hit record highs. Kenneth Minogue recently wrote of Sullivans's book that support for homosexual marriage would strike most people as "mere parody," one that could further weaken an already strained institution.

To me, the chief limitation of Sullivan's view is that it presupposes that marriage would have the same, domesticating, effect on homosexual members as it has on heterosexuals, while leaving the latter largely unaffected. Those are very large assumptions that no modern society has ever tested.

Nor does it seem plausible to me that a modern society resists homosexual marriages entirely out of irrational prejudice. Marriage is a union, sacred to most, that unites a man and woman together for life. It is a sacrament of the Catholic Church and central to every other faith. Is it out of misinformation that every modern society has embraced this view and rejected the alternative? Societies differ greatly in their attitude toward the income people may have, the relations among their various races, and the distribution of political power. But they differ scarcely at all over the distinctions between heterosexual and homosexual couples. The former are overwhelmingly preferred over the latter. The reason, I believe, is that these distinctions involve the nature of marriage and thus the very meaning—even more, the very possibility—of society....

* * *

Let us assume for the moment that a chance to live openly and legally with another homosexual is desirable. To believe that, we must set aside biblical injunctions, a difficult matter in a profoundly religious nation. But suppose we manage the diversion, perhaps on the grounds that if most Americans skip church, they can as readily avoid other errors of (possibly) equal magnitude. Then we must ask on what terms the union shall be arranged. There are two alternatives—marriage or domestic partnership.

Sullivan acknowledges the choice, but disparages the domestic-partnership laws that have evolved in some foreign countries and in some American local-

ities. His reasons, essentially conservative ones, are that domestic partnerships are too easily formed and too easily broken. Only real marriages matter. But—aside from the fact that marriage is in serious decline, and that only slightly more than half of all marriages performed in the United States this year will be between never-before-married heterosexuals—what is distinctive about marriage is that it is an institution created to sustain child-rearing. Whatever losses it has suffered in *this* respect, its function remains what it has always been.

The role of raising children is entrusted in principle to married heterosexual couples because after much experimentation—several thousand years, more or less—we have found nothing else that works as well. Neither a gay nor a lesbian couple can of its own resources produce a child; another party must be involved. What do we call this third party? A friend? A sperm or egg bank? An anonymous donor? There is no settled language for even describing, much less approving of, such persons.

Suppose we allowed homosexual couples to raise children who were created out of a prior heterosexual union or adopted from someone else's heterosexual contact. What would we think of this? There is very little research on the matter. Charlotte Patterson's famous essay, "Children of Gay and Lesbian Parents" (*Journal of Child and Development*, 1992), begins by conceding that the existing studies focus on children born into a heterosexual union that ended in divorce or that was transformed when the mother or father "came out" as a homosexual. Hardly any research has been done on children acquired at the outset by a homosexual couple. We therefore have no way of knowing how they would behave. And even if we had such studies, they might tell us rather little unless they were conducted over a very long period of time.

But it is one thing to be born into an apparently heterosexual family and then many years later to learn that one of your parents is homosexual. It is quite another to be acquired as an infant from an adoption agency or a parent-for-hire and learn from the first years of life that you are, because of your family's position, radically different from almost all other children you will meet. No one can now say how grievous this would be. We know that young children tease one another unmercifully; adding this dimension does not seem to be a step in the right direction.

Of course, homosexual "families," with or without children, might be rather few in number. Just how few, it is hard to say. Perhaps Sullivan himself would marry, but, given the great tendency of homosexual males to be promiscuous, many more like him would not, or if they did, would not marry with as much seriousness.

That is problematic in itself. At one point, Sullivan suggests that most homosexuals would enter a marriage "with as much (if not more) commitment as heterosexuals." Toward the end of this book, however, he seems to withdraw from so optimistic a view. He admits that the label "virtually" in the title of his book is deliberately ambiguous, because homosexuals as a group are *not* "normal." At another point, he writes that the "openness of the contract" between two homosexual males means that such a union will in fact be more durable than a heterosexual marriage because the contract contains an *"understanding of the need for extramarital outlets"* (emphasis added). But no such "understanding" exists in hetero-

sexual marriage; to suggest that it might in homosexual ones is tantamount to saying that we are now referring to two different kinds of arrangements. To justify this difference, perhaps, Sullivan adds that the very "lack of children" will give "gay couples greater freedom." Freedom for what? Freedom, I think, to do more of those things that heterosexual couples do less of because they might hurt the children.

* * *

The courts in Hawaii and in the nation's capital must struggle with all these issues under the added encumbrance of a contemporary outlook that makes law the search for rights, and responsibility the recognition of rights. Indeed, thinking of laws about marriage as documents that confer or withhold rights is itself an error of fundamental importance— one that the highest court in Hawaii has already committed. "Marriage," it wrote, "is a state-conferred legal-partnership status, the existence of which gives rise to a multiplicity of rights and benefits...." A state-conferred legal partnership? To lawyers, perhaps; to mankind, I think not....

Our challenge is to find a way of formulating a policy with respect to homosexual unions that is not the result of a reflexive act of judicial rights-conferring, but is instead a considered expression of the moral convictions of a people.

POSTSCRIPT

Should Gay Marriage Be Legalized?

It is conceivable, if improbable, that Randy Rohl and Grady Quinn, the homosexual couple from Sioux Falls, South Dakota, who received permission to attend their prom together in 1979, are living together in their home town. If so, they may soon be able to solemnize their union in Hawaii, then fly back to Sioux Falls and enjoy the status of married people, including the right to adopt children and raise them in accordance with their own moral principles and practices. The Defense of Marriage Act was meant to head off this eventuality, but the law will almost certainly be challenged in the courts and may be struck down as unconstitutional. If so, the nation will be brought face to face with what may be the toughest of all the issues involving human sexuality.

William N. Eskridge, in *The Case for Same-Sex Marriage* (Free Press, 1996), develops at greater length some of the arguments made by Sullivan. In particular, he stresses Sullivan's point that Americans should extend the right of marriage to gay couples because of the stabilizing influence of the marriage bond. Mark Strasser, in *Legally Wed: Same-Sex Marriage and the Constitution* (Cornell University Press, 1997), looks at the legal aspects of same-sex marriage and argues that the usual objections to such unions are either weak or irrelevant. Other arguments in favor of gay marriage include Jonathan Rauch, "For Better or Worse?" *The New Republic* (May 6, 1996), and Gabriel Rotello, "To Have and to Hold: The Case for Gay Marriage," *The Nation* (June 24, 1996). Diana Schaub, in "Marriage Envy," *The Public Interest* (Winter 1996), makes some of the same points as Wilson in her critique of same-sex marriage. For a comprehensive collection of opinions supporting and opposing gay marriage, see Andrew Sullivan et al., eds., *Same Sex Marriage, Pro and Con: A Reader* (Vintage Books, 1997). See also Robert M. Baird and Stuart E. Rosenbaum, eds., *Same-Sex Marriage: The Moral and Legal Debate* (Prometheus Books, 1997).

Note that the title of Sullivan's book is *Virtually Normal*. Virtually, but, in Sullivan's estimation, "not entirely normal." In gay relationships, he suggests, there is a "greater understanding of the need for extramarital outlets." Is there really such a "need" within marriage? If so, perhaps the "gay marriage" movement has uncovered a long-repressed truth. If not, perhaps Wilson is right to worry about the corrupting effects of the movement.

On the Internet . . .

Department of State

View this site for understanding into the workings of a major U.S. executive branch department. Links explain exactly what the department does, what services it provides, and what it says about U.S. interests around the world, as well as provide much more information.
http://www.state.gov/

Marketplace of Political Ideas/University of Houston Library

Here is a valuable collection of links to campaign, conservative/liberal perspectives, and political party sites. There are general political sites, Democratic sites, Republican sites, third-party sites, and much more.
http://info.lib.uh.edu/politics/markind.htm

National Journal's Cloakroom

This is a major site for information on American government and politics. There are reportage and discussion of campaigns, a congressional calendar, a news archive, and more for politicos and policymakers. Membership is required, however, to access much of the information.
http://www.Cloakroom.com/

American Diplomacy

American Diplomacy is an intriguing online journal of commentary, analysis, and research on U.S. foreign policy and its results around the world.
http://www.unc.edu/depts/diplomat/

Cato Institute

The Cato Institute presents this page to discuss its Project on Social Security Privatization. The site and its links begin from the belief that privatization of the U.S. Social Security system is a positive goal that will empower workers.
http://www.cato.org/research/ss_prjct.html

Foreign Affairs

This page of the well-respected foreign policy journal is a valuable research tool. It allows users to search the journal's archives and provides indexed access to the field's leading publications, documents, online resources, and so on. Links to dozens of other related Web sites are possible from here.
http://www.foreignaffairs.org/

PART 4

America and the World

What is the role of the United States in world affairs? From what premise—realism or idealism—should American foreign policy proceed? What place in the world does America now occupy, and in what direction is it heading? American government does not operate in isolation from the world community, and the issues in this section are crucial ones indeed.

- Will America Dominate Tomorrow's Global Economy?

- Does China Threaten Vital American Interests?

- Should the United States Put More Restrictions on Immigration?

- Is Democracy Desirable for All Nations?

ISSUE 17

Will America Dominate Tomorrow's Global Economy?

YES: Mortimer B. Zuckerman, from "A Second American Century," *Foreign Affairs* (May/June 1998)

NO: Paul Krugman, from "America the Boastful," *Foreign Affairs* (May/June 1998)

ISSUE SUMMARY

YES: Publisher Mortimer B. Zuckerman maintains that America's entrepreneurial genius will keep the nation economically dominant in the twenty-first century.

NO: Economist Paul Krugman asserts that American economic dominance in the world can easily be upset by even a mild national recession combined with moderate recovery in Europe and Asia.

In the 1987 book *The Rise and Fall of the Great Powers* (Random House), historian Paul Kennedy warned that the Soviet Union and the United States were treading the fateful path of previous great powers, into a spiral of decline. "Relative to such expanding states as Japan, China, etc.," Kennedy wrote, the economies of the two countries were steadily losing ground.

Kennedy understated the Soviet Union's problem. Within the next decade the Soviet Empire not only declined but vanished. But by the end of the century, as the "expanding states" of Japan and the rest of Asia were on financial life-support and Europe was stagnating, America's economy was soaring: the stock market remained bullish, unemployment and inflation were the lowest since the 1960s, and business and consumer confidence had never been higher.

How long would it all last? In conjuring up visions of American economic decline, Kennedy may have been unduly pessimistic. But at other times it has been the optimists who have wound up with egg on their faces. In 1929 Yale University economics professor Irving Fisher declared, "Stock prices have reached what looks like a permanently high plateau." His view was echoed by many other financial analysts and experts at the time. Yet within months the stock market crashed, ushering in the worst economic depression in the nation's history.

As the new century begins the good news is that America, free from cold war rivalry with the Soviet Union, can concentrate on modernizing its do-

mestic peacetime industries and expanding its industrial base. After getting through a troubled period of downsizing and restructuring, American capitalism has surged forward, creating tens of millions of new jobs. It has accomplished this with negligible inflation, which in turn has kept interest rates low and encouraged capital investment. The more sober news is that productivity growth (output per worker) is slow compared to what it was in the past; workers' wages have stagnated, and their benefits have been squeezed; and the wage gap between skilled and unskilled workers is growing.

Although Japan and Asia's emerging economies are now facing serious crises, the energy and resourcefulness of their populations should not be underestimated. European economies, too, have shown considerable resilience since the end of World War II. They have narrowed the gap in productivity with the United States, and their technology in some areas (e.g., cellular telephones) is superior to America's.

It is far from clear, then, whether America will retain its economic dominance in the world. In the following selections, publisher Mortimer B. Zuckerman argues that America is in a "virtuous cycle"—the opposite of a vicious cycle—in which low inflation produces lower interest rates, which translates into more capital investment, rising productivity, and higher growth. More basically, he traces America's prosperity to "a culture that has long valued individualism, entrepreneurialism, pragmatism, and novelty." These, he believes, are the qualities that have produced the dynamic capitalism that will make the twenty-first century, like the twentieth, an American century." Economist Paul Krugman suggests that even a mild recession in the United States combined with moderate recovery in Europe and Asia could make America "first among equals" at best. In his view, the current assumption of continued dominance "is based on a huge exaggeration of the implications of a few good years here and a few bad years elsewhere."

YES

Mortimer B. Zuckerman

A SECOND AMERICAN CENTURY

WHY WE WILL REMAIN NUMBER ONE

The American economy is in the eighth year of sustained growth that transcends the "German miracle" and the "Japanese miracle" of earlier decades. Everything that should be up is up—GDP [gross domestic product], capital spending, incomes, the stock market, employment, exports, consumer and business confidence. Everything that should be down is down—unemployment, inflation, interest rates. The United States has been ranked number one among major industrial economies for three years in a row. America is riding a capital spending boom that is modernizing its existing industrial base and expanding its industrial capacity. The Dow Jones Industrial average is more than four times as high as it was six years ago. The New York and NASDAQ stock exchanges have added over $4 trillion in value in the last four years alone—the largest single accumulation of wealth in the history of the United States. By contrast, Europe is stagnating and burdened with double-digit unemployment, and Asia is floundering in the wake of financial collapse.

This is no fluke. The unique American brand of entrepreneurial bottom-up capitalism is made up of structural elements that have wrought the stunning economic success of the 1990s and are likely to provide the basis for extending America's comparative advantage over time.

Consider where the country has come from and where it is undoubtedly going. America was all but written off in the 1980s because of its apparently uncontrollable fiscal deficit and its products' steady loss of competitiveness in the global economy. Downsizing and restructuring depressed everyone, but that valley is now largely traversed. In a literal application of Schumpeter's notion of creative destruction, the United States lost some 44 million jobs in the process of adjusting its economy but simultaneously created 73 million private-sector jobs—a net gain of over 29 million jobs since 1980. A stunning 55 percent of the total work force today is in a new job, some two-thirds of them in industries that pay more than the average wage. Contrast all of continental Europe, with its larger economy and work force. It has created an estimated 4 million jobs in the same time period, virtually all of which are in

the public sector. Since 1991, the European Union has lost about 5 million jobs while the U.S. economy has created more than 14 million new ones. Today a record 64 percent of American adults are working, the unemployment rate has fallen to 4.6 percent, and GDP growth has accelerated at the rate of close to 4 percent over the last two years.

In the past, such figures have raised the red flag of inflation. But inflation is at a 30-year low and, like unemployment, is still falling. This contradicts the historical experience of the late phase of a traditional business cycle, where accelerated growth usually correlates with higher inflation. Disinflation is emerging in commodities, which are hitting record lows, and was present in manufactured goods even before the impact of cheaper Asian exports. All this is happening despite an economy that seems close to the maximum sustainable level of growth. Nowhere does there seem to be an imminent inflationary threat. The markets do not anticipate it, and many in the private sector accept what many economists, including Chairman Alan Greenspan of the Federal Reserve, believe—that the official consumer price index overstates inflation by at least a percentage point. If that is correct, it means the United States is closing in on a zero-inflation economy.

Low inflation means lower interest rates, more capital investment, rising productivity, and higher growth—a virtuous cycle not likely to be broken by external forces. Despite a slowing and riskier global economy, the United States remains a balanced economy with the world's most buoyant domestic demand and a more limited exposure than other major industrial nations to exports, which account for only 13 percent of U.S. GDP. Moreover, U.S. exports are less vulnerable because they are diversified around the world and consist primarily of value-added goods, worldwide branded products that incorporate sophisticated technology and intellectual capital and do not have to compete on price alone. Exports are rising three times as fast as the overall economy, which is especially notable because it takes place not as a result of dollar devaluation but in the face of dollar appreciation. Exports are growing even more rapidly in the sectors where America dominates, such as advanced semi-conductors, computer network servers, personal computers, software and services, entertainment, finance, and telecommunications. The United States dominates the knowledge industries of the future. Americans spend vastly more on research and development in these areas than their competitors, and the gap between the United States and the rest of the world will grow, not contract. America dominates the world of the Internet. Some 90 percent of web sites are American. U.S. companies are the major suppliers of the information age's silicon brains and sinews.

On the brink of the 21st century, the United States is at a point reminiscent of its entry into the twentieth. Frederick Jackson Turner pronounced the end of the American frontier in 1893. The newly settled continent, linked by rail, lay open as a vast, tariff-free marketplace, conducive to mass-produced products at prices the masses could increasingly afford—Edison's electric lights, Singer's sewing machines, Bell's speaking tubes, Ford's automobiles. Unimpeded access to that burgeoning marketplace was the one indispensable condition for the flowering of American enterprise.

EXPLAINING SUCCESS

Today, of course, the new frontier is the global economy. Evidence is growing that the United States is as well placed to exploit that as it was the new continental marketplace of a century ago. There are structural strengths that explain U.S. economic success and why it can be sustained.

An examination of these structures of advantage can begin with the improvement of American management skills. American managers were unprepared when global competition began to emerge in the 1970s and 1980s. Long sheltered by domestic regulation, lucrative contracts with the Defense Department, and earnings and growth boosted by inflation, they had a nasty awakening. Foreign competition took market share at both the high end and the low. Profits plummeted, thousands of companies failed or fell to takeovers, and famous brand names were humbled. Business managers, shocked out of their smug parochialism, began years of restructuring, reengineering, and cost-cutting that saw their companies become vastly more efficient. America is now the lowest-cost, most flexible producer among the industrial nations, with something like a $10-an-hour cost per worker advantage, fully loaded, over Japan and a $20-an-hour cost advantage over Germany.

To bring this about, American managers invested in new technologies, high-tech training to exploit these new advances, increased quality control, and improved information systems to adjust supply, prices, and output more quickly to market conditions. U.S. companies were the first to realize the importance of computers and information technologies and have invested massively in them, accounting for over 40 percent of the world's investment in computing. They spend more than twice as much per capita on "infotech" as Western European firms and eight times the global average; there are more than five times as many computers per worker in the United States as in Europe and Japan. U.S. manufacturing has replaced large mass-produced consumer products with sophisticated goods derived from intellectual output in knowledge-based industries, the fastest-growing segment of the world's economy. Management has been assisted by labor flexibility that is the envy of both Europe, where the legacy of the steam age is craft, union, and management demarcations that limit management's role, and Asia, where management is stifled by large oligopolistic networks and government mandates. Management incentives were increased by linking compensation to shareholder returns through stock options.

These are some of the reasons why profit margins in American corporations, once among the world's worst, are now among its best. Return on equity has more than doubled, to over 20 percent, and retained earnings have become the principal source of America's capital regeneration. This microeconomic vitality has translated into the macroeconomic success of the American economy.

RUGGED INDIVIDUALISM

The achievements of business in America grew out of a culture that has long valued individualism, entrepreneurialism, pragmatism, and novelty. This legacy has outlived the passing of the frontier and still inspires millions. American culture nourishes its mavericks, cherishes its young, welcomes newcomers, and dramatically

opens to energy and talent rising from the bottom up. In the nineteenth century, men like Carnegie, Frick, Rockefeller, and Morgan seized their chances. Today, their heirs are Bill Gates, Ted Turner, Larry Ellison, Craig McCaw, and the many others who vie for the top of *Forbes'* list of the 400 richest people in America.

American history uniquely encouraged the development of a management culture. The anthropologist Lionel Tiger showed that the development of American corporate management was America's response to a huge market, vast distances, and diverse populations, and the administrative and economic challenges they presented. Furthermore, what has dominated our business world is contract and law rather than kinship and custom, not primogeniture but an impersonal, monetized market economy and a belief in technology and scientific management. Indeed, the science of management was invented by an American, Frederick Winslow Taylor, who pioneered the time-and-motion study and was the father of mass-production techniques. No other country met the requirements of an emerging industrial system that needed people to be mobile, both physically and psychologically. No other country, for example, shares the American belief in numbers and statistics as the basis for decision-making. No other country has a population so prone to self-help, self-improvement, and even self-renovation in a manner that carries over into business life. No other country invests so much in the business training and retraining of its people—some $100 billion a year—in addition to having the largest and best graduate and undergraduate business schools in the world. And no other country sees its most talented move so overwhelmingly into the private

sector, where the most successful are celebrated and rewarded as symbols in a nation of doers.

Entrepreneurialism and individual initiative in this country are so widely accepted that in the 1990s approximately 1.8 million businesses will have been started, on top of 1.5 million in the 1980s. Smaller companies have demonstrated their capacity to compete in this swiftly changing environment with flexibility, rapid response, openness, innovation, and the ability to attract the best people. Blue chip, large-scale companies no longer have a lock on recruiting the best and brightest graduates of elite business schools. Thousands of these smaller companies have had the potential to blossom and grow, even as thousands have gone belly-up. And as soon as new products and services are developed, American business' unique marketing and advertising skills establish their success at home and abroad.

From among these business start-ups have emerged the smaller companies that have provided the energy in our economy and the sources of our job growth. In contrast, the sprawling *Fortune* 500 companies lost approximately 3 million jobs in the 1980s and are expected to lose another million in the 1990s.

America's economy is even better suited for today's rapidly changing knowledge-based economy than it was for the mass production, industrial economy of earlier times. The new bottom-up economic environment is tantamount to a giant information processing system that enhances its capacity to absorb, adapt to, and manage ongoing revolutions in technology, information, and logistics that are too dynamic and complex to be handled by a top-down system, no matter how talented its bureaucracy, government, or

corporate oligopoly. The marriage of a new economy and an older American culture promises a comparative advantage that will endure.

A THOUSAND POINTS OF FINANCIAL LIGHT

The energy in the business economy is matched by a unique and remarkable world of finance capital. This realm has proven its capacity to provide the multiple sources of entrepreneurial capital needed by entrepreneurial management, thereby demonstrating its ability to meet the needs of a modern, rapidly changing, globalized economy. The "old-boy" financial institutions—primarily the major banks and insurance companies—proved to be less entrepreneurial, more risk-averse, and more bureaucratic than was necessary for American growth in a dramatically changing economic environment. They tended to concentrate their lending to investment-grade companies when approximately 95 percent of American companies were not investment-grade.

In the 1970s and 1980s, access to capital was thrown open by the burgeoning American middle class. In the 1970s, they watched the decline in the stock and bond markets; in the 1980s, they witnessed the focus on shareholder values and superior market performance of the Fidelities, the Alliance Capitals, and investors like George Soros. Their capacity to invest was enhanced by the ERISA pension legislation, and especially by 401(k)s, which gave some individuals the right to direct their investments. With scorecards to measure performance, middle-class Americans voted with their savings and abandoned the practice of investing their money with elite banking and insurance firms with illustrious pasts. Instead, as the American middle class gained economic sophistication, they increasingly trusted their funds to those who demonstrated a capacity to respond to change and whose relative performance could be measured by regular calculations of their gains and losses. The result was an explosion of the share of their household wealth that has gone into stocks—now 28 percent, compared with just 12 percent in 1990.

The diversification of investment outlets means that elite institutions no longer dominate the commanding heights of finance as they did earlier and still do in countries like Germany and Japan. American elite banks' involvement in both lending and managing financial assets dropped precipitously, while those of mutual funds and other managers rose correspondingly. As a result, the number of places to go for money exploded. Accompanied by financial market deregulation and financial product innovation, the stock and bond markets, mutual funds, investment managers, hedge funds, opportunity funds, high-yield funds, bridge funds, venture capital funds, and initial public offerings (IPOs) grew in amounts and varieties that vastly exceeded the total in all other countries—a veritable thousand points of financial light. . . .

The United States is reaping the benefits of the best political climate in 50 years for the practice of such noninflationary fiscal and monetary policies. The structural element here is demographics—the rising proportion of our population that is retired or will be over the next several decades. The elderly and the baby boomers are making government listen to their anxieties about inflation. As some 70 million baby boomers approach retirement, they are putting their savings into

mutual funds and other equities, determined to protect these savings from inflation. Their desire for a stable dollar is more politically important today than the pressure for job creation for the young, which dominated policy for most of the postwar era.

Public policy has also significantly sharpened competition and reduced inflation through deregulation—a trend that is unlikely to be reversed. Today oil, gas, transportation, railroads, airlines, and telecommunications companies have to compete or die. The steel, textile, and auto industries are no longer fully protected by tariffs and "voluntary" quotas. Even agriculture is facing deregulation.

Finally, there are the gains from a public policy that articulates not just what government does but what government does not do. In the United States, unlike Asia, the government is not involved in the formulation of industrial policy or in mandating funding or other support to specific industries or companies. Nor is there the intimacy between government and business characteristic of much of Europe. In the United States, the private sector makes the overwhelming majority of strategic and tactical business decisions. This is all to the good in a rapidly changing economic ecology in which only the markets have the capacity to process vast amounts of information rapidly enough to make the best decisions for allocating resources and developing products and services. Other dimensions of the limited role of government are reflected in the ease with which new companies can be started and new products introduced. This systemic difference between the United States and the rest of the world serves U.S. economic prospects well.

IGNORE THE CASSANDRAS

Pessimists say U.S. growth is not really so impressive and cannot be sustained. If inflation is lower, the argument goes, the United States may just be on the verge of a wage-increase-driven inflation. If U.S. productive capacity is growing, they warn, it is not growing fast enough. Bottlenecks and price increases lie ahead. The pessimists find discomfort even in the fact that today's productivity improvements may be understated for an information economy, rather than an industrial economy. That would mean growth is even faster, enhancing the risk of inflation.

The practical experience of U.S. business leaders suggests otherwise. They understand that the low level of inflation Americans are enjoying is self-perpetuating. With long bonds at their lowest levels since the government started to issue 30-year Treasury bonds in 1977, companies are laying down an even better future by investments in machinery and systems that will enable them to prosper without raising prices. The gains in productivity offer the chance to simultaneously increase profits and wages and decrease inflation. Business leaders assert that productivity increases are genuine and revealed in the form of rising profits, despite stable prices. If statistics suggest that productivity increases are still around 1.5 percent annually, far less than the 3 percent rises of the 1950s and 1960s, then business leaders say something is wrong with the numbers —numbers that are more relevant to an industrial economy than to a service and information economy, where so much investment goes to improve quality and speed of output....

This litany of America's economic successes may sound tinny to those who feel their lives buffeted by forces over which they have virtually no control. People are working harder than ever before. The gap between the well-to-do and the poor has been growing. The options for unskilled workers keep shrinking, as does the safety net that is supposed to protect them if they fall out of the economy altogether. Yet other benefits do, in fact, radiate from the flourishing economy. Young families today are two-thirds better off than their parents were at the same age. If today's material abundance feels inadequate, it is only because Americans today view as essential many things that used to be considered luxuries. But who can doubt that the quality of life has improved? Lower crime rates, dramatic reductions in the welfare rolls, more varied leisure activities, greater opportunity (even in a society renowned for equality of opportunity), record numbers of people entering colleges and universities—all feed a national optimism and sense of renewal that rides over the potholes of politics and defies predictions of calamity.

There are many explanations for this buoyant, confident mood. One is the get-up-and-go spirit that has always typified America. But surely another is prosperity. This survey of the American economy shows that this is not a transient prosperity but one that derives from a series of structural advantages that today only America enjoys. The rest of the world may improve their public policies through accelerated deregulation and prudent fiscal policy. They may reform their closed and opaque financial systems; they may embrace more fully the technological and logistical revolutions sweeping the business world; they may send their sons and daughters to business schools; they may strive to open up their more parochial business and national cultures. But America will not be standing still. If anything, American business should widen its lead over the rest of the world. France had the seventeenth century, Britain the nineteenth, and America the twentieth. It will also have the twenty-first.

NO

Paul Krugman

AMERICA THE BOASTFUL

WHAT HAS NOT GONE RIGHT

The late 1980s were a good time for Europe: growth accelerated, unemployment fell, and dreams of European unity seemed within reach. A mood of almost giddy optimism—Europhoria—swept the continent. Even non-Europeans were caught up in the spirit. As late as 1992 the economist Lester Thurow's bestseller *Head to Head* proclaimed that "future historians will record that the 21st century belonged to the House of Europe."

So in 1987, when the Brookings Institution published a collection of papers entitled *Barriers to European Growth: A Transatlantic View*, which focused on the syndrome of slowing growth and rising unemployment that had become evident over the previous 15 or so years, many European commentators dismissed the volume as a case of fighting the last war. Europe, they insisted, was on the move; energized by the transition to a single market, it had entered a period of renewed growth and technological vigor.

In retrospect, European elation was, to say the least, premature. The structural problems that underlay Eurosclerosis had not been resolved; they had merely been masked by an upswing in the business cycle. When the next recession arrived—and there is always a next recession—it raised unemployment rates not merely to their previous peaks but, in most of Europe, to levels not seen since the 1930s. All in all, it was an object lesson in the difference between cycle and trend: one swallow does not make a spring, and a few good years of growth do not necessarily signal a turnaround in economic fundamentals.

While Europeans may have learned that lesson, Americans have not. Although until quite recently titles like Donald Bartlett and James Steele's *America: What Went Wrong?* typified commentary about the U.S. economy, and economic journalism was dominated by scare headlines about downsizing, after a mere two years of good news America's mood has become startlingly triumphalist. In the view of many business and political leaders America has entered the era of the New Economy, in which traditional limits to economic expansion are no longer relevant. And because America has a New Economy

and the rest of the world does not, it is once more indisputably number one, and the rest of the world must adopt its values and emulate its institutions if it wants to compete.

To anyone with a sense of history, this is all deeply worrying. If pride goeth before a fall, the United States has one heck of a comeuppance in store. Yet the strengths of the U.S. economy are not merely a matter of boasting. The task is to separate the realities from the myth. What has gone right with America, and what has not?

HOW NEW AN ECONOMY?

By any standard, 1997 was a very good year for the U.S. economy. GDP grew by almost 4 percent, well above the 2.4 percent average over the past 20 years. Unemployment fell to 4.6 percent, a 25-year low. Meanwhile inflation remained quiescent, at less than 2 percent.

How should we view this success? A year of fast growth, even without inflation, is not that unusual: in 1983 the economy grew by almost 7 percent, also without inflationary pressure. Yet morning in America did not signal a long-term increase in the economy's growth rate: growth over the following decade averaged only 2.4 percent annually. How can we tell whether 1997 was a similarly temporary surge or something to which we should become accustomed?

To answer this question, it is essential to take on board a bit of economics that, though rudimentary, is often ignored in public discussion: the distinction between growth in the economy's productive capacity and fluctuations in the utilization of that capacity—or, to put it another way, the difference between trend and cycle.

Think of the economy as a machine that can be run at variable speed. It may sometimes be possible to increase what is produced by running the machine faster; however, if it is run too fast, it will overheat. Thus while it is possible in the short run to get more output by using the economy's capacity more intensively—especially if the economy starts from a point where capacity is severely underused—over the long run the only way to achieve a sustained increase in production is to increase what the machine is capable of making, that is, to increase the amount it can produce at a given speed.

This discussion may sound abstract, but it is possible to make a fairly clear distinction in U.S. economic data between growth due to fuller use of existing capacity and growth due to expanded capacity. The unemployment rate turns out to be a pretty good indicator not only of the utilization of the labor force but of the utilization of economic capacity in general. There is a remarkably good (though not exact—this is economics, not physics) rule of thumb known as Okun's Law, which relates changes in the economy's utilization of capacity, as measured by the unemployment rate, to its growth rate. Here is how Okun's Law works. In a year in which the unemployment rate does not change, the economy typically grows about 2.4 percent; every percentage point decline in unemployment adds 2 percent to that growth rate (while every percentage point rise subtracts 2 percent). That 2.4 percent growth when the unemployment rate is constant is the growth in the economy's capacity; the extra growth when the unemployment rate declines (or growth shortfall when unemployment rises) represents a change in the utilization of that capacity.

Okun's Law works well in accounting for the growth surge of 1983. As the economy recovered from the recession that had raised unemployment to a postwar high of 10.7 percent in the fourth quarter of 1982, the unemployment rate fell by 2.2 percentage points. The rule says that the economy should therefore have grown by 2.4 + (2 × 2.2) = 6.8 percent—very close to the actual growth. The same rule also works well for [1997]: since the unemployment rate fell from 5.3 percent in late 1996 to 4.7 percent in late 1997, we should have expected growth of 2.4 + (2 × 0.6) = 3.6 percent—close enough to the actual 3.9 percent to be well within the normal fuzziness of economic statistics.

The point of these exercises in arithmetic is that because the same rule that accounted for fluctuations of growth around its long-run average 15 years ago continues to work today, there is no reason to believe that the rate of growth of the economy's capacity—and therefore its long-run growth rate—has accelerated.

What may have changed is the ability of the economy to make use of capacity without getting overheated. Until a few years ago, typical estimates suggested that any unemployment rate below about 6 percent would lead to a gradual but inexorable acceleration of inflation. But here we are with an unemployment rate of less than 5 percent, and with prices still stable. Does this situation represent a fundamental improvement in the economy's ability to deliver full employment?

The answer is definitely ambiguous. Some have argued that tight labor markets no longer cause inflation because international competition now prevents companies from passing on increases in wages or other costs in higher prices.

However, there is no evidence for this view (which is dubious in any case for an economy dominated by non-traded services). Rather, the proximate explanation for low inflation in recent years has been that costs themselves have, for a variety of reasons, risen less than one might have expected given how hot the economy is running. The most important restraint on inflation has been a squeeze on worker benefits, mainly due to the switch to managed health care. In the last two years the strength of the dollar and the economic woes of Asia have also pushed down import prices, helping keep inflation low. But for these special and necessarily temporary factors inflation would probably already have started to show clear signs of returning. Wage increases have been accelerating steadily since 1995, and, with the shift to health maintenance organizations more or less complete, benefits have started to rise again. Sooner or later the need to keep inflation in check will probably force the Federal Reserve to allow (or engineer) a rise in the unemployment rate....

A HIDDEN BOOM?

... [W]hen businessmen enthuse about the supposed technological revolution in America, they also tend to enthuse about the institutions that supposedly make that revolution possible: an entrepreneurial culture, capital markets eager to back risky start-ups, labor markets that do not burden employers with annoying regulations (or unions), and so on. They also congratulate themselves on having become lean, mean, and competitive.

Perhaps the main point to make about this institutional optimism is that it involves a lot of implicit theorizing. Do

we really know that highly flexible capital and labor markets are such wonderful things? As recently as five years ago the conventional wisdom was exactly the opposite: Japanese companies, in particular, were supposed to be superior to their Western counterparts because they were insulated from the pressure of capital markets and hence able to take a long view, and because inflexible labor markets, also known as the lifetime employment system, made them better at accumulating human capital. Why such a reversal of opinion? The answer, presumably, is that now we can see that American institutions foster higher productivity—except that the productivity surge is itself merely hypothetical, invisible in the data.

While a sense of history might lead one to be agnostic about claims of a productivity revolution in the United States, doesn't the experience of high growth without inflation show that something new and good is happening? Well, no. For one thing, the quiescence of inflation in the face of declining unemployment seems to be fully explicable in terms of other, less glamorous factors—mainly the sluggish growth in wages and benefits. Furthermore, a technical point is critical here: official estimates of productivity are constructed using the same data that are used to construct estimates of GDP. Indeed, official estimates of productivity are nothing more than GDP per worker. Any understatement of one must therefore imply an equal understatement of the other—hence unmeasured productivity growth cannot be responsible for the high measured GDP growth.

This seems to be a surprisingly difficult point to grasp. A parable may help. Imagine a New Economy advocate who discovers that he has a problem with his car. Whenever he drives too fast—

whenever the needle on his speedometer goes above 40—the car develops a dangerous shimmy. So he carefully drives the car to his mechanic, never letting the needle go past 39. Alas, the mechanic informs him not only that he cannot fix the shimmy, but that the car has another problem: something is wrong with the speedometer, which is consistently understating the car's speed. Indeed, when the needle is at 40, the car is actually going 55. To the mechanic's surprise, the New Economy advocate is delighted with this news: "What you're telling me is that the shimmy doesn't start until I'm actually going 55. That means I can drive home 15 miles an hour faster than I drove here!"

Nobody would make this mistake in daily life, but many New Economy advocates make exactly the same mistake with regard to productivity and growth. [In 1997] U.S. economy grew by 3.9 percent, which is about 1.5 percent more than its long-run sustainable rate. But New Economy enthusiasts argue that productivity growth is severely understated. And suppose, they say, that productivity is actually growing 1.5 percent faster than the numbers say; then the sustainable rate of growth of the U.S. economy is really 3.9 percent, not 2.4. And doesn't that mean that last year's growth did not put any strain on capacity after all—which explains why it did not cause inflation (the shimmy)?

The point should now be obvious: since measured productivity growth is simply GDP per worker, if productivity has been understated, so has GDP, by exactly the same amount. So if productivity growth was really 1.5 percent higher than the numbers say, even though the sustainable rate of growth would be 3.9 percent, the economy would really have grown by 5.4 percent—and the failure to show signs

of inflation is as much (or as little) of a puzzle as ever.

That means that the recent ability of the United States to combine high measured growth with low inflation provides no evidence for the putative hidden boom in productivity. Even if official statistics understate true productivity increases, the economy's rapid measured growth over the last two years has sharply increased its capacity utilization—just as driving with the speedometer needle at 55 means driving faster than with the needle at 40, even if the speedometer consistently understates your true speed. So invoking unmeasured productivity growth does not help explain why the acceleration of inflation that normally occurs when capacity utilization is high has not yet materialized; that good news must and can be explained by other factors. Conversely, the fact that inflation has remained low despite high growth offers no evidence in support of claims of a hidden productivity boom—if A can't cause B, then observing B provides no evidence in favor of A. The supposed productivity revolution remains purely hypothetical.

What, then, is left of the New Economy? We have had a favorable turn in the business cycle, abetted by some temporary factors that have helped keep inflation down, and probably also by shifts in the labor market that have reduced the bargaining power of workers and therefore allowed fuller employment without accelerating wage increases. The New Economy, in short, looks a lot like the Old Economy. It has about the same long-run growth rate but can run at slightly lower unemployment. Things could be worse, but nothing fundamental has changed— the amount of good news is not enough to justify the triumphant rhetoric one now hears so often. . . .

AMERICA: FIRST AMONG EQUALS

Suppose that you had made a realistic assessment of the economic prospects of the world's major economies circa late 1992—say, at the time of President-elect Bill Clinton's famous economic summit in Little Rock. You would have noted that the one-time dominance of the United States—that postwar peak of influence when America produced as much as all other market economies together, when American technology was superior in almost every industry—had long since passed. Instead, we were in a world in which Europe, Japan, and the United States were all more or less on the same technological level and in which the economy of Europe as a whole was about the same size as that of the United States. But the U.S. economy was still larger than that of any other country, and it seemed likely to remain so for at least several decades. Europe was growing no faster than America. Japan was growing faster (4 percent versus 2.5 percent), but since its economy was less than half the size of America's, it would take more than half a century to close the gap even if that growth differential persisted. The only way the United States might be displaced as the world's leading economic power would have been for Europe to form a true federal union (which would have given it a political weight comparable to its already huge economic weight), something that looked almost as unlikely in 1992 as it does now.

How much has that assessment changed in the five years since? Hardly at all: Certainly there has been no revolutionary improvement in the performance

of the United States. The U.S. economy is doing better than most economists expected, but as we have seen, the good news, while real, is fairly modest. Europhiles do have grounds for dismay, but mainly because their expectations five or six years ago were unrealistically high. Only in Asia has there been a true reversal of fortune, but it is too soon to count emerging Asia out, and even Japan may yet stage a recovery.

None of this is meant to suggest that the United States is in any sense on the verge of crisis; its economy does seem fundamentally sound. But the current sense that the United States is on top of the world is based on a huge exaggeration of the implications of a few good years here and a few bad years elsewhere. Let there be even a mild recession in the United States, a moderate recovery in Europe and Japan, and a rebound in emerging Asia, and talk of the return of American dominance will start to sound silly indeed. Future historians will not record that the 21st century belonged to the United States.

POSTSCRIPT

Will America Dominate Tomorrow's Global Economy?

Both Zuckerman and Krugman concede certain "inconvenient facts," facts that lend support to the other side. Zuckerman admits that his rosy account of the American economy "may sound tinny" to those who have to work harder to make the same wages they did before, to those unskilled workers who are lagging ever further behind in wages, and to unemployed people who fall through the increasingly fragile "safety net." But it is Krugman who is the most generous in his admissions. The U.S. economy, he says, "does seem financially sound," and the only way the United States could be displaced as the world's leading economic power would be if Europe forms "a true federal union"—which Krugman considers unlikely.

Paul Kennedy's gloomy warnings in 1987 about American economic decline are still worth perusing because of Kennedy's larger historical account of the decline of nation-states. They also serve as cautionary tales of a different sort, demonstrating the risk of writing histories of events before they happen. The full title of Kennedy's book is *The Rise and Fall of the Great Powers: Economic Change and Military Conflict from 1500 to 2000* (Random House, 1987).

As the twenty-first century begins, all kinds of prophesies on where the United States is headed can be read. In *The End of the Twentieth Century and the End of the Modern Age* (Ticknor & Fields, 1993), historian John Lukacs suggests that American authority (as opposed to power) in the world will decline. Lukacs revisits his thesis at various places in his more recent book *A Thread of Years* (Yale University Press, 1998). In a somewhat similar vein, Jean-Marie Guehenno, in *The End of the Nation-State* (University of Minnesota Press, 1995), argues that the European Union and other organizations have failed to protect the nation-state from the centrifugal forces of race, ideology, corruption, and tribalism. In *The Clash of Civilizations and the Remaking of the World Order* (Simon & Schuster, 1996), which was written before the crash of the economies of East Asia, political scientist Samuel P. Huntington argues that the rise of Asian countries and the population explosion in Muslim countries will challenge Western dominance and promote opposition to the ideals of the West. David Rothkopf sees this less as a threat than as an opportunity. In "In Praise of Cultural Imperialism?" *Foreign Policy* (Summer 1997), he writes that the United States "is in a position not only to lead in the 21st century as the dominant power of the Information Age but to do so by breaking down the barriers that divide nations."

ISSUE 18

Does China Threaten Vital American Interests?

YES: Richard Bernstein and Ross H. Munro, from "The Coming Conflict With America," *Foreign Affairs* (March/April 1997)

NO: Robert S. Ross, from "Beijing as a Conservative Power," *Foreign Affairs* (March/April 1997)

ISSUE SUMMARY

YES: Book critic Richard Bernstein and Ross H. Munro, director of the Asia program at the Foreign Policy Research Institute, argue that China, while disguising or minimizing its actual military expenditures, is rapidly modernizing its land, air, and naval forces and still pursues its aim of dominating East Asia.

NO: Professor of political science Robert S. Ross argues that China, with an obsolete air force, primitive missiles, and a miniscule navy with no aircraft carriers, has neither the means nor the will to challenge U.S. hegemony in the Pacific.

China's emperors used to think of their country as the center of the world, to which all other nations were to pay tribute. By the middle of the nineteenth century, however, China found itself invaded and victimized by foreigners, forced to pay reparations, and made to sign treaties allowing Western traders to sell opium to its people.

Not until the early years of the twentieth century did China start recovering some degree of autonomy. By this time Chinese reformers had deposed the last of the Confucian emperors, who had ruled their country for 2,000 years. But the new government quickly splintered into warring factions, and for the rest of the twentieth century the alternative to anarchy in China was some form of despotism: rule by generals, mystagogues, and party bureaucrats.

Since the 1940s America's relations with China have undergone a series of flip-flops. During World War II, China was America's ally. (Shortly after the Japanese attack on Pearl Harbor in 1941, *Time* magazine ran a piece on Japanese and Chinese racial profiles entitled "How to Tell Your Friends from the Japs.") But after the Communist revolution in 1949, China became an enemy, and by the 1960s it was seen in the United States as the most fanatical of its enemies. The threat of eventual Chinese control of Vietnam was one of

the reasons cited by officials in the Johnson and Nixon administrations for continued American involvement in the Vietnam War.

Then, in 1972, President Richard Nixon stunned friend and foe alike by announcing that he was to visit China and meet its leader, Mao Zedong. Soon Nixon was in Beijing, dining and exchanging toasts with the man he had once depicted as a murderous tyrant. At a stroke, Nixon had changed the whole tone of U.S.-Chinese relations, and over the next two decades those relations continued to improve. After Mao's death in 1976, China seemed to lose its ideological fanaticism; doctrinaire communism gave way to what appeared to be pragmatic, state-controlled capitalism, which was congenial to American business interests. The possibility of huge, new markets for America's high-tech industries added to the allure.

A new setback to Sino-American relations occurred in June 1989, when Chinese tanks and machine guns crushed student prodemocracy demonstrations in Beijing's Tiananmen Square, killing, wounding, and imprisoning thousands of peaceful protesters. As a result, President George Bush suspended all high-level government exchanges and banned the export of weapons to China; Congress later extended the sanctions. A year later, however, Bush met with China's minister of foreign affairs, and relations seemed to be mending. But a year after that the State Department issued a critical report on China's human rights record, and in August 1993 the United States imposed new sanctions on China, this time for China's sales of nuclear-capable technology to Pakistan. Then a new thaw began when, starting in 1994, President Bill Clinton annually renewed China's most-favored-nation trading status, guaranteeing privileged Chinese access to U.S. markets.

New concerns in the United States about Chinese strategies and intentions have surfaced more recently: press reports and congressional investigations have suggested that the Chinese attempted to influence the 1996 presidential and congressional elections through secret campaign contributions. (One of the more startling news items in 1998 was a *New York Times* report of a $100,000 contribution to the Democrats by leaders of China's People's Liberation Army.) As Congress pursued its investigation of these charges, Americans pondered the question of Chinese aims and policies. Was China a nation with which America could safely do business? What were its intentions? Had it finally renounced the triumphalism of Marxism-Leninism, or was it simply disguising it? Did it have the capability and desire to engage in military aggression?

The following selections draw very different conclusions on these questions. Richard Bernstein and Ross H. Munro argue that China, while disguising or minimizing its actual military expenditures, pursues its aim of intimidating its neighbors and displacing American influence in the region. Robert S. Ross argues that China, with an obsolete air force, primitive missiles, and a miniscule navy, has neither the means nor the will to challenge the United States anywhere in Asia.

YES

Richard Bernstein and Ross H. Munro

THE COMING CONFLICT WITH AMERICA

THE RISING ASIAN HEGEMON

For a quarter-century—indeed, almost since Richard Nixon signed the Shang-hai Communiqué in 1972—a comforting, even heart-warming notion has prevailed among many policymakers and experts on American policy to-ward the People's Republic of China. They believe that China will inevitably become more like the West—non-ideological, pragmatic, materialistic, and progressively freer in its culture and politics. According to them, China is militarily weak and unthreatening; while Beijing tends toward rhetorical ex-cess, its actual behavior has been far more cautious, aimed at the overriding goals of economic growth and regional stability.

While this vision of China, and especially its diplomatic and economic be-havior, was largely true until the middle to late 1980s, it is now obsolete, as it ignores many Chinese statements and actions that suggest the country is emerging as a great power rival of the United States in the Pacific. True, China is more open and internationally engaged than at any time since the commu-nist revolution of 1949. Nevertheless, since the late 1980s Beijing's leaders, especially those who have taken over national policy in the wake of Deng Xiaoping's enfeeblement, have set goals that are contrary to American inter-ests. Driven by nationalist sentiment, a yearning to redeem the humiliations of the past, and the simple urge for international power, China is seeking to replace the United States as the dominant power in Asia.

Since the late 1980s, Beijing has come to see the United States not as a strategic partner but as the chief obstacle to its own strategic ambitions. It has, therefore, worked to reduce American influence in Asia, to prevent Japan and the United States from creating a "contain China" front, to build up a military with force projection capability, and to expand its presence in the South China and East China Seas so that it controls the region's essential sea-lanes. China's sheer size and inherent strength, its conception of itself as a center of global civilization, and its eagerness to redeem centuries of humiliating weakness are propelling it toward Asian hegemony. Its goal is to

From Richard Bernstein and Ross H. Munro, "The Coming Conflict With America," *Foreign Affairs* (March/April 1997). Excerpted from *The Coming Conflict With China* by Richard Bernstein and Ross H. Munro (Alfred A. Knopf, 1997). Copyright © 1997 by Richard Bernstein and Ross H. Munro. Reprinted by permission of Alfred A. Knopf, Inc. Notes omitted.

ensure that no country in the region—whether Japan seeking oil exploration rights in the East China Sea, Taiwan inviting the Dalai Lama for an official visit, or Thailand allowing American naval vessels to dock in its ports—will act without taking China's interests into prime consideration.

TACTICALLY TACTFUL

China and the United States have, to be sure, been through phases of friendship and tension, with some of the latter unrelated to China's hegemonic goals. At times relations have soured because of inconsistent American policies, especially on human rights and trade matters, that have irritated China's leaders and produced a nationalistic reaction among intellectuals and ordinary Chinese alike. China's current leaders understand the value of stable relations with Washington and under the right terms will accept, as President Jiang Zemin recently did, a resumption of the ceremonies of high-level exchanges.

But China's willingness, even eagerness, to improve the Sino-American mood represents a tactical gesture rather than a strategic one. Since its setback in the Taiwan crisis of early 1996—when China's decision to stage large-scale military exercises in the Straits of Taiwan during Taiwan's presidential election drew harsh criticism from the international community and led the United States to deploy two aircraft carrier task forces to the region—Beijing has tempered its confrontational rhetoric and retreated from some of the actions that most annoyed Washington. China's deference reflects its continued interest in the burgeoning trade and technology transfer relationship with the United States and

its hope of quelling anti-Chinese sentiment in Congress and among the American public. When Jiang Zemin comes to Washington in the next year or two, many Americans will likely regard the visit as a sign of a restored sense of common interests. Influential Chinese planners like General Mi Zhenyu, vice-commandant of the Academy of Military Sciences in Beijing, on the other hand, will see it as the next step in bringing China's strength and influence up to par with the United States. "For a relatively long time it will be absolutely necessary that we quietly nurse our sense of vengeance," Mi wrote last year. "We must conceal our abilities and bide our time."

China's goal of achieving paramount status in Asia conflicts with an established American objective: preventing any single country from gaining overwhelming power in Asia. The United States, after all, has been in major wars in Asia three times in the past half-century, always to prevent a single power from gaining ascendancy. It seems almost indisputable that over the next decade or two China will seek to become the dominant power on its side of the Pacific. Actual military conflict between the United States and China, provoked, for example, by a Chinese attempt to seize Taiwan by force or to resolve by military means its territorial claims in the South China Sea, is always possible, particularly as China's military strength continues to grow.

Even without actual war, China and the United States will be adversaries in the major global rivalry of the first decades of the century. Competition between them will force other countries to take sides and will involve all the standard elements of international competition: military strength, economic well-being, influence among other nations and

over the values and practices that are accepted as international norms. Moreover, the Chinese-American rivalry of the future could fit into a broader new global arrangement that will increasingly challenge Western, and especially American, global supremacy. China's close military cooperation with the former Soviet Union, particularly its purchase of advanced weapons in the almost unrestricted Russian arms bazaar, its technological and political help to the Islamic countries of Central Asia and North Africa, and its looming dominance in East Asia put it at the center of an informal network of states, many of which have goals and philosophies inimical to those of the United States, and many of which share China's sense of grievance at the long global domination of the West. Samuel Huntington of Harvard University has argued that this emerging world order will be dominated by what he calls the clash of civilizations. We see matters more in the old-fashioned terms of political alliance and the balance of power. Either way, China, rapidly becoming the globe's second most powerful nation, will be a predominant force as the world takes shape in the new millennium. As such, it is bound to be no strategic friend of the United States, but a long-term adversary.

MIGHT LEANS RIGHT

One common view of China holds that its integration into the world economy will make it more moderate and cautious in its foreign policy and more open and democratic at home. But the alternative view sees China's more aggressive behavior of the last five years as a consequence of its growing economic and military strength and as linked to its intensifying xenophobic impulses. China's more modern econ-

omy and its greater economic influence are already giving it the power to enhance its authoritarianism at home, resist international dissatisfaction with its policies and practices, and expand its power and prestige abroad in ways hostile to American interests.

China's ability to resist and ultimately beat back efforts by the Clinton administration to protest Chinese human rights abuses by withholding most-favored-nation status is a case in point. While complaining bitterly about the American use of economic pressure for political goals, the Chinese applied powerful economic and political pressure on both the United States and elsewhere—notably in Europe and the United Nations—to force President Clinton to retreat from his earlier position. The irony in Sino-American relations is that when China was in the grip of ideological Maoism and displayed such ideological ferocity that Americans believed it to be dangerous and menacing, it was actually a paper tiger, weak and virtually without global influence. Now that China has shed the trappings of Maoism and embarked on a pragmatic course of economic development and global trade, it appears less threatening but is in fact acquiring the wherewithal to back its global ambitions and interests with real power. . . .

THE NUMBERS GAME

Nothing could be more important in understanding China's goals and self-image than its military modernization program. China's official position, which is given credence in many Western analyses, is that its primary goal is to develop a world-class economy while maintaining a defensive military force. The official annual defense budget of

$8.7 billion—compared to the $265 billion spent annually by the United States or even the $50 billion spent by Japan—seems to support that claim. In reality, almost every major study of Chinese military spending, whether conducted by the U.S. Government Information Office or the International Institute for Strategic Studies, has concluded that actual spending is at least several times Beijing's official figure.

The official budget, for example, does not include the cost of the People's Armed Police, even though it consists mostly of former soldiers demobilized to reduce the size of the army and serves as a reserve available for use in an international conflict. The official budget also excludes nuclear weapons development and soldiers' pensions. When the Chinese purchased 72 SU-27 fighterjets from Russia in 1995 for about $2.8 billion, the entire amount was covered by the State Council and was not deemed a defense expenditure. The official numbers also exclude the cost of research and development. Part of the funding for the development of nuclear weapons, for example, comes from the Ministry of Energy budget, and part of the money for aircraft development comes from the Ministry of Aeronautics and Astronautics Industry. Beijing also excludes proceeds from arms sales, which totaled nearly $8 billion between 1987 and 1991 alone, as well as income from businesses and industries owned and operated by the army, which, with unknown and largely unaccounted-for resources, has quietly become a major player in the global economy.

Realistic analyses of China's defense budget (or those of any other country's, for that matter) must also take into account purchasing power parity—the difference between what something would cost in China and what it would cost elsewhere. As much as 68 percent of Chinese expenditures, from soldiers' salaries and pensions to weapons systems and supplies, which the PLA purchases at artificially low state-set prices, cost a fraction of their equivalent American value. Taking all these factors into account, a conservative estimate of China's actual military expenditures would be at least ten times the officially announced level. In other words, China's real annual defense budget amounts to a minimum of $87 billion per year, roughly one-third that of the United States and 75 percent more than Japan's. Moreover, the figure was 11.3 percent higher in 1996 than in 1995, and 14.6 percent higher in 1995 than in 1994. Even adjusting for inflation, that is still an exceptionally high rate of growth. No other part of the Chinese government budget has increased at a rate anywhere near that, whether adjusting for inflation or not.

It is true, as the more optimistic analysts point out, that China poses little direct military threat to the United States. But comparing the two countries to highlight Chinese shortcomings is a pointless and misleading exercise, and not only because China's actual military expenditures are a moving target. Whatever the exact figures, China is now engaged in one of the most extensive and rapid military buildups in the world, one that has accelerated in recent months even as China's rhetoric has softened and Beijing has moved to improve its ties with the United States. Driven by its setback in the Taiwan crisis last year and disturbed by the awesome power of the two American aircraft carrier task forces dispatched to the waters near the Straits of Taiwan, China

has stepped up its efforts to acquire two capabilities: a credible Taiwan invasion force and the capacity to sink American aircraft carriers should the United States interfere militarily in the China-Taiwan issue.

Even before the Straits of Taiwan incident, China was acquiring airborne early warning technology in Europe and Israel and developing its own in-flight refueling techniques to extend the range of its warplanes. Since the incident, it has sealed a deal with Russia to acquire two destroyers equipped with modern cruise missiles. In the past several years, China has acquired SU-27 fighter-bombers and Russian Kilo-class submarines. In the last three years, China has built 34 modern warships on its own and developed a fleet of M-9 and M-11 mobile-launched missiles of the sort fired near Taiwan during the crisis. It has also expanded its rapid reaction force from 15,000 to 200,000 men and built an airfield in the Paracel Islands and an early warning radar installation on Fiery Cross Reef in the Spradys. China is the only Asian country to deploy nuclear weapons and the world's third-largest nuclear power in terms of the number of delivery vehicles in service, having surpassed Britain and France by the late 1970s.

As time passes, in other words, it will become far riskier for Washington to pre-empt Chinese aggression with the kind of overwhelming show of force made during the Straits of Taiwan crisis. With the largest army, navy, and air force in Asia, China spends more both relatively and absolutely than any of its neighbors, with the possible exception of Japan, whose modern forces are untested and whose operations could be severely hampered by pacifist leanings at home. In short, China's relative strength gives it the abil-ity to intimidate regional foes and win wars against them. If it continues its rapid military modernization, China will soon become the only country capable of challenging American power in East Asia —and only the United States will have the influence to counterbalance China's regional ascendancy. Moreover, China's goals go a long way toward explaining its tactical attitude toward its relations with the United States, where an annual trade imbalance approaching $40 billion has helped China finance its arms acquisitions. China's mercantilist policies, which include large-scale technology transfers from American sources and the purchase of dual-use technologies in the American market, are likely to become a major source of Sino-American conflict as Beijing grows stronger.

A DEMOCRATIC PEACE?

Of course, if China became a democracy its military build-up would be far less threatening than if it remained a dictatorship. But while the forces pushing toward global democracy are probably too powerful for China to remain unaffected by them forever, there is no reason to believe that China will become democratic in the near future. In the first place, that would be contrary to Chinese political culture. In its entire 3,000-year history, China has developed no concept of limited government, no protections of individual rights, no independence for the judiciary and the media. The country has never operated on any notion of the consent of the governed or the will of the majority. Whether under the emperors or the party general secretaries, China has always been ruled by a self-selected and self-perpetuating clique that operates in secret and treats opposition as treason....

The most likely form for China to assume is a kind of corporatist, militarized, nationalist state, one with some similarity to the fascist states of Mussolini or Francisco Franco. China already has a cult of the state as the highest form of human organization, the entity for whose benefit the individual is expected to sacrifice his or her own interests and welfare. The army is emerging as the single most powerful institution in the country. It has ultimate political authority and has created a large number of influential business enterprises. Unlike the Soviet Union, China is not becoming a powerful military power founded on a pitifully weak economy, but a powerful economy creating a credible military force. It promises to be a state based on the continued rule of a disciplined party that controls information and demands political obedience.

Completing this picture of China is a wounded nationalism, a sense of unredeemed historical suffering, and a powerful suspicion of foreigners. Given the decline of ideology and the passing of the country's charismatic leaders, the government encourages and exploits such sentiments in an effort to enhance its legitimacy and control. When those sentiments prove insufficient to maintain order, the army and the leaders can turn to a vast, intrusive security and police system operating in close cooperation with a compliant judiciary to maintain their undisputed power....

THE NEW STRATEGIC TRIANGLE

The primary American objective in Asia must be to prevent China's size, power, and ambition from making it a regional hegemon. Achieving that goal requires maintaining the American military presence in Asia and keeping it vastly more powerful and effective than China's armed forces. Furthermore, preventing China from expanding its nuclear weapons arsenal should clearly be an American goal. In the worst-case scenario, Sino-American relations would witness the reappearance of a nuclear standoff reminiscent of the Cold War, with each side relying on the doctrine of mutually assured destruction to prevent an attack from the other. In fact, China has numerous incentives to avoid a nuclear arms race. The United States should play a quiet but effective role in building international pressure to persuade China to make its current moratorium on nuclear weapons testing permanent. Washington should also actively fight against nuclear proliferation in China and elsewhere. The third element in maintaining a balance of power involves Taiwan —specifically, ensuring that it maintains a credible defensive deterrent such that reunification, should it occur, would be voluntary.

The growth of Chinese power has made America's overarching attitude toward Japan obsolete. The United States can no longer operate on the assumption that a weak Japan is a good Japan. If that was once true, it was only because China was poor and weak. In the post-Cold War world, it is Japan's weakness that threatens peace and stability by creating a power vacuum that the United States alone can no longer fill. A strong Japan, in genuine partnership with the United States, is vital to a new balance of power in Asia. A weak Japan benefits only China, which wants no stabilizing balance of power but Chinese hegemony, under which Japan would be little more than Beijing's most useful tributary state.

The difficulties here are considerable. The United States cannot block Chinese

hegemony in Asia unless Japan is an equal and willing partner in the process. But if it pushes Japan, the result could well be an anti-American reaction there. Resolving that dilemma might be the single most important task of American diplomacy in the near future. The United States must demonstrate that it is a reliable ally—as it did last spring in the waters near Taiwan—while waiting for Japan to come to grips with an increasingly threatening security environment. China's determination to achieve hegemonic status in Asia will probably facilitate this. But the United States and Japan must realize they need each other.

NO

Robert S. Ross

BEIJING AS A CONSERVATIVE POWER

BALANCING ACT

In the late 1980s, the People's Republic of China emerged as one of the most powerful countries on the East Asian mainland. It had established its strategic authority on the Korean peninsula in the early 1950s, when it held the U.S. military to a standstill and inflicted unacceptable casualties on American soldiers. Since then its capabilities in northeast Asia have grown, giving it a strong voice in peninsular affairs. After the demise of the Soviet Union and the disintegration of the Russian armed forces, China established conventional military control along the full length of its border with Russia and projected a powerful presence throughout the region. What is most striking about this development is that the United States and its allies have accommodated themselves to Chinese power in northeast Asia. Because of a continued U.S. regional presence, America's allies have not considered China's strategic power a threat to the regional balance.

China has also established superiority in Indochina with the acquiescence of the United States. Indeed, the United States welcomed China as a substitute for American power in Indochina throughout the 1970s and 1980s. In an era of declining U.S. capability, the Nixon Doctrine explicitly called for American reliance on regional powers as counterweights to the U.S.S.R. In Indochina and much of Southeast Asia, China was the regional power of choice. Washington was grateful for Beijing's ability to reassure Thailand against the Soviet Union and Vietnam in the wake of its withdrawal from the Vietnam War. Throughout the 1980s Washington supported Chinese efforts to roll back Soviet influence in Southeast Asia by helping the Khmer Rouge to resist the Soviet-sponsored Vietnamese occupation of Cambodia.

In 1989, when the Vietnamese military finally withdrew from Cambodia, Indochina fell within China's strategic sphere of influence. Having ousted the French, the Americans, and the Russians, China no longer confronts a rival in this region. As in northeast Asia, America and its allies accommodated themselves to China's preeminence. Neither the United States nor its traditional partners in Southeast Asia have considered the substitution of Chinese

strategic dominance for Soviet power a challenge to their vital security interests.

Chinese strategic authority on mainland East Asia is a long-established characteristic of the region's balance of power. Since the early 1970s, it has not elicited fears of Chinese regional hegemony or calls for China's containment. On the contrary, East Asia's status quo is widely considered an appropriate foundation for a stable regional order. Concern over a Chinese challenge to the regional balance of power—the most vital U.S. interest in East Asia—must focus on the rise of Chinese power beyond the mainland and into the maritime regions of East Asia. Specifically, it must focus on China's ability to become a military power in the East China Sea or the South China Sea.

CHINA AT SEA

China's authority in the East China Sea relies on airpower. Its proximity to the East China Sea allows it to use land-based airpower to influence naval activities in the region. But China's air force remains a primitive war-fighting machine. Its inventory is composed mainly of 1950s-and l960s-generation aircraft. While China is working to develop modern planes, its most advanced domestically produced fighter, the F8-11, is the equivalent of a late 1960s U.S. warplane. Even this primitive plane has yet to enter fully into operation. Besides American airpower, China must also contend with the Japanese air force, one of the most advanced in the world. Japanese production of the F2 fighter jet will assure it of defensive air superiority over the East China Sea for the foreseeable future. Moreover, Japanese aircraft are armed with air-to-air missiles far more advanced than their Chinese counterparts, and they enjoy the support of advanced AWACS aircraft and other sophisticated defense technologies. Add to this imbalance in air capability Japan's large fleet of advanced surface warships, its vastly superior technological base, and its self-restraint in defense spending as a share of GNP, and it becomes clear not only that China cannot dominate the East China Sea, but that it is not even a player in the naval balance. Recent acquisitions of Soviet SU-27S, a late 1970s fighter jet, fail to alter this reality since China cannot offset Japan's indigenous ability to manufacture 21st century aircraft. Should a Sino-Japanese arms race develop, Japan could easily augment its superiority in regional waters.

Chinese power could also destabilize the South China Sea, which comprises two distinct military theaters. Its northern reaches include the waters east of Vietnam and the Paracel Islands, territory contested by China, Vietnam, and Taiwan. Here, absent outside influence, Chinese military modernization and arms imports can make a difference. Because this part of the South China Sea is within range of Chinese land-based aircraft, improved Chinese capabilities would challenge Vietnam's ability to defend its coastal waters and its claims to the Paracel Islands. But such a development would merely reinforce current trends in Sino-Vietnamese relations, not destabilize the existing order.

The southern reaches of the South China Sea, including Malaysia, Singapore, Indonesia, and the Philippines, comprise another distinct military region, well beyond the reach of China's land-based aircraft. Air support for Chinese ground forces and naval vessels in the distant waters of the South China Sea would require carrier-based air support. Even air refueling of SU-27S is insuffi-

cient. Air refueling is complex and does not enable aircraft to loiter over distant waters, providing around-the-clock support for troops and surface vessels deployed near potential adversaries. The Chinese navy would lose a battle in this region against Singapore, Malaysia, or Indonesia, all of which possess advanced American or British aircraft. This fact explains the evident willingness and ability of these countries to occupy Chinese-claimed islands in the South China Sea. Indonesia, for example, has used a show of force to warn China from contesting its claim to the economic zone surrounding Natuna Island....

China will need aircraft carriers to become a great power in the distant waters of the South China Sea, capable of challenging America's influence in the maritime countries of Southeast Asia and its access to the region's strategic shipping lanes. It is not clear that China could meet such an enormous challenge. Construction and deployment of an aircraft carrier requires the most modern technology, advanced pilot skills, and astronomical funding. Moscow did not deploy its first true aircraft carrier until after the Cold War. China is far from possessing the power plant, avionics, and metallurgy technologies required to manufacture a plane that can take off and land on an aircraft carrier in any weather. Its pilots have minimal training over blue water and little experience flying without ground control. Its systems engineers cannot manage the logistics of supplying resources to a carrier and its half dozen support vessels, the equivalent of a small city at sea. The expense of outfitting a carrier group would require China to skew its defense procurement toward naval power or divert significant resources from important civilian infrastructure projects.

Power projection cannot be purchased abroad. Not only would the expense be prohibitive, requiring import of aircraft carriers, appropriate aircraft, and high-technology avionics, but the necessary managerial expertise is not for sale. Moreover, there are limits to what countries will export to China. Obsolete sample carriers from France, for example, may become available, but the hardware for full power projection can only be developed indigenously.

Despite the obstacles and costs, China might still decide to build an aircraft carrier. Experts estimate that if China began today, the vessel would become operational between 2005 and 2010. And that would be only one carrier. The U.S. Navy estimates that keeping one carrier on location at all times requires a fleet of three. China could not build a third carrier until approximately 2020. Due to inferior managerial skills and logistical facilities, China would probably need more than three carriers to keep one on location in the distant regions of the South China Sea. Moreover, these first-generation Chinese carriers would be half the size of an American carrier, deploying aircraft inferior to those currently deployed by the maritime Southeast Asian countries, much less those deployed by the United States on its far larger and more sophisticated vessels.

Finally, even if China does pursue significant military advancements, its rivals will not be standing still. Given its head start and cooperation with Japan and other regional allies, the United States could maintain its current defense posture and the South China Sea would remain an "American lake" well into the 21st century. But the United States

continues to modernize all branches of its military. In developing power projection capability, China would risk a U.S.-Japanese arms buildup, leaving itself relatively weaker, while diverting scarce funds from more pressing military objectives, such as securing its coastal waters.

CHINA'S WILD CARD

... Beijing can use military power to destabilize Taiwan and regional politics. China had a similar ability in the 1950s, when its shelling of the offshore islands caused a crisis in Sino-American relations. Similarly, Chinese missiles can threaten U.S. naval vessels. But this capability is shared by the most primitive militaries, including those of Iran and Argentina. As Iraq showed during the 1991 Persian Gulf War, even a 1960s Scud missile can disrupt local economies and menace U.S. forces. Indeed, the gravest danger posed by China's 1996 missile tests was their obsolescence: the missiles were so primitive that they could have veered off course and hit Taiwan. America must be concerned by Chinese military power not because China will develop hegemonic power but because it can raise the cost of defending American interests and spoil the prospects for a cooperative regional order.

CHINA'S CONSERVATIVE FOREIGN POLICY

China's ability to wreak havoc is not new to East Asia. Since 1949 the United States has had to cope with U.S.-Chinese conflicts of interest. In many respects, it is easier to deal with these conflicts today than ever before. Indochina is no longer an issue. China is collaborating with South Korea to encourage North Korean moderation. Even the conflict with Taiwan has become more manageable. Taiwan now has a stable government, a prosperous economy, and a vastly improved military. The mainland's ability to challenge Taiwan's security is less today than ever before. Moreover, the mainland is no longer allied with a global superpower that can shield it in a conflict with the United States over Taiwan. Nor is it an antagonist in a polarized East Asian balance of power. Participation in the global economy and a stake in regional stability encourage China to avoid confrontations with the United States over Taiwan.

Despite cooperative relations with almost all of its neighbors in Asia, Chinese foreign relations have not been perfectly harmonious. But the friction does not reflect Beijing's restlessness. It is true that China's Taiwan policy contains significant coercive elements and that Beijing has not relinquished its right to use force against the island. But China's intent is to deter Taipei and Washington from changing the status quo, not to compel Taiwan to expedite the pace of formal reunification. Beijing has made clear that it is prepared to return to the rules that governed U.S.-Taiwan-mainland relations prior to 1994, when Washington did not allow Taiwan's senior officials to visit the United States but supplied it with large quantities of advanced weapons. The friction in Sino-American relations since June 1989 has stemmed primarily from bilateral trade relations, U.S.-Taiwan relations, and American criticism of China's human rights record. Moreover, China has acquiesced to U.S. pressure regarding weapons proliferation. With the exception of its security relationship with Pakistan, since the end of the Cold

War Beijing has not exported any missiles in violation of international agreements, nor has it exported technology for use in nuclear reactors not under the International Atomic Energy Agency's supervision.

China's relationship with Japan has become more difficult, but this primarily reflects changes in Japanese politics. Japan's development of a competitive multiparty electoral system has politicized its policy toward Taiwan and Sino-Japanese territorial disputes and promoted linkage between Japanese aid and China's human rights record. Japan has also become a more confident country, less willing to abide Chinese demands that it maintain a low international profile as penance for its military expansionism in the 1930s and 1940s. During the 1996 dispute over the Diaoyu (Senkaku) islands, China adopted a cautious policy, waiting for Japanese policy to change after the November general elections....

Since the early 1980s, the world's major industrial economies have been eager to participate in Chinese modernization. The prospect of China's economic growth and greater domestic employment has encouraged them to expand trade and investment ties with China. They have also been willing to extend considerable foreign aid and technical assistance through bilateral and multilateral institutions. The accompanying technology and capital transfers have played an important role in modernizing Chinese industry and stimulating economic growth. Beijing realizes that conservative international behavior was the precondition that encouraged the advanced industrial countries to participate in China's economy. They also realize that provocative policies risk ending China's economic success story.

A stable regional order is conducive to Chinese ambitions insofar as it allows Beijing to focus its domestic resources on the economic foundations of strategic power. The growth of the Chinese military budget since the late 1980s has been significant, if only because it has allowed China to import advanced Russian weaponry. Recent increases in the military budget partially reflect high inflation affecting soldiers' salaries and the cost of consumer goods purchased by the Chinese military. Nonetheless, estimates of the overall size of China's military budget indicate that China's defense spending remains relatively low, both as a share of gross national product and compared with the spending of other great powers.

THE LUXURY TO ENGAGE

Thus far, post-Cold War international relations have not hardened into opposing blocs. The opportunity still exists to establish a stable international order. But the sine qua non of such an order is Chinese participation in its creation. Chinese leaders remain committed to seeking constructive relations with all their neighbors. Given the costs that China can impose on America and its allies, U.S. policy should take advantage of that posture to reinforce China's interest in regional stability and strengthen its commitment to global stability. Engagement, not isolation, is the appropriate policy.

Engagement must mean more than simply offering China the opportunity to follow the rules. It requires acknowledging Chinese interests and negotiating solutions that accommodate both American and Chinese objectives. In bilateral relations, this will entail compromise approaches over the future of Taiwan. It

will require mutual accommodation to prevent nuclear proliferation on the Korean peninsula and accommodation of Chinese interests in Sino-Pakistani security ties. Washington must acknowledge the economic sources of trade imbalances and the Chinese government's limited ability to enforce its domestic laws and international commitments...

There is no guarantee that engagement will work. It will often involve acrimonious negotiations as the two sides make difficult policy adjustments and seek compromise solutions. At times, Washington will have to protect its interests unilaterally. It will also have to maintain its current military deployments in Asia. U.S. strategic retrenchment would do far more to alter the Sino-American bilateral balance of power and the regional balance of power than any combination of Chinese military and economic policies. But it is also clear that reliance on purely coercive measures will not elicit Chinese cooperation. Rather, it would almost guarantee renewed tension in Sino-American relations and heightened instability in East Asia. Given the strategic head start the United States and its allies enjoy, Washington has the luxury of observing Chinese modernization before adopting a more assertive posture.

POSTSCRIPT

Does China Threaten Vital American Interests?

Although Ross minimizes China's threat to U.S. interests, he recognizes the need for American military preparedness: "U.S. strategic retrenchment would do far more to alter the Sino-American bilateral balance of power and the regional balance of power than any combination of Chinese military and economic policies." But if he is right that China is now in a cooperative posture (he mentions China's help in encouraging North Korean moderation and in generally acquiescing to U.S. demands for nonproliferation), why is there a need for American armaments? Perhaps Ross shares the view of the famous gangster Al Capone, who once ventured the view that "you get more with a kind word and a gun than with a kind word alone."

Roger Garside, in *Coming Alive: China After Mao* (McGraw-Hill, 1981), offers the view that "there is now in place a group of experienced and relatively pragmatic leaders" running China. That, of course, was his view at the beginning of the 1980s. Is it still valid? Ross thinks it is. With coauthor Andrew J. Nathan, Ross has written a more expanded version of the essay reprinted here. In *The Great Wall and the Empty Fortress* (W. W. Norton, 1997), Ross and Nathan portray China as a vulnerable power crowded on all sides by rival powers and facing serious security problems within its own borders. Obviously, Bernstein and Munro disagree. They have also further developed their arguments in the book *The Coming Conflict With China* (Alfred A. Knopf, 1997). Ross Terrill, *China in Our Time* (Simon & Schuster, 1992) combines the author's personal reportage (he witnessed the crackdown on the prodemocracy demonstrations in 1989) with his analysis of the erratic course of China on the world stage since the 1949 Communist takeover.

President Bill Clinton came into office in 1993 after having taken a fairly hard line toward China in his campaign. He accused President George Bush of "coddling" the Chinese regime and repeatedly called attention to China's human rights abuses. But by 1998 Clinton was being accused of turning a blind eye to China's internal abuses, its export of dangerous weaponry, and its aggressive behavior in the international arena. Some of his critics even suspect that Clinton tolerates China's misbehavior because of secret Chinese campaign contributions to his party Eventually, it is to be hoped, facts and fantasies will be sorted out and distinguished.

ISSUE 19

Should the United States Put More Restrictions on Immigration?

YES: Daniel James, from "Close the Borders to All Newcomers," *Insight* (November 22, 1993)

NO: Stephen Moore, from "Give Us Your Best, Your Brightest," *Insight* (November 22, 1993)

ISSUE SUMMARY

YES: Daniel James, an adviser to Carrying Capacity Network in Washington, D.C., wants a moratorium on immigration, which, he claims, is taking away jobs from American workers, threatening the environment, and breaking up American culture.

NO: Economist Stephen Moore insists that immigrants have created more jobs than they have taken away and have greatly enriched the economy and culture.

In 1949 a delegation of Native Americans went to Washington to tell lawmakers about the plight of America's original occupants. After meeting with Vice President Alben Barkley, the delegation got up to leave. But one old Sioux chief stayed a moment longer to deliver a parting word to the vice president. "Young fellow," he said, "let me give you a little advice. Be careful with your immigration laws. We were careless with ours."

As America prospered and offered the hope of opportunity and freedom, increasing numbers of immigrants came to the United States. In the last two decades of the nineteenth century, Congress barred further immigration by convicts, paupers, idiots, and Chinese. That, however, did not stem the tide.

In the half-century between 1870 and 1920, more than 26 million people came to live in the United States. The National Origins Act was adopted in 1924 to restrict the number of new immigrants, ban east Asian immigration (directed at Japan), and establish a European quota based on the population of the United States in 1890, when there had been far fewer new arrivals from eastern and southern Europe. The total number of legal immigrants was later cut again, but still they came.

In 1965 the national origins formula was abandoned, but strict limits on the number of immigrants were retained. The end of quotas spurred a dramatic increase of immigrants from Central and South America and Asia. Between 1965 and 1995, nearly one-half of all immigrants came from Mexico, the Car-

ibbean, and the rest of Latin America, and nearly one-third arrived from Asia. Because they fear deportation, illegal arrivals accept very low wages and poor living conditions.

The number of illegal arrivals from Latin America prompted passage of the Immigration Reform and Control Act of 1987, requiring that employers confirm the legal status of their employees. At the same time, undocumented workers who had entered the United States before 1982 were granted amnesty. However, the flood of illegal immigrants has not been stemmed.

Why do so many people want to come to the United States? They come to flee tyranny and terrorism, to escape the ravages of war, and to join relatives already here. Above all, they come because America offers economic opportunity, in stark contrast to the poverty they endure in their native countries.

Do immigrants endanger or improve the American standard of living? Critics fear that the new immigrants, willing to work longer hours at lower pay, will take jobs away from American workers. Supporters of immigration believe that the new immigrants fill jobs that most Americans do not want and that they stimulate economic growth. Do poor, often uneducated immigrants contribute to urban crowding and the decline of cities? Do they introduce new diseases or reintroduce old ones that have been conquered here?

Do immigrants undermine or enrich American culture? The changing face of the United States has been dramatic in the last quarter-century. California, the most populous state, no longer has a single racial majority. Hispanics defined as whites and blacks who identify themselves as being of Hispanic origin make up the fastest-growing major category. Currently, whites make up 73.6 percent of the population; blacks make up 12 percent; Hispanics, 10.2 percent; and Asians, 3.3 percent. If we project present population trends forward, we can see that still greater change will take place among these populations: By the year 2050 whites will make up 52.8 percent of the population; blacks 13.6 percent; Hispanics, 24.5 percent; and Asians, 8.2 percent. (American Indians are not included here, because they are likely to continue to be less than 1 percent of the population.)

What, if anything, is to be done? California's voters adopted Proposition 187 to cut off all state assistance to illegal immigrants, but its implementation has been blocked in the courts. Congress has acted to deny welfare to illegal immigrants and public education to their children. Some have argued that children born in the United States to illegal immigrants should be denied citizenship. Others have argued that a great wall should be built between the United States and Mexico to discourage illegal entry.

Some of these issues are touched upon in the debate that follows, although the authors place greatest emphasis on economic considerations. Daniel James worries that recent immigration adds immeasurably to America's economic problems. Stephen Moore insists that "immigrants don't just take jobs, they create jobs."

YES

Daniel James

CLOSE THE BORDERS TO
ALL NEWCOMERS

Strip the rhetoric from the evolving immigration debate and the bottom line becomes crystal clear: We may desire more and more immigrants, but can we afford so many of them? In his recently published memoirs, *Around the Cragged Hill*, George F. Kennan, perhaps [America's] most eminent statesman, goes to the heart of the matter:

> "We are already, for better or for worse, very much a polyglot country; and nothing of that is now to be changed. What I have in mind here are sheer numbers. There *is* such a thing as overcrowding. It has its psychic effects as well as its physical ones. There *are* limits to what the environment can stand."

The sheer numbers are indeed mind-boggling:

- 10.5 million immigrants, including those arriving illegally, entered the U.S. in the 1980s. That topped the previous record of 8.8 million who came here from 1901 to 1910.

- 15 to 18 million more newcomers, both legal and illegal, are projected to reach America in the 1990s, assuming our present immigration policy remains unchanged. Already, the number arriving in this decade is greater than for the same period in the previous decade. And there were nearly 1.2 million immigrants in 1992, 20 percent more than in 1991.

- 30 million immigrants—perhaps as many as 36 million—are expected to arrive in the first two decades of the next century, according to demographic projections and extrapolation of 1991–92 Census Bureau data.

The last two projections indicate that between 45 million and 54 million people—almost equal to the population of Great Britain—will be entering the U.S. in little more than a generation.

Add the 20 million immigrants who arrived from 1965 to 1990, and the grand total who will have entered the U.S. in just over a half-century (1965–2020) will be 65 million to 74 million.

There is no precedent for these numbers anywhere in the world. They constitute the biggest wave of immigration ever to a single country. Called the "fourth wave" of immigration to the U.S., it is really a tidal wave.

Yet the numbers are conservative. Unforeseeable trends in countries that generate immigrants could swell the tidal wave even higher than projected. It is likely, for example, that the demise of Cuba's communist dictatorship would send a flood of refugees to Miami comparable to the 125,000 *Marielitos* who inundated it in 1980.

Mexico is an even bigger concern. In the 1980s, it sent the U.S. nearly 4 million immigrants, more than the total for all of Asia. Two great "push" factors will drive ever more of them northward: high population growth—Mexico's present 90 million inhabitants will become 110 million by 2000—and unemployment/underemployment levels of 40 to 50 percent.

The North American Free Trade Agreement [NAFTA] ... may generate a temporary upsurge in illegal border crossings. It would draw more Mexicans to the relatively affluent north and make entering the U.S. affordable. Meanwhile, an expected rise in imports of cheaper U.S. corn would bankrupt Mexico's peasant class, the *campesinos*, and drive them to seek work stateside. Only years from now would NAFTA create enough jobs to keep Mexicans at home.

The cost to U.S. taxpayers of accepting endless numbers of immigrants is intolerable. We learn from a new study, "The Costs of Immigration," by economist Donald Huddle, that the net 1992 public assistance cost of the 19.3 million immigrants who have settled here since 1970 was $42.5 billion, after subtracting $20.2 billion they paid in taxes.

Huddle examined costs in 22 categories of federal, state and local assistance available to immigrants, including a package of 10 county welfare and health services. The largest net costs for immigrants in 1992 were $16 billion for education (primary, secondary and bilingual), $10.6 billion for health and welfare services and $8.5 billion for Medicaid.

Criminal justice and corrections costs for immigrants were found by Huddle to total more than $2 billion in 1992. The social price was greater: A disproportionately large number of illegals were in prison for committing felonies. In California, they made up 11 percent of all inmates.

Huddle also found that immigrants in 1992 displaced—probably forever—2.07 million American workers. This should answer the oft-debated question: Do immigrants take jobs away from Americans?

It is true that American workers frequently turn down tasks that immigrants willingly perform, such as picking fruit and vegetables under inhumane conditions or making garments in urban sweatshops. But that hardly explains the virtual elimination of blacks from jobs in entire industries. In Los Angeles, unionized blacks have been displaced by nonunion Hispanics in janitorial services, and in Washington, D.C., by Latino immigrants in hotels and restaurants.

The puzzling question is: Why does the U.S. continue to import competition for American workers at a time of high unemployment? The Labor Department reports that 8.5 million Americans, about 6.7 percent of our work force, are unemployed. Our two principal minorities suffer most from joblessness—12.6 percent

of blacks and 9.7 percent of Latinos—and they are the most vulnerable to displacement.

Immigration costs will rise further in this decade, Huddle forecasts. He projects that from 1993 to 2002, 11.1 million legal and illegal immigrants will be added to the 19.3 million post-1970 immigrants already here, for a total of 30.4 million. Their net cost to taxpayers during the next decade would come to $668.5 billion, which is larger than the $496 billion of the national deficit that President Clinton and Congress have pledged to erase over five years.

Indeed, the savings from reducing immigration could be applied to cutting the deficit considerably, with less pain to the taxpayer than paring public services and raising taxes, as the administration proposes. Alternatively, Huddle suggests, such savings could be used to finance investment tax credits to create and maintain 4.1 million private sector jobs, or 1.4 million public works and service jobs, throughout the decade.

Impossible to quantify, but perhaps more devastating in the long run, is the cost of excessive immigration to the environment. As more and more people are added to our population—already excessive at 260 million—the greater the environmental degradation will be. The immigrants will contribute to increasing energy use, toxic waste, smog and urban crowding, all of which affect our mental and emotional health as well as the ecosystem.

Our population is increasing by 3 million a year, a rate faster than that of any other advanced country. California provides an example of what can happen to a nearly ideal environment when it is overwhelmed by too many people. Since 1980, its population has zoomed from 23.7 million to more than 31 million, an increase of almost one-third. As a consequence, Los Angeles and its once pristine bay are all but hopelessly polluted, and San Diego and Orange counties are fast becoming sad miniatures of Los Angeles.

Equally alarming is the impetus that uncontrolled immigration provides to separatism and its obverse, multiculturalism. Those living in areas where there are many other immigrants, such as Los Angeles and Texas's Rio Grande Valley, see no need to learn English and so live in virtual isolation from the general population. As long as these barrios are constantly replenished with newcomers from Mexico—virtually a stone's throw away—their inhabitants will feel less and less need or desire to assimilate. This process encourages a kind of natural separatism that could lead to political separatism.

Richard Estrada, a journalist and scholar, sees an ominous parallel with Quebec: "If Francophone Quebec can bring the Canadian confederation to the brink of disintegration even though France lies an ocean away, should there not at least arise a certain reflectiveness about our Southwest, which lies contiguous to an overpopulated Third World nation?"

A growing number of Americans of all classes and ethnic groups share these concerns about immigration and favor reducing it. For at least two decades, a majority of Americans have expressed in various polls their desire to stop or reduce immigration. In January 1992, a Gallup Poll found that 64 percent of registered voters would vote for a presidential candidate who favored tougher laws on immigration. In December, the Latino National Political Survey discovered

that Hispanics overwhelmingly believed there is too much immigration.

* * *

Even politicians who previously shunned immigration as a taboo subject are jumping onto the immigration reform bandwagon. From President Clinton, a Democrat, to California's Gov. Pete Wilson, a Republican, most are clamoring to curb illegal immigration. We can hope that they soon will understand that the main problem, as the public generally has perceived, is legal immigration.

Serious though illegal immigration is, *legal* immigration poses a much graver problem. We receive more than three times as many legal immigrants, including refugees, as illegal ones. Their numbers are projected to grow exponentially, because under the 1990 Immigration Act they are permitted to bring in an endless procession of family members. In 1992, for example, family-related immigrants totaled 594,000, or 49 percent of the 1.2 million immigrants who entered the U.S. that year.

Legal immigrants account for almost three-quarters of the total costs calculated by the Huddle study. Thus, of the $668.5 billion projected net cost to taxpayers for all immigrants from 1993 to 2002, legal immigrants would account for $482 billion. Illegal aliens would cost $186.4 billion.

The most effective way to curb illegal immigration is to declare a moratorium on *all* immigration. Why? If the U.S. clamps down on illegals but permits legal immigration to continue uncontrolled, that tells the world we are not serious about solving either problem, for it is easier to reduce or halt the legal flow than to hunt down those who arrive undercover. To do so would require a mere stroke of the pen and wouldn't cost taxpayers extra—Congress could just reform the Immigration Act of 1990, which is directly responsible for the 40 percent increase to immigration. That would send the unequivocal message to anyone who plans to enter the U.S. that we cannot afford to receive them—at least for the time being.

The message would ring loud and clear to would-be illegal immigrants that we mean business. It must be backed up, however, by a whole range of law enforcement measures that are now on the books but are ignored or not used effectively. In addition, to smoke out illegals and also eliminate the racket in fraudulent documents, Congress should approve a universal ID, much like the health security card that President Clinton displayed when he presented his health plan.

The ID cards would identify those who are legally in the U.S. and entitled to work and receive benefits. Local and state authorities should be directed to share information on illegals with the Immigration and Naturalization Service to aid in apprehending them; at present, authorities deny such information to the INS, in effect protecting illegals.

Instead of sending the National Guard to patrol the border as advocated by some lawmakers. it would be more effective to give the Border Patrol sufficient personnel to do its job. At least 2,000 new agents should be added to the current force of about 4,000, as well as equipment such as better night sensors and new vehicles. The Customs Service will also require additional personnel, particularly if NAFTA is put into effect and vehicular traffic from Mexico increases as expected.

A vital component of any program to curb immigration must be the cooper-

ation of the Mexican government. The White House should take advantage of our cordial relations with Mexico and our growing economic clout to request that our southern neighbor cease its traditional (though unwritten) policy of regarding the U.S. as a safety valve.

A U.S. moratorium on immigration would yield highly positive gains by allowing the 20 million immigrants now within our borders time to assimilate into the mainstream. It would remove the pressure of new millions crowding into inner-city barrios and encourage existing inhabitants to break out of them. This would mitigate the danger of separatism, counter multiculturalist trends, defuse interethnic tensions and reduce crime and violence.

If this prescription sounds like a pipe dream, let us recall that restrictive legislation in 1924 cut immigration to a trickle, allowing enough time for the masses of immigrants the U.S. had then to overcome the obstacles to assimilation. That literally saved America. For when the Japanese struck at Pearl Harbor in 1941 and the U.S. was confronted by their military might plus that of Ger-many, which already had conquered Europe and had just invaded the Soviet Union, our nation stood united against them. Sadly, one doubts whether today's America, torn by an identity crisis spawned by divisive forces, would be capable of meeting a similar threat.

The United States is headed for a crisis of incalculable magnitude if mass immigration continues unchecked. The argument of those who favor an open border is that immigrants have always contributed to our society, and so they have. But we no longer can afford the world's "huddled masses" when our own are so often homeless and jobless. If we permit immigration to continue uncontrolled, it will explode in a full-blown crisis that will extend beyond the vociferous separatism/multiculturalism debate to engulf us in a violent civil conflict.

America is under siege. It is threatened from without by international terrorism and from within by centrifugal forces that already have revealed their capacity for destruction in bloody riots from Los Angeles to Miami, from Washington to Manhattan.

NO

Stephen Moore

GIVE US YOUR BEST, YOUR BRIGHTEST

For many Americans, the word "immigration" immediately conjures up an image of poor Mexicans scrambling across the border near San Diego to find minimum-wage work and perhaps collect government benefits. Recent public opinion polls confirm that the attitude of the American public toward immigration is highly unfavorable. Central Americans are perceived as welfare abusers who stubbornly refuse to learn English, Haitians are seen as AIDS carriers, Russian Jews are considered to be mafiosi, and Asians are seen as international terrorists. The media reinforce these stereotypes by battering the public with negative depictions of immigrants.

The conception of immigrants as tired, poor, huddled masses seems permanently sketched into the mind of the public, just as the words are sketched irrevocably at the feet of the Statue of Liberty. But the Emma Lazarus poem simply does not describe the hundreds of thousands of people who are building new lives here in the 1990s. It would be more appropriate if the words at the base of the statue read: "Give us your best, your brightest, your most energetic and talented." Why? Because in large part those are the people who come to the United States each year.

Before we start slamming shut the golden door, it might be worthwhile to find out who the newcomers are and how they truly affect our lives.

Anyone who believes that immigrants are a drain on the U.S. economy has never visited the Silicon Valley in California. Here and in other corridors of high-tech entrepreneurship, immigrants are literally the lifeblood of many of the nation's most prosperous industries. In virtually every field in which the United States asserted global leadership in the 1980s—industries such as computer design and softwear, pharmaceuticals, bioengineering, electronics, superconductivity, robotics and aerospace engineering—one finds immigrants. In many ways these high-growth industries are the modern version of the American melting pot in action.

Consider Intel Corp. With profits of $1.1 billion in 1992, it is one of the most prolific and fast-expanding companies in the United States, employing tens of thousands of American workers. It is constantly developing exciting,

cutting-edge technologies that will define the computer industry in the 21st century.

And it is doing all of this largely with the talents of America's newest immigrants. Three members of Intel's top management, including Chief Executive Officer Andrew S. Grove, from Hungary, are immigrants. Some of its most successful and revolutionary computer technologies were pioneered by immigrants, such as the 8080 microprocessor (an expanded-power computer chip), invented by a Japanese, and polysilicon FET gates (the basic unit of memory storage on modern computer chips), invented by an Italian. Dick Ward, manager of employee information systems at Intel, says: "Our whole business is predicated on inventing the next generation of computer technologies. The engine that drives that quest is brainpower. And here at Intel, much of that brainpower comes from immigrants."

Or consider Du Pont-Merck Pharmaceutical Co., an $800 million-a-year health care products company based in Wilmington, Del., which reports that immigrants are responsible for many of its most promising new product innovations. For example, losartan, an antihypertensive drug, was developed by a team of scientists that included two Chinese and a Lithuanian. Joseph Mollica, Chief Executive Officer of Du Pont-Merck, says that bringing together such diverse talent "lets you look at problems and opportunities from a slightly different point of view."

Intel and Du Pont-Merck are not alone in relying on immigrants. Robert Kelley Jr., president of SO/CAL/TEN, an association of nearly 200 high-tech California companies, insists: "Without the influx of Asians in the 1980s, we would not have had the entrepreneurial explosion we've seen in California." David N. K. Wang, vice president for worldwide business operations at Applied Materials Inc., a computer-technology company in California, adds that because of immigration, "Silicon Valley is one of the most international business centers in the world."

Take away the immigrants, and you take away the talent base that makes such centers operate. Indeed, it is frightening to think what would happen to America's global competitiveness if the immigrants stopped coming. Even scarier is the more realistic prospect that U.S. policymakers will enact laws to prevent them from coming.

New research has begun to quantify the contributions of immigrants to American industry. The highly respected National Research Council reported in 1988 that "a large fraction of the technological output of the United States [is] dependent upon foreign talent and that such dependency is growing." Noting that well over half of all scientists graduating with doctorate degrees from American universities and one in three engineers working in the United States are immigrants, the report states emphatically: "It is clear ... that these foreign-born engineers enrich our culture and make substantial contributions to the U.S. economic well-being and competitiveness."

The United States' competitive edge over the Japanese, Germans, Koreans and much of Europe is linked closely to its continued ability to attract and retain highly talented workers from other countries. A 1990 study by the national Science Foundation says, "Very significant, positive aspects arise from the presence of foreign-born engineers in our society."

For example, superconductivity, a technology that is expected to spawn hun-

dreds of vital new commercial applications in the next century, was discovered by a physicist at the University of Houston, Paul C. W. Chu. He was born in China and came to the U.S. in 1972. His brilliance and inventiveness have made him a top contender for a Nobel Prize.

Of course, if Chu does win a Nobel, he will join a long list of winners who were immigrants in America. In the 20th century, between 20 percent and 50 percent of the Nobel Prize winners, depending on the discipline involved, have been immigrants to the United States. Today there are more Russian Nobel Prize winners living in the U.S. than there are living in Russia.

Public opinion polls consistently reveal that a major worry is that immigrants take jobs from American workers. The fear is understandable but misplaced. Immigrants don't just take jobs, they create jobs. One way is by starting new businesses. Today, America's immigrants, even those who come with relatively low skill levels, are highly entrepreneurial.

Take Koreans, for example. According to sociologists Alendro Portes and Ruben Rumbaut, "In Los Angeles, the propensity for self-employment is three times greater for Koreans than among the population as a whole. Grocery stores, restaurants, gas stations, liquor stores and real estate offices are typical Korean businesses." Cubans also are prodigious creators of new businesses. The number of Cuban-owned businesses in Miami has expanded from 919 in 1967 to 8,000 in 1976 to 28,000 in 1990. On Jefferson Boulevard in Dallas, more than 800 businesses operate, three-quarters of them owned by first- and second-generation Hispanic immigrants. Just 10 years ago, before the influx of Mexicans and other Central Americans, the neighborhood was in decay, with many vacant storefronts displaying "for sale" signs in the windows. Today it is a thriving ethnic neighborhood.

To be sure, few immigrant-owned businesses mature into an Intel. In fact, many fail completely. Like most new businesses in America, most immigrant establishments are small and only marginally profitable. The average immigrant business employs two to four workers and records roughly $200,000 in annual sales. However, such small businesses, as President Clinton often correctly emphasizes, are a significant source of jobs.

It should not be too surprising that immigrants are far more likely than average U.S. citizens to take business risks. After all, uprooting oneself, traveling to a foreign culture and making it requires more than the usual amount of courage, ambition, resourcefulness and even bravado. Indeed, this is part of the self-selection process that makes immigrants so particularly desirable. Immigrants are not just people—they are a very special group of people. By coming, they impart productive energies on the rest of us.

This is not just romanticism. It is well-grounded in fact. Countless studies have documented that immigrants to the United States tend to be more skilled, more highly educated and wealthier than the average citizen of their native countries.

Thomas Sowell, an economist and senior fellow at the Hoover Institution in Stanford, Calif., reports in his seminal study on immigration, "Ethnic America," that black immigrants from the West Indies have far higher skill levels than their countrymen at home. He also finds that the income levels of West Indies immigrants are higher than those of

West Indies natives, American blacks and native-born white Americans.

Surprisingly, even illegal immigrants are not the poverty-stricken and least skilled from their native countries. Surveys of undocumented immigrants from Mexico to the United States show that only about 5 percent were unemployed in Mexico, whereas the average unemployment rate there was about three times that level, and that a relatively high percentage of them worked in white-collar jobs in Mexico. In addition, surveys have found that illiteracy among undocumented Mexicans in the U.S. is about 10 percent, whereas illiteracy in Mexico is about 22 percent.

Perhaps the greatest asset of immigrants is their children, who tend to be remarkably successful in the U.S. Recently, the city of Boston reported that an incredible 13 of the 17 valedictorians in its public high schools were foreign-born—from China, Vietnam, Portugal, El Salvador, France, Italy, Jamaica and the former Czechoslovakia. Many could not speak a word of English when they arrived. Public high schools in Washington, Chicago and Los Angeles also report remarkably disproportionate numbers of immigrant children at the top of the class. Similarly, Westinghouse reports that over the past 12 years, about one-third of its prestigious National Science Talent Search winners have been Asians. Out of this group might emerge America's next Albert Einstein, who himself was an immigrant.

So one hidden cost of restricting immigration is the loss of immigrants' talented and motivated children.

In the past century, America has admitted roughly 50 million immigrants. This has been one of the largest migrations in the history of the world. Despite this infusion of people—no, because of it

—the United States became by the middle of the 20th century the wealthiest nation in the world. Real wages in America have grown more than eightfold over this period. The U.S. economy employed less than 40 million people in 1900; today it employs nearly 120 million people. The U.S. job machine had not the slightest problem expanding and absorbing the 8 million legal immigrants who came to this country in the 1980s. Eighteen million jobs were created.

But what about those frightening headlines? "Immigration Bankrupting Nation." "Immigrants Displacing U.S. Workers." "Foreigners Lured to U.S. by Welfare."

Here are the facts. The 1990s census reveals that roughly 6 percent of native-born Americans are on public assistance versus 7 percent of the foreign-born, with less than 5 percent of illegal immigrants collecting welfare. Not much reason for alarm. Because immigrants tend to come to the United States when they are young and working, over their lifetimes they each pay about $20,000 more in taxes than they use in services, according to economist Julian Simon of the University of Maryland. With 1 million immigrants per year, the nation gains about $20 billion more than cost. Rather than fiscal burdens, immigrants are huge bargains.

Nor do immigrants harm the U.S. labor market. A comprehensive 1989 study by the U.S. Department of Labor concluded "Neither U.S. workers nor most minority workers appear to be adversely affected by immigration—especially during periods of economic expansion." In the 1980s the top 10 immigrant-receiving states —including California, Florida, Massachusetts and Texas—recorded rates of unemployment 2 percentage points below the U.S. average, according to the

Alexis de Tocqueville Institution in Arlington, Va. So where's the job displacement?

We are now witnessing in America what might be described as the return of the nativists. They are selling fear and bigotry. But if any of their allegations against immigrants are accurate, then America could not have emerged as the economic superpower it is today.

In fact, most Americans do accept that immigration in the past has contributed greatly to the nation's economic growth. But they are not so sanguine in their assessment of present and future immigrants. It is strangely inconsistent that Americans believe that so long-standing and crucial a benefit is now a source of cultural and economic demise.

Shortly before his death, Winston Churchill wrote, "The empires of the future are the empires of the mind." America is confronted with one of the most awesome opportunities in world history to build those empires by attracting highly skilled, highly educated and entrepreneurial people from all over the globe. The Andrew Groves and the Paul Chus of the world do not want to go to Japan, Israel, Germany, France or Canada. Almost universally they want to come to the United States. We can be selective. By expanding immigration but orienting our admission policies toward gaining the best and the brightest, America would enjoy a significant comparative advantage over its geopolitical rivals.

By pursuing a liberal and strategic policy on immigration, America can ensure that the 21st century, like the 20th, will be the American century.

POSTSCRIPT

Should the United States Put More Restrictions on Immigration?

There is no accurate census of illegal immigrants, but the best estimate is that 5 million persons have entered the United States illegally within the past 10 years. What are the consequences for American society? The issue of immigration encompasses both legal and illegal immigrants. Immigration policy should begin by examining who comes and the consequences for the nation. Who are they, and what impact do they have? What do they cost, and what do they contribute?

Until the early years of the new republic, immigrants were predominantly white, English-speaking, Protestant Europeans and African slaves who were forcibly brought to the New World. This soon changed, and for a half-century —until the adoption of laws restricting immigration in the 1920s—Catholics and Jews, southern and eastern Europeans, most of them non-English speakers, came to the United States. Since World War II, Asian and Hispanic immigrants have come in ever-increasing numbers. George Henderson and Thompson Olasiji's *Migrants, Immigrants, and Slaves: Racial and Ethnic Groups in America* (University Press of America, 1995) is a useful introduction to the patterns of immigration into the United States.

Nicalaus Mills has edited the anthology *Arguing Immigration: The Debate Over the Changing Face of America* (Simon & Schuster, 1994), which presents a wide variety of contemporary viewpoints on the costs, benefits, and consequences of immigration policies. Leon F. Bouvier and Lindsey Grant, in *How Many Americans? Population, Immigration and the Environment* (Sierra Club Books, 1994), examine the consequences of population growth, which threatens grave environmental damage, including acid precipitation and climatic warming. The authors conclude that restrictions on immigration are imperative.

Georgie Anne Geyer's *Americans No More* (Atlantic Monthly Press, 1996) is a lament on the decline of civic life in America as a result of both legal and illegal immigration. Geyer does not deplore illegal immigration but the recent tendency of legal immigrants to resist assimilation. Peter Brimelow, in *Alien Nation: Common Sense About America's Immigration Disaster* (Random House, 1995), catalogs what he perceives to be the consequences of what he calls America's "immigration disaster." Brimelow argues that no multicultural society has lasted.

In opposition to Brimelow's view, Sanford J. Ungar, in *Fresh Blood: The New American Immigrants* (Simon & Schuster, 1995), argues, "To be American means being part of an ever more heterogeneous people and participating in

the constant redefinition of a complex, evolving cultural fabric." Somewhere in between multiculturalists like Ungar and assimilationists like Brimelow and Geyer is Peter D. Salins. In *Assimilation, American Style* (Basic Books, 1997), Salins argues that the naturalization process is the best means for absorbing the flood of immigrants who arrive in America each year.

Americans confront a choice. On the one hand, there are the ethical and political consequences of restricting immigration into a country whose attraction to poor or persecuted people is as great as its borders are vast. On the other hand, there are the problems of absorbing new, generally non-English-speaking populations into an economy that may have to provide increasing public support and a society whose traditions and values may clash with those of the newcomers.

ISSUE 20

Is Democracy Desirable for All Nations?

YES: Robert Kagan, from "Democracies and Double Standards," *Commentary* (August 1997)

NO: Robert D. Kaplan, from "Was Democracy Just a Moment?" *The Atlantic Monthly* (December 1997)

ISSUE SUMMARY

YES: Author and editor Robert Kagan argues that democracy has taken root in many nations that never had it before, in large measure due to American intervention, with desirable consequences for American security and prosperity.

NO: Foreign correspondent Robert D. Kaplan contends that recent experience demonstrates that not all nations have the conditions in which democracy can thrive, that some nations prosper without it, and that democracy may be less important in the future.

The most thoughtful advocates of democracy do not claim that it provides a cure for all that ails us. Rather, they argue, it is simply the best way—far and away the best, say its most ardent advocates—of organizing societies to deal with public issues. Winston Churchill acknowledged that he was not the first to express the sentiment in his famous observation, "No one pretends that democracy is perfect or all-wise. Indeed, it has been said that democracy is the worst form of government except all those other forms that have been tried from time to time."

Writing about the United States more than 150 years ago, Alexis de Tocqueville expressed his belief that the spread of democracy was irresistible, but he also concluded that the American example of the 1830s might not be the best for either America's future or the rest of the world. Tocqueville warned that democracy must "adapt its government to time and place, and to modify it according to men and conditions." With the belief of hindsight and an awareness of the ways in which democracy has developed, we may ask, Can those adaptations and modifications be sufficient to meet the needs of all nations and cultures? Is it possible that democracy is neither inevitable nor desirable at some times, under some circumstances, and in some places?

The evidence of the past quarter century is encouraging to those who believe in the triumph of democracy. President Bill Clinton has asserted that, for the first time in human history, more people live in democracies than any

other form of government. Throughout Latin America and in parts of Asia, Africa, and Eastern Europe in which democracy was previously unknown, personal freedoms, free elections, and a free press have become familiar. By contrast, Freedom House, a private organization devoted to the spread of democracy, estimated in 1996 that only one-fifth of the world's population lived in free societies, two-fifths in partly free nations, and another two-fifths in countries that were not free.

What are the necessary conditions for democracy? The most basic requirement is economic: the existence of a minimally adequate standard of living that provides enough food and other basic necessities. No population would choose a ballot over bread or other basic dietary staples. Implicit is the existence of employment that is adequate to ensure that individuals will continue to be able to meet these needs.

The fundamental political requirement for democracy is literacy, which goes beyond the ability to read and write to an awareness of one's responsibilities and rights in a democratic society. Political pundit Walter Lippmann observed, "No amount of charters, direct primaries, or short ballots will make a democracy out of an illiterate people." In this respect, democracy sets a high standard that many nations may not be able to meet.

More debatable is the claim of a social requirement: the sense of a shared destiny that cuts across racial, ethnic, and religious differences to create a common bond that ensures stability and a willingness to abide by the results of the last election, no matter how opposed the losers may be. The idea is that although the best public policy may not be made by counting heads, it is far better than breaking them, as appeals court judge Learned Hand once said.

Should America seek to export democracy? "The world must be made safe for democracy," was President Woodrow Wilson's plea when he urged Congress to involve the United States in World War I. Since then America has often sought the expansion of democracy, but it has also given military and economic assistance to governments that were undisguisedly antidemocratic. America's foreign policy often hinges on a choice between morality (what's good?) and practicality (what's good for America?). Those who urge American commitment to the spread of democracy argue that the idealistic and pragmatic approaches now coincide because the security of the United States is endangered by the presence of authoritarian regimes.

In the first of the following selections, Churchill's argument for democracy is echoed by Robert Kagan, who concludes, "Democracy is not the solution to the world's problems. But it is a better solution than the alternatives." He adds, relevant to America's relations with the rest of the world, "And it is the only solution the United States can ever support with a modicum of enthusiasm or consistency." In the second selection, Robert D. Kaplan suggests that democracy may be rendered irrelevant as a result of the globalization of economic enterprise, culture, electronic communications that transcend all boundaries, and material prosperity that leaves less time and thought for public concerns.

YES

Robert Kagan

DEMOCRACIES AND DOUBLE STANDARDS

For citizens of the world's most powerful democracy, it ought to be a source of satisfaction, and even of pride, that peoples all over the planet have struggled to adopt our model of government—and, in recent years, have succeeded in doing so at an astonishingly high rate. In the wave of democratization that swept the world between the late 1970's and early 1990's, more than 30 nations of widely diverse cultures and locales became democratic. Many of these transformations would once have been unimaginable: democracy in Taiwan? in Nicaragua? in Romania? in South Africa? Although some have since faltered and slipped back toward dictatorship, in most democracy has sunk its roots deeply and appears to be settling in for a long stay.

The United States played a central part—indeed, an indispensable part—in spurring and supporting this global transition. To be sure, in Latin America and Asia, growing economies and indigenous political forces made dictatorship more precarious. Within the Soviet empire, stagnation and decay hollowed out Communist tyranny from within. But in the absence of American exhortation, pressure, and in some cases direct intervention, these broad historical trends could easily have been cut short by guerrilla victories, military coups, or violent repression. Instead, they were seized upon by local leader after local leader, from Corazon Aquino and José Napoleon Duarte to Lech Walesa and Boris Yeltsin, each of whom was favored with American support at the crucial turning point.

Can anyone doubt that the spread of democracy these past twenty years has been a good thing, both for the United States and for the world? To contemplate today's situation is to appreciate anew the wisdom of American policy-makers in the late 70's and throughout most of the 1980's who placed a special value on promoting democratic governance abroad as part of America's grand strategy. Indeed, given the remarkable success of this policy,

one would have every reason to expect that it continues to command a great deal of support in the foreign-policy establishment and among American public officials.

But one would be wrong.

* * *

Over the past four or five years, a new pessimism, a new indifference, and even a new distaste for the promotion of democracy abroad have rippled through intellectual circles and out into the political arena. The assault comes from many different directions: from both the Right and the Left, from isolationists and internationalists, from the avatars of realism and the apostles of free-trade liberalism. But for all its diversity, the trend is unmistakable. The policies that helped shape the present, democratic era are losing legitimacy.

As one rather remarkable illustration, consider two "data points." In 1991, the distinguished Harvard political scientist Samuel P. Huntington published a book, *The Third Wave: Democratization in the Late Twentieth Century*, which exhaustively chronicled and unapologetically celebrated the advance of democracy around the world from the late 1970's onward. Although Huntington recognized some significant obstacles to the further extension of this trend—not least, the limits on political pluralism and individual rights that might be imposed by certain cultures, especially the Islamic and the Confucian—he reminded his readers that similar arguments had once been made about the inhibiting effects of Catholicism, and had been proved wrong in Spain, Portugal, Poland, and Latin America. Cultures need not be "permanent obstacles to development in one direction or another," he wrote. "Cultures evolve."

Thanks to broad, impersonal forces like economic growth, "time," Huntington concluded in 1991, was "on democracy's side." Still, though economic development and modernization helped make democracy possible, only "political leadership makes it real." Democracy would continue to spread only "to the extent that those who exercise power in the world and in individual countries want it to spread." Urging the United States to take a leading role in the process, Huntington departed from the analytic mode of the social scientist to propose, at several points in his book, "Guidelines for Democratizers."

Now for our second data point. It could not have been very long before the Huntington who wrote ringingly in 1991 that "I believe . . . democracy is good in itself and . . . has positive consequences for individual freedom, domestic stability, international peace, and the United States of America" began revising his optimism downward. By 1994, he had published an article in *Foreign Affairs*, "The Clash of Civilizations," in which he outlined the view—later developed in a book of the same title—that culture, or civilization, pretty much determined politics after all. As he would put it in another article in *Foreign Affairs* two years later, such hallmarks of democracy as the separation of spiritual and temporal authority, pluralism, the rule of law, representative government, and respect for individual rights and liberties were a product of European civilization, and "the belief that non-Western peoples should adopt Western values, institutions, and culture is, if taken seriously, immoral in its implications." The message now was that the United States and the West should stay out of the affairs of other civilizations and tend to their own—which happened,

by the way, to be in a perilous state of decline.

* * *

Huntington's may be the starkest but is far from the only example of the swift journey traveled by many foreign-policy thinkers from optimism to skepticism, and from participation, however qualified, in the euphoria occasioned by the spread of democracy and the downfall of Soviet Communism to denunciation of that euphoria. One can discern the origins of the new dourness in the virtually uniform response among intellectuals to Francis Fukuyama's 1989 article, "The End of History." In that now-famous work, Fukuyama suggested that the collapse of Communism augured nothing less than "the end point of mankind's ideological evolution and the universalization of Western liberal democracy as the final form of human government." Although Fukuyama conspicuously did *not* say this spelled an end to all human troubles, he was taken as saying it, and the reaction was fierce. It was not enough to prove that Fukuyama had exaggerated the good news; it was necessary to declare that he was entirely wrong, and that the news was in fact bad.

The harbingers of bad news have multiplied in the intervening years. We have been told that the world, far from being in somewhat greater harmony as a result of the spread of democratic government, is really *Out of Control* (the title of a 1993 book by Zbigniew Brzezinski) or in a state of *Pandaemonium* (the title of a book by Daniel Patrick Moynihan in the same year). The Yale historian Paul Kennedy, undeterred by history's refutation of his 1988 work, *The Rise and Fall of the Great Powers* (in which he had warned of the impending bankruptcy of the

United States under the weight of "imperial overstretch"), produced, in *Preparing for the Twenty first Century* (1993), a new catalogue of global horrors: population explosions, disease, growing disparities of wealth, environmental catastrophe, the breakdown of nation-states. In "The Coming Anarchy," an influential article in the *Atlantic Monthly* later fleshed out in the portentously titled book, *The Ends of the Earth*, Robert D. Kaplan gave "personal meaning" to Kennedy's tale of miseries by providing a worldwide tour of the future now awaiting us: "Poverty, the collapse of cities, porous borders, cultural and racial strife, growing economic disparities, [and] weakening nation-states."

Although Huntington himself has not fully endorsed the new "chaos paradigm," the picture he has painted in the last few years suggests the futility of any efforts at amelioration. In a world in which, as he wrote last year, "the word 'genocide' has been heard far more often ... than it was in any half-decade during the cold war," talk of supporting the further spread of democracy seems not only silly but misguided. In a *New York Times* op-ed piece, Robert Kaplan has suggested that we "shift our emphasis in the third world from holding elections to promoting family planning, environmental renewal, road building, and other stabilizing projects." What many third-world countries now need, in Kaplan's view, is not democracy, which tends rather to weaken than to strengthen society, but a dictatorship that can lead them through the stages of economic development necessary before democratic government becomes thinkable.

Kaplan is not alone in proposing that democracy may not only be too difficult for some people to achieve but actually bad for them. Two political scientists from

Columbia University, Edward D. Mansfield and Jack Snyder, have discovered a hitherto unknown "historical pattern" linking "democratization, belligerent nationalism, and war." Reinterpreting the origins of the Crimean war, World War I, and such modern conflicts as the wars between Serbia and Croatia and between Armenia and Azerbaijan; and citing the fact that "the electorate of Russia's partial democracy cast nearly a quarter of its votes [in 1993] for the party of radical nationalist Vladimir Zhirinovsky," Mansfield and Snyder have concluded, with mathematical precision, that

> states that make the biggest leap, from total autocracy to extensive mass democracy—like contemporary Russia—are about twice as likely to fight wars in the decade after democratization as are states that remain autocracies.

Indeed, the splitting-up of the Soviet behemoth into fifteen new states has provided ample fodder for the new debunkers of democracy. In seven of those states democracy is intact though precarious, while in the remaining eight it is either increasingly flawed or absent. But these eight make up fully half of a worldwide list compiled by Thomas Carothers of the Carnegie Endowment as proof positive of a "retrenchment" that "is stripping away the illusions that have surrounded the pro-democratic enterprise of recent years." Similarly with the breakup of Yugoslavia, where, according to Mansfield and Snyder, the "inexorable pressure for democratization" is what allowed the old elites to create "a new basis for legitimacy through nationalist propaganda and military action." After all, Fareed Zakaria, the managing editor of *Foreign Affairs*, pointed out in early 1996, it was through the quintessentially democratic procedure of elections that a "xenophobic dictator," Slobodan Milosevic, could consolidate his power in Serbia.

To the list of bad things produced by democracy has been added, finally, the deeply problematic outcome of elections in the Islamic world. In Algeria in 1992, such elections seemed certain to yield a victory by Muslim radicals, and were therefore canceled by the military. In Turkey, elections in 1995 produced a victory for the Welfare party, whose leader, Necmettin Erbakan, upon taking power in 1996, set about encouraging Islamic fundamentalism at home and courting the radical governments of Iran, Iraq, and Libya abroad; he was forced from his perch this year by the secular Turkish military. In both cases, it took a violation of democratic process to put a halt to what the democratic process had alarmingly yielded, and in both cases many observers and government officials heaved a sigh of relief: surely, they reasoned, it is better to have in place an orderly authoritarian government we can work with than a radical one we cannot.

* * *

Irronically, that is the kind of reasoning that Jeane J. Kirkpatrick pursued many years ago in these pages in "Dictatorships and Double Standards,"[1] the seminal and wide-ranging article which led to her appointment as U.S. ambassador to the United Nations and influential adviser on foreign policy to the newly elected Ronald Reagan.

Kirkpatrick came at the issue from within the context of that historical moment. Specifically, her article was aimed at the blunderings of the Carter administration in foreign affairs over the pre-

ceding three years, and the "double standard" referred to in her title was this: the administration, and its liberal supporters, had reacted with punitive outrage to violations of human rights perpetrated by right-wing regimes allied to the United States, while taking a relatively accommodating view of the far more systematic abuses of Communist tyrannies that were actively threatening American interests around the world. Worse, by hectoring our allies and pressuring them to democratize overnight, the Carter administration, she argued, had transformed two such allies, Iran and Nicaragua, into hostile, radical dictatorships.

But much of Kirkpatrick's essay also transcended the particular issues of the day and was meant to enunciate durable political truths, however hard she thought they might be for some Americans to swallow. One of these was that dictatorships, like the poor, would always be with us. At a time when the number of democracies outside Western Europe, the United States, and Canada could be counted on one hand, Kirkpatrick declared, quite accurately, that "most governments in the world are, as they always have been, autocracies of one kind or another." And yet, she went on, "no idea holds greater sway in the mind of educated Americans than the belief that it is possible to democratize governments, anytime, anywhere, under any circumstances."

This idea, in Kirkpatrick's judgment, was simply false. In "Dictatorships and Double Standards" she took sharp issue with the notion of modernization's inevitability (an idea associated with the work of Samuel P. Huntington), and went out of her way to slam Zbigniew Brzezinski, the main foreign-policy intellectual in the Carter administration, for his insistence on viewing the world not from the "perspective of American interests or intentions" but from that of "the modernizing nation and the 'end' of history." Although Kirkpatrick did not deny that U.S. policy could "encourage [the] process of liberalization and democratization" in some autocratic regimes, she came close to doing so. The attempt should certainly not be made, she wrote, "at a time when the incumbent government is fighting for its life against violent adversaries." Moreover, the proposed reforms would have to be "aimed at producing gradual change rather than perfect democracy overnight." And "gradual" did not mean a few years. "Decades, if not centuries" might be "required for people to acquire the necessary disciplines and habits.

* * *

Eighteen years and more than 30 new democracies later, Kirkpatrick's intellectual followers include, amazingly enough, some of the main targets of her criticisms in 1979—and on both the Left and the Right. On the Left, especially in the giddily optimistic crowd of free-trade liberals, some of the same people who wanted the United States to topple Somoza and the Shah in 1979, and who denounced "constructive engagement" with South Africa in the 1980's, today argue with equal passion for "constructive engagement" with China. A hefty portion of the Right similarly defends a tolerant attitude toward China, as well as other dictatorial regimes, on the solid Kirkpatrickian grounds that we cannot and must not expect "perfect democracy overnight."

To be sure, the new debunkers of democratization have had to digest the inconvenient fact that democracy can, indeed, spring up "anytime, anywhere,

under any circumstances." But this does not appear to have fazed them. Whether the subject is Indonesia, a classic authoritarian government, or, more incongruously, China, which still retains many of the defining characteristics of a totalitarian society, the current wisdom holds that tyrannies should be given time to evolve naturally, which is to say, as Kirkpatrick explained, "slowly."

In one sense, of course, the return of the Kirkpatrick thesis is only part of a broader resurgence of an older and more established tradition in foreign policy: namely, "realism." In the 1950's and 1960's, the leading prophets of this influential school of thought, Hans J. Morgenthau and George E. Kennan, constantly warned against "crusades" on behalf of democracy, which they thought would lead either to nuclear holocaust or to the immoral dominance of one power—the United States—over every other.[2] Kennan, for one, did not much care for democracy, believing that, in Latin America and other less developed parts of the world, it made for weak and untrustworthy allies in the fight against Communism. And as for democracy in the United States, he once compared it to a dinosaur with a "brain the size of [a] pin."

Today, modern realists from Huntington to Owen Harries, the editor of the *National Interest*, complain about the "arrogance" of American efforts to impose our values on others, while some echo Kennan's view that democracies may be too weak to withstand the onslaught of radicals (in today's circumstances, these are usually not Communists but religious fundamentalists). Still others, like Henry Kissinger, admire the "Asian values" which allegedly form the basis of political society in Singapore, Indonesia,

and China: in particular, the emphasis on "order" and "community" over individual rights and freedoms. And the aversion to promoting democracy abroad is also heavily influenced, just as it was in the past, by a deep pessimism about the health of democracy here at home.

This is especially, but not exclusively, true among conservatives. If, in the 1950's, the realists' hostility to ideological crusades was closely related to their disgust at what they perceived to be the wild and irresponsible behavior on display during the McCarthy era, today many conservatives are worried about the balkanization of American culture, about the impact of immigration and multiculturalism on our national identity, about threats to the American family, about an overweening government bureaucracy on the one hand and rampant individual license on the other. "The central issue for the West," Huntington warns in *The Clash of Civilizations*, "is whether, quite apart from any external challenges, it is capable of stopping and reversing the internal processes of decay."

* * *

It is hard to say just how much this pessimism about democracy at home has influenced the reorientation of attitudes toward foreign policy, but one suspects it is quite a bit. What is clear, in any case, is that this reorientation has spread far beyond the think tanks and the universities and has profoundly affected the world of policy-makers.

A year ago, a panel of experts, former senior officials, and members of Congress produced a report on American interests in the post–cold-war era.... The panel listed those interests under the categories of color-coded poker chips.

Blue-chip interests were "vital," that is, "strictly necessary to safeguard and enhance the well-being of Americans in a free and secure nation." Red-chip interests, deemed "extremely important," represented conditions that "if compromised would severely prejudice but not strictly imperil the ability of the U.S. government to preserve American well-being. There were five of the former sorts of interest, eleven of the latter.

Then came the white chips, among which, at last, democracy made its appearance: the panel deemed it "just important" that the United States promote this interest, but only in "strategically important states" and only "as much as feasible without destabilization." A broader approach, "enlarging democracy elsewhere or for its own sake," was listed at the very bottom, as a translucent chip—something "intrinsically desirable" but having no major effect on the ability of the U.S. government to safeguard the freedom, security, and well-being of Americans.

A decade ago, these conclusions, by these people, would surely have provoked considerable discussion. They would have been taken, and rightly, as a strong repudiation of the policy followed by the Reagan administration, which had made a very high priority out of promoting democracy in such places as El Salvador, Chile, the Philippines, and South Korea, as well as in Eastern Europe and within the Soviet Union. Today, however, the report's hierarchy of interests aroused not the smallest hint of controversy. Nor was it meant to: rather, it was a conventional representation of conventional thinking.

* * *

It is true that the Clinton administration, at least until recently, has tilted against this prevailing wind. Indeed, the President and his top advisers have declared the "enlargement" of the democratic sphere to be something of a red-chip or even a blue-chip goal, and in some areas their rhetoric has been complemented by action. Thus, the administration has devoted considerable energy to supporting democratic forces in Russia, often in the face of indifference and skepticism in Congress and the foreign-policy establishment. It has used the process of NATO enlargement as a means of both preserving and encouraging democratic reforms in former Warsaw Pact countries. It played an important role in the continuing transition to democracy in South Africa. In Latin America, it helped support a crucial, second free election in Nicaragua, blocked a military coup in Paraguay and another in Guatemala, and, in a very bold move for which it was harshly condemned by Republicans, even used force to restore a democratically-elected president in Haiti.

More recently, though, the administration's commitment has faltered. Instead of treating the "enlargement" of the democratic world as a high American priority, it has increasingly settled into the establishment view that democracy is only a white or translucent chip and hence subject to barter in return for other benefits, especially of the economic or commercial variety. As Thomas Carothers correctly notes, the administration has "shied away" from pushing hard for democratic reform in Nigeria (which has oil); it has kept largely silent about the move toward authoritarian rule in Kazakhstan (which also has oil); it has

been unwilling to take a hard line against the increasingly authoritarian president of Armenia, Levon Ter-Petrosian (there is a domestic constituency for continuing aid to Armenia); and it has been sporadic, at best, in its support for democratic reforms in Croatia and Serbia. In Asia, though willing to apply sanctions against tiny and inconsequential Burma for suppressing the democratic movement of Aung San Suu Kyi, Clinton has placed the avidity of American business for "emerging markets" in China and Indonesia ahead of concerns about those regimes' tyrannical practices.

In short, what we are seeing in the administration's moves, as in the experts' report, is the emergence of a new consensus, created more by default than by design and based on today's version of a double (or, rather, multiple) standard. Democracy is to be supported in Western Europe and parts of Central and Eastern Europe, but not necessarily in Southeastern Europe. It is to be celebrated in those Asian nations, like Taiwan, Japan, and South Korea, which have already chosen the democratic path; but in those that have not, we are to respect the dictators' right to impose "Asian values" on their people. (In Hong Kong, this may require some particularly uncomfortable contortions, but the pain will pass.) In Latin America, democracy is to be supported almost everywhere, except (if you are a conservative) Haiti or (if a liberal) Cuba. Democracy is altogether too dangerous to support in the Islamic world, except, partially, in Turkey, which is a member of NATO. In the states that once made up the former Soviet Union, the issue is largely one of culture: the peoples of the Baltic states, Russia, and Ukraine are to be held to a much higher standard than the peoples of the Caucasus and Central Asia. As for the African nations, if they hold elections, we will be happy; if they cancel them, or start slaughtering each other, we can rest content in the knowledge that they were not ready for elections in the first place.

* * *

Two decades ago, it may have made sense to be pessimistic about the prospects for democracy. As Jeane Kirkpatrick noted at the time, autocracy in one form or another was the norm, democracy the rare and fragile exception. Much less understandable is today's dour and cynical view, which is so at odds with the global experience of the intervening two decades.

Are some of the world's new democracies unstable or faltering? Of course they are. But the largest chunk of these troubled nations lies in a part of the world—the former Soviet Union—that possesses a number of unique qualities. The main problem is not that such newly independent states as Tajikistan, Uzbekistan, Turkmenistan, Belarus, and Kazakhstan have no history of democracy; there is plenty of evidence from elsewhere in the world that this need not be an insuperable obstacle to democratization. The far greater problem is that they have no history of independent nationhood. Their institutions, such as they are, are the provincial remnants of the Soviet system. As Alexander J. Motyl notes in this year's Freedom House survey, most of the non-Russian Soviet republics began their lives lacking almost everything—"elites, civil society, rule of law, and the market"— necessary to support almost *any* form of government. It is certainly disappointing that democracy in about half of these countries is in trouble, but the miracle is that it continues to survive in so many.

And in any case it is an analytical error to lay disproportionate stress on these failures in any objective global assessment....

That the African picture is a mixed one is powerfully proved by the horrors of Rwanda and Burundi, the brutal tyranny of Nigeria, and the turmoil of the Democratic Republic of Congo (formerly Zaire). But given Africa's history, and given the long-term failure of the United States and other democracies to address themselves to its political problems, the wonder once again is that the continent's record is as mixed as it is.

If it is one kind of mistake to overstate the bad news by measuring today's much-improved reality against some imagined utopia, a much bigger mistake is to shape our policy around the failures. The notion, for instance, that we would do better to focus on economic development, on establishing the alleged "prerequisites" of democracy rather than democracy itself, simply ignores the lessons of the recent past. As the political analyst Adrian Karatnycky has noted, the states of the former Soviet empire that "have made the greatest progress in creating market economies" have, for the most part, also been those "that have made the greatest progress in consolidating their democratic transitions." Conversely, the failure to achieve economic reform has been most notable in states showing the least progress toward political reform. These findings, Karatnycky argues,

> contradict the argument that economic reform can successfully be implemented by authoritarian rulers who [allegedly] can take decisive and unpopular steps because they are not inhibited by public opinion, ... rival political parties and movements, or free trade unions.

What about the idea that democracy leads to instability, bloody ethnic conflict, and war? Surely no one can seriously believe it would have been better to preserve the Soviet or Titoist tyrannies intact after 1989—let alone that this would have been possible. The collapse of these regimes did, indeed, unleash ethnic conflicts and innumerable border disputes. But was democratization to blame? Absent the firm intervention of outside powers, would the break-up of Yugoslavia have been more peaceful if the successor governments had been more uniformly tyrannical? If this century has taught us anything, it is that dictators are perfectly capable of whipping up ethnic and/or nationalist hysteria, and of initiating genocide, for their own purposes.

Finally, the claim by Edward Mansfield and Jack Snyder that states in transition to democracy are twice as likely to engage in war cannot withstand scrutiny. Even leaving aside their interpretation of earlier historical events, it is simply wrong to conclude that today's Russia is more warlike because nearly a quarter of the Russian electorate voted in 1993 for a radical nationalist, or because Boris Yeltsin used murderous force against the breakaway republic of Chechnya. The fact is that Zhirinovsky reached his political zenith in 1993, and his support has dwindled ever since. Russia's new democratic system, meanwhile, has compelled the Kremlin to give up its disastrous effort to crush the Chechen revolt. (In the czarist era, Russia fought wars of this nature for decades.) And democratic Russia has likewise peacefully negotiated a settlement with democratic Ukraine for control of Sevastopol and the Black Sea fleet; somehow, one doubts that Stalin, or even Gorbachev, would have been so ac-

commodating. If, in sum, today's Russia offers evidence of anything, it is the generally pacifying effect of democracy on a leadership not traditionally known for its pacific policies.

* * *

Democracy is not the solution to the world's problems. But it is a better solution than the alternatives. And it is the only solution the United States can ever support with a modicum of enthusiasm or consistency.

This, certainly, was the hard-learned lesson of the Reagan era. Contrary to what everyone expected at the time, the Reagan administration did not ultimately conduct its foreign policies according to the Kirkpatrick thesis, though for a time it tried to do so by instituting closer ties, or at least less hostile relations, with certain dictatorial regimes in Latin America and elsewhere. (Reagan himself had fond feelings for the Philippine dictator, Ferdinand Marcos.) But the practice proved unsustainable, and for a simple reason.

Reagan, who was no realist in the Kissingerian mode, elevated the global struggle with Communism to a high priority; rather than accept a condition of permanent coexistence, he took steps to try to undo Communism whenever and wherever the opportunity beckoned. A couple of years into his first term, however, administration officials began to realize that such a battle against the world's most formidable tyranny could not be won by a policy that was officially sanguine about lesser and friendlier tyrannies. It could not be won, that is, under a double standard. And so, instead of accepting the permanence and legitimacy of friendly dictatorships, the administration set about pressing them to

reform, often not under conditions of relative calm and safety but when, precisely, they were engaged in "fighting for [their] life against violent adversaries," and not over decades or centuries but quickly.

In El Salvador, in the Philippines, in Chile, and elsewhere, the Reagan team found a way to accomplish this without suffering the fate of the Carter administration in Iran and Nicaragua. In the countries where the "Reagan doctrine" was applied, democratic reformers did indeed gain strength and guerrillas and terrorist groups were indeed weakened. This record looks all the more impressive in the light of today's sober warnings that we should support democracy abroad only when the risks to our security, or to our oil, or to our export markets, are negligible.

One area in which the Reagan-era experience holds obvious implications today is the Islamic world. Clearly it is in our interest to prevent radical fundamentalist regimes from taking power there. In fact, the battle against the radicals in Iran, in Sudan, and in Afghanistan should be waged more tenaciously than it has been. Simultaneously, however, we could and should be holding authoritarian regimes in the Middle East to higher standards of democracy, and encouraging democratic voices within those societies, even if it means risking some instability in some places. At the height of the cold war, the strategic risks in Central America and in Asia were at least as great as they are today in the Middle East—and the gamble, once taken, paid off.

The real question before us today is the same question Samuel P. Huntington posed, in Lincolnesque fashion, seven years ago: "How long can an increasingly interdependent world survive part-democratic and part-authoritarian?"

Huntington's point was not that the world would ever *become* completely one or the other, but that a modern, closely interconnected world must move generally either in one direction—i.e., toward greater liberty—or in another—toward greater tyranny. Although the United States may not have the final say over the outcome, as the leading power our say can well be determinative. If we act wrongly, we may lose something even more valuable than our relative security.

* * *

For the day we adopt a neutral attitude toward the fate of democracy in the world is the day we deny our own essence, an essence rooted in a commitment to certain principles which we believe to be universal. Anyone worried about our national identity, and about the challenge posed to it by the balkanization of our culture, must know that we can hardly expect to unite our own country if we decide that those principles apply only in a few, rare circumstances and to a limited number of fortunate peoples. Nor can we expect to achieve renewal at home if we conduct ourselves abroad in a mood of despair and cynicism about the very things we hold most dear.

It is often argued that vitality abroad depends first on vitality at home. But the reverse is also true: the active defense of our principles abroad has encouraged us to support them even more vigorously at home. The fight against Nazism and Communism in the 1940's and 50's helped build a national consensus behind the civil-rights movement. In the Reagan era, confidence about America's beneficial role in the world was closely linked with confidence about the democratic project at home. This is a point on which the Samuel P. Huntington of 1991 needed no instruction. "Other nations," he wrote,

> may fundamentally change their political systems and continue their existence as nations. The United States does not have that option. Hence Americans have a special interest in the development of a global environment congenial to democracy.

There is no stasis in international affairs. Some day, the world may well turn back toward autocracy. The United States, the world's leading democratic power, could lose a major war to some rising, nondemocratic power. Or some calamity, whether man-made or not, may devastate the civilization we have created. But precisely because nothing lasts forever, and in the full knowledge that democracy is not inevitable but requires constant effort by those who mean to sustain it, the task facing us is to preserve and extend the democratic era as far into the future as possible. As it happens, and precisely because of the success of earlier policies, the present moment is one of relative safety, and therefore one that offers special opportunities. It would be a timeless human tragedy if, out of boredom, laziness, carelessness, or unfounded gloom, we failed to seize them.

NOTES

1. November 1979.

2. I have written on the realists at greater length in "American Power—A Guide for the Perplexed," COMMENTARY, April 1996.

3. "1997 Freedom Around the World," *Freedom Review,* January 1997.

NO
Robert D. Kaplan

WAS DEMOCRACY JUST A MOMENT?

In the fourth century A.D. Christianity's conquest of Europe and the Mediterranean world gave rise to the belief that a peaceful era in world politics was at hand, now that a consensus had formed around an ideology that stressed the sanctity of the individual. But Christianity was, of course, not static. It kept evolving, into rites, sects, and "heresies" that were in turn influenced by the geography and cultures of the places where it took root. Meanwhile, the church founded by Saint Peter became a ritualistic and hierarchical organization guilty of long periods of violence and bigotry. This is to say nothing of the evils perpetrated by the Orthodox churches in the East. Christianity made the world not more peaceful or, in practice, more moral but only more complex. Democracy, which is now overtaking the world as Christianity once did, may do the same.

The collapse of communism from internal stresses says nothing about the long-term viability of Western democracy. Marxism's natural death in Eastern Europe is no guarantee that subtler tyrannies do not await us, here and abroad. History has demonstrated that there is no final triumph of reason, whether it goes by the name of Christianity, the Enlightenment, or, now, democracy. To think that democracy as we know it will triumph—or is even here to stay—is itself a form of determinism, driven by our own ethnocentricity. Indeed, those who quote Alexis de Tocqueville in support of democracy's inevitability should pay heed to his observation that Americans, because of their (comparative) equality, exaggerate "the scope of human perfectibility." Despotism, Tocqueville went on, "is more particularly to be feared in democratic ages," because it thrives on the obsession with self and one's own security which equality fosters.

I submit that the democracy we are encouraging in many poor parts of the world is an integral part of a transformation toward new forms of authoritarianism; that democracy in the United States is at greater risk than ever before, and from obscure sources; and that many future regimes, ours especially, could resemble the oligarchies of ancient Athens and Sparta more than they do the current government in Washington. History teaches that it is exactly at such prosperous times as these that we need to maintain a sense of the tragic, however unnecessary it may seem.

From Robert D. Kaplan, "Was Democracy Just a Moment?" *The Atlantic Monthly* (December 1997). Copyright © 1997 by Robert D. Kaplan. Reprinted by permission.

... Those who think that America can establish democracy the world over should heed the words of the late American theologian and political philosopher Reinhold Niebuhr:

> The same strength which has extended our power beyond a continent has also... brought us into a vast web of history in which other wills, running in oblique or contrasting directions to our own, inevitably hinder or contradict what we most fervently desire. We cannot simply have our way, not even when we believe our way to have the "happiness of mankind" as its promise.

The lesson to draw is not that dictatorship is good and democracy bad but that democracy emerges successfully only as a capstone to other social and economic achievements. In his "Author's introduction" to *Democracy in America*, Tocqueville showed how democracy evolved in the West not through the kind of moral fiat we are trying to impose throughout the world but as an organic outgrowth of development. European society had reached a level of complexity and sophistication at which the aristocracy, so as not to overburden itself, had to confer a measure of equality upon other citizens and allocate some responsibility to them: a structured division of the population into peacefully competing interest groups was necessary if both tyranny and anarchy were to be averted.

The very fact that we retreat to moral arguments—and often moral arguments only—to justify democracy indicates that for many parts of the world the historical and social arguments supporting democracy are just not there....

The demise of the Soviet Union was no reason for us to pressure Rwanda and other countries to form political parties—though that is what our post–Cold War foreign policy has been largely about, even in parts of the world that the Cold War barely touched. The Eastern European countries liberated in 1989 already had, in varying degrees, the historical and social preconditions for both democracy and advanced industrial life: bourgeois traditions, exposure to the Western Enlightenment, high literacy rates, low birth rates, and so on. The post–Cold War effort to bring democracy to those countries has been reasonable. What is less reasonable is to put a gun to the head of the peoples of the developing world and say, in effect, "Behave as if you had experienced the Western Enlightenment to the degree that Poland and the Czech Republic did. Behave as if 95 percent of your population were literate. Behave as if you had no bloody ethnic or regional disputes."

States have never been formed by elections. Geography, settlement patterns, the rise of literate bourgeoisie, and, tragically, ethnic cleansing have formed states. Greece, for instance, is a stable democracy partly because earlier in the century it carried out a relatively benign form of ethnic cleansing—in the form of refugee transfers—which created a monoethnic society. Nonetheless, it took several decades of economic development for Greece finally to put its coups behind it. Democracy often weakens states by necessitating ineffectual compromises and fragile coalition governments in societies where bureaucratic institutions never functioned well to begin with. Because democracy neither forms states nor strengthens them initially, multiparty systems are best suited to nations that already have efficient bureaucracies and a middle class that pays income tax, and where primary issues such as borders

and power-sharing have already been resolved, leaving politicians free to bicker about the budget and other secondary matters.

Social stability results from the establishment of a middle class. Not democracies but authoritarian systems, including monarchies, create middle classes—which, having achieved a certain size and self-confidence, revolt against the very dictators who generated their prosperity. This is the pattern today in the Pacific Rim and the southern cone of South America, but not in other parts of Latin America, southern Asia, or sub-Saharan Africa....

Foreign correspondents in sub-Saharan Africa who equate democracy with progress miss this point, ignoring both history and centuries of political philosophy. They seem to think that the choice is between dictators and democrats. But for many places the only choice is between bad dictators and slightly better ones. To force elections on such places may give us some instant gratification. But after a few months or years a bunch of soldiers with grenades will get bored and greedy, and will easily topple their fledgling democracy. As likely as not, the democratic government will be composed of corrupt, bickering, ineffectual politicians whose weak rule never had an institutional base to start with: modern bureaucracies generally require high literacy rates over several generations. Even India, the great exception that proves the rule, has had a mixed record of success as a democracy, with Bihar and other poverty-wracked places remaining in semi-anarchy. Ross Munro, a noted Asia expert, has documented how Chinese autocracy has better prepared China's population for the economic rigors of the post-industrial

age than Indian democracy has prepared India's.

Of course, our post–Cold War mission to spread democracy is partly a pose. In Egypt and Saudi Arabia, America's most important allies in the energy-rich Muslim world, our worst nightmare would be free and fair elections, as it would be elsewhere in the Middle East. The end of the Cold War has changed our attitude toward those authoritarian regimes that are not crucial to our interests—but not toward those that are. We praise democracy, and meanwhile we are grateful for an autocrat like King Hussein, and for the fact that the Turkish and Pakistani militaries have always been the real powers behind the "democracies" in their countries. Obviously, democracy in the abstract encompasses undeniably good things such as civil society and a respect for human rights. But as a matter of public policy it has unfortunately come to focus on elections....

The current reality in Singapore and South Africa, for instance, shreds our democratic certainties. Lee Kuan Yew's offensive neo-authoritarianism, in which the state has evolved into a corporation that is paternalistic, meritocratic, and decidedly undemocratic, has forged prosperity from abject poverty. A survey of business executives and economists by the World Economic Forum ranked Singapore No. 1 among the fifty-three most advanced countries appearing on an index of global competitiveness. What is good for business executives is often good for the average citizen: per capita wealth in Singapore is nearly equal to that in Canada, the nation that ranks No. 1 in the world on the United Nations' Human Development Index. When Lee took over Singapore, more than thirty years ago, it

was a mosquito-ridden bog filled with slum quarters that frequently lacked both plumbing and electricity. Doesn't liberation from filth and privation count as a human right? Jeffrey Sachs, a professor of international trade at Harvard, writes that "good government" means relative safety from corruption, from breach of contract, from property expropriation, and from bureaucratic inefficiency. Singapore's reputation in these regards is unsurpassed. If Singapore's 2.8 million citizens ever demand democracy, they will just prove the assertion that prosperous middle classes arise under authoritarian regimes before gaining the confidence to dislodge their benefactors. Singapore's success is frightening, yet it must be acknowledged.

Democratic South Africa, meanwhile, has become one of the most violent places on earth that are not war zones, according to the security firm Kroll Associates. The murder rate is six times that in the United States, five times that in Russia. There are ten private-security guards for every policeman. The currency has substantially declined, educated people continue to flee, and international drug cartels have made the country a new transshipment center. Real unemployment is about 33 percent, and is probably much higher among youths. Jobs cannot be created without the cooperation of foreign investors, but assuaging their fear could require the kind of union-busting and police actions that democracy will not permit. The South African military was the power behind the regime in the last decade of apartheid. And it is the military that may yet help to rule South Africa in the future. Like Pakistan but more so, South Africa is destined for a hybrid regime if it is to succeed. The abundant coverage of South Africa's impressive attempts at coming to terms with the crimes of apartheid serves to obscure the country's growing problems. There is a sense of fear in such celebratory, backward-looking coverage, as if writing too much about difficulties in that racially symbolic country would expose the limits of the liberal humanist enterprise worldwide....

"WORLD GOVERNMENT"

Authoritarian or hybrid regimes, no matter how illiberal, will still be treated as legitimate if they can provide security for their subjects and spark economic growth. And they will easily find acceptance in a world driven increasingly by financial markets that know no borders.

For years idealists have dreamed of a "world government." Well, a world government has been emerging—quietly and organically, the way vast developments in history take place. I do not refer to the United Nations, the power of which, almost by definition, affects only the poorest countries. After its peacekeeping failures in Bosnia and Somalia—and its $2 billion failure to make Cambodia democratic—the UN is on its way to becoming a supranational relief agency. Rather, I refer to the increasingly dense ganglia of international corporations and markets that are becoming the unseen arbiters of power in many countries....

Of the world's hundred largest economies, fifty-one are not countries but corporations. While the 200 largest corporations employ less than three fourths of one percent of the world's work force, they account for 28 percent of world economic activity. The 500 largest corporations account for 70 percent of world trade. Corporations are like the feudal domains that evolved into nation-states;

they are nothing less than the vanguard of a new Darwinian organization of politics. Because they are in the forefront of real globalization while the overwhelming majority of the world's inhabitants are still rooted in local terrain, corporations will be free for a few decades to leave behind the social and environmental wreckage they create—abruptly closing a factory here in order to open an unsafe facility with a cheaper work force there. Ultimately, as technological innovations continue to accelerate and the world's middle classes come closer together, corporations may well become more responsible to the cohering global community and less amoral in the course of their evolution toward new political and cultural forms....

The level of social development required by democracy as it is known in the West has existed in only a minority of places—and even there only during certain periods of history. We are entering a troubling transition, and the irony is that while we preach our version of democracy abroad, it slips away from us at home.

THE SHRINKING DOMAIN OF "POLITICS"

I put special emphasis on corporations because of the true nature of politics: who does and who doesn't have power. To categorize accurately the political system of a given society, one must define the significant elements of power within it. Supreme Court Justice Louis Brandeis knew this instinctively, which is why he railed against corporate monopolies. Of course, the influence that corporations wield over government and the economy is so vast and obvious that the point needs no elaboration. But there are other, more covert forms of emerging corporate power.

The number of residential communities with defended perimeters that have been built by corporations went from 1,000 in the early 1960s to more than 80,000 by the mid-1980s, with continued dramatic increases in the 1990s. ("Gated communities" are not an American invention. They are an import from Latin America, where deep social divisions in places like Rio de Janeiro and Mexico City make them necessary for the middle class.) Then there are malls, with their own rules and security forces, as opposed to public streets; private health clubs as opposed to public playgrounds; incorporated suburbs with strict zoning; and other mundane aspects of daily existence in which—perhaps without realizing it, because the changes have been so gradual—we opt out of the public sphere and the "social contract" for the sake of a protected setting. Dennis Judd, an urban-affairs expert at the University of Missouri at St. Louis, told me recently, "It's nonsense to think that Americans are individualists. Deep down we are a nation of herd animals: micelike conformists who will lay at our doorstep many of our rights if someone tells us that we won't have to worry about crime and our property values are secure. We have always put up with restrictions inside a corporation which we would never put up with in the public sphere. But what many do not realize is that life within some sort of corporation is what the future will increasingly be about."...

Corporations, which are anchored neither to nations nor to communities, have created strip malls, edge cities, and Disneyesque tourist bubbles. Developments are not necessarily bad: they provide low prices, convenience, efficient work forces,

and, in the case of tourist bubbles, safety. We need big corporations. Our society has reached a level of social and technological complexity at which goods and services must be produced for a price and to a standard that smaller businesses cannot manage. We should also recognize, though, that the architectural reconfiguration of our cities and towns has been an undemocratic event—with decisions in effect handed down from above by an assembly of corporate experts.

"The government of man will be replaced by the administration of things," the Enlightenment French philosopher Henri de Saint-Simon prophesied. We should worry that experts will channel our very instincts and thereby control them to some extent. For example, while the government fights drug abuse, often with pathetic results, pharmaceutical corporations have worked *through* the government and political parties to receive sanction for drugs such as stimulants and anti-depressants, whose consciousness-altering effects, it could be argued, are as great as those of outlawed drugs.

The more appliances that middle-class existence requires, the more influence their producers have over the texture of our lives. Of course, the computer in some ways enhances the power of the individual, but it also depletes our individuality. A degree of space and isolation is required for a healthy sense of self, which may be threatened by the constant stream of other people's opinions on computer networks.

Democratic governance, at the federal, state, and local levels, goes on. But its ability to affect our lives is limited. The growing piles of our material possessions make personal life more complex and leave less time for communal matters. And as communities become liberated from geography, as well as more specialized culturally and electronically, they will increasingly fall outside the realm of traditional governance. Democracy loses meaning if both rulers and ruled cease to be part of a community tied to a specific territory. In this historical transition phase, lasting perhaps a century or more, in which globalization has begun but is not complete and loyalties are highly confused, civil society will be harder to maintain. How and when we vote during the next hundred years may be a minor detail for historians....

UMPIRE REGIMES

This rise of corporate power occurs more readily as the masses become more indifferent and the elite less accountable. Material possessions not only focus people toward private and away from communal life but also encourage docility. The more possessions one has, the more compromises one will make to protect them. The ancient Greeks said that the slave is someone who is intent on filling his belly, which can also mean someone who is intent on safeguarding his possessions. Aristophanes and Euripides, the late-eighteenth-century Scottish philosopher Adam Ferguson, and Tocqueville in the nineteenth century all warned that material prosperity would breed servility and withdrawal, turning people into, in Tocqueville's words, "industrious sheep."

... The mood of the Colosseum goes together with the age of the corporation, which offers entertainment in place of values. The Nobel laureate Czeslaw Milosz provides the definitive view on why Americans degrade themselves with mass culture: "Today man believes that there is *nothing* in him, so he accepts *anything*, even if he knows it to be bad, in

order to find himself at one with others, in order not to be alone." Of course, it is because people find so little in themselves that they fill their world with celebrities. The masses avoid important national and international news because much of it is tragic, even as they show an unlimited appetite for the details of Princess Diana's death. This willingness to give up self and responsibility is the sine qua non for tyranny....

A continental regime must continue to function, because America's edge in information warfare requires it, both to maintain and to lead a far-flung empire of sorts, as the Athenians did during the Peloponnesian War. But trouble awaits us, if only because the "triumph" of democracy in the developing world will cause great upheavals before many places settle into more practical—and, it is to be hoped, benign—hybrid regimes. In the Middle East, for instance, countries like Syria, Iraq, and the Gulf sheikhdoms —with artificial borders, rising populations, and rising numbers of working-age youths—will not instantly become stable democracies once their absolute dictators and medieval ruling families pass from the scene. As in the early centuries of Christianity, there will be a mess.

Given the surging power of corporations, the gladiator culture of the masses, and the ability of the well-off to be partly disengaged from their own countries, what will democracy under an umpire regime be like?

THE RETURN OF OLIGARCHY?

... [T]he differences between oligarchy and democracy and between ancient democracy and our own could be far subtler than we think. Modern democracy exists within a thin band of social and economic conditions, which include flexible hierarchies that allow people to move up and down the ladder. Instead of clear-cut separations between classes there are many gray shades, with most people bunched in the middle. Democracy is a fraud in many poor countries outside this narrow band: Africans want a better life and instead have been given the right to vote. As new and intimidating forms of economic and social stratification appear in a world based increasingly on the ability to handle and analyze large quantities of information, a new politics might emerge for us, too—less like the kind envisioned by progressive reformers and more like the pragmatic hybrid regimes that are bringing prosperity to developing countries.

... If democracy, the crowning political achievement of the West, is gradually being transfigured, in part because of technology, then the West will suffer the same fate as earlier civilizations.

POSTSCRIPT

Is Democracy Desirable for All Nations?

The questions raised by Kagan and Kaplan are as complex as they are important. At least one prominent American political scientist, Samuel P. Huntington, has shifted his position from a positive view of the likelihood of democratic domination in the future in *The Third Wave: Democratization in the Late Twentieth Century* (University of Oklahoma Press, 1991) to a more negative outlook in *The Clash of Civilizations and the Remaking of the World Order* (Simon & Schuster, 1996). Another analysis that argues that democracy has not established the claim of its ultimate triumph is found in Albert Somit and Steven A. Peterson, *Darwinism, Dominance, and Democracy* (Praeger, 1997).

Evidence regarding the successes and failures in the transition from autocracy to democracy can be found in recent studies. Barry M. Hager, in *Limiting Risks and Sharing Losses in the Globalized Capital Market* (Johns Hopkins University Press, 1998), examines Mexico's 1994–1995 financial crisis and the 1997 Asian crisis affecting Thailand, Indonesia, Korea, and Japan, and considers how the world's response to crises is related to other aspects of international relations, including support for democracy. Walter O. Oyugi et al., eds., *Democratic Theory and Practice in Africa* (Heinemann, 1998), offers a wide-ranging examination of new African democracies.

What will be the impact of electronic information and entertainment on democracy? It is likely that the rise of global corporations and the worldwide communications made possible by the Internet will diminish the importance of national boundaries and, to a considerable extent, homogenize national and ethnic cultures. Will such changes adversely affect the movement toward democracy? A pessimistic answer is offered by Donald N. Wood in *Post-Intellectualism and the Decline of Democracy: The Failure of Reason and Responsibility in the Twentieth Century* (Praeger, 1997). Wood believes that America is moving away from the conviction that enlightened citizens can govern with reason and responsibility and toward a society marked by a decline in critical thinking, the substitution of information for knowledge, specialization, psychological isolation, and moral anarchy.

For many thoughtful analysts, the pressing question is not whether or not democracy will triumph but whether or not it will survive. Jean Bethke Elshtain, in *Democracy on Trial* (Basic Books, 1996), contends that the gridlock and cynicism that ail democracy are the result of a loss of faith in democratic institutions and that these are made worse by the public's appetite for scandal and a society that has become litigious, suspicious, and selfish.

President John F. Kennedy's ringing proclamation in 1961 that the United States was ready to "pay any price, bear any burden, meet any hardship,

support any friend, oppose any foe, to assure the survival and the success of liberty" suggested that America has a unique role in spreading democracy. Consider the following facts, which are much more evident now than when Kennedy spoke four decades ago: English has become the language that links educated people throughout the world. The United States is the sole military superpower. American movies and music threaten to overwhelm the popular culture of other nations. And, despite the challenge of Japan, America is the world's only information superpower. Perhaps the decline of cultural distinctions and the evolution of a global culture of shared interests is a measure of enhanced communications and understanding. Insofar as this is occurring, it provides for the United States not only an enormous commercial opportunity but also the opportunity to promote American values, including freedom of conscience and expression, the universal and secret ballot, and the other liberties identified with democracy. But the question remains: Can America—should America—play this role in promoting democracy everywhere in the world?

CONTRIBUTORS
TO THIS VOLUME

EDITORS

GEORGE McKENNA is a professor of political science and chair of the Department of Political Science at City College, City University of New York, where he has been teaching since 1963. He received a B.A. from the University of Chicago in 1959, an M.A. from the University of Massachusetts in 1962, and a Ph.D. from Fordham University in 1967. He has written numerous articles in the fields of American government and political theory, and his publications include *American Populism* (Putnam, 1974) and *American Politics: Ideals and Realities* (McGraw-Hill, 1976). He is the author of the textbook *The Drama of Democracy: American Government and Politics,* 3rd ed. (Dushkin/McGraw-Hill, 1998).

STANLEY FEINGOLD holds the Carl and Lily Pforzheimer Foundation Distinguished Chair for Business and Public Policy at Westchester Community College of the State University of New York. He received his bachelor's degree from the City College of New York, where he taught courses in American politics and political theory for 30 years, after completing his graduate education at Columbia University. He spent four years as Visiting Professor of Politics at the University of Leeds in Great Britain, and he has also taught American politics at Columbia University in New York and the University of California at Los Angeles. He is a frequent contributor to the *National Law Journal* and *Congress Monthly,* among other publications.

STAFF

David Dean   List Manager
David Brackley   Senior Developmental Editor
Juliana Poggio   Associate Developmental Editor
Rose Gleich   Administrative Assistant
Brenda S. Filley   Production Manager
Juliana Arbo   Typesetting Supervisor
Diane Barker   Proofreader
Lara Johnson   Design/Advertising Coordinator
Richard Tietjen   Publishing Systems Manager

AUTHORS

RICHARD BERNSTEIN is a book critic for the *New York Times* and coauthor, with Ross H. Munro, of *The Coming Conflict With China* (Alfred A. Knopf, 1997). He was the first Beijing Bureau chief for *Time* magazine.

CARL T. BOGUS is an associate professor at Roger Williams University School of Law in Bristol, Rhode Island. He is also a contributor to *The American Prospect.*

ROBERT H. BORK is the John M. Olin Scholar in Legal Studies at the American Enterprise Institute in Washington, D.C., a privately funded public policy research organization. He is also a former U.S. Court of Appeals judge for the District of Columbia Circuit.

DANIEL CASSE is senior director of the White House Writers Group, a public policy communications firm.

ARCHIBALD COX is the Carl M. Loeb University Professor Emeritus of Law in the School of Law at Harvard University. He is the author of *The Warren Court* (Harvard University Press, 1968), *Freedom of Expression* (Harvard University Press, 1981), and *The Court and the Constitution* (Houghton Mifflin, 1988). He was a special Watergate prosecutor in 1973.

CHRISTOPHER C. DeMUTH is president of the American Enterprise Institute for Public Policy Research.

RONALD DWORKIN is a professor of law at New York University in New York City and University Professor of Jurisprudence at Oxford University in Oxford, England.

PETER EDELMAN is a professor of law at Georgetown University, and he was the assistant secretary for planning and evaluation in the Department of Health and Human Services from 1995 to 1996.

JAMES FALLOWS is editor of *U.S. News and World Report.* He is the author of *Looking at the Sun: The Rise of the New East Asian Economic and Political System* (Pantheon Books, 1994) and *More Like Us: Making America Great Again* (Houghton Mifflin, 1989).

LOIS G. FORER (d. 1994) served as judge of a trial court of general jurisdiction in Philadelphia, Pennsylvania. She received the American Bar Association's 1985 Silver Gavel Award, and she is the author of five books, including *Unequal Protection: Women, Children, and the Elderly in Court* (W. W. Norton, 1993).

MARY ANN GLENDON is the Learned Hand Professor of Law in the School of Law at Harvard University. She is the author of *A Nation Under Lawyers: How the Crisis in the Legal Profession Is Transforming American Society* (Farrar, Straus, & Giroux, 1994).

MARY GORDON is a novelist and short-story writer. She is the author of *Penal Discipline: Female Prisoners* (Gordon Press, 1992), *The Rest of Life: Three Novellas* (Viking Penguin, 1993), and *The Other Side* (Wheeler, 1994).

DANIEL JAMES is an adviser to Carrying Capacity Network in Washington, D.C., an organization that focuses on issues pertaining to the carrying capacity of the Earth, including immigration, population, and the environment. He is the author of *Illegal Immigration—An Unfolding Crisis* (University Press of America, 1991).

ROBERT KAGAN is the Alexander Hamilton Fellow at American University and a contributing editor of *The Weekly*

Standard. He is also the author of *A Twilight Struggle: American Power and Nicaragua 1977–1990* (Free Press, 1996).

VICTOR KAMBER is president of the Kamber Group, a political consultant firm in Washington, D.C.

ROBERT D. KAPLAN is a contributing editor of *The Atlantic Monthly* and the author of several books, including *To the Ends of the Earth: A Journey at the Dawn of the Twenty-First Century* (Vintage Books, 1997).

JON KATZ is a media critic for *Rolling Stone* magazine, a commentator for National Public Radio, and a contributing editor of the *Columbia Journalism Review.* He is a former executive producer for CBS News, and he has also been a newspaper editor and a managing editor. He is the author of *Sign Off* (Bantam Books, 1991) as well as two mysteries, *Death by Station Wagon* (Doubleday, 1993) and *The Family Stalker* (Doubleday, 1994).

ANTHONY KING is a professor of political science at the University of Essex and the author of *Running Scared: Why America's Politicians Campaign Too Much and Govern Too Little* (Martin Kessler Books, 1997).

IRVING KRISTOL is publisher of *The National Interest* and a fellow of the American Enterprise Institute, a privately funded public policy research organization located in Washington, D.C.

PAUL KRUGMAN is a professor of economics at the Massachusetts Institute of Technology. He is the author of many books, including *Pop Internationalism* (MIT Press, 1996) and *The Accidental Theorist: And Other Dispatches from the Dismal Science* (W. W. Norton, 1998).

CHARLES R. LAWRENCE III is a professor in the School of Law at Georgetown University in Washington, D.C.

DANIEL LAZARE is a freelance writer based in New York City, who has written for *The Village Voice, Dissent,* and *In These Times.*

ROBERT W. LEE is a contributing editor of *The New American* and the author of *The United Nations Conspiracy* (Western Islands, 1981).

STEPHEN MOORE is director of fiscal policy study at the Cato Institute in Washington, D.C., a public policy research foundation.

ROSS H. MUNRO is director of the Asia program at the Foreign Policy Research Institute. He is coauthor, with Richard Bernstein, of *The Coming Conflict With China* (Alfred A. Knopf, 1997).

CLARENCE PAGE is a Pulitzer Prize–winning journalist for the *Chicago Tribune.*

DANIEL D. POLSBY is the Kirkland and Ellis Professor of Law at Northwestern University in Evanston, Illinois. He has also held academic positions at Cornell University, the University of Michigan, and the University of Southern California. He has published numerous articles on a number of subjects related to law, including employment law, voting rights, broadcast regulation, and weapons policy.

SAMUEL L. POPKIN is a professor of political science at the University of California, San Diego. He has been an active participant in and an academic analyst of presidential elections for over 20 years, and he served as a consultant to the Clinton campaign in 1992, for which he worked on polling and strategy.

JONATHAN RAUCH is a writer for *The Economist* in London and the author of *Kindly Inquisitors: The New Attacks on Free Thought* (University of Chicago Press, 1993).

JANET RENO is the attorney general of the United States.

ROBERT S. ROSS is a professor of political science at Boston College and a research associate at the John King Fairbank Center for East Asian Research at Harvard University. He is coauthor, with Andrew J. Nathan, of *The Great Wall and the Empty Fortress: China's Search for Security* (W. W. Norton, 1997).

ANTONIN SCALIA is an associate justice of the U.S. Supreme Court. He taught law at the University of Virginia, the American Enterprise Institute, Georgetown University, and the University of Chicago before being nominated to the U.S. Court of Appeals by President Ronald Reagan in 1982. He served in that capacity until he was nominated by Reagan to the Supreme Court in 1986.

BRADLEY A. SMITH is an associate professor at the Capital University Law School in Columbus, Ohio.

SHELBY STEELE is a professor of English at San Jose State University in San Jose, California, and the author of *The Content of Our Character: A New Vision of Race in America* (St. Martin's Press, 1990).

MATTHEW L. STEPHENS is a pastor at the Ninth Street United Methodist Church in Covington, Kentucky, and a chaplain at Ohio's Lebanon Correctional Institute. He is also chair of the National Interreligious Task Force on Criminal Justice, an organization of the National Council of Churches of Christ.

ANDREW SULLIVAN is a former editor of *The New Republic*. He received a B.A. in modern history and modern language from Oxford University in 1984 and an M.A. in public administration and a Ph.D. in political science from Harvard University in 1986 and 1990, respectively. His articles have been published in the *New York Times*, the *Wall Street Journal*, *Esquire*, *The Public Interest*, and the *Times* of London. He is also the author of *Virtually Normal* (Alfred A. Knopf, 1995).

GEORGE F. WILL is a contributing editor of *Newsweek*, an ABC News commentator, and the author of several books.

JAMES Q. WILSON, a criminologist and sociologist, is the James Collins Professor of Management and Public Policy at the University of California at Los Angeles, where he has been teaching since 1985. He has studied and advised on issues in crime and law enforcement for nearly 25 years, serving on a number of national commissions concerned with public policy, and he has authored, coauthored, or edited numerous books on crime, government, and politics, including *Bureaucracy: What Government Agencies Do and Why They Do It* (Basic Books, 1989), *American Government* (Houghton Mifflin, 1996), and *The Moral Sense* (Simon & Schuster, 1997).

JAMES WOOTTON is president of Safe Streets Alliance in Washington, D.C.

MORTIMER B. ZUCKERMAN is chairman and editor-in-chief of *U.S. News and World Report*. He is also publisher of the *New York Daily News*.

INDEX

DATE DUE

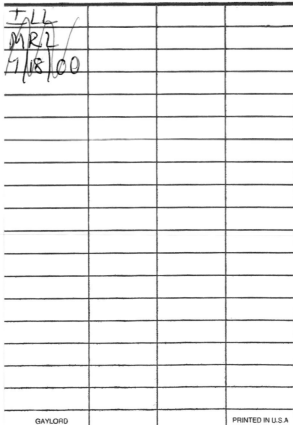

GAYLORD   PRINTED IN U.S.A